D0873946

The Chinese People's
Liberation Army

The
Chinese People's
Liberation Army

SAMUEL B. GRIFFITH, II

A VOLUME IN THE SERIES,
"THE UNITED STATES AND CHINA IN WORLD AFFAIRS"

PUBLISHED FOR THE COUNCIL ON FOREIGN RELATIONS BY THE

McGRAW-HILL BOOK COMPANY

New York · Toronto · London · Sydney

The Council on Foreign Relations is a nonprofit institution devoted to the study of political, economic, and strategic problems as related to American foreign policy. It takes no stand, expressed or implied, on American policy.

The authors of books published under the auspices of the Council are responsible for their statements of fact and expressions of opinion. The Council is responsible only for determining that they should be presented to the public.

To Robert Blum, Friend and Counselor

Foreword

This is the sixth volume in the series on The United States and China in World Affairs, which is being sponsored by the Council on Foreign Relations through a generous grant from the Ford Foundation. In supporting this research program, the Council seeks to encourage more active and better-informed considerations of one of the most important areas of foreign policy for the United States.

The Council program was under the able direction of Robert Blum until his untimely death, and it was he who envisioned the total project, arranged for the authors of the separate studies, and counseled them during the formative stages of their work. The appearance now of the completed studies constitutes appropriate memorials to his deep concern for a more enlightened public understanding of Asia.

This project, which has been guided by a Steering Committee under the chairmanship of Allen W. Dulles, has not sought to produce any single set of conclusions on a subject as complex as that of America's relations with China. Each study in the series, therefore, constitutes a separate and self-contained inquiry written on the responsibility of the author, who has reached his own judgments and conclusions regarding the subject of his investigations and its implications for U.S. policy. The list of authors includes persons with a variety of backgrounds in Chinese affairs and foreign policy. Some have had long personal experience in China. Others have studied China and Far Eastern problems during recent years or dealt with them as officials and administrators. In each case, they have been able to consult with a group of qualified persons invited by the Council on Foreign Relations to meet periodically with them.

Of all the issues relating to Communist China, the one which perhaps arouses the greatest anxieties among the American public is that of Chinese military capabilities and how they will be used. Much of the concern over our involvement in Vietnam stems from the unanswered question of the possibilities and consequences of Chinese intervention. How adventuresome are the Chinese likely to be in military matters? Under what conditions would the rulers in Peking order the People's Liberation Army into battle? And how strong is the largest army in the world?

It has been peculiarly difficult for Westerners to evaluate Asian military power accurately. With respect to Japan, we underestimated her capabilities before Pearl Harbor and overestimated her remaining strength immediately before she surrendered. In the case of Communist China, we discounted the fighting qualities of her forces before she entered the Korean War, and then, by the end of that war, we were inclined to exaggerate what she was capable of doing. At present, as we work to achieve a more stable pattern of relations in Asia, it is critically important that we have a realistic understanding of exactly what Chinese power represents under different possible contingencies, for American military power today must serve as the main deterrent to Chinese power because of the relative weakness of China's Asian neighbors.

The great merit of this broad-ranging study by Brig. Gen. Samuel B. Griffith, U.S. Marine Corps (Ret.), is that it seeks to set Communist Chinese military developments within the context of the Chinese revolution. In Book I General Griffith brings together his unique skills as an academic student of Chinese history and as a Marine long stationed in China to write a fascinating military history of the PLA. He demonstrates what a significant accomplishment it was, within the context of China's society, for the Communists to build up the forces they had at the time of Korea. This was no mean achievement.

In Book II General Griffith turns to an evaluation of current Chinese capabilities. His estimates indicate that as impressive as the Communist accomplishments have been in comparison with modern Chinese tradition, the pace of developments in military technology has left the Chinese still far behind the more advanced countries of the world, particularly the United States and the Soviet Union. At the same time, however, she has progressed sufficiently to cast menacing shadows over her smaller and less powerful neighbors in Asia.

Measured against all objective standards, the PLA today has

serious limitations which the decision makers in Peking no doubt recognize. What is uncertain is how far the men in Peking believe that they can overcome these objective considerations by calling upon the subjective forces of sheer will power and ideological determination. As General Griffith explains, Mao Tse-tung and the men of the Long March have had long experience in calling upon the human spirit to overcome deficiencies in machine power.

It would be wrong to assume that a study of military affairs deals with a marginal or esoteric aspect of Chinese communism. Throughout the history of the Chinese Communist Party there has been an intimate relationship between military and party affairs, and military considerations have shaped domestic policies in innumerable areas of Chinese life. And this feature of Chinese communism is one which is likely to survive Mao.

Thus, General Griffith's contribution to our understanding of China encompasses both foreign policy and domestic Chinese developments. He provides us with a perspective for appreciating the dynamics of Chinese power in the past and for evaluating Chinese capabilities in the future.

LUCIAN W. PYE, *Director*
The United States and China in
World Affairs

Preface

I am indebted to the Council on Foreign Relations for grant of a two-year fellowship (including a six-month trip to the Far East) which made it possible for me to write this book. During this time I was fortunate to have enjoyed a close personal and professional association with Robert Blum, to whom the book is dedicated, and who, until his death in July 1965, sympathetically and energetically directed the work of those engaged in the Council's project, The United States and China in World Affairs.

The major portion of my manuscript was read in draft form by members of a study group, of which Hanson W. Baldwin was the chairman. I wish here to thank him, and those other friends and critics named below, who gave so generously of their time and contributed a number of thoughtful suggestions at the meetings of the study group: Frank E. Armbruster, Hamilton Fish Armstrong, Maj. Gen. C. Stanton Babcock, USA (Ret.), A. Doak Barnett, Davis Bobrow, Maj. Gen. John B. Cary, USAF (Ret.), O. Edmund Clubb, Tillman Durdin, Harold Ford, Raymond L. Garthoff, Brig. Gen. Gordon Gayle, USMC, Col. Robert N. Ginsburgh, USAF, A. M. Halpern, Morton Halperin, Samuel P. Huntington, Col. William R. Kintner, USA, David W. MacEachron, Maj. George K. Osborn, USA, Ralph L. Powell, Col. Wilfred J. Smith, USAF.

Additionally, I must express particular gratitude to Lucian W. Pye, Gen. Matthew Ridgway, USA (Ret.), Col. David D. Barrett, USA (Ret.), John S. Service, Lieut. Col. William W. Whitson, USA, David Albright, and William F. Dorrill, who read all or parts of the various drafts of the manuscript and provided cogent comment.

I am also grateful to Lieut. Jack G. Downing, U.S. Marine Corps, Maj. Pierre Krebs of the French army, and Alexander L. George of the RAND Corporation for allowing me to read unpublished studies relating to various aspects of my own research. Conversations with Dr. Ralph Lapp, an eminent nuclear physicist, enhanced my appreciation of the manifold scientific and engineering problems connected with the Chinese development of a nuclear capability.

Mrs. Anne B. Clark and Donald W. Klein of Harvard University kindly made biographic materials available.

Neither the Council nor any of those named is responsible for conclusions and interpretations, which are, of course, entirely my own.

The staff of the Library at the Council on Foreign Relations proved indispensable, and to all of them, especially to Miss Janet Rigney, I wish to extend my appreciation for the many hours spent locating countless vaguely defined brochures and long-forgotten magazine and newspaper articles.

I should like here also to express my thanks to Ernest Adelberg, who prepared the maps and charts which appear in this book.

Without the expert clerical assistance of Mrs. Ruth Drilling Pashman and Miss Adrienne Sullivan this book would probably never have reached the printer.

Finally, I would remind readers that the situation in the People's Republic of China, and in her defense establishment, has been, is now, and for an indefinite time will continue to be, in a state of flux. Thus, we must expect a variety of interpretations of events that have taken place, as well as those that will occur affecting Communist China's world outlook and her conduct of strategy.

Samuel B. Griffith, ii
BRIGADIER GENERAL, U.S. MARINE CORPS (RET.)

Norcross Lodge
Mt. Vernon, Maine
September 1966

Contents

LIST OF MAPS AND ILLUSTRATIONS

The Chinese People's
Liberation Army

Introduction

On February 12, 1912, the Empress Dowager Lung Yü renounced in the name of the child Emperor Hsüan T'ung the Mandate of Heaven his imperial ancestor Shun Chih had acquired in 1644. Although the abdication of the last Ch'ing ruler marked the formal end of a centuries-old dynastic tradition in China, it did not—as Sun Yat-sen and many other Chinese revolutionaries ardently hoped—herald the birth of a modern state. That laborious event was to be delayed for many years, years in which the rotting fabric of the country would be further shredded by ambitious generals, intriguing politicians, a full-scale invasion by the Japanese, and finally by four years of civil war.

For a few months in 1926 and early 1927 there appeared to be a reasonable chance that a vital new revolutionary force would arrest the processes of social decay and political disintegration that had been working in China for three-quarters of a century. But this hope, too, turned out to be illusory, for the base that Chiang Kai-shek's Revolutionary Army succeeded in establishing in the Yangtze Valley was limited in terms of both geography and effective political authority. And no sooner was this regional authority born than it was challenged internally on the one hand by venal, power-hungry war lords and radicals of the Nationalist Party—the Kuomintang (KMT)—and on the other by the Communists, who at Moscow's behest had allied themselves with the left wing of the KMT with the mission of working as "a bloc within."

Momentarily, at least, the Japanese were restrained by a *modus vivendi* which restricted their economic infiltration to Manchuria, where Marshal Chang Tso-lin acted the part of benevolent despot. His relationship with the ambitious young Kuomintang general was frigid and formal. The Mongols of Suiyuan, Chahar, and Ningsia,

1

detesting central authority as a matter of principle, paid no attention either to pleas for national unity or to the threatening manifestos issued by the upstart in the Yangtze Valley.

From T'aiyuan, his capital in Shansi province, "Model Governor" Yen Hsi-shan exercised exclusive writ in a realm of 25 million. Of these, the great majority were illiterate and poverty-stricken peasants. The governor of Shantung, secure in his own domain, collected taxes for a decade in advance, surrounded himself with a bodyguard of White Russian gunmen, and luxuriated in the pleasures of a harem staffed with women assembled from virtually every country in the world. The unprincipled "Christian General" Feng Yü-hsiang, who had introduced his mercenaries to the mysteries of the Christian faith in wholesale baptismal ceremonies involving fire hoses, had but recently debouched from his arid stronghold in the northwest to occupy the more inviting plains of Central China.

In South China, opposition cliques flourished. Leaders there, too, had plans for their personal futures—plans which did not include subordination of themselves, their armies, or their domains to the whims of a central government dominated by Chiang Kai-shek.

Yünnan, "South of the Clouds," a province bordering on Indo-China, produced one major cash crop: opium poppies. Crude opium, shipped almost openly to Canton, Wuhan, and Shanghai and discreetly smuggled south to French Indo-China, provided the governor a revenue sufficient to maintain himself and his entourage in a state of quasi-regal independence and to buy the loyalty of his impressed soldiers. The 60 million in distant Szechwan, a province larger than France, were misgoverned by a trio of local war lords whose bloated personal armies swallowed money faster than the tax collectors could wring it out of the peasants.

This chaotic situation, in which war-lord groupings coalesced and dissolved only to re-form with completely different casts of characters, was further aggravated by the fact that China was, to use Mao Tse-tung's words, no more than "a semi-colony." Foreigners controlled the principal revenue-producing agencies in China. French, British, American, and Italian nationals administered the salt *gabelle* and controlled the customs and the postal services. A large share of the income from these sources was paid directly to various foreign governments to liquidate the preposterous indemnities they had imposed on China after the Boxer Uprising or to service loans advanced for construction of railways, purchase of locomotives and rolling stock, harbor improvements, and so forth. Until 1926, the scale of import tariffs devised and enforced by the foreign powers effectively prevented the progressive development of indigenous industry. Foreign banks, shipping companies, oil, spinning, mining, and cigarette combines controlled and manipulated China's economy to their profit. The foreigners graciously permitted the Chinese a miniscule share of this pie. China's foreign trade was not exactly flourishing; the country had little to export but coal, soybean products, tungsten, dried eggs, tung oil, peanuts, embroidery, silk, pig bristles, poorly-cured furs, and tea. What she could sell abroad was invariably carried in foreign bottoms.

Managers and staffs of the foreign concerns which benefited from these lucrative arrangements lived in protected privacy in "concessions" their governments had at one time or another extorted from a supine Peking. Here they were isolated completely from the Chinese people. Nor were they subject to Chinese administration or law. The sanctity of the concessions was guaranteed by foreign troops, cruisers, and gunboats. This pattern was undeniably satisfactory to almost everybody but the half-billion Chinese who happened, by some mischance, to own the country.

One had to escape the cities to discover what lay under the riven, purposeless, and corrupt surface, for about 85 per cent of China's huge population lived in the rural countryside. This vast sea of peasant humanity, usually so deceptively calm, concealed within its depths a latent force that, when periodically aroused, rolled with furious energy across the country and blindly destroyed everything that lay in its path.

Since the earliest days rebellions against indifferent and corrupt imperial tyrannies had been a recurring pattern in the texture of Chinese history. The most dramatic of these, the T'aiping rebellion of the mid-nineteenth century lasted, with its subsequent episodes, for twenty years. This massive peasant protest was put down with indescribable cruelty, thanks in measurable degree to the intervention of foreign mercenaries, including such questionably motivated figures as Britain's "Chinese" Gordon and the American adventurer Frederick T. Ward. A later paroxysm, the Boxer Uprising (1899–1900), which germinated as an anti-dynastic, peasant-based rebellion, was craftily converted by the xenophobic dowager Empress Tz'u Hsi into a crusade to end the creeping encroachment of foreigners and to evict them from the country. These volcanic disturbances were portents.

In accordance with Marxist theory, the Chinese Communist Party, founded in 1921, used the word "feudalism" to describe the socioeconomic structure that prevailed in a countryside where the landed gentry sat on top of the heap. At the bottom was the poor peasant, the protagonist in recurring desperate uprisings. It is difficult, if not indeed impossible, for anyone unfamiliar with the Chinese countryside of thirty or forty years ago to visualize the conditions under which the peasant masses struggled to survive. Agents of war-lord governors and the gentry levied exorbitant taxes in kind with small regard for basic food and seed needs of peasant households. Usury was endemic, interest rates appalling. Natural disasters —plague, floods, droughts, blights, and insects—to say nothing of bandits and pillaging soldiery, afflicted the countryside in one or another part of China with increasing frequency and severity. Illiteracy, grinding poverty, unceasing toil, and malnutrition were four constants in the life of a Chinese peasant, and female infanticide a generally accepted practice in rural areas. Technically, this society was not "feudal" in the European sense of that word. Chinese feudalism had been destroyed centuries before, in 221 B.C., by Ch'in Shih Huang Ti, the "First Universal Emperor." But many characteristics of feudal society were present in twentieth-century China. "Hope" was a word not included in the peasant's vocabulary.

The message got through to Mao Tse-tung, a dedicated young Communist activist and agitator who had himself sprung from a middle-peasant family. When Mao wrote his "Report on the Peasant Movement in Hunan" in March 1927, he was already convinced that he had discovered a force capable of transforming China, a force which if organized and directed could rescue his country from the chaos which arrogant war lords, grasping gentry, and selfish foreigners had created and promoted to their profit, and restore to it the attributes of sovereignty and dignity imperial China had once enjoyed.

He could not then have known that this torrential force, one he was destined to direct, would one day shake the world.

The history of the rise to power of the Chinese Communist Party (CCP) is also the history of the development of the People's Liberation Army (PLA).* The two stories are inextricable. In twenty-two

---

* This appellation is somewhat misleading, for the PLA includes air, naval, and embryonic missile forces as well as ground forces. In Chinese usage, "PLA" is equivalent to "military forces."

years of struggle against odds often appearing insurmountable, the Party and its army traveled together from the tumbled mountains of southern Kiangsi, first to safety in a cave city in Shensi, a desolate province in Northwest China, and finally, in 1949, to imperial Peking. The Chinese people are rightfully proud of the PLA, for it has a history of remarkable and often brilliant achievement.

Born in revolution, the Red Army was a "class" army from the beginning; the PLA is distinctively a "class" army today. The first Chinese Red Army was not, however, the proletarian army envisioned by European Marxists, but an army of peasants with rifles. This tradition, too, has been maintained, except that many of the "peasants" now fly jet aircraft, man 54-ton tanks, operate complicated electronic equipment, and crew diesel-powered submarines and speedy motor-torpedo boats.

From the trying days in the Chingkang mountains the Party has always exercised rigid control over its army: "The Party commands the gun." A "purely military viewpoint" has never been tolerated. The PLA, indeed, is a politically conscious army. "Politics is the heart and the soul," the director of the Eighth Route Army's Political Department, Jen Pi-shih, told a visitor to Yenan in 1937. A slogan common since those days has been: "Use the Party to Guide the Army." This guidance insures that members of the armed forces are "red" before they are "expert." Ideological work in the armed forces never ceases: about 40 per cent of the time available for training is devoted to it. Other pressures—combat, marches, technical, training, professional schooling—do not infringe on time allotted for indoctrination and study. Periodic "rectification" campaigns are designed to maintain ideological purity and promote "unity of the party and the army" and "unity of the army with the people."

Chinese Red armies have never existed "merely to fight." As was the first army to carry the hammer and sickle flag in China, so is the PLA today a mechanism for agitation, organization, and control of the masses. As many Chinese armies have been since antiquity, the PLA is an "armed producer." Communist China's soldiers, sailors, and airmen grow the bulk of the cereals and vegetables they eat; raise their own hogs, cattle, ducks, and chickens; manufacture uniforms, shoes, and equipment; build barracks, warehouses, and airfields, and operate arsenals.

For one hundred and twenty days of every year the PLA takes time off from military training to engage in projects assigned by the government. The army is perhaps the party's single most valuable tool, as the slogan "Use the army to supplement government" suggests. Extracurricular tasks assigned the armed forces vary from helping peasants prepare their fields and rice paddies for planting and assisting them to gather the harvest, to afforestation, terracing, flood control, and irrigation work, construction of mills and foundries, and siting and building roads and airfields. It would be safe to surmise that the PLA provided the greater part of the labor force, skilled and unskilled, mobilized to build China's first gaseous diffusion plant.

The PLA is responsible, too, for organizing and training the People's Militia that is one of the distinctive features of contemporary Chinese society. Nor is this a new function. From the day it was founded, the army has been intimately associated with the peasant masses. "Unity of the army and the people" is, as we have observed, a party watchword.

As the army developed from its original primitive state, so did the body of doctrine that has guided its field operations as well as its less martial activities. This doctrine did not, as some presume, spring fully formed from the brain of Mao Tse-tung as Athena had from the forehead of Zeus. Rather, it is a product of varied revolutionary experience, Chinese tradition, continual trial and error; of repeated combining of theory with practice; of assimilation of some tested principles and methods, rejection of others, and the addition (in Mao's words) of "what is essentially our own."

This doctrine—"the glorious military thought of Comrade Mao Tse-tung"—began to germinate during 1927 and 1928 when the ragged Communists, existing from one day to the next in the mountains, initiated their peasant-based struggle for power against Chiang Kai-shek's Nationalists. From 1930 to 1934, the doctrine was tested and refined in the laboratory of five "bandit-extermination campaigns" the Generalissimo conducted against the Communists. The first five months of the Long March, the great strategic retreat from Kiangsi to Shensi, provided further opportunities for development. In the fall of 1936, safe at last in his Yenan cave, Mao completed "Strategic Problems of China's Revolutionary War," the first of a series of discourses and essays in which he sought to give expression to the theories he was convinced would guide a protracted peasant-based revolution to victory.

Many features which contribute to the distinctive character of the contemporary PLA are rooted in its progenitor Red armies.

Thus no serious study of the Party's modern military establishment can be undertaken without consideration of the historical background. It is the purpose of the first ten chapters of this book to establish this frame of reference, to bring the army from the night of its birth in Nanch'ang in August 1927 to the end of the dynamic phase of the Korean War.

In these chapters I do not presume to present a definitive history of the army's growth and operations over a span of two decades. This would require probably twenty thick volumes based on records no Western writer will be able to see for many years, if at all. Documents dealing with the army's early years were lost irretrievably during the Long March. Conditions during the Yenan period were not conducive to compilation of data or to preparation and preservation of operational histories. Much was never recorded. Recently the Party has made strenuous efforts to re-create, in both popular literature and more serious historical studies, the periods of the early Soviets in China and of the Long March. All general officers, for example, were in 1961 ordered to prepare "objective" memoirs. Some of this material may eventually appear, but much will never be publicly available. What does emerge will undoubtedly be highly colored. Use of Nationalist materials stored in Taiwan presents problems, too. Not the least of these is obtaining permission to see the records, many of which are not yet available to foreign researchers. Despite these circumstances, enough material exists to permit us to trace the major themes constant in the PLA's growth.

In the second part of this book I have attempted to deal with the current state of the Chinese Communist armed forces and (with considerable trepidation) to assess China's capabilities to project a developing military power beyond her borders. A caveat in respect to these assessments is mandatory, however, for Peking releases no hard data relating to national defense matters.

In 1961, the U.S. government acquired a number of copies of *The Bulletin of Activities*, a publication issued by the General Political Department of the People's Liberation Army. These *Bulletins*, marked "Secret" and restricted in distribution to regimental and higher headquarters, provided some valuable information on the prevailing state of discipline and morale, training, schooling, and standards of equipment in the ground, air, and naval forces. They clearly revealed the Party's apprehension that its armed forces were not sufficiently indoctrinated with the thought of Mao Tse-tung, that training standards left much to be desired, and that there was small hope—at least for some years—for drastic improvement in the unsatisfactory equipment situation. But the *Bulletins* showed, too, that the many problems besetting the armed forces are recognized at the highest party and government levels and are carefully and realistically examined there. They reflected, as well, the Party's determination to create a strong, completely modern military establishment.

The Chinese appreciate the magnitude of the obstacles that must be overcome before this ambition can be realized. And they know that many years must pass before they dare challenge the United States directly. In the meantime, they will use indirect and ambiguous methods to erode U.S. positions whenever and wherever possible.

It is true that the Chinese are operating from what we would consider an extremely limited defense-industry base, that their strategic options are restricted and their choices hard. But we must not conclude that this situation will continue to prevail for the indefinite future. Nor should we seek comfort in the fond delusion that the People's Liberation Army may cast off the inflexible bonds the Party has fastened on it.

Finally, any assessment of Chinese military capabilities, present or future, must take into account the facts that the Communist Party of China is imbued with a martial spirit and driven by international revolutionary ambitions. These are qualitative factors that will bear significantly on both the rate of China's domestic progress and her future relations with this country and its allies and consequently on the future of world order.

It is sometimes held that Peking would moderate her bellicosity and be amenable to arms-control discussions if she were brought into the United Nations. But far from exhibiting any desire to enter the United Nations, the Chinese have made it abundantly clear that they consider this international body a creature of the United States. Their position is that the People's Republic of China has been illegally deprived of its legitimate rights in the United Nations by U.S. machinations. Moreover, Peking has frequently asserted, in categorical terms, her determination not to take a seat in the United Nations until the "Chiang Kai-shek clique" has been evicted.

It has often been said that we must learn to live with a militant, totalitarian China. This is true. But it is equally true that China must learn to live with us and with the world community. At the present time she shows slight indication of wishing to do either.

Book I

CHAPTER ONE

"We Must Have a Regular Red Army"
Mao Tse-tung

On the first day of October each year, the Chinese celebrate the birthday of the People's Republic. In every city massive parades and rallies last for hours; bombastic and bellicose speeches last even longer; street theatricals glorify Mao Tse-tung, the Chinese Communist Party, the "invincible" People's Liberation Army.

In Peking the first of an interminable series of parades forms before dawn. The participants, in their tens of thousands, are ordered into place by shouting cadres. Finally, the march to the great square before the T'ien An Men—"The Gate of Heavenly Peace"— begins. As rank after rank of students, workers, farmers and militia pour past the red walls of the Imperial City, senior Party members take allotted places on a monumental flag-draped reviewing stand. Behind them, monster pictures of Marx, Lenin, Stalin and Mao Tse-tung contemplate the spectacle with expressions of benign approbation. Facing them, on the south side of this huge plaza, packed thousands roar songs and slogans drowned intermittently by the cacophonies of clashing cymbals, gongs and drums.

In the evening, the Party elite, its military hierarchy, and foreign guests enjoy a lavish state banquet set in the splendor of Peking's imperial palaces. Outside the majestic walls and in public parks around the *Pei Hai* everyone enjoys the fireworks. The Chinese love a good show, and on the first day of October each year, the Party provides one.

The People's Liberation Army (PLA) has traveled a long road from Nanch'ang, Kiangsi province, where it was officially born a few hours before dawn on August 1, 1927. Three of the four men who planned and directed this nocturnal event are very much alive

11

today. They are Chu Teh and Ho Lung, formerly marshals of the P.R.C., and Chou En-lai, Premier of the People's Republic.* Party mythology has endowed them and others who were in Nanch'ang on that night with a special aura.

In the beginning, an army was the least of the Chinese Communist Party's concerns, if indeed it was a concern at all. For the first two years of its existence, from July 1921 into 1922, the CCP was a small and ineffectual group which resembled an academic debating society more than a revolutionary party.[1] Most of the members were intellectuals; none had any military background. All bracketed militarism with foreign imperialism as twin afflictions which had reduced Chinese society to a state of chaos. These two cancers must be excised before the nation could hope to cast off its humiliation and become a healthy, modern state.[2] Aside from habitual excoriation of militarism as manifested in China by feudal war lords, Party members scarcely mentioned military matters in their interminable discussions. At no time in these early years did the leadership conceive the formation of a regular army under party control as possible, desirable, or necessary in the existing revolutionary context.

The CCP was then—and for some years would continue to be—wholly subservient to the Third Communist International. The Chinese Party generated no independent policies and did not dare take any initiative that could conceivably jeopardize its position as an obedient satellite, a status which brought in a monthly subsidy of U.S. $12,000 from the Comintern. The Party spent this money promoting the Comintern's China "line," which demanded concentration of effort on propagandizing and organizing the urban proletariat as "vanguard of the revolution."

The infant CCP depended on the International not just for financial support but for guidance and advice. The Chinese leadership then looked to Moscow much as another leadership would thirty years later: as "elder brothers"—experienced, talented, and courageous. In the context of this relationship, the Chinese role was that of "younger brother"—*hsiung ti*—trusting, dependent, eager to learn. Events were to show that the Russian comrades would not hesitate to take advantage of their "younger brothers."

In 1922, the Comintern began working to infiltrate members of

* All ranks were abolished in 1965. Officers are now addressed as "Comrade Company Commander"; "Comrade Division Commander." Similarly, more senior officers are addressed by the title of the office held. For the sake of convenience, the ten men made marshals of the People's Republic of China in 1955 will be so described.

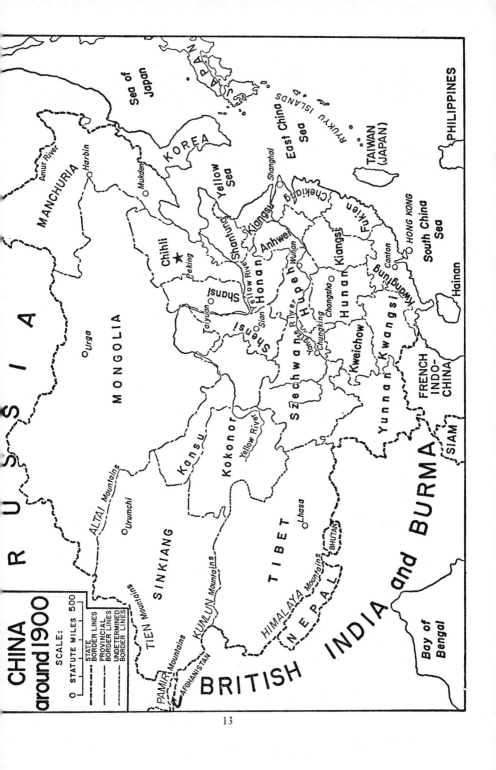

CHINA around 1900

SCALE:

0   STATUTE MILES   500

STATE BORDER LINES
PROVINCIAL BORDER LINES
UNDETERMINED BORDER LINES

RUSSIA

MANCHURIA

Amur River

Harbin

Mukden

MONGOLIA

Urga

Sea of Japan

KOREA

JAPAN

RYUKYU ISLANDS

East China Sea

TAIWAN (JAPAN)

PHILIPPINES

Yellow Sea

Shanghai

Chekiang

Chihli

★ Peking

Shansi

Taiyuan

Shensi

Sian

Yellow River

Shantung

Kiangsu

Anhwei

Honan

Wuhan

Hupeh

Kiangsi

Fukien

HONG KONG

South China Sea

Hainan

Canton

Kwangtung

Kweichow

Changsha

Hunan

Chungking

Szechwan

Yangtze River

Kwangsi

Yunnan

FRENCH INDO-CHINA

SIAM

Kansu

Kokonor

Yellow River

SINKIANG

Urumchi

ALTAI Mountains

TIEN Mountains

PAMIR Mountains

AFGHANISTAN

KUNLUN Mountains

TIBET

Lhasa

HIMALAYA Mountains

NEPAL

BHUTAN

BRITISH INDIA and BURMA

Bay of Bengal

13

the CCP into Sun Yat-sen's Nationalist Party, the Kuomintang (KMT), on an individual basis; in January 1924, Michael Borodin, senior Comintern adviser, prevailed upon "the father of the Chinese revolution" to accept individual Communists as members of his revolutionary party. Borodin's object was to create "a bloc within." Many leading Nationalists, correctly suspecting that Moscow's aim was to seize control of their party by this means, vigorously opposed the policy. But their objections were futile. Dr. Sun, desperate for the cash, arms, military equipment, and advisers only Moscow would supply, was in no position to reject suggestions emanating from the source of this indispensable assistance. Thus, in 1924, the first Nationalist-Communist "united front" was consummated by Moscow's brokers in revolution.[3] This *mariage de convenance*, unhappy almost from the beginning, was destined to disintegrate in violence three years later.

The Russians who came to Canton at Dr. Sun's request had three projects which they at once took in hand. The first was to reorganize the Kuomintang on the model of Lenin's party; the second, to establish a military academy to train commanding personnel and political officers; the third, to design a political structure for the revolutionary army they proposed to create.

In the spring of 1924, Whampoa Military Academy was founded. Dr. Sun Yat-sen's secretary, a young and ambitious officer named Chiang Kai-shek, was appointed commandant of cadets; Chou En-lai, an aristocratic intellectual who had joined the Communist Party in France, was named deputy director of the Political Department. General Galin, chief of the Soviet Military Mission, was senior military adviser, ex-officio. The Russian on the spot, Cherapanov, was said to be "an experienced soldier and seasoned diplomat." Altogether, the quality of officers Moscow sent to advise the Chinese was of the highest.

At Whampoa's opening exercises, Sun Yat-sen stated the objectives of the academy to the first cadet class:

We have established this academy in the hope that the revolutionary movement may be revitalized. Therefore you, the cadets of this academy, must dedicate yourselves to forming the backbone of the revolutionary army. Otherwise, failing to achieve this armed might, the Chinese revolution will be foredoomed from its beginning. This academy, therefore, has the sole purpose of creating a new revolutionary army for the salvation of China.[4]

From the first day, the curriculum placed emphasis on ideological indoctrination with the avowed aim of instilling in the young cadets a sense of dedication to the revolution. The Soviet experience had demonstrated that highly motivated, idealistic, and politically conscious junior officers could successfully convey this spirit to the men they commanded. The performance in battle of Whampoa graduates and their units confirmed the expectations of Dr. Sun, who did not live to see the first victory of the cadets, officers, and men of the academy's Training Regiment.

Less than a year after the first cadets entered Whampoa, the young army had won Kwangtung province for the revolution. There was now no shortage of applicants for admission to the academy or of men eager to join the ranks of an "ever victorious" army. In July 1925, the Kuomintang established the National Revolutionary Army (*Kuo-min Ke-ming-chün*) with Chiang Kai-shek as commander in chief. Galin was appointed his senior Soviet adviser. The relationship between these two men was one of mutual respect and confidence. Chiang wrote of Galin, later known as Marshal Vassili Blücher, commander in chief of the Soviet Far Eastern Army, as one does of a trusted friend.

The Soviet advisers applied the system of political controls they knew to the new army. Political officers were inserted at levels of command from army to regiment. Most were Communists who held concurrent membership in the Kuomintang. Scores of junior officers had also joined the Communist Party. To assert that the National Revolutionary Army was infested with Communists would be a considerable exaggeration, but to say that they—and particularly the zealous young political cadres (*hsia-chi kan-pu*) at lower levels —exerted an influence out of all proportion to their numbers would not. The success of these cadres reflected a superior ideological commitment and derived, too, from the fact that the ordinary peasant recruit proved particularly susceptible to vague but appealing pronouncements on agrarian reform. The major thrust of the propaganda, however, was "anti-imperialist" and nationalistic.

But purveying revolutionary slogans and a patriotic line was by no means the sole function of the cadres. They were then— as they are in the PLA today—educators, welfare and recreation officers, and confidants to whom the men turned, as they frequently do to chaplains in other armies, with troubling personal problems. It is not difficult to appreciate the influence these dedicated young men exerted on uneducated, unsophisticated, and impressionable peasants.

Nevertheless, the Russian advisers were not entirely satisfied with the rate of progress. One reported to Moscow that political work in the army was "poor in many respects"; that it was "still in the initial stages"; that a "unified commissar system" had not yet been established; and that "military courts" did not exist. In December 1925, the Revolutionary Military Council of the Kuomintang published regulations designed to correct these defects.[5]

On July 1, 1926, Chiang Kai-shek issued a mobilization order to the National Revolutionary Army. The Generalissimo was then at Canton, where with Russian help he drew up final plans for the "Northern Expedition," the crusade "to unify China and revive the nation." The major objective was the key Wuhan industrial complex (Hankow-Wuch'ang-Hanyang) on the Yangtze. After seizing this, with its valuable Hanyang arsenal, the central column of the Revolutionary Army would unite with forces commanded by General Feng Yü-hsiang north of the river. In the meantime, the right (east) wing was to advance north through Fukien and Chekiang, seize Nanking and Shanghai, and consolidate the revolution in the coastal provinces.

As it happened, the central column was that in which Communist influence was strongest. As the army marched north, CCP agitators crossed the countryside and carried the revolutionary message to cities and towns along its route. For the first time—and the last time, too, for many years—the Chinese masses responded with tremendous enthusiasm.

The army had always been a dreaded and hated thing in China. But the Nationalist Army was hailed by the people everywhere as the liberator. The forces of the enemy were thus caught between two fires. Surrounded by the hostile people, they flew in all directions, even before being attacked by the Nationalist troops. Many enemy commanders declared their adhesion to the Nationalist cause, that being the only means by which they could hold their forces together. . . .[6]

On October 10, the central column entered Wuch'ang in triumph.

And in this triumph the CCP could justly claim a share. The soldiers, deeply affected by the missionary work of the cadres, fought with courage. Their exemplary behavior won the admiration and active support of the people, a support which contributed in decisive measure to victory. At the same time, the membership of the CCP, its youth organizations, and Party-directed unions and peasant associations increased dramatically.[7] But whatever satisfaction the Party derived from these successes would be transitory, and whatever hopes it built upon them, illusory; for from this peak, the Party's fortunes were destined to take a drastic plunge, which swept the CCP to the edge of oblivion.

One aspect of this decline—indeed, the crucial aspect—was that the CCP, although ostensibly strong, did not control an instrument of power: an army. This fact apparently did not worry the Party leadership as much as it did the Party's masters in Moscow. At the November 1926 Plenum of the Executive Committee of the Communist International (ECCI), Stalin called upon the Chinese Communists "to devote special attention to work in the army" and to "use every means to intensify political work" there; to make "a special study" of military matters, which he emphasized "must not" be regarded as questions "of secondary importance." Comrade Petroff, in a discussion of Stalin's speech, declared that the CCP "must increase its work in the armies; it must give this work its greatest attention"; it must not spare "the most strenuous efforts to obtain a firm foothold in the armies; to entrench its influence there; to educate the armies to political consciousness, and to prevent their becoming pliant tools in the hands of individual militarists." [8]

There was only one thing wrong with this otherwise sound advice: it was utterly irrelevant to the existing situation. The CCP could no longer possibly "obtain a firm foothold in the armies" or "entrench its influence" in them. Commanders were beginning to distrust the Communists and to suspect their motives. It was too late for the leaders to devote time to "a special study" of those military questions which, from the day the Party was founded, they had regarded as matters of "secondary importance." It was also too late to act upon the words of the American comrade, Duncan, who in support of Stalin's thesis said: "The armies—the men with the guns—perform those deeds which mean the fate of the revolution." [9]

The complex political background of the Nanch'ang insurrection does not require detailed analysis here. Briefly, the April 1927 split between the "left" and "right" wings of the Kuomintang gave birth to two power centers—that at Hankow, "the center of the revolution," which included the Communists; and that at Nanking, "the center of counterrevolution," over which Chiang Kai-shek presided. So Stalin, in his thesis of April 21, 1927, on the Chinese revolution, described the situation. This appraisal did not reflect the fact that the ranks of the Hankow group were daily becoming more disordered as the "Left" Kuomintang and the Communists jockeyed for control. In mid-June, the Comintern realized that the situation was moving to a crisis; new instructions were required. The Comintern sent these to its representative lately dispatched to Hankow, the Indian Communist M. N. Roy.[10]

In these instructions, the CCP's Moscow masters directed immediate "liquidation of dependence upon unreliable generals" and called on the CCP "to mobilize about 20,000 workers and peasants from Hunan and Hupeh, form several new army corps, utilize the students of the school for military commanders, and organize your own reliable army before it is too late. Otherwise there can be no guarantee against failure. It is a difficult matter, but there is no other course." [11] It was already "too late." The high tide of revolutionary fervor had subsided. Not even a remote possibility to organize "a reliable army" existed. Moscow was completely out of touch with reality.

The only military force available to the Hankow government was the Second "Front" (Group) Army, the celebrated "Iron Army" (*T'ieh Chün*), commanded by Chang Fa-k'uei. The Communists had infiltrated its ranks to a degree but had no control over General Chang, who, although he had no particular use for Chiang Kai-shek, was unsympathetic both to the objectives of the CCP and its methods. Several of his subordinates who did not fully share his views were, however, ready to act.[12]

In late July 1927, the 24th Division of Chang's army, commanded by the Communist general Yeh T'ing, had moved into Nanch'ang, an important provincial city on the Kan River in northern Kiangsi. Party political officers and propagandists had been active in the division for almost two years, and the majority of men in two of its regiments were indoctrinated and reliable Communists. Of other units present, several were liberally salted with Communists and their sympathizers. One such was the so-called 20th Army, commanded by Ho Lung, a suave, dignified officer whose appearance and manner belied his background. This recent and not altogether welcome addition to Chang's "Iron Army" was in fact a ragtag collection of some 4,000 poor peasants and ex-bandits, only half of whom were armed. All, however, were intensely loyal to their general, who had invariably lived up to his promise to provide them with "iron rice bowls." The chief of public security of Nanch'ang at the time, General Chu Teh, controlled a small force aggregating several companies; a younger colleague, Chou En-lai, commanded the provincial military academy.

These four men, acting on instructions of the Party's Central Committee, planned and executed the August 1 insurrection (*paotung*) which the Chinese Communist Party officially commemorates as the birth date of the PLA. Others whose names are now equally familiar were at the scene: Lin Piao, then a junior officer and currently Defense Minister; Ch'en Yi, now Foreign Minister; P'eng Teh-huai, a company commander, later Defense Minister; and two others who later became marshals of the P.R.C., Nieh Jung-chen and Liu Po-ch'eng (the "One-eyed Dragon").

The coup was well coordinated and speedily executed. There was very little shooting; nonparticipating troops laid down their arms without argument. Dawn of August 1 discovered a quiet city. Citizens who ventured into the streets on that morning found the walls plastered with posters announcing the creation of a Revolutionary Committee. One of the senior officers listed as a member was General Chang Fa-k'uei.

The General, at Front Army Headquarters in Kiukiang, was as yet entirely unaware of the events of the preceding night. True, he had suspected that trouble of some sort was brewing at Nanch'ang, and when he discovered that telegraph and telephone lines to that city, about 75 miles to the south, had been cut, he ordered two reliable divisions to march. These arrangements naturally took some time.

Later, General Chang stated:

I had suspected something was going on in Nanch'ang as I had ordered Yeh T'ing and Ho Lung to come to Kiukiang two days before to attend a conference and they had made all sorts of excuses, saying that it was not convenient to leave their commands at the moment. Still, I did not think they had any idea of mutiny, and even less did I give them any authority to use my name. This was a surprise to me, and also very embarrassing, and I immediately disavowed it.

I knew that Yeh T'ing was a Communist and that two regiments of his division were well indoctrinated, but I did not suspect him capable of disloyalty to the Hankow government or to me. Yeh T'ing had participated in the Northern Expedition and was a trusted officer. He was alert, intelligent, and a good commander. Ho Lung, a capable soldier, had secretly joined the Communist Party only a short time previously. I did not know that he was a member of the Party.[13]

The residents of Nanch'ang did not respond to the Communist *pronunciamento* with any enthusiasm. As soon as they discovered what was afoot, practically all the male inhabitants made themselves as inconspicuous as possible. During the day, Communists from the 24th Division called rallies which were not particularly well attended. Fewer than 400 workers responded to their exhortations to join the army. On the morning of August 5, as Chang Fa-k'uei's loyal troops approached, the mutineers left the apathetic city and headed south. The people, unaware that they had slept through an event of considerable symbolic importance, tore down the wall posters and resumed their normal occupations.[14]

If the *pao-tung* was intended to usher in what Stalin defined as the "second stage" of the Chinese revolution, it was a total failure. It did not, as the Comintern and its authors had hoped, spark an uprising "of the millions of the *working* and *peasant* masses—the *agrarian* revolution" which would "strengthen and extend the struggle against imperialism, against the gentry and feudal landlords, against the militarists and the counterrevolutionary Chiang Kai-shek group." [15]

What did develop was a situation almost the opposite of that prognosticated in Moscow. The Chinese peasants were sick of civil war. As the Communists marched south, they encountered a hostile population. The peasants not only failed to rally to the ranks but fled from their villages as the Communists approached.

Neither food nor drink could be bought . . . it was difficult to get a bit of gruel. When thirsty we drank from the ditches . . . a great many soldiers died of disease; men fell over and died along the road continuously . . the soldiers' morale was very shaky . . . a great many of them deserted . . . half the ammunition was abandoned . . . the mortars were completely thrown away . . . several of the large cannon were also lost. The soldiers who deserted and died of illness approached four thousand . . . for many days we didn't see a person . . . soldiers who dropped from the ranks because of illness were frequently killed by the peasants.[16]

After resting for three days at Lin Ch'uan, the army resumed the march to the south. Now the Reds, reasonably safe from any pursuers, could afford to slacken the pace. As they approached Jiuchin, they encountered a well-trained enemy force which resisted stubbornly and withdrew only after severe fighting. With the main body of the army assembling in the city of Jiuchin, Chu Teh drove the retreating enemy to the southwest. This action was inconclusive; to remove the threat to their right flank, the Communists mounted an attack on Hiuch'ang on August 24. After an "extremely fierce" battle, the enemy dispersed; the Communists picked up more than 1,000 rifles and quantities of equipment abandoned in the field. On the 27th, the army set out for Swatow.

It is interesting to observe that even during this trying period, when the Revolutionary Committee and the Army Command faced daily emergencies, nothing interfered with indoctrination: "Whenever we rested . . . we had public lectures . . . we constantly held conferences of Party members. . . . Party work never stopped even during marches or battles." [17]

On September 24, the army arrived at Swatow. In fifty-one days the troops had marched more than 500 miles and won victories in two major engagements. This ability to endure—to march and fight, to march again and fight, and to march yet again—was a presentiment of things to come. Total strength, drastically reduced by desertions and death from disease and battle casualties, was less than 6,000 men, of whom only one-third were armed. On the last day of September 1927, with powerful Nationalist forces closing on the city, the Communists withdrew toward Lufeng, 100 miles southwest of Swatow.

The Communists had saved the hard core of the army and extorted a considerable sum of money from merchants, small landlords, and rich peasants, but they had failed to arouse the poor peasants along the route of march. Their hopes "to butcher counterrevolutionaries on a large scale" had not been realized. In all, they had managed to catch and execute fewer than 60. "Several tens" awaiting slaughter in the Swatow jail escaped the knife and after their release became "even more fiercely counterrevolutionary" than ever! [18]

However, the Party was pleased to discover that the peasants in Kwangtung were more responsive to propaganda than those in Kiangsi. A band of peasants led by one Comrade Fang fully justified the expectations of the leadership. In Ch'aoyang *hsien*, they "extensively slew counterrevolutionaries," and in another nearby county, they "gave the landlords one big burning and slaying." [19]

But altogether, the episode had been a colossal failure. In his report Comrade Li Li-san wrote:

. . . revolt is an art created by the masses and if there are no masses, it simply cannot be called a revolt, but in each place where we revolted there was only military preparation, we completely failed to stir up the masses, and furthermore, when we were preparing for revolt we put all our energy into military organization and let existing mass organizations all be abandoned. The so-called revolt of the workers' and peasants' army was nothing more than a transformed [should read "transitory"?] military adventure. . . .[20]

Li Li-san exhorted all comrades to "deeply comprehend" the "precious lessons" of August and warned that if they failed to do so, they would "continue to be criminals who would irretrievably lose the revolution." Li Li-san's later action proved that he himself did not deeply comprehend the "precious lessons" of this abortive affair. But another, one destined to become the leader of the CCP, did.

During this hot August, Mao Tse-tung, a Hunanese Communist, was stirring up the rural masses in his native province. As his earlier "Report on an Investigation into the Peasant Movement in Hunan" demonstrates, Mao knew the peasants and their problems, and he sensed the tremendous revolutionary potential of these illiterate, poverty-stricken masses. Indeed, he had described the peasant movement as "a colossal event . . . in a very short time several hundred million peasants will rise like a tornado or a tempest, a force so extraordinarily swift and violent that no power, however great, will be able to suppress it. They will break all trammels . . . rush forward along the road to liberation . . . send all imperialists, war lords, corrupt officials, local bullies, and bad gentry to their graves. . . ." What position should the Party take? "To march at their head and lead them . . . or to follow at their rear . . . or to face them as opponents? Every Chinese is free to choose . . . but circumstances demand that a quick choice be made." [21] The future head of the People's Republic and of the Party had made his choice: "Without the poor peasants there can be no revolution. To reject them is to reject the revolution. To attack them is to attack the revolution." [22]

At the end of 1927, the fortunes of the CCP reached an all-time low. Not only did the "Autumn Harvest Uprising" led by Mao Tse-tung fail miserably, but the Canton Commune, established in a Communist coup on December 11, 1927, lasted only three days and was then liquidated in a blood bath. As Yeh T'ing reported the event:

The masses took no part in the insurrection. All shops were closed, and the employees showed no desire to support us. Most of the soldiers we disarmed dispersed in the city. The insurrection was not linked to the difficulties of the railway workers. The reactionaries could still use the Canton–Hankow line. The workers of the power-plant cut off the light, and we had to work in the dark. The workers of Canton and Hongkong as well as the sailors did not dare join the combatants. The river sailors placed themselves shamefully at the service of the Whites [Nationalists and provincial commanders]. The railway workers of the Hongkong and Canton–Hankow line transmitted the telegrams of the enemy and transported their soldiers. The peasants did not help us by destroying the tracts [sic], and did not try to prevent the enemy from attacking Canton. The workers of Hongkong did not display the least sympathy for the insurrection.[23]

Roy later described the Canton uprising as

the most tragic event in the entire history of the Chinese Revolution . . . the greatest mistake ever committed . . . its bloody suppression was inevitable . . . a foolhardy, ill-conceived, dilettantly prepared offensive . . . a typical adventure. The Nanchang insurrection had its historical significance. It marked the break of the Communist party from its fateful opportunistic past. But since the break took place much too late, it should not have been the starting point for an offensive on the whole front. The mistakes in the past could not be rectified by plunging headlong into a desperate offensive; the proper course for the moment was to beat a strategic retreat with the object of saving the defeated and demoralized forces and marshalling them for an eventual offensive in the next favorable opportunity. The impossibility of holding Nanchang, the fact that the peasants did not join the insurgents' army during its long march through Kiangsi, the abortive occupation of Swatow—all these showed that the Communist slogans of "general armed uprising" and "Soviet Republic" did not find the necessary response from the masses. In those circumstances, it was a serious mistake to go in for an uprising in Canton under the banner of "Soviets." While admiring the heroism of the fallen insurgents of Canton, and honouring their memory, it must nevertheless be said that the mistake did incalculable harm to the revolution. It completed the defeat of the working class and placed it out of combat for a long time.[24]

We may surmise that Mao was not surprised when he learned of this débâcle. He had earlier become convinced that the urban proletariat could not carry out the Chinese revolution, that the conquest of power in China was the ordained task of millions of faceless peasants. And as their vanguard would march a disciplined and politically conscious Red Army.[25]

CHAPTER TWO

The First Six Years

At a clandestine meeting at Kiukiang on August 7, 1927, the Politburo of the CCP had designated Mao to lead an Autumn Harvest Uprising in Hunan and Kiangsi. "The reason for staging the Autumn Harvest Uprising was to take advantage of the harvesting period to intensify the class struggle in the villages," to transfer political power to the peasant associations, and to redistribute the land. These goals having been accomplished, Mao and a motley "army" he had collected were to take Ch'angsha.[1]

This ill-considered plan turned into a fiasco. Two of Mao's four regiments, not exactly compatible, attempted to resolve their differences in a pitched battle. While they were thus engaged, the other two were attacked by Nationalist forces and practically destroyed. Mao himself fled only to be captured by a band of landlord militia, whose leader released him. By the time the militia commander realized that he had made an egregious mistake, "it was too late for regrets." Mao eluded pursuit and in early October began rounding up the dispersed remnants of his "army." These he organized as the 1st Regiment, 1st Division, First Workers' and Peasants' Revolutionary Army. During the month, he arrived with his nondescript and poorly equipped rabble—indeed, it was little better than that—in the Losiao Mountains astride the borders of Hunan and Kiangsi provinces. Here he hoped to find a haven, rest, recruit, reorganize, and prepare for the next revolutionary "upsurge" that Leninist theory assured him was inevitable.

Mao's later conduct testifies that he had learned a great deal from the failure of the Harvest Uprising, which exemplified the "adventurist" tactics he would in the future so consistently condemn. In another sense, the experience was valuable, for it marked Mao's

24

introduction to combat. We have reason to believe that he relished
the challenge and the danger of the battlefield.

Those who have seen scroll paintings of the mountains of South
China may picture Chingkangshan: convoluted, heavily forested
hills, their heights wrapped in drifting fog rising wraith-like from
deep gorges down which tumbling waters rush. Such isolated spots
were traditionally favored, particularly by Taoists and Buddhists, as
retreats to which those sated with worldly things could retire to
contemplate the beauties of nature, paint, perfect their calligraphy,
and compose poetry or music.

Mao, who had not fled to the wild and lonely mountains to pursue
his aesthetic bents, found the area otherwise suitable. There were,
however, certain preliminary arrangements to be made with local
bandits who claimed proprietary rights derived from long possession
of the territory. Negotiations were conducted, and conclusions satisfactory to both Communists and bandits reached. The two leaders,
Yuan Wen-ts'ai and Wang Tso, placed their groups, each with
about sixty rifles in bad repair, under Mao's orders. The army
ejected the priests from their scattered temples and moved in. Chu
Teh with a few poorly armed men soon joined.

"Chingkangshan proved to be an excellent base for a mobile army
such as we were building. It had good natural defenses, and grew
enough crops to supply a small army. It had a circuit of about 500 *li*
[170 miles] and was about 80 *li* [26 miles] in diameter." [2] From this
remote and circumscribed stronghold detachments of the Red
Army sallied forth to organize Red Guards in surrounding farm villages, conduct propaganda, collect food, clothing, and money, and
ambush small bodies of provincial troops. Organizational activities
left little time for fighting, but as Mao once observed, the Red
Army did "not exist merely to fight."

On Chingkangshan, the army had to fight solely to exist. Meat
and salt were hard to get, a bowl of rice a rare treat. The army sub-
sisted much of the time on squash. The men were often without
shoes. Even simple medicines were not to be had, nor were doctors
or surgeons available. [3] A soldier seriously wounded in battle had a
poor chance of surviving. It is little wonder that men deserted.
What should be remarked is that relatively few did.

The 4th Red Army—the now legendary "Chu-Mao army" (commanded by Chu Teh with Mao Tse-tung as political commissar)—
was formed in May 1928; with the accession of hundreds of

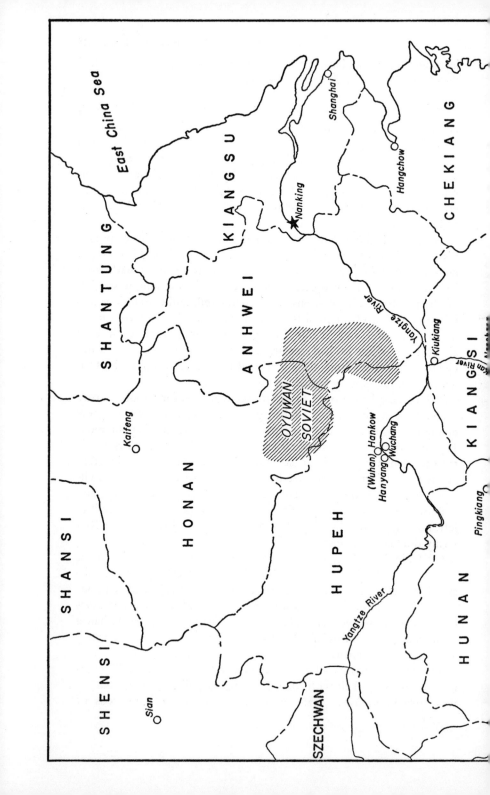

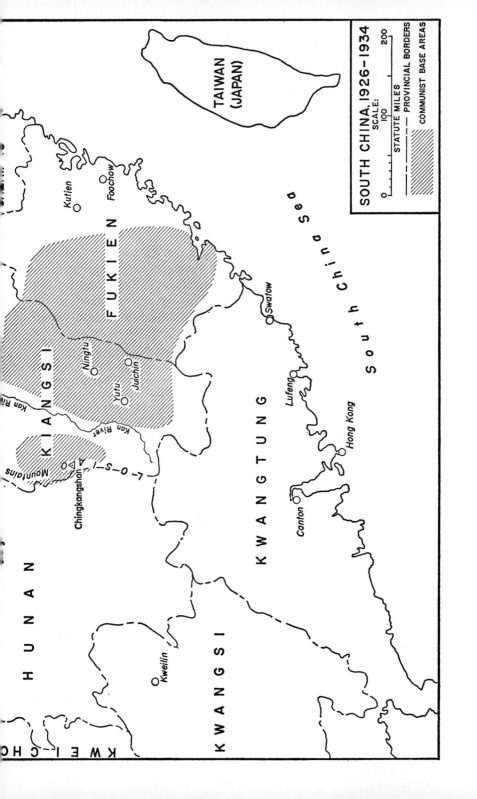

SOUTH CHINA, 1926-1934

SCALE:
STATUTE MILES
0   100   200

——— PROVINCIAL BORDERS
▨ COMMUNIST BASE AREAS

TAIWAN
(JAPAN)

South China Sea

FUKIEN

Kutien

Foochow

Swatow

Lufeng

Hong Kong

KIANGSI

Ningtu

Yütu

Juichin

Kan River

Kan River

Chingkangshan

Mountains

KWANGTUNG

Canton

HUNAN

KWEICHOW

KWANGSI

Kweilin

deserters from the army of Ho Chien, the provincial war lord of Hunan, the Communists created shortly thereafter the 5th Army, commanded by P'eng Teh-huai. Both were "armies" in name only —neither came to a strength of 5,000 officers and men, and only about two-thirds of the total were armed. Machine guns, mortars, and ammunition were always in short supply. The only source of replenishment was the enemy. "The Whites," the Communists said, "supplied our weapons, our ammunition, horses, radios, and other equipment, and actually delivered them to us—on the battlefield." The enemy, both Nationalist and Japanese, was to be the principal source of weapons for many years; U.S. forces in Korea were not exempt from this type of requisition.

The summer of 1928 was profitably spent: the territory under the independent regime was expanded; the agrarian revolution deepened, the people's political power extended; the Red Army and the Red Guard strengthened. So Mao Tse-tung was to report to the Central Committee in November 1928. In elaboration Mao wrote:

The policies of the Border Area Special Party Committee (with Mao Tse-tung as secretary) and the Army Party Committee (with Ch'en Yi as secretary) were then as follows: struggle resolutely against the enemy, establish a regime in the middle section of the Losiao mountain range and oppose flight-ism; deepen the agrarian revolution in areas under the independent regime; promote the development of the local Party organisation through the help of the army Party organisation, and the development of the local armed forces through the help of the regular army; adopt a defensive strategy for Hunan where the ruling power was comparatively strong and offensive strategy for Kiangsi where the ruling power was comparatively weak: devote great efforts to the development of Yungsin, set up an independent regime of the masses there and make preparations for a prolonged struggle; concentrate the Red Army to fight at opportune moments the enemy confronting it and oppose the division of the forces in order to avoid their being smashed separately by the enemy; and adopt the policy of advancing in a series of waves for the expansion of the area under the independent regime and oppose the policy of venturesome advance. Thanks to these appropriate policies, plus the terrain in the border area (which is favourable to our struggle) and the absence of perfect coordination between the invading troops from Hunan and those from Kiangsi, we were able to win a number of military victories and expand the independent regime of the masses in the four months from April to July.[4]

Military weakness did not deter the Communists from taking the initiative when an opportunity presented itself. They adjusted tactics to the political situation existing in adjacent White territory. Chu Teh later described the pattern:

> Our tactics were to attack the Kiangsi troops only. We selected Kiangsi for attack because in the Kiangsi troops under Chu Pei-teh we still had some Party workers, so his men often deserted to us and were influenced by our ideas. We first defeated the expedition from Kiangsi, then the Hunan and Kwangtung armies retreated without fighting.
> The second drive was commanded by Chu Pei-teh, and we concentrated all our forces to annihilate his expedition. The Hunan troops did not cooperate with Chu Pei-teh because of mutual antagonisms, so he failed to maintain his power.
> During the third of these small campaigns, P'eng Teh-huai led an uprising of his Kuomintang troops in P'ingkiang, Hunan, Liu Yang *hsien*, and joined the Red Army. This helped us at Chingkanshan very much because it made the Kuomintang troops immobile and they could not maneuver. So we were able to take a rest on Chingkanshan and reorganize our forces.[5]

If the army were to be the instrument to bring the Party to power, the army had to be the armed extension of the Party: politically conscious, literate, motivated, and thoroughly indoctrinated —an army that respected the people and was respected and actively supported by them. To create an army of this type from the human material available was a challenging task, to say the least. And unlike the Russian Bolsheviks, who absorbed more than 30,000 former Czarist officers into the Red Army, the Chinese Communists had to start virtually from scratch. They had few bricks and little straw, but they had a clearly defined goal and the determination and perseverance needed to attain it.

Since these early days, the Chinese Communists have claimed that theirs is a "democratic" army. In one sense of that word, their claim is true. The officers did not beat or physically mistreat the soldiers; officers and men lived together, ate the same food, and dressed alike. No particular deference was paid an officer. Everyone was socially —and financially—equal. Mess money was administered by a soldiers' committee; mess savings were spent for the common benefit.

> All these measures [Mao wrote] were very satisfactory to the soldiers. . . . The newly captured soldiers in particular feel that our army and the Kuomintang's army are worlds apart. They feel that, though in material life they are worse off in the Red Army than in the White Army, spiritually they are liberated. The fact that the same soldier who was not brave in the enemy army yesterday becomes very brave in the Red

Army today shows precisely the impact of democracy. The Red Army is like a furnace in which all captured soldiers are melted down and transformed the moment they come over.[6]

Mao described others who gravitated to the Chu-Mao army in the early years as *Lumpen proletariat*—riffraff of all descriptions: former bandits, escaped criminals, paupers; the proscribed, the homeless, the outcasts, the dispossessed. A fairly large proportion of recruits were deserters from the *min t'uan*—the landlords' private militia—or from provincial armies. Most officers and men who surrendered to the Communists fully expected to be shot. Instead, they found themselves welcomed, especially if they brought with them guns and bullets. The soldier deserters shared a poor peasant background—which is to say that they had probably never seen as much as five silver dollars at one time or eaten more than half-a-dozen decent meals in their entire lives. What they *were* thoroughly habituated to eating was "bitterness." These short, scrawny, thin-legged men were tougher than jerked meat; they could endure. Still, they did not appear to be exactly the sort from which to forge an "iron army." A U.S. recruiting sergeant would have turned them all away from his door. He would have been making an egregious mistake.

The experienced officers, veteran enlisted men, and cadres took this unpromising material in hand. They imposed strict discipline: orders to be obeyed promptly and without question; no confiscations from the peasantry; prompt delivery to the authorities of anything confiscated from landlords.[7] Condign punishment—death by shooting—was adjudged against officers or men guilty of rape, robbery, or wanton shooting and burning. Evidences of "guerrillaism" were to be extirpated: ". . . the tendency to destroy cities and kill, burn, and rob purposelessly . . . is only a reflection of the *Lumpen proletariat* and peasant mentality *which may hamper the development of the party among the peasant masses* . . . every effort should be made to erase this erroneous concept . . . purposeless killing and burning . . . are irrelevant to our revolutionary mission." [8]

After discipline came political indoctrination and military training, which proceeded simultaneously. If any subject suffered, it was training. The Communists had no ammunition to shoot at anything but live targets. Mao once observed that training was mostly conducted in combat—a system which, although no doubt efficacious, generally turns out to be rather costly.

Political control and indoctrination went hand in hand. The Communists had earlier learned from the Kuomintang's Russian advisers and adopted the basic system the Russians had applied first to Bolshevik armies during the civil war and later to Chiang's Revolutionary Army before it set out from Canton for the north. The mechanism in the structure was the "Party Committee"; the key figure, the "political representative." These committees and officers functioned at every level in the army. One may suspect that many difficulties would arise between the Party's watchdogs and commanding personnel, and many did.

But "experience has proved that the system of Party representatives must not be abolished," Mao wrote in 1928. "As the Party branch is organized on the company basis, the Party representative at the company level is particularly important. He has to supervise the soldiers' committee in carrying out political training, to direct the work of the mass movement, and to act at the same time as the secretary of the Party Branch." [9] Mao neglected to mention other crucial duties of the Party representative: those of ideological ferret and petty inquisitor. The Party representative's responsibilities required him to find out everything he could about every officer and man in the company—his background, the webs of his family and personal relationships, his predilections. Such duties represented a considerable development, a refinement, of the system imposed by the Bolsheviks, whose political officers spent much of their time during the early years of the Red Army's existence keeping tabs on former Czarists.

The representative was assisted by a "Party Branch Committee" (in which the representative, the only permanent member, held the key position of secretary), by "soldiers' committees" in platoons, and by activists in squads. Meetings and discussions took place every day—often two or three times a day. In camp and during rest periods, the soldiers soaked up Party policies relating to organization of peasant associations, debt cancellation, rent reductions, tax remissions, and confiscation and redistribution of land. At the same time, they were indoctrinated to hate landlords, Whites, and "imperialists." To understand this army, one must realize that hatred of "class enemies" has been a prime motivator from the beginning. After only a year, Mao was able to report that Red Army soldiers had all become class conscious.

During this formative period serious conflicts of opinion arose between Chu and Mao, fighting in the mountains, and the Party Central, hiding in Shanghai. These reflected irreconcilable views on two fundamental questions. First was an argument over the direction and nature of the Party's main thrust. Was it to be in urban areas, in organization of "the toiling masses," as the Comintern obstinately demanded, or in rural areas, in organization of the peasants, as Chu and Mao urged? The social and political situation provided the answer clearly enough. But Moscow was far away, and the dogmatic panjandrums of the Comintern poorly advised. Revolutionary temperature ran high in the countryside; in the cities, the wave of 1926 had subsided. Workers were not just apathetic, but—as the catastrophe of Canton had demonstrated—hostile. The KMT had smashed the Party's urban machinery.

An equally important question was the military policy to be adopted. Was there to be a regular professional Red Army, which Chu and Mao believed necessary, or was the Party by clandestine means to prepare peasants and workers for armed insurrection—a *levée en masse*—at some indefinite future date, as Moscow directed? As Stuart R. Schram has written in his analysis of Mao's "military deviation" (for which Mao was deprived of membership on the Central Committee):

It is perhaps not an exaggeration to say that as early as August 1927 a conflict was emerging between a conception of the Chinese revolution based to a considerable extent on the model of the Russian October Revolution, and upheld by the Comintern and the CCP Central Committee, and an as yet ill-defined model of revolution for an agricultural nation, based on guerrilla warfare in the countryside, toward which Mao was groping.[10]

This long-range factional feuding did not, however, interfere with military operations, during which the Red command began to work out the pattern of a doctrine later to be associated with the Eighth Route Army. This doctrine was based essentially on precise and carefully evaluated information, meticulous planning, rapid secret movement, retention of the initiative, creation of favorable tactical situations by simulation and dissimulation; sudden, short-range surprise attacks, rapid disengagement, and speedy withdrawal. The pattern was dynamic: concentrate, disperse, and concentrate again. The Communists rarely engaged unless victory was certain; if a situation developed to their disadvantage, they broke off the action. They always sought surprise, for as one ancient master of the art of war had written: "With the lightning flash, there is no chance to shield the eye; with the thunderclap, no time to cover the ears."

Although the fact has been deliberately obscured by contemporary Chinese Communist hagiographers, the small Chu-Mao army did enjoy certain distinct military advantages. First, it occupied an inaccessible and readily defensible redoubt in provincial borderlands. Since the last thing local war-lord governors could conceive was coordination of military effort under unified direction, the Soviet area was, as Chu Teh observed, blessed with immunity from effective converging attacks. Second, the base area was ringed with a generally friendly population which provided essential food and timely information of enemy projects. Thus the Communists, operating on interior lines, were able to anticipate the movement of White detachments and fall upon them unexpectedly with decisively superior forces. Third, as the Communists knew the surrounding areas intimately, they were able to move at night and with extreme rapidity. Finally, a psychological factor entered into the equation: the landlord militia and many White provincial troops, poor peasants, too, were fundamentally sympathetic to the Communists and deserted to them before, during, and after battle. White commanders, reluctant to expend their "personal" military capital, hesitated to take the field with troops whose loyalty was at best questionable. Some Communist "victories" were in fact victories in sham battles; some of the arms "captured," in fact bought.

The trying Chingkang era, although short, was fruitful. Here many of the operational principles that would guide the Party and its small but already redoubtable army crystallized. The revolutionary temper of the leaders and the rank and file was tested—and found not wanting. Mao certainly never lost an iota of his characteristic confidence, as his poem commemorating a series of battles fought in the Huangyangchieh district testifies:

CHINGKANG MOUNTAIN

Below the hills were our flags and banners,
To the hilltop sounded our bugles and drums.
The foe surrounded us thousands strong,
But we were steadfast and never moved.

Our defence was strong as a wall already,
Now did our wills unite like a fortress.
From Huangyangchieh came the thunder of guns,
And the enemy army had fled in the night.[11]

In the early winter of 1929, Chu and Mao were faced by increasing pressure to forsake the Chingkangshan base for a safer haven. They chose the western border area of Fukien province, where better opportunities for supply, organization of the peasants, and expansion of Soviet areas existed. In early December, they set out. For the time being, P'eng Teh-Huai remained at Chingkanshan. As for the army "there were still many bad tendencies" to be eradicated, and in December 1929, the leaders convened a conference at Kut'ien, in west Fukien. Here the Party "laid the foundations for a high type of ideological leadership in the Red Army" and launched the first of its countless "rectification campaigns" within the armed forces.

At this conference, Mao Tse-tung presented a lengthy resolution entitled "On the Rectification of Incorrect Ideas in the Party." [12] Mao's concepts, clearly expressed in this early document, have exerted a lasting influence on the character of the army. They are, therefore, worthy of examination.

What were some of the "nonproletarian ideas" of which Mao disapproved? First, a "purely military viewpoint . . . unusually widespread among a number of comrades." These comrades, for example, regarded military work and political work as mutually exclusive; they failed "to recognize military work as only one of the means for accomplishing political tasks." Mao declared that "when the Red Army fights it fights not merely for the sake of fighting but to agitate the masses, to organize them, to arm them, and to help them establish revolutionary political power; apart from such objectives, fighting loses its meaning and the Red Army the reason for its existence." He saw the Red Army primarily as an instrument to accomplish a political task, and he did not intend to permit political organs in the army to be subordinated to military organs. Politics was to be firmly in command.

Other attitudes also attracted Mao's condemnation. Too many officers, for instance, became conceited after a battle was won and dejected when one was lost. The balanced commander must be imperturbable, given neither to undue optimism, which induces rashness, nor undue pessimism, which induces excessive caution, hesitation, and vacillation. Some comrades permitted "revolutionary impetuosity" to prevail over calm judgments, wished "only to do big things," and were "chock full of illusions." This criticism constituted a direct attack on Li Li-san's "line," which stressed efforts to seize control of urban areas. In Mao's view, such a line was irrelevant to prevailing "subjective and objective conditions." It was necessary to assess these carefully, to go slowly, to "take pains" with "minor, detailed work."

To correct these and other erroneous and dangerous ideas which reflected "the purely military viewpoint," Mao proposed "to raise the level of political work in the army," to intensify ideological indoctrination and thus eradicate "remnant bourgeois" and mercenary concepts. (Even today, after almost forty years, the People's Liberation Army is still apparently cursed with some who harbor these "remnant concepts.")

The dangers of "extreme democratization," a natural development in a revolutionary army, were as apparent to Mao Tse-tung as they had been earlier to Leon Trotsky when he presided over the formation and development of the Soviet Red Army. Mao was determined that the army would not degenerate into a congeries of debating societies. Nor would it elect its officers. Plans and orders would be generated at the top, just as they were in "imperialist" armies. There would be "democratization," but under centralized control and with definite limitations. The proper function of lower levels was neither to formulate policies nor to question orders received but to discuss them constructively and devise the most effective methods of executing them.

Mao was also concerned with the spirit of "absolute equalitarianism" which pervaded the Red Army. The rank and file, he noted, had carried this to excess: soldiers objected to officers riding horses, to the better billets assigned headquarters staffs, and even to loads carried on the march. There could be no such thing, said Mao, as "absolute equalization." The revolutionary soldier's deep conviction on this subject was of course not peculiar to members of the Chu-Mao army. It is a characteristic manifest in any army inspired by revolutionary ideology. Trotsky had wasted no time stamping it out in the Bolshevik forces he commanded.

Mao also attacked extreme "guerrillaism":

The political idea of the roving insurgents arises in the Red Army because the vagabond elements form a very large proportion of it and because there are enormous numbers of vagabonds in the country, especially in the southern provinces. This idea manifests itself as follows: (1) To be unwilling to expand our political influence by strenuous work in founding base areas and establishing the political power of the masses of the people, but to try to expand it by applying only mobile guerrilla methods. (2) In expanding the Red Army, to follow not the line of first expanding the local detachments of the Red guards, then the local units of the Red Army, and finally the main forces of the Red Army, but the line of "hiring men and buying horses" and "recruiting deserters and taking in mutineers." (3) To be impatient in carrying on hard struggle together with the masses, and to hope only to go to the big cities and indulge in eating and drinking. All such manifestations of the idea of the roving insurgents seriously hamper the Red Army in accomplishing its proper task; thus the elimination of this idea is indeed one of the important aims of the ideological struggle of the Party organization in the Red Army.

As methods of rectification, Mao proposed:

1. To intensify education, criticize incorrect ideas, and eliminate the idea of the roving insurgents.
2. To intensify education against the vagabond outlook among the basic sections of the Red Army and the newly captured soldiers.
3. To strive to draw into the ranks of the Red Army active workers and peasants experienced in struggle in order to change the composition of the Red Army.
4. To create new units of the Red Army from among the masses of workers and peasants who are in the midst of struggle.

The "Resolutions and Spirit of the Second Plenum of the CC [Central Committee]" of July 9, 1929, had made it clear that the Party intended to adhere to the line prescribed by the Comintern and proposed to continue to devote major effort to capturing the urban proletariat. At the same time, the Plenum had acknowledged (in rather deprecatory phraseology) that "certain Soviet areas as well as the Red Army commanded by Chu and Mao are still in existence." [13] But even had the Central Committee wished to do anything concrete to help the Red Army expand the Soviet areas —and at this time it did not particularly wish to do so—its efforts could not have been successful. The Communist areas were distant from cities, isolated, blockaded, and under intermittent attack. Occasional couriers slipped through the cordon, but traffic in goods was impossible.

In the spring of 1930, the intra-Party struggle entered its decisive phase. The Party leadership, dominated by Li Li-san, "was still not directing its main attention to Red Army warfare and Comrade Mao Tse-tung was still not recognized as leader of the Party." [14] Nor was Mao as yet strong enough to challenge what he and Chu Teh believed to be the "adventurist" and dangerous strategy concocted by Li Li-san. Later, Mao wrote of this debate:

[Our] tactics were severely criticized by Li Li-san who . . . wanted attacks rather than consolidation; advances without securing the rear; sensational assaults on big cities, accompanied by uprisings and extremism. The Li Li-san line dominated the Party then, outside Soviet areas, and was sufficiently influential to force acceptance to some extent, in the Red Army, against the judgment of its field command.[15]

In the late spring of 1930, in response to directives from the Party Central, the Red armies were reorganized and ordered to prepare for a general offensive against the Ch'angsha-Wuch'ang-Nanch'ang triangle. These operations were to be coordinated with Party-led workers' insurrections. The newly organized 1st Army Corps with Chu Teh in command and Mao as political commissar, was to attack Nanch'ang. Ho Lung (2nd Army Corps) in conjunction with Hsü Hsiang-ch'ien (4th Army Corps) was to threaten Hankow and take Wuch'ang; P'eng Teh-huai (3rd Army Corps) was to attack Ch'angsha. This unrealistic scheme lacked even a modicum of strategic coherence and subjected the several corps to the danger of defeat in detail. But Party discipline was sufficiently strong to override any objections entertained by the field commanders.

Of the three attacks, only P'eng Teh-huai's was successful. He took Ch'angsha on July 28; three days later, the 1st Army Corps was bloodily repulsed under the walls of Nanch'ang. Chu Teh and Mao called off the operation. Ho Lung's attack on the Wuhan complex never materialized, and after holding Ch'angsha for ten days, P'eng was forced to withdraw.

These checks did not, however, have any perceptible effect on Li Li-san, who ordered a second attack on Ch'angsha.

But the second attack on Ch'angsha proved to be a failure. Great reinforcements had been sent to the city, and it was heavily garrisoned. . . . [The Red Army] could not take the city of Ch'angsha and after a few weeks withdrew to Kiangsi.

This failure helped to destroy the Li Li-san line and saved the Red Army from what would probably have been a catastrophic attack on Wuhan, which Li was demanding.[16]

The near debacle at Ch'angsha confirmed the belief of Mao and his colleagues that they, not a remote Central Committee or an even more remote Comintern, had the practical solution to the problems of the Chinese revolution. Not for seventeen years would the Communists again attack a well-defended city. This, Sun Tzu had written centuries before, was the worst possible strategy: "Attack cities only when there is no alternative." Mao had sometime earlier found the alternative: an army which in the first phase of development would be capable of conducting coordinated mobile and guerrilla operations over a vast and friendly countryside and in the process fighting only when and where the "subjective and objective situations" guaranteed victory. The cities could wait; the Red Army would get them eventually, and at a minimum cost in lives and treasure.

Li Li-san's abortive strategy had failed before the walls of Nanch'ang and Ch'angsha. But it scared the Kuomintang, whose senior members for the first time began to realize that the Communists constituted something more than an ephemeral menace. The government's victory at Ch'angsha had averted an immediate threat, but offensive action, and on a major scale, was now obviously demanded.

The Fourth Plenary Conference of the KMT, held in Nanking November 1–28, 1930, unanimously decided to suppress the Communist bandits (*kung-fei*) "completely"; "to dispatch government forces against the Red Army in order to exterminate it, and to reoccupy the Sovietized areas." [17] The delegates conceived that this task, the most important the government faced, could be concluded "in from three to six months." This optimistic hope was to be frustrated; the campaigns dragged on for almost four years. Their history, a large part of which is a depressing catalogue of Nationalist mistakes, is at the same time a fascinating page in the story of the growth of the Red Army and the development of its tactics. For this reason, the "Extermination Campaigns" and their culminating episode—"The Long March"—necessarily find a place in these pages.

For the planned operation, Nanking fielded a striking force of eleven provincial divisions under command of Lu Ti-p'ing. His strategy, designed to surround, compress, and annihilate the Communists in Kiangsi, was uncoordinated. The general was inept; his troops apathetic. The Communists trapped the 18th Division on December 30, captured (and later tried and executed) its commander, Chang Hui-tsan, and took thousands of weapons. Four days later, they attacked the rear guard of the 50th Division at Tung Shao in southern Kiangsi, trapped the main body, attacked it from two directions, and inflicted crippling losses. They had defeated the "First Extermination Campaign" in less than two weeks.[18] Mao celebrated the victory with a poem set to the music of an ancient melody.

The Nationalists reacted on April 1, 1931, with the "Second Extermination Campaign." For this, they mustered almost 200,000 troops under command of Ho Ying-ch'in, Chiang's Minister of War. General Ho, determined to avoid the fate that had overtaken his predecessor, advanced slowly and methodically. This tactic played into the hands of the fast-moving Communists, who slipped between and around his columns, cut out and destroyed the weakest elements, inflicted heavy casualties on six divisions, and captured thousands of rifles and machine guns.[19] The Nationalists, thoroughly beaten for the second time in four months, retreated to northern Kiangsi. In May, Mao wrote another martial poem in praise of the Red Army which had swept away thousands of enemy troops "like rolling up a mat." [20]

The Communists were now flourishing. Nanking's estimate of May 1931 put their strength at 117,400, with almost 60,000 rifles, 768 machine guns, 29 cannon, and 74 trench mortars.[21] Ninety per cent of these weapons had been taken from the Nationalists. Of the total Communist force, about 35,000 were serving in the 2nd, 3rd, and 5th armies, commanded respectively by Ho Lung, Chu Teh, and P'eng Teh-huai, all generals of proven competence.

It is not possible to reconstruct the Extermination Campaigns in detail from the few, inexact, and frequently contradictory sources available.[22] Nor is it necessary to do so here except as their conduct sheds light on Communist strategy and tactics. As we have seen, the first two major campaigns, characterized on the part of the Nationalists by inept generalship and a decided disinclination of the troops to fight, resulted in serious but not critical defeats.

For the third attempt, Chiang mounted about 300,000 men; he also made the mistake of giving Ho Ying-ch'in command of the "Central Route" to which he assigned the best-equipped and most reliable forces. On July 1, 1931, the Nationalists marched. General Ho was optimistic; he had some reason to be, for the Nationalists enjoyed overwhelming superiority both in numbers and in weapons.

Chiang's concept was to move deliberately, to hem the Communists in on north, east, and west and press against them simultaneously from three directions. Eventually, he hoped, the Reds would have to stand and fight. And in a "set-piece" battle, superior groundfire power and aircraft would tell the story. The Communists naturally had no intention of accommodating the overconfident Generalissimo.

General Ho's first encounter with the Reds was unpropitious: an isolated Nationalist brigade went over to the enemy, lock, stock and barrel. As before, their amazing mobility enabled the Reds to evade Nationalist enveloping maneuvers and to trap several enemy units in the process. Still, by the end of July the Nationalists had made some progress. A few weeks later, the campaign bogged down in the rains. In early September, with the weather again favorable, General Ho's columns resumed the advance, achieved some tactical successes, and were in position to threaten Juichin. Unfortunately for Chiang, developments which demanded his attention suddenly occurred elsewhere. He withdrew his columns to the north, and practically all Kiangsi south of Nanch'ang again fell to the Communists.[23]

During the Third Campaign, Communist commanders demonstrated imaginative boldness, great flexibility, and tenacity of purpose. Even their opponents conceded that the troops were well led and were highly disciplined, loyal, and ferocious fighters. The mobility of their enemy amazed Kuomintang commanders. The Communists seemed to appear from the void, strike always the flanks or rear, and melt away before the surprised and reeling Nationalists could recover from the shock.

But had the Generalissimo not been diverted by events which forced him to close down the Third Campaign prematurely, he might have liquidated the Communists. On September 18, the Japanese Kwantung Army seized Mukden, and Chiang's colleagues immediately pressured him to cease internal warfare and concentrate on ejecting the invaders from Manchuria. This, however, was by no means within his capabilities at the time. The Generalissimo, fully conscious of his military weakness, cherished the hope that he could localize the encroachment and, after announcing a policy of "non-resistance," referred China's case to the League of Nations. As the Japanese had correctly anticipated, this impotent body took no action to restrain their blatant aggression.

The Party took note of these successes on December 20, 1931, when the first All-China Congress of Soviets (the First National Congress of the Representatives of Chinese Workers', Peasants', and Soldiers' Soviets), in session at Juichin, Kiangsi, proclaimed the Constitution of the Chinese Soviet Republic. This document, signed by Mao Tse-tung as president of the Central Executive Committee of the Chinese Communist Party, described the Red Army as "the front-rank fighter in defense of the Soviet government and the overthrow of the rule of imperialism."

The Congress also adopted a "'Final Decision Concerning Red Army Problems." This resolution declared that success or failure of the "historic class struggle will be decided by armed strength" and called upon "the worker and peasant masses" to put forth all their efforts to strengthen the Red Army. The "Final Decision" continues:

The Red Army is the most important defender of the Soviet political power; it is a class army, and in mission or in spirit, it is fundamentally dissimilar from the Kuomintang army and the imperialist armies.

The imperialist armies and war lord armies are isolated from the masses; they are instruments to oppress the workers and peasants and to ravage colonies, and they are advancing aggressive wars and war lord coalition wars. But the Red Army is the army of the masses of workers and peasants themselves; it is the armed power of liberation of the masses of workers and peasants, and, moreover, it is the army which has a great international mission. The armed might of the Red Army is the armed might which is capable of accelerating the collapse of the reactionary ruling class and of destroying the capitalist and imperialist armies.

The Red Army is the army which is trained and acts in obedience to the international mission and spirit of the toiling masses, and in the history of China it is the one organized with consciously revolutionary warriors. . . .

The Red Army Political Commissariat is the direct representative of the Communist Party and the Soviet Government in the Red Army, and the Communist Party and the Communist Youth League are inseparable organizational constituents of the Red Army.

All toilers, workers, hired farmers, poor peasants, middle peasants, and urban poor have the right and privilege to take up arms to defend the Soviet political power; all who belong to the ruling classes and flayers— war lords, landlords, bullying gentry, bureaucrats, capitalists, rich peasants, and those who belong to their families—are not permitted to join the Red Army.

To serve the interests of the revolution, a strict, self-conscious discipline must be established in the Red Army. All command, managerial, and supply organizations must be completely integrated; they must use all their power regularly to strengthen and raise the fighting capacity of the Red Army, and at the same time, with all their power, they must increase the ability of the Soviet political power to maintain its authority within the Red Army.[24]

The "Final Decision Concerning Red Army Problems" is a document of fundamental importance in the development of the Party's armed forces. In fact, it may be regarded as the "charter" of the Red Army. It stated that the army was to be a "class" army, one based on the masses and united with them. The "right and privilege" to serve in the army were restricted to workers and peasants. The "charter" also assigned the army an international mission: to accelerate the collapse of the ruling classes and to destroy "capitalist" and "imperialist" armies. In addition, it firmly established the positions of the "political commissariat" and party organizations in the army and devised a relentless campaign designed to insure the authority of the Party in the army.

The Communists and the Japanese were not the only daggers in Chiang's side. For months he had been waging a political battle with a Cantonese group determined to displace him. This feud was not settled until mid-January 1932.

The Communists were the immediate beneficiaries of the complicated situation. Time, that invaluable commodity in war, had unexpectedly been accorded them. They used it to good advantage to reorganize and rebuild the Red Army. As of June 1932, Nanking's "enemy order of battle" showed a Communist strength of almost 100,000: [25]

Army Corps	Strength	Rifles	Commander
1	21,000	12,000	Chu Teh
2	9,000	6,000	Ho Lung
3	12,000	9,000	P'eng Teh-huai
4	6,000	2,000	Li Nien-Hui
5	7,000	5,000	Ki Chen-Tou
6	8,000	6,000	Hsu Chi-Shen
7	5,000	4,000	Lin Piao
8	7,200	6,000	Tuan Te-Chang
9	5,000	5,000	Li Keh
10	4,500	2,000	Chou Kien-Pei
11	4,000	3,000	Lo Pin-Hui
12	2,000	1,200	Tou Chen-Tan
13	2,200	2,100	Tien Tse-Huei
Total	92,900	63,300	

Although the Nationalists continued to announce that the Communists had been liquidated, this was far from the fact.

In the summer of 1932, Chiang launched yet another campaign to clear the Communists from a base area in southern Honan, Hupeh, and Anhwei provinces. Here the Fourth Front Army (Chang Kuo-t'ao and Hsü Hsiang-ch'ien) had established the Oyüwan Soviet. In the face of constantly increasing Nationalist pressure, they retired westward into Szechwan, where the unstable political situation promised almost a free hand to organize the peasants and to recruit.

No satisfaction could be derived from a review of the Third Campaign, but Chiang drew some solace from the successes achieved in Honan, Hupeh, and Anhwei. On December 1, 1932, he reported to the Third Plenary Session of the KMT's Central Executive Committee that operations had progressed satisfactorily. The Communists, he announced, had been "invariably defeated and routed." In the process, "thousands were killed . . . large quantities of military booty captured." [26] This statement was a misrepresentation of fact. The Communists had not been "invariably defeated and routed." Perhaps the Generalissimo felt the need to "save face," or perhaps he had not yet recognized harsh reality.

In April 1933, Nanking mounted a Fourth Campaign. Another disaster ensued—this time under the immediate aegis of General Ch'en Ch'eng, who had risen in favor since the temporary eclipse of Ho Ying-ch'in. Three Central divisions, the 11th, 52nd, and 59th, were eliminated.

Whether or not the Nationalists received any advice from General von Seeckt, chief of the German military mission, in planning for the Fifth Campaign is not clear.[27] Nationalist authorities have frequently asserted that they did not. Whatever the facts are, the Nationalists now followed, with solid success, a strategy they had first applied tentatively in the Third Campaign and with limited, localized success in the Fourth. For what he designed as a conclusive effort, the Generalissimo planned a gigantic compression, an almost literal "walling in" of the Communists. To accomplish this end, he set out to construct thousands of mutually-supporting blockhouses and excavate hundreds of miles of barrier ditches. At the same time, the entire population was moved from the area of operations. New roads were built, and new airfields constructed.

The Communists could not cope with this strategy. Several times they launched ill-conceived local offensives. The Nationalists, supported by the grid of blockhouses, aircraft, and artillery, repeatedly fought them to a standstill and inflicted terrible casualties on them. L. M. Chassin, a French historian, has summarized this last campaign in these words:

Chiang's troops, protected by aircraft and artillery, advanced methodically from the solid bases afforded by their blockhouses. Little by little the Red territory shrank, and the effect of this blockade, and above all, the lack of salt in the area, made itself felt severely. As the Red Army levied requisitions on the peasants, their condition became progressively more miserable.

Early in 1934 the Reds tried to push into Fukien province. They succeeded in advancing to a point only fifty kilometers from Foochow. But this time, the Nanking troops counterattacked them and threw them back. The Red Army had lost 60,000 men; famine had caused hundreds of thousands of deaths. It was necessary to take a definite decision.[28]

The Communists now had but two possible courses of action: to remain in Kiangsi—a once rich province but now a desert—and die, or to break the encirclement.

As August 1934 wore on, the situation in the Kiangsi Soviet deteriorated rapidly. Nationalist pressure on the ground continued, and aircraft bombed the capital with impunity. Sometime during this month, the Central Committee tentatively decided to move to a new base. What part Mao and Chu Teh played here is unclear. The Commander in Chief of the Red armies, eager to reinforce Ho Lung's debilitated 2nd Army Corps and create a safe refuge for the Kiangsi Soviet government if—as seemed inevitable—it soon moved, dispatched Hsiao K'o's 6th Army Corps of 10,000 to northern Hunan. There, in September 1934, Ho Lung formed the Second Front Army.

At about this time, the final decision was made. The army and government, altogether some 110,000 people (including several hundred women), would leave Kiangsi. There could have been little doubt about which direction they would take. To the north and east, vastly superior Nationalist forces walled them in. To the south, there was only Kwangtung, a geographical pocket and graveyard as well as the birthplace of revolutions. They had to go west.

In any review of the Bandit Extermination Campaigns, one question persistently arises: Why in five attempts could the Nationalists not satisfy the Generalissimo's consuming ambition to extirpate the Communists in Kiangsi? Besides the obvious fact that it gave the Communists a chance to survive, Chiang's inability to accomplish his purpose was politically and psychologically damaging to the Nationalists, both domestically and internationally. Equally, his failure enhanced the military reputation of the Communists.

The answer to this perplexing question, one which must occasionally return to haunt the Generalissimo in his island retreat, is at least partially obscure. Certainly one contributing factor, however, was the mental attitude of the opposing leaderships. Until they were defeated in the Third Campaign, the Nationalists were contemptuous of the Communists. Not until then did Chiang begin to take his enemy seriously. The deprecatory term *kung-fei*, "Communist bandits," which was habitually applied to the Communists, was an unfortunate choice of terminology, as was *ch'ing-hsiang*, "cleansing of the countryside," an idiom used since ancient times to describe anti-bandit operations. As the Nationalists learned to their great cost, the Red Army was something more than a collection of ragged vagabonds and escaped criminals.

The average Nationalist general of the time, inclined to be arrogant, had been schooled professionally in conventional methods of warfare and was psychologically unable to adjust to the unusual pattern he encountered when he operated against the Red Army. Chiang's commanders wanted to fight the war in Kiangsi (as French generals later wanted to fight one in Indo-China) as wars are "supposed" to be fought. There was only one flaw: the Communists did not propose to accommodate them.

Relatively much weaker than their opponents in terms of men, arms, and equipment, the Communist commanders were forced to seek formulas which canceled Nationalist superiority. Formula number one was information: information both timely and accurate. A related formula was the obverse—security: to deny equivalent information to the enemy. This they succeeded in doing by vertical and horizontal organization of the population, by enrolling literally thousands of men, women, and children as spies.

But it was not enough to deny the enemy information; he must also constantly be deceived. The Communists were students of Sun Tzu, who twenty-three hundred years before had written: "All warfare is based on deception. Therefore, when capable, feign incapacity; when active, inactivity. When near, make it appear that you are far away; when far away, that you are near." [29] In Kiangsi, Communist commanders quickly became past masters of the complementary arts of simulation and dissimulation.

Sun Tzu had also advised offering the enemy baits to lure him into a trap. This formula the Communists commonly used; Mao described the tactic as "luring deep." Such a tactic created opportunities for the Communists to fragment Nationalist columns and destroy them in detail.

"Surprise" was a fundamental principle. The Communists attacked when and where their enemies were unprepared, moved secretly and with unexampled speed to appear suddenly when the

Nationalists believed them to be a hundred miles away. For the Communists in Kiangsi, Sun Tzu was the operational bible.

The Nationalists, too, were groping for related formulas and, as the Fifth Campaign demonstrated, finally found them. To choke off information, the Nationalists moved several million people from the periphery of the Communist-controlled area and created what in a later war was described as "an administrative desert." With their sources of information choked off, the Communists were denied any chance to exercise the initiative. It was now the turn of Chu Teh's army to stumble in the dark. As Mao would write, they were "reduced to a state of complete passivity."

If an inferior force long remains in this state, there is but one end: annihilation. To escape this inexorable fate, the Communists marched into the west—marched so that some place else, on some other day, they could regain freedom of action.[30]

The Nationalists lost no time broadcasting the news that they had expelled the Communists from the Kiangsi Soviet district. The Fifth Campaign, they announced, had accomplished its objectives; surviving Communists were fleeing in disorder. Their final "extermination," now a certainty, was but a matter of time.

CHAPTER THREE

"*March on! March on! March on and on!*": *The Long March*

The celebrated 6,000-mile Long March of the "Chu-Mao army" (the First Front Red Army) from South China to the northwest inevitably recalls the ordeal, recounted in Xenophon's *Anabasis*, of the 10,000 Greeks who twenty-three hundred years earlier had fought their way from deep in the hostile Persian empire to the shores of the Black Sea. In an even more majestic achievement, the Chinese Communists repeatedly tested and confirmed man's ability to undergo indescribable hardship, to overcome every challenge placed in his path by a nature determined to thwart him; to triumph over enemies equally determined to destroy him; and to reach his goal. Alike, Greeks and Chinese endured scorching heat, bitter cold, thirst, and hunger. Alike, they climbed snow-covered mountains, ate roots, slept in the snow, marched, fought, and marched again. Alike, they reconciled internal disputes that threatened to tear them apart. Alike, they survived.

To name the men who led this march is practically to call the roll of those who in the past thirty years have led the Party and its army: Mao Tse-tung, Chou En-lai, Chu Teh, P'eng Teh-huai, Yeh Chien-ying, Liu Ya-lou, Lin Piao, Hsiao Hua, Liu Po-ch'eng, Lo Ping-hui, Nieh Jung-chen. Others, who will one day replace these men, marched with them. At the time, they all sensed the magnitude of their achievement. Shortly after they had come to safety in Shensi, Mao, addressing a meeting of Party cadres, asked if "since P'an Ku divided heaven from earth, and the Three Sovereigns and

47

Five Emperors reigned" there had ever been in history a march to equal it:

> For twelve months we were under daily reconnaissance and bombing from the air by scores of planes; we were encircled, pursued, obstructed, and intercepted on the ground by a big force of several hundred thousand men; we encountered untold difficulties and great obstacles on the way, but by keeping our two feet going we swept across a distance of more than 20,000 *li* through the length and breadth of eleven provinces. Well, has there ever been in history a long march like ours? No, never.[1]

Every school child and every soldier in the People's Liberation Army today studies the story of the march. To the eighteen-year-old peasant conscript, the tale should prove a constant source of inspiration and kindle a desire to emulate the men whose dedication, endurance, and courage wrote a page in history which any army might envy.

For at least a month before the army set out, it was apparent to officers and soldiers that something was in the wind. Regular troops, withdrawn from the front secretly at night and replaced by partisan groups and militia, were ordered to concentrate near Yütu, a *hsien* seat in southwest Kiangsi. The Communists tightened security measures. Teams scoured the area for donkeys and horses to carry heavy machine guns, mortars, and ammunition. Hand-operated machinery used in the primitive Juichin arsenal and printing presses, sewing machines, and other items essential to establish a base in a new area were carefully dismantled. Cannon and shells captured from the Nationalists were buried, as was all other equipment too heavy for donkeys to pack or carriers to transport in baskets suspended from shoulder poles.

On September 30, 1934, the Chairman of the Provisional Government of the Soviet Republic left his quarters in the outskirts of Juichin for the last time. One of Mao's bodyguards has recalled that even the Chairman was prepared to travel in light marching order, for he "did not take his nine-compartment knapsack with him. His entire equipment consisted of two blankets, a cotton sheet, an oil-cloth, a warm overcoat, a broken umbrella, and a bundle of books." [2] At five in the afternoon of October 18, Mao and an escort of some 20 men left Yütu and headed west. "It was the first step on the Long March." [3]

At this time, no one, including Mao Tse-tung, Chu Teh, Chou En-lai, or other members of the Party's Central Committee, knew precisely where the columns were going or when they would reach safety. The story, sanctified by time and the unremitting labors of Party historians and propagandists, is that the leaders intended to march toward Northwest China to prosecute the war the Chinese Soviet Republic had declared against Japan in 1932. The Chairman has been more honest than some of the Party's sycophantic historians. In December 1936, Mao wrote that during the Fifth Nationalist "Encirclement and Supression Campaign," the Communist armies "milled around between the enemy's main forces and his blockhouses and were reduced to complete passivity. All through our fifth counter campaign against 'encirclement and suppression,' which lasted a whole year, we showed not the slightest initiative or drive. In the end we had to withdraw from our Kiangsi base area." [4] Better than most, Mao understood that the army must move not simply to save itself from imminent destruction, but so that it could once again take the offensive, "the only means of destroying the enemy, and . . . the principal means of self-preservation." [5]

The night the Communists set off, they knew only that they were heading west to establish a new base. Hsü Meng-ch'iu, the official historian of the Long March (during which he lost both legs, first frozen in the "Great Snowy Mountains"), recalled in 1937 that the original plan was to join Ho Lung's Second Front Army in northern Hunan.[6] This involved slipping westward along the northern borders of Kwangtung and Kwangsi for more than 400 miles and then cutting north for about 300 more. Alternatively, the columns could fight westward through Kweichow and northern Yunnan, swing north into Szechwan, and there join Hsü Hsiang-ch'ien's Fourth Front Army. Here, in a well-established Soviet area administered by Chang Kuo-t'ao, the Chu-Mao army could rest, reorganize, and plan for the future. Neither prospect was alluring.

For eight nights, the columns marched; in the daytime, they hid. On the ninth day, they shattered a screen of provincial troops and broke into Kwangtung.[7] Then began three days of "fast march" during which the troops traveled four hours and rested four. The prescribed rate of advance was 120 *li*, or almost 35 miles a day. It was soon apparent the train could not meet this pace, and piece by piece, heavier equipment was reluctantly jettisoned and buried.

The Nationalists were now fully alive to what was going on, and Chiang Kai-shek hastily threw fresh units across the routes he presumed the Communists must take. Curiously, the Communists did

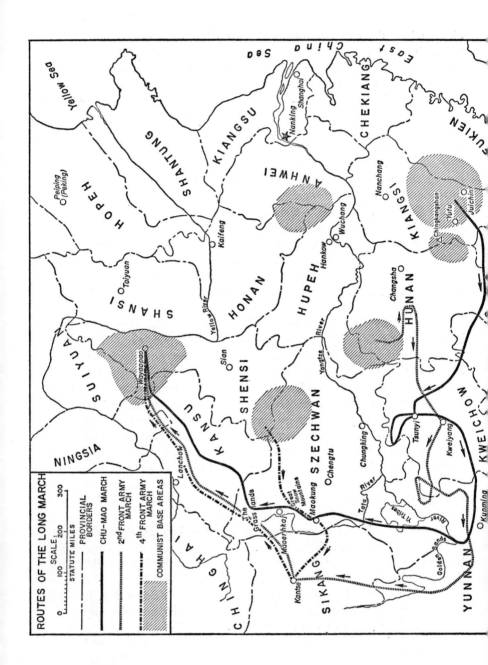

ROUTES OF THE LONG MARCH

SCALE:
STATUTE MILES
0   100   200   300

- PROVINCIAL BORDERS
- CHU-MAO MARCH
- 2nd FRONT ARMY MARCH
- 4th FRONT ARMY MARCH
- COMMUNIST BASE AREAS

not respond to these challenges with maneuver but chose to meet them. This decision may have speeded the march, but in terms of lives, it was terribly costly. The bloodletting lasted for weeks.

At this critical stage, "Mao Tse-tung came forward with a plan which saved the Red Army." [8] Mao proposed to the Central Committee that the army give up the idea of joining Ho Lung and swing south into Kweichow. There, the Nationalists were weak; to the north, they were strong and every day getting stronger. And the army could not risk any more head-on collisions with them. Since leaving Kiangsi ten weeks before it had been bled white. More than 60,000 officers and men, two-thirds of its original strength, had been lost.

The repeated setbacks, in sharp contrast with the situation prior to the fourth campaign against the enemy's encirclement and suppression, gradually opened the eyes of the cadres to the fact that the campaign was being misdirected and that the military tactics were contrary to the correct line as expounded by Mao Tse-tung. The rank and file began to voice doubts and dissatisfaction.[9]

The "correct line as expounded by Mao Tse-tung" was adopted, and his "firm demand for a change of policy saved the remaining 30,000 Red Army men from extermination." [10]

In January 1935, the army took the city of Tsunyi. Here, while the troops rested, the Party's Central Committee met, and the leadership convened an enlarged conference of the Politburo. At this historic conference, Mao mustered enough support to gain the unchallengeable position which is still his. To this day, no one outside the tight circle at the top of the Party knows precisely what went on behind closed doors at Tsunyi. Obviously, there was some frank —and probably heated and acrimonious—discussion. We are told only that the conference rectified "predominant mistakes in military and organizational work"; that it rejected the "incorrect military line . . . responsible for defeat" during the Fifth Campaign in Kiangsi in favor of a strategy based on mobile and guerrilla warfare; that proponents of the "leftist line" in the Central Committee were "overthrown," and that a new leadership was set up with Mao Tse-tung at its head. According to Liu Po-ch'eng, who was then chief of staff to Chu Teh, "the decisions of the Tsunyi Conference were like a tonic to the Red Army units, raising morale"—which after the frightful losses of November and December must have been at a very low ebb—"and sweeping aside all misgivings and discontents." [11]

While the Party's future (and the future of China) was being re-solved at Tsunyi, political workers were busy arresting and executing "evil gentry" and confiscating their land, grain, animals, and farm equipment for subsequent division among the poor peasants. As they had done in other areas, the Communists during their stay in Kweichow destroyed land titles, deeds, and tax records, shot any Kuomintang officials and sympathizers they could lay their hands on, and released prisoners from local jails. They disarmed and dispersed the *min t'uan* (the landlords' private militia) and gave its rifles to Red Guards. Propagandists held mass meetings to assist the army's campaign for recruits, and thousands of young men joined the ranks, although not enough by any means to make up for those who had been lost. The 20,000 who now for the first time put on black caps with the red star were destined to receive their basic training under fire.

Although the available literature does not explicitly state so, a basic decision made at the Tsunyi conference was to press on into Szechwan where under the leadership of Chang Kuo-t'ao and Hsü Hsiang-ch'ien, the Fourth Front Army had established a Soviet district in 1933 after the demise of the Oyüwan Soviet.

This district was ideally situated in a rich and populous province, remote from Nationalist centers of power, difficult of access, and torn apart by a family quarrel between Liu Wen-hui and his nephew, Liu Hsiang, the governor—each of whom claimed the province as a personal satrapy. Other factions also entered the picture from time to time to create a situation of no benefit to anyone but the Communists. Although the squabbling war lords eventually sank their differences in the face of the common danger, it was then too late. Under Chang Kuo-t'ao's energetic leadership, the Fourth Front Army rapidly expanded from some 25,000 to a strength of 60,000. By mid-1934, it consisted of the 4th, 9th, 30th, 31st, and 33rd "armies," each nominally of three "divisions." [12]

Against the Szechwan generals the Communists used the same tactics they had elsewhere applied successfully. Their basic secret was an astounding mobility. They "came like the wind." Their "thunder attacks," always delivered under conditions which favored an attacker with a locally superior force, invariably took the Whites by surprise. Constant marching and maneuvering, combined with an unsurpassed system for gathering information, enabled them to retain the initiative and strike at targets of their own choosing. During the Szechwan campaign, Hsü Hsiang-ch'ien, a graduate of Whampoa then in his early thirties, first established in reputation as an original and brilliant commander.

If the forces from Kiangsi could reach Szechwan, Mao reasoned, the Party would then control well-equipped, battle-experienced armies sufficiently powerful to induce the Generalissimo to think twice before seriously challenging them. It was Mao's intent to consolidate these two forces; Chiang's, to prevent him from doing so, and in the process to exterminate the Chu-Mao army.

Nationalist troops were but one of the many obstacles that lay in the Communists' path. First, there was the problem of crossing the upper reaches of the Yangtze or, as it was called in Yunnan province, "The River of Golden Sands." This would not be easy. The Generalissimo was mustering blocking forces on all sides. Mao and Chu Teh, masking their ultimate design, maneuvered for several weeks in Kweichow. During this time, the Communists skirmished almost daily with Chiang's troops but successfully avoided a major battle.

Suddenly, the Communist columns turned west and headed for the capital of Yunnan province. This sudden move, completely unanticipated, pulled Nationalist forces from blocking positions and cleared the way to the river. Within sight of the provincial capital, the Communists abruptly turned ninety degrees north and in a series of amazing "fast marches" approached their goal. By an amusing stratagem, an advance patrol disguised in Nationalist uniforms got control of one boat, crossed the river, and seized the others, which contrary to Chiang's instructions had not been burned. The army ferried the river into Szechwan without incident and left behind it in K'unming a frustrated Generalissimo.

There now remained but one major obstacle, the Tatu River. In an operation distinguished by individual initiative, courage, and skill, a few Communist soldiers seized a narrow chain bridge which was inadequately guarded. This ancient bridge, swaying 300 feet above the waters churning below, was the means by which, on May 30, 1935, the army crossed. On July 12, 1935, after conquering mountains covered with snow and ice, the Communist vanguards arrived in Maokung *hsien* in northwest Szechwan, headquarters of the Fourth Front Red Army.

The army that marched into Maokung was not the army that had left Yütu nine months earlier. Of the original commanders, leaders, and fighters, but 25,000 remained. Perhaps 20,000 men had joined en route. Again and again, the First Front Army had proved itself a superb combat instrument, but the incessant strain and the frightful losses had told. For officers and men worn out physically and depleted emotionally, rest was a necessity: the road ahead, 2,000 miles long, held many perils. But for the leaders there was to be little rest.

Even as the troops stacked arms, disputes arose between Mao and Chang Kuo-t'ao. The succeeding weeks were devoted to futile discussions which raged around the question of the united army's ultimate destination. In mid-August, Mao asserted himself. He would depart with two corps of the First Front Army to the Soviet area Li Chih-tan had built in northern Shensi. Chu Teh would remain in Szechwan in command of the situation there and await the arrival of Ho Lung, Jen Pi-shih, and Hsiao K'o from Hunan with their Second Front Army. Then all would proceed together to Shensi. With some variations, some altercations, and considerable marching and countermarching, this plan was ultimately followed.[13]

During the last week of August 1935, the First Front Army, with P'eng Teh-huai in command, Yeh Chien-ying as chief of staff, and Mao as political commissar, set out. Lin Piao and Chou En-lai, together with practically the entire membership of the new Central Committee installed at Tsunyi, were in the column. Now began the last and most dangerous phase of the march.

The terrain they had to cross was in places desolate and mountainous, in places nothing but a vast bog known as "the Grasslands." Not only the land was hostile; the fierce tribesmen who occupied it were even more so. Here were no peasants to help them, no provincial troops or *min t'uan* to replenish ammunition, no landlords to despoil, no towns, no habitations, no stocks of food. The army was truly marching in the wilderness.

Unlike the Lolo tribesmen they had earlier encountered, the Mantzu and Tibetans were implacably hostile. For the first time, the Communists discovered that being ambushed is an unpleasant experience. The tribesmen were not only expert shots, they were expert thieves who infiltrated camps at night and stabbed and beheaded sleeping soldiers and made off with everything portable.

The Grasslands, a great bog in which the soldiers sank to their calves in clinging muck, was the army's final ordeal. A young woman who made the march described "these hideous yellow and black marshes" in which the pack animals foundered in "deep boggy pools of black mud."[14] This experience made an indelible impression: "The soldiers hated the Grasslands very bitterly." They were depressed, and "the Army's Political Department had to work very hard to conquer pessimism among the troops, and the Communist Party members had to measure up to carrying the burdens of the weak." [15]

At last, in October 1935, the lean columns swung singing into Wayaopao in Li Chih-tan's Shensi Soviet. The last line of the song they sang on that historic day was: "March on! March on! March on and on!"

In December 1935, Mao, in speaking of the Long March, asked "What is its significance?" He answered:

The Long March is a manifesto. It proclaims to the world that the Red Army is an army of heroes and that the imperialists and their jackals, Chiang Kai-shek and his like, are perfect nonentities. It announces the bankruptcy of the encirclement, pursuit, obstruction, and interception attempted by the imperialists and Chiang Kai-shek. The Long March is also an agitation corps. It declares to the approximately two hundred million people of eleven provinces that only the road of the Red Army leads to their liberation. Without the Long March, how could the broad masses have known so quickly that there are such great ideas in the world as are upheld by the Red Army? The Long March is also a seeding machine. It has sown many seeds in eleven provinces, which will sprout, grow leaves, blossom into flowers, bear fruit, and yield a harvest in the future. [16]

Later, in a less polemical mood, the Chairman wrote a *lü shih*, a Chinese poem in eight lines, each of seven characters:

THE LONG MARCH

The Red Army fears not the trials of a distant march;
To them, a thousand mountains, ten thousand rivers
   are nothing:
To them the Five Ridges ripple like little waves,
And the mountain peaks of Wumeng roll by like mud
   balls.
Warm are the cloud-topped cliffs washed by the River
   of Golden Sand,
Cold are the iron chains that span the Tatu River.
The myriad snows of Minshan only make them happier,
And when the Army has crossed, each face is smiling. [17]

The Long March placed its peculiar and irrevocable mark on the Party and the Red Army. The experience of incredible trials surmounted and dangers overcome confirmed the positions of the leaders who shared them. Ever since those days, days when each man repeatedly faced an ultimate test in one form or another, the "Long Marchers" have until recently practically monopolized top positions in the hierarchies of the Party and its army. From this trial emerged a group of tested leaders, supremely confident of their ability to shape the destiny of their Party and their country. And from it, too, sprang an indoctrinated army endowed with a rich experience, convinced of the righteousness of its cause and equipped with a dynamic doctrine of guerrilla and mobile war.

"On the Eve of a Great New Revolution": The Red Army's "War of Resistance" Against Japan

One hundred thousand left Kiangsi in October 1934. After three hundred and sixty-six days and hundreds of battles and skirmishes, 20,000 arrived in North Shensi. They had marched something more than 6,000 miles. The march had accomplished its purpose. The Party had preserved the hard core of its army and its political and military leadership. In these barren and remote highlands, so different from the southland they knew, the Communists could rest, renew their strength, organize the peasants, and rebuild the army that had eluded its pursuers with consummate skill and frustrated every attempt to stop its march.

If Juichin had little to recommend it as the seat of an ambitious Soviet government, Pao-an ("Protected Peace"), the site selected for the new capital, had even less. Centuries before the Communists arrived, the town had been an outpost guarding the northwest approaches to Shensi and Shansi from the mounted barbarians who periodically swept in from the plains to collect loot and Chinese women. But now both provinces were poor and undeveloped; only Sian (capital of Shensi), T'aiyuan (capital of Shansi), and a few other cities boasted public utilities—to say nothing of amenities usually taken for granted elsewhere. Communications were equally primitive.

Such superficial disadvantages were greatly outweighed by fundamental advantages. In strategic terms, North Shensi was a good choice. Distant from Chiang's power centers in the Yangtze Valley, it was close to the borders of the Soviet Union, from whence some material help might hopefully be expected. Shansi, the mountain redoubt on the eastern flank, afforded excellent base areas for forays into the plain of North China, where 60 million peasants waited.

By February 1936, the Communists had recovered sufficiently to go into action. Under the guise of prosecuting the war against Japan, three Red Army columns—some 34,000 men—crossed the Yellow River into Shansi. There they thoroughly reconnoitered prospective base areas, repeatedly defeated the feckless provincial troops fielded by "Model Governor" Yen Hsi-shan, collected grain and money, shot rich landlords and tax collectors, recruited thousands of peasants for their armies, and began organizing the rural masses. Peasant responses to their propaganda, which stressed nationalism and resistance to Japan, was instantaneous and widespread. The entire province north of T'aiyuan was soon fermenting.[1]

The Communists also slanted their appeals for unity to the intellectuals—particularly the students—the shopkeepers, government employees, workers, and soldiers. When they withdrew, hundreds of students returned with them to Shensi. Many of Yen's troops defected; some units went over intact. The Communists later claimed they enrolled 8,000 selected volunteers during their Shansi operations.[2]

The success of these forays made it unmistakably clear to Nanking that the rejuvenated Communists were again on the warpath. Although it was no easy matter to reach the heart of the new Soviet area, the Generalissimo began laying plans for a final drive against it. As a preliminary measure, he deployed about 150,000 troops along the Yellow River and set up a new "Bandit Suppression Headquarters" at Sian. This *cordon sanitaire* was held by "Young Marshal" Chang Hsüeh-liang's Northeast (*Tung-pei*) Army and Yang Hu-ch'eng's Northwest (*Hsi-pei*) Army, with the "Young Marshal" in supreme command.

For some time, however, the Young Marshal had been in secret communication with the Communists. Indeed, he and his confidential emissaries had held numerous conferences with Communist leaders, and with his permission, a number of Communist cadres were covertly working in the *Tung-pei* Army. The soldiers in this army, practically all Manchurians, had understandably never been particularly interested in suppressing Communists while the Japanese Kwantung Army remained in uncontested possession of their homeland.

When in the middle of 1936 the Generalissimo issued a directive to the Young Marshal to exterminate the Communists, Chang Hsüeh-liang vigorously protested the order and pointed out that continued Japanese encroachment on China's territory and sovereignty demanded not a resumption of costly internecine war but a national united front against the invader. The Generalissimo would not entertain this advice, which coincided with the Communist line. His policy gave priority to "national unification," by which he meant extirpation of the Red Army. The Japanese could wait. It was to explain the necessity for this program that he flew to Sian from Nanking on December 7, 1936.

The Young Marshal and his generals listened respectfully to their commander in chief. They were not impressed by the arguments Chiang adduced. The Generalissimo was equally stubborn when his nominal subordinates repeatedly urged him to cancel the proposed operations and unite with the Communists to repel the Japanese. These fruitless discussions went on for five days.

To Chang Hsüeh-liang and his commanders there seemed but one obvious way to resolve the impasse—to use a method the Chinese euphemistically describe as "military persuasion" (*ping chien*). And this they proceeded to do. In the early morning of December 12, they arrested members of Chiang's military and personal staffs, disarmed Nationalist troops in Sian, and finally, after a brief clash with his bodyguard, took the Generalissimo into "protective custody." This term is correctly descriptive. Chiang Kai-shek's life was in danger. Younger officers of the *Tung-pei* Army attacked him as a traitor, a "country-selling thief" (*mai-kuo-tsei*), and demanded a speedy public trial. The Young Marshal kept his head and saved the Generalissimo's.

It is not relevant here to narrate the details of this dramatic kidnaping or the course of the parleys which culminated in Chiang's safe return to Nanking. The event and subsequent negotiations which terminated on Christmas Day have been described with varying degrees of authority by a number of foreign observers as well as by the distinguished victim.[3] What may be noted is that Chou En-lai, vice-chairman of the Party's Military Affairs Committee, whom the Young Marshal had hastily summoned to Sian, played a prominent—if not, indeed, a decisive—role in procuring Chiang's release. Substantially, the demands of the rebellious officers, in which the Communists concurred, were met. If the Generalissimo's word was good, the putative agreement paved the way for the "united front" the Communists had been vociferously demanding.

While Chou En-lai lingered in Sian, Mao Tse-tung occupied himself composing and inscribing an epistle to Chiang Kai-shek. In this letter, made public on December 26, Mao reminded his enemy of almost ten years' standing that he "owed his safe departure from Sian to the mediation of the Communist Party." In blunt language, Mao informed Chiang that "the people throughout the country" would not "tolerate" any further "procrastination or modification of the terms" which he had accepted at Sian in exchange for his freedom. If, Mao concluded, Chiang did not "cease waging wars at home . . . oppressing the people . . . and immediately join the anti-Japanese front," the "revolutionary tide" would certainly sweep him away. On the other hand, if he would at once end his policy of attempting to annihilate the Communists and "enter into an alliance with the Red Army to resist Japan," the Party would "naturally extend its assistance to him." [4]

Although there is no record that the Generalissimo replied to this statement, he did call a halt to scheduled operations against the Communist-held area. At the time, he took no other public steps to heal the breach. This, it appeared, might require a *deus ex machina*, a role which the Japanese China Garrison Army (Lieutenant General Tashiro Kan'ichirō) obligingly played at Marco Polo Bridge, some ten miles west of Peking, on July 7, 1937.

The Lukouchiao "incident," which rapidly expanded into a full-scale invasion of North and Central China, brought the question of practical agreement between Nanking and Yenan to a head, and by mid-August the two had reached a preliminary understanding to integrate the Communists' three Front armies into a national force which was designated the Eighth Route Army (*ti-pa-lu-chün*) and assigned for operations to the Second War Zone, commanded by the aging Governor Yen. Chu Teh was named vice-commander of the war zone and commander in chief of the Eighth Route Army.

Officially, the army was not formally constituted until September 22, but it began to operate under its new—and soon to become famous—designation in late August. At that time, it had an official strength of 45,000 and was organized as follows:

HEADQUARTERS

Commander	Chu Teh
Vice-Commander	*P'eng Teh-huai
Chief of Staff	Yeh Chien-ying
Director, Political Department	**Wang Chia-hsiang

115TH DIVISION—15,000

Commander	***Lin Piao
Vice-Commander	Nieh Jung-chen
Political Commissar	Nieh Jung-chen
343rd Brigade	Ch'en Kuang
344th Brigade	Hsü Hai-tung

120TH DIVISION—15,000

Commander	Ho Lung
Vice-Commander	Hsiao K'o
Political Commissar	Kuang Hs'iang-ying
358th Brigade	Hsiao K'o
359th Brigade	Wang Chen

129TH DIVISION—15,000

Commander	Liu Po-ch'eng
Vice-Commander	Hsü Hsiang-ch'ien
Political Commissar	Teng Hsiao-p'ing
385th Brigade	Hsü Hsiang-ch'ien
386th Brigade	Chen Keng

* Later, Field Commander
** Replaced in November 1937 by Jen Pi-shih
*** Concurrently president, Yenan Anti-Japanese Political and Military Academy

It may be noted that the over-all size of the Communist forces at this time was 80,000 to 90,000. Nanking, naturally desiring to limit effective Communist strength, had been unwilling to subsidize more than three divisions totaling 45,000. The Communists, who had no intention of observing a limitation they considered entirely academic, accepted the central government's figure in order to collect the monthly subsidy. They did not reduce their forces to the stipulated strength, but rather continued to increase them. Sizable amounts of Nationalist money designed for pay, allowances, and operational expenses were diverted to the training of political cadres.

Mao and Chu Teh did not wait for formal approval from Nanking to send the Eighth Route Army into action. All three divisions crossed the Yellow River from Shensi into Shansi in early September 1937. At that time, one Japanese column threatened Shansi from the north; another was pushing westward from the Hopeh plain. The common objective of these coordinated thrusts was T'aiyuan. Lin Piao led the 115th Division toward the Wut'ai Mountains to block the former, which consisted of the Japanese 5th Division (Lieut. Gen. Itagaki Seishirō) advancing south from Kalgan via a single motorable road. The other two divisions, Ho Lung's 120th and Liu Po-ch'eng's 129th, were not committed against the Japanese. As we shall see later, they had other fish to fry.

In his speech at Wayaopao in December 1935, Mao had indicated that the Communists intended to follow a prudent military policy: "Before the time is ripe for a decisive battle, or before we have adequate strength for it, we must not rashly wage a decisive battle." [5] In the contexts of both the recently concluded united front agreement and the existing war situation, with Central and provincial forces in continuous retreat, the time was "ripe." Although its military effect might be transitory, a Communist victory gained against a sizable Japanese force—particularly one commanded by such a well-known soldier as Itagaki—would have tremendous moral and psychological impact. We may be sure that these factors were most carefully weighed at councils of war in Yenan before Lin Piao was assigned his mission.

Another factor which undoubtedly influenced the decision to take this initiative was the relative state of intelligence available to the Japanese and to the Communists. During his unopposed move up the P'ing-Sui (Peip'ing–Suiyuan) railway toward Kalgan and since departing from that city for the thrust into North Shansi, Itagaki had no way of getting reliable information about the Communists. If he trusted reports and estimates prepared at headquarters of the Area Army in Tientsin, he could have had no better than a fragmentary conception either of where major elements of the Eighth Route Army were or what they were doing. The Communists, on the other hand, had complete, correct, and timely information as to where the 5th Division was and precisely what it was doing.

Finally, the Communists assessed Itagaki's character correctly. This Japanese general was an imperious, conceited, and arrogant man. These characteristics were obvious to anyone who encountered him even briefly.[6] Contemptuous of his Chinese opponents and supremely confident in his skill and the fighting qualities of his division, Itagaki blithely approached the passes leading through the Wut'ai Mountains. The General was stumbling in the dark in a strange, forbidding, and hostile land and was too unimaginative to conceive the dangers that might attend his march.

On September 25, 1937, the 115th Division ambushed Itagaki's long column in a defile known as P'inghsingkuan. The battle was a stunning victory for the Chinese, who struck the Japanese as they advanced laboriously and with completely inadequate security down a sunken road overlooked by low-lying hills. Nieh Jung-chen, vice-commander of the 115th Division, conducted the battle. As Chu Teh later described the successful action: ". . . two regiments struck the enemy's flank and two battalions enveloped his rear. The Japanese were caught in a trap." [7] They were indeed. Itagaki's division suffered almost 5,000 casualties and lost many rifles, pistols, automatic weapons, and mortars; much ammunition, and a brigade train loaded with food, winter clothing, and the paymaster's money chests. These contained a quarter of a million very negotiable yen.

On the basis of the mythology that has grown up about P'inghsingkuan, one might imagine that it was another Cannae, a Blenheim, a Gettysburg, or a Marne—which it was not. It was a small-scale battle that had no military effect whatsoever on subsequent operations. But it was the first victory of the united front. It served as a badly needed tonic to Chinese morale and showed that the Japanese "dwarfs" could be beaten.

The jubilant Communists naturally lost no time in trumpeting the claim that their original and unique tactics of mobile warfare had produced this triumph. This is nonsense. Itagaki's carelessness contributed quite as much as did any other factor to the debacle his division suffered. General Nieh adapted classic tactics to terrain and circumstances, took advantage of his adversary's laxity, and surprised him. The victory enhanced Nieh's reputation as an imaginative and bold combat commander able to recognize and seize opportunity. But it was a battle only half won. Itagaki's division should have been annihilated.

Nevertheless, P'inghsingkuan is a landmark for the People's Liberation Army. And it has another claim to distinction: it was the first, last, and only occasion during the Anti-Japanese War when the Communists committed a unit as large as a division to formal battle —despite the fact that there were many opportunities to have done so. P'inghsingkuan, then, was a battle of considerable psychological

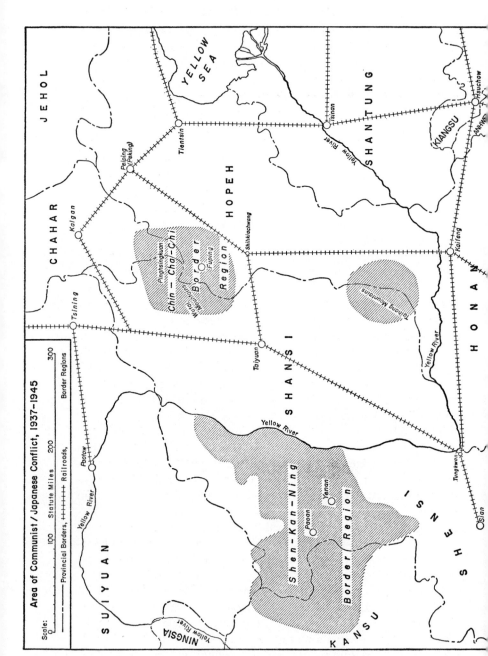

Area of Communist / Japanese Conflict, 1937–1945

Scale:
0   100   200   300
Statute Miles

— · — Provincial Borders, ┼┼┼┼┼ Railroads,

[shaded] Border Regions

JEHOL

YELLOW SEA

SHANTUNG

Peiping (Peking)

Tientsin

Tsinan

Yellow River

Hsuchow

KIANGSU

Nanking

CHAHAR

Kalgan

HOPEH

Shihkiachwang

Kaifeng

Tsining

Pinghsingkuan

Chin – Cha – Chi
Border Region
Fuping

Wutai Mountains

Taiyuan

Taihang Mountains

SHANSI

Yellow River

HONAN

Yellow River

Packow

Yellow River

Shen – Kan – Ning
Border Region

Yenan

Paoan

Tungkwan

SIAN

Sian

SHENSI

SUIYUAN

NINGSIA

Yellow River

KANSU

64

import but of negligible military significance. The Communists lived on the reputation they had made there for a long time—until 1945, in fact, when the divisions they had so carefully husbanded during the Anti-Japanese War took the field once again against their original enemy, the Generalissimo.

What sort of an army was it which excited the unqualified admiration of the few Westerners who visited it during the first years of the Anti-Japanese War? The immediately noticeable characteristics were that the Eighth Route was a young, tough, and enthusiastic army. The average age of the "fighters" (*chan shih*) was in the early twenties. The great majority were veterans of the Long March. And so were the junior officers—the "leaders"—and the political cadres. All "commanders"—a title reserved for those commanding units larger than companies—had been on the Long March, and all were members of the Party, as were many noncommissioned "leaders" and "fighters."

The enthusiasm of the soldiers and the evident spirit of fundamental democracy which pervaded the army deeply impressed foreign observers. Col. Evans Carlson of the U.S. Marine Corps, the first foreign military observer to get into Communist-held areas, commented repeatedly on these characteristics as well as on the self-discipline of the individual soldier. "The explanation," he wrote, "lay in the ethical indoctrination of the individual. Each man possessed the *desire* to do what was right; it was right to perform his duty." [8]

Political work in the army had been standardized at the time of Carlson's visits. Trained cadres in sufficient numbers staffed Party committees at all echelons. The basic Party unit was at company level, and political indoctrination sessions were an important feature of the daily training schedule. But full benefit could not be derived from these classes unless the soldiers were literate, and education at the primary level was emphasized. Carlson describes one ingenious "educational aid": "When units are on the march lesson papers are pinned to the back of the cap of the man ahead so that the soldier may study as he walks." [9]

In conversation with Carlson, Jen Pi-shih, director of the Political Department of the army, described political work as the "life line of the army" and "the heart and soul of our resistance to the invasion. Our weapons are antiquated and inferior, but we can compensate for this handicap by emphasizing political indoctrination." [10] (This theme, developed earlier by Mao Tse-tung, is a constant. One finds contemporary reflection of it in such statements as: "The atom bomb is a paper tiger"; "We have the spiritual atomic bomb"; "Weapons decide nothing; man decides everything.")

To a foreign correspondent who visited Yenan at about this time, Mao described political work in the army as one of its "very significant and distinctive" features. This work was guided by three "basic principles":

First, the principle of unity between officers and men, i.e., eradicating feudal practices in the army, abolishing the practice of beating and bullying the men, building up a conscious discipline, and leading a life in which weal and woe are shared by all alike—as a result of which the whole army is perfectly united. Secondly, the principle of unity between the army and the people, i.e., enforcing such discipline in dealing with the masses as forbids the army from violating even in the slightest degree the property rights of the people, carrying out propaganda among the masses and organizing and arming them, lightening the financial burden of the people, and dealing blows to the traitors and collaborators who undermine the army and the people—as a result of which the army and the people are perfectly united and the army everywhere welcomed by the people. Thirdly, the principle of disintegrating the enemy troops and giving lenient treatment to prisoners of war. Our victory depends not only upon the operations of our troops, but also upon the disintegration of the enemy troops.[11]

Carlson traveled on foot for more than 2,000 miles with Eighth Route Army guerrillas in 1937 and 1938. He was particularly struck by the uncomplaining endurance of the soldiers during long and dangerous marches behind Japanese lines. On one occasion, he records a march of 58 miles in thirty-two hours—a feat the more remarkable because it was performed in mountainous country by a battalion of 600 men. Most of the distance was covered in moonlight. From the top of a mountain where the battalion had stopped to catch a few hours' sleep, "the descent was steep and the footing precarious. Slipping and sliding down the mountain, we entered a valley which we followed to the north. The pace again became rapid and rhythmic. As the hours wore on the mind became numb to everything but the task of placing one foot ahead of the other. We resolved into automatons. . . ."[12] It need not be emphasized that the amazing mobility which excited Carlson's admiration did not arouse the same response from the Japanese.[13]

After the victory at P'inghsingkuan, the Eighth Route Army abruptly switched major emphasis from combating the Japanese to organizing the masses. In his address at Wayaopao in December 1935, Mao had told the working cadres that China was "on the eve of a great change" and had defined the Party's new task as one of "integrating the activities of the Red Army with all the activities of the workers, peasants, students, and petty bourgeoisie and the national bourgeoisie throughout the country." [14] The army now addressed itself to the task assigned by the Chairman.

The Communists had selected three general areas in Shansi for major bases: the rugged Wut'ai Mountains, which dominate the plains of central Hopeh; the Taihang range in the southeast part of the province; and the thinly-populated northwest districts. By January 1, 1938, the army had succeeded in establishing "border governments" in two of these areas. At Fup'ing, in western Hopeh, Nieh Jung-chen presided over the *Chin-Ch'a-Chi* (Shansi-Chahar-Hopeh) Border Region; in the northwest, Ho Lung deployed his 120th Division over a huge area, the *Shen-Kan-Ning* (Shensi-Kansu-Ningsia) Border Region.[15] Liu Po-ch'eng based his 129th Division in the Taihang range. In these areas, the Red Army began the "integrating activities" which before the end of the Anti-Japanese War expanded to embrace vast areas in North and Central China with a population of 100,000,000.

The establishment of "guerrilla areas" as adjuncts to the three major "base areas" was the next step in a long-range program designed to mobilize the masses and create the ocean in which guerrillas could swim with impunity. Mao defined a "guerrilla area" as one which at the beginning "the guerrillas could not completely occupy"—which belonged to the guerrillas only as long as they were physically present and which reverted to "puppet" control as soon as they left.

Such guerrilla areas will be transformed into base areas when they have gone through the necessary processes . . . that is, when a large number of enemy troops have been defeated or annihilated, the puppet regime destroyed, the activity of the people called forth, popular anti-Japanese organizations formed, the people's armed forces developed, and an anti-Japanese political power established.[16]

Mao observed that to convert a guerrilla area into a base area was "a painstaking process of creation," for it depended "on how far the enemy is annihilated and how far the masses of the people are aroused." [17] To initiate this "painstaking process," elite detachments of the Eighth Route Army began slipping quietly down from their Shansi bases into Hopeh in early October 1937.

The direction of thrust: the countryside. The target: the peasant. As soon as a Red Army detachment moved into a rural district, it applied a well-tested organizational pattern across the board. Cadres of the Political Department's "Mass-Movement Branch" presented the Party's program for resistance to the Japanese at village meetings the entire populace was summoned to attend. Here the cadres called on the people to provide able-bodied recruits for the Red Army, to enroll in the militia (*min-ping*), the People's Self-Defense Corps (*jen-min tzu-wei-tui*), or "voluntarily" to join one of the numerous auxiliary groups. A particular appeal was made to the youth and to children. At the same time, the Propaganda Branch saw to the posting of anti-Japanese *ta-tzu-pao* (slogans in large characters) and wall newspapers; set up a school for illiterates; and arranged for theatricals and other entertainments. The anti-Japanese theme predominated.

Concurrently, the army's Political Department established administrative organs staffed by reliable inhabitants; the Security Section rounded up suspected collaborators, overt Nationalist sympathizers, "local bullies," "evil landlords," and rich peasants whose social attitudes were suspect and who lacked the good sense to have sought a more salubrious atmosphere. During this period, the Communists applied terror with cautious and selective discrimination. There was some shooting, but the circumstances demanded moderation. Although most landlords escaped with their lives, they paid for them. The Communists imposed heavy fines on all those whom the peasants accused of oppressive and usurious habits.

Organization of guerrilla activities in these "liberated areas" required decentralization of command and dispersion of forces, and for almost three years after P'inghsingkuan, the Communists conducted no major military operations. During this period, the Eighth Route Army and its partisan groups confined themselves to raids and other variants of what they called *yü-chi-chan*—"mobile-striking war." These tactics harassed and irritated the Japanese and tied thousands of troops, who might otherwise have been employed to better advantage, to static guard duties.

During this time the united front began to show very definite cracks. The behavior of the Communists during 1938 and 1939 and particularly the increasing scope and tempo of their work in rural areas, where local Communist regimes "sprang up like bamboo shoots after a rain," alarmed the Generalissimo and confirmed his opinion that they were intent on building up strength for the eventual inescapable trial at arms with the Nationalists. Therefore, in the summer of 1939 he imposed a stringent blockade on Communist-held areas. Travel to and fro, as well as passage of goods of any description, including medicines, was strictly prohibited. Skirmishes between Nationalist and Communist partisan detachments, each seeking to win support of the peasants, broke out like a rash and soon became endemic in the countryside of North and Central China.

Each side naturally accused the other of violations of the united front agreement. But in examining available evidence, one can only conclude that the Communists deliberately accelerated the rate of discord. Mao's acerbic "Notice by the Government of the Shensi-Kansu-Ningsia Border Region and the Rear Headquarters of the Eighth Route Army," written May 15, 1938, "with a view to counteracting the disruptive activities of the Chiang Kai-shek clique," is a good example of the insulting diatribes the Communists now began to direct at the central government.[18] Needless to say, the Nationalists counterattacked. These exchanges did nothing to compose fundamental differences, nor were they designed to do so.

The Communists at this time labored under a severe disadvantage. Diplomatic representatives of foreign powers and newsmen were accredited to Chungking. As a consequence, Chungking was the only source of information on the progress (or lack of it) of resistance, and the news generated by the KMT was not exactly slanted to enhance the Communist image. Government spokesmen accused the Communists of a "two-faced" policy and produced damaging documentary evidence to substantiate the allegation that Yenan was devoting 70 per cent of its military effort to expansion, 20 per cent to skirmishing with the Nationalists, and 10 per cent to resisting Japan.[19] By the summer of 1940, it had thus become politically expedient for the Communists to take offensive action and so demonstrate to those beginning to question their motives that they were very much in the Anti-Japanese War.[20]

Another development made action imperative. This was the new anti-guerrilla strategy put into effect by Lieut. Gen. Tada Hayao shortly after he took command of the North China Area Army in late September 1939. Tada's "cage policy" was a refinement of the strategy of "fortism" Chiang had used so effectively to lever the Communists out of Kiangsi in 1934. Tada proposed no less than to alter the entire countryside of North China. To carry out this scheme, the Japanese mobilized thousands of Chinese peasants. As American Military Intelligence later reported:

Deep and wide ditches or moats were dug and high walls built along the sides of the railways and highways in Central and Southern Hopeh in order to protect them from attacks and, more important, to blockade and to break up the Communist base areas. At the same time, hundreds of miles of new roads with protecting ditches were built with the object of cutting up the guerrilla bases into small pieces which would then be destroyed one by one. The number of blockhouses along the railways and roads, manned by Japanese soldiers, was greatly increased. . . . The Eighth Route Army clearly saw the danger of Tada's new tactics.[21]

The Communists had an additional self-serving motive for action. They were aware that any operation on a large scale would provoke severe reprisals against the villages suspected of harboring or supporting guerrillas. These reprisals would naturally sharpen the enmity of the peasants toward the invaders and consequently render them the more susceptible to Communist propaganda and organizational efforts.

The Communists launched the "Hundred Regiments Offensive," their major effort of the Anti-Japanese War, on the night of August 20, 1940. This coordinated operation continued, with several interludes, for three months. In its overt aspects, the campaign was a success. Guerrillas made hundreds of cuts in rail lines; derailed trains, blew up small bridges and viaducts, attacked and burned stations; destroyed switches, water towers, and signal-control equipment, and otherwise seriously damaged and temporarily disarranged the railway system in North China. As a substantial dividend, Japanese garrison forces, necessarily concentrating on counterguerrilla operations and major restoration projects, were unable to get into the countryside to confiscate the autumn harvest.

The Communists announced that the "Hundred Regiments Offensive" had been a great victory. They reported more than 20,000 Japanese killed; 5,000 puppet troops killed and wounded; 281 Japanese officers captured, and 18,000 puppet prisoners. They claimed that almost 3,000 forts and blockhouses had been destroyed and large quantities of arms and ammunition taken.[22] A more realistic appraisal indicated that the Japanese, taken by surprise, were indeed hurt but not to the extent Yenan claimed.

From the Hundred Regiments Offensive, the Communists also reaped some less tangible advantages. The campaign somewhat ameliorated the central government's suspicions and got the Communists a good press. The anticipated brutal reprisals were carried out by the Japanese, the hatred of the peasants was aroused, and Communist efforts to organize them were thereby greatly facilitated.[23]

Actually, the Japanese reprisals were much fiercer than the Communists had expected. When he assumed command of the North China Area Army in July 1941, General Okamura Yasuji instituted the "three-all" policy—"kill all, burn all, destroy all." This was scorched earth with a vengeance.

Okamura did not, however, confine his activities to burning villages, shooting the inhabitants, and slaughtering the livestock. Mobile Japanese columns took to the hills in search of the Eighth Route Army and inflicted severe casualties on the Communists, who had not bargained for such a violent reaction. The active counterguerrilla program which Okamura pursued during 1941 and 1942 severely restricted Eighth Route Army partisan activity. Not again would the Communists mount an operation on the scale of the "Hundred Regiments."

The paper war Yenan conducted with the central government crescendoed in 1941–42. Although as far as diplomatic usage was concerned the tone of Communist communications left something to be desired, the Nationalists tended to conform to normal standards. But in another sense the missives the Nationalists sent to Yenan were quite as irritating as those they received. During this time, government correspondence exuded an attitude of pious rectitude: "tolerance," "sincerity," "leniency," "magnanimity," "forbearance," earnestness," and similar expressions dot Nationalist statements, manifestos, and communiqués like raisins in a pie. If the CCP would only "realize and correct" its errors; "abandon its present policy of forcibly occupying our national territory," "obstructing the prosecution of the war," "assaulting government troops," "fulfill its promises," and "prove its good faith," the central government would "take note of its sincerity and loyalty" and "once more treat it with sympathy and consideration." [24] A prime minister of the era of Warring States would have felt at home with letters of this type, overflowing as they were with meaningless moral aphorisms culled from the classics. The Communists had no use for the language of the classics. Revolutionary vitriol suited them better.

The bulk of this correspondence dealt with two matters: first, an agreed strength for the Eighteenth Group Army (the official Nationalist designation of the Eighth Route Army),[25] and second, an agreed delineation of areas in which the Communists could operate. Neither problem was ever settled.

In essence, the Communists kept raising the ante. For example, in the fall of 1937, they had accepted three divisions. In early May 1943, Lin Piao, in a memorandum to General Chang Chih-chung, stated the desire of the Communists that their troops "be reorganized into four armies with 12 divisions."[26] This demand suggests a regular force in being of well over 120,000. Fifteen months later, Yenan was insisting upon at least five armies with a total of 16 divisions—a figure indicating a force in being of about 200,000 front-line troops.[27]

At the end of 1943, the strength of the Eighth Route Army, according to Communist figures, stood at about 325,000. Of this number, two-thirds operated as guerrillas. The core of the army, however, was organized into regular triangular divisions—that is, three squads of 12 to 16 men formed a platoon; three platoons, a company; three companies, a battalion; three battalions, a regiment; three regiments (and sometimes four), a division; and three divisions, an army. This structure was not then universal but later became so. In addition, there were a number of independent brigades, regiments, and detachments. The Communists were thus flexible in their organizations; they had developed the "task-force" concept and shifted subordinate units freely to compose forces or groups deemed appropriate to the mission assigned.

One organizational feature was particularly noteworthy: the "3 for 3" squad structure. Each squad in the Red Army consisted of three "small teams" of three, four, or five men plus a squad leader. The squad leader was normally a Party member, and the group leaders (when possible) were either members or aspirants to membership. This squad structure (which prevailed in the PLA during the Korean War) was effective in both its institutional and tactical aspects. In terms of the former, it provided a mechanism for assured control and constant surveillance. As the members of the small group ate, lived, slept, studied, marched, trained, and fought together, they developed a distinct cohesion, cemented by commitment to common ideology and shared aspirations and experiences. Incipient "deviations" could be detected early by group and squad leaders and "rectified" before they developed dangerously. Tactically, a squad so organized provided great flexibility at the lowest level. It permitted a squad leader to exploit the terrain and to take advantage of the enemy situation by the classic methods of fire and movement. The inherent virtues of this organizational innovation were not lost on foreign observers.[28]

In view of this strength and structural flexibility, one might have presumed that some time in 1943 or certainly by early 1944, the Communists would have switched from guerrilla missions to "regular warfare . . . in its mobile form." In 1938 in his now celebrated essay "On the Protracted War," Mao had said: "In the course of the prolonged, ruthless war, guerrilla warfare should not remain its old self but must develop into mobile warfare." [29] He had also defined this transition as "the strategic task" for guerrilla warfare. Mao regarded "mobile" warfare as the "higher form of warfare" because "the issue of the war" would be "mainly decided by regular warfare especially in its mobile form" undertaken "by regular army corps along an extensive front in a vast theater of war." [30] Nevertheless, he asserted that during the period of transition from guerrilla to "mobile" warfare, there would be constant interplay between the two. This is reminiscent of the *Yin-Yang* concept in Chinese philosophy, which postulates a state of flux in which sometimes the *Yin*, sometimes the *Yang* exerts a predominant influence. As the "protracted war" entered its final phase, however—that stage when the enemy's offensives reached terminal points, lost impetus, and could no longer be sustained—"mobile" warfare would become dominant and decisive, and guerrilla warfare would be secondary and "supplementary."

Although the Japanese had reached this stage in China in 1941, the transition from guerrilla to "mobile" warfare did not take place. Why? This question was asked repeatedly during the last years of the war.

The answer must be sought in the contexts of the contemporary international and internal situations. To both the Chinese Communists and Chinese Nationalists, America's entry into the war seemed to make Japan's ultimate defeat a virtual certainty. As one anonymous observer in the bombed-out Nationalist capital of Chungking is said to have remarked: "Pearl Harbor Day in America was Armistice Day out here." Indeed, "the Chinese felt they need only wait until the enemy crumbled before American strength." [31] Thus, the mandarins of Chungking and Yenan alike found themselves in the situation of those ancient ministers who craftily "used barbarians to control barbarians" (*i i chih i*).

In these happy circumstances, nothing was to be gained by commitment of major forces against the Japanese invaders, who would ultimately be made to disgorge what they had gobbled. For the Communists as for the Nationalists, the imperative dictated by the international situation was to preserve their forces for the ultimate trial of strength in China's civil conflict.

Moreover, in strategic terms the Anti-Japanese War was static by the end of 1941. The Japanese held almost all the principal cities of China and, aside from mounting an occasional "punitive expedition" into Communist hinterlands, were content to defend their acquisitions. The only way the Communists could restore fluidity to the situation was seriously to threaten positions the Japanese could not afford to lose, to drive significant garrison forces out of the cities they were defending. But the Communists had neither the strength nor the equipment to mount such attacks or to drive them home. In sum, the Communists were incapable of creating a dynamic situation and hence incapable of conducting mobile war. Under such circumstances, to have embarked on major operations against the Japanese in North or Central China—to have tried to make the transition from guerrilla to "mobile" warfare—would have placed the Party's entire future in jeopardy and been rash in the extreme.

And as the difficulties imposed by the external aggressor would be solved by the interposition of the United States, it was only necessary for the Communists to be patient, to expand the areas under their control, to consolidate their holdings, and to build the Red Army.

On April 25, 1945, General Chu Teh, commander in chief of the Chinese Communist armies, addressed the Seventh Party Congress in Yenan regarding the military situation.[32] The tenor of his report reflected the optimistic spirit which then prevailed in Mao Tse-tung's city of caves. The General praised the performance of the 910,000 officers and men who marched with the Eighth Route Army, the New Fourth Army, the South China Anti-Japanese Column, and the Anti-Japanese Allied Forces in the northeast provinces and extended his greetings to a militia numbering almost 2.25 million.[33] These "great people's armies," he declared, had waged a war "of unparalleled heroism, fought bitter, magnificent, and triumphant battles, and become the kingpin of China's War of Resistance." They had gone from victory to victory, he asserted, because they had religiously followed Chairman Mao Tse-tung's "correct political policy in combination with his correct military policy."

The occasion provided a convenient opportunity for a violent attack on the "mistaken policies" of the Kuomintang government and its high command. Chu accused the Kuomintang of adopting a "stupid," "defeatist strategy" which had resulted only in "tremendous losses" of manpower and of many "key points" in North, Central, and South China. While Kuomintang armies were "beating a mass retreat," the Eighth Route and New Fourth armies "with unparalleled heroism . . . launched counteroffensives in the enemy's rear and won victory after victory. They tied the enemy down, established strategic bases, created liberated areas, and raised the fighting morale of the whole Chinese people." Until 1943, the Communists, said Chu, pinned down "65 per cent of the puppet troops."

While these exaggerated claims made effective propaganda at the time—and still do today—they are gross distortions of historical fact. No authentic records support the proposition that Communist military operations succeeded in forcing the Japanese invaders from any extensive territory they physically occupied and wanted to hold. The North China Area Army (successively commanded after December 1938 by Generals Sugiyama, Tada, Okamura, and Shimamura) never attempted to occupy the countryside in North China on a permanent basis. The Japanese were content to seize the large cities and key communication points (*chiao-t'ung-tien*) and to hold railway lines and principal highways (*chiao-t'ung-hsien*). They garrisoned rural cities and towns with puppet troops of negligible combat efficiency and questionable loyalty.

Furthermore, after January 1, 1943, Japanese offensive capabilities in the China theater were stringently limited by the number and quality of troops available. During late 1942 and early 1943, seven first-line divisions experienced in conducting counterguerrilla operations were redeployed from North China to the Pacific theater. They were replaced with second-line formations of considerably lower combat efficiency. Imperial General Headquarters also levied arms and equipment requisitions on General Okamura, who remarked to the author:

If you people had not come into the Pacific when you did, there would be no Communists in Peking. My operations in 1942 and 1943 reduced their strength by more than 100,000. But the troops that replaced my good divisions were worthless. For one thing, the average age of the men was ten to fifteen years older. These older men could not campaign as the youngsters could. And they had no heart in it all.[34]

On rare occasions, Chinese Communist troops drove greatly inferior Japanese units from strong points in *hsien* towns or along the railways. But when the Japanese wished, they could invariably return in sufficient strength to force Communist withdrawals. As the Red Army's information of Japanese movements was always precise and detailed, such withdrawals were usually planned to avoid contact and were executed in an orderly fashion. When they pulled out of an area in response to Japanese pressure, the Communists stripped it of everything useful: sewing machines, small printing presses, portable power tools, what money they could get, medical supplies and equipment, excess grain, salt, and so forth. True, they paid for what they took, but with paper or cloth money and coins negotiable only in areas under Communist control. One need scarcely wonder why this "money" was not too popular—a peasant caught by the Japanese with "liberation" currency on him carried a death warrant in his pocketbook.

With one notable exception—the period of the Hundred Regiments Offensive—the Eighth Route Army did not launch counter-offensives "in the enemy's rear," successfully "open new fronts," or "recover a vast amount of lost territory." [35] In terms of both lives and ammunition, the Hundred Regiments Offensive was an expensive affair for the Communists, who thereafter confined themselves to less grandiose operations. The new policy put into effect in 1941, essentially political in nature, was to fill vacuums created by the withdrawal of Japanese garrison troops, to seep into rural areas administered by Chinese traitors and collaborators and "defended" by puppet ("bogus") troops whom the Communists described as *wei-ping* or *wei-chün*. Collaborators and "bogus" troops speedily acquired the prudent habit of taking to their heels before the Communists fired a shot. When "bogus" troops were captured, they were indoctrinated and integrated.

Truly, in Mao's words, the Red Army did not "exist merely to fight." After the Hundred Regiments Offensive, fighting the Japanese enemy became an incidental task. The primary mission of this unique and essential mechanism for agitation and organization was to bring Mao's revolution to almost 100 million peasants living in the plains, valleys, and mountains of North China. [36]

American diplomatic and military observers in Yenan were well aware of Communist activities in Shensi, Shansi, Hopeh, Chahar, and Shantung and their implications for the future. For example, on August 3, 1944, John S. Service wrote the Department of State an objective summary reporting that the Communists were actively supporting the war "because this gives them an opportunity to mobilize, organize, and indoctrinate the people and to create and train an efficient army." [37] Two months later, another Chinese specialist, John Paton Davies, wrote: "The Communists are now so strong between the Great Wall and the Yangtze that they can look forward to the postwar control of at least North China." [38]

Subsequent events were soon to prove the prescience of these observations.

CHAPTER FIVE

"We Can Defeat Chiang Kai-shek": The Civil War in China, 1945-49

This chapter does not purport to present an operational history of the civil war which spread over China with progressively increasing intensity between the summer of 1946 and the critical autumn of 1948. Significant operations will be described briefly; those less so, omitted. Nor will any attempt be made to treat the wearisome and ultimately futile negotiations which General George C. Marshall conducted in an effort to mediate the deep differences which divided the antagonists.

As the story of what the Communists call the "Third Revolutionary War" unfolds, it will become evident that what had happened so many years before in Kiangsi during the first three Bandit Extermination Campaigns happened again in Manchuria and in North and Central China. The only differences were in scale: a stage infinitely larger; casts numbered in millions; the prize in contention not a few *hsien* or even a few provinces but an empire, an empire of vast extent, with resources unmeasured, and with a population of more than 500 million intelligent and industrious men and women.

Again the Party's armies—this time the famous Eighth Route and the New Fourth—were challenged by numerically superior Nationalist forces, which now included some American-trained and -equipped infantry divisions, competent artillery and armored units, and an expanding air force.

Three of the infantry divisions had fought under Lieut. Gen. Joseph W. Stilwell, U.S. Army, in the Second Burma Campaign. There, under conditions that demanded the most of every officer and man, they had conquered all obstacles imposed by nature and had sought out, brought to battle, and after bitter, vicious close-range fighting—in the jungle, there is no other—defeated some of the best divisions of the Japanese Imperial Army. Their performance more than justified Stilwell's confidence in the latent potential of the Chinese soldier. In Burma, these three fighting divisions inflicted more military damage on the Japanese than the Eighth Route Army had done in eight years of hit-and-run operations. The Chinese New First Army, commanded by Sun Li-jen, left Burma proved and confident. Officers and men were battle-tested and tough. They were good and they knew it.

Other Nationalist divisions had fought on the Salween front. These, too, were well trained and fully equipped. The officers, loyal and courageous, had led their men to victory in battle against an enemy who fought to the death. They were ready to meet the Communists.

But between these relatively few tested commanders and troops and the great remainder of the Nationalist army, tremendous gaps in experience, morale, leadership ability, and equipment existed. Most of the men were semi-trained, illiterate conscripts in poor physical condition who had no idea why they were fighting and no stomach for the job. The leadership was little better. Lieut. Gen. Albert C. Wedemeyer, Chiang's last American chief of staff, described many senior officers as elderly incompetents who were uneducated and not versed in modern combat.[1] Measured in terms of the factors which constitute the amalgam of combat efficiency, the Nationalists were not ready to engage in decisive battle with much hope of success against soldiers led by such redoubtable generals as Chu Teh, Lin Piao, Ch'en Yi, Liu Po-ch'eng, Hsü Hsiang-ch'ien, P'eng Teh-huai, Ho Lung, and Su Yü.

On August 6, 1945, an atomic bomb exploded over the Japanese city of Hiroshima. Two days later, the Soviet government declared war on Japan, and three Soviet armies poised on the border of Manchuria launched concerted drives toward Harbin, Changchun, and Mukden. On August 9, a U.S. B-29 aircraft dropped an atomic bomb which exploded over Nagasaki.

News that Russia had entered the war evoked an enthusiastic response from Yenan, where, on August 9, Mao Tse-tung issued a call to arms, "The Last Round with the Japanese Invaders." It was obvious that Japan was on her knees; Mao made it equally apparent that the Communists were going to move fast to take advantage of golden opportunity:

The Eighth Route Army, the New Fourth Army and all other People's troops should seize every chance to launch extensive offensives against all invaders and their jackals who refuse to surrender, annihilate their forces, capture their arms and material, put forth the most energetic efforts to expand our liberated areas and reduce the areas under enemy occupation. They must boldly form armed squads which, by hundreds and by thousands, should penetrate deep into the rear of the enemy-occupied areas to organize the people *for the wrecking of the enemy's communication lines* and to support the operations of the regular armies. They must boldly rouse the tens of millions of the people in the enemy-occupied areas, and *immediately proceed to organize underground forces*, prepare armed uprisings, and annihilate the enemy in coordination with the regular forces attacking at the front. *The consolidation of the liberated areas should not be overlooked.*[2]

As an afterthought, Mao paid lip service to the moribund (if not technically defunct) concept of national unity: he adjured "all the people" in the country to "make efforts to prevent civil war and expedite the formation of a democratic coalition government.[3]

Clearly, at this time there could be only one purpose in wrecking lines of communication: to prevent the Nationalist "enemy" from making use of them. And what "enemy" were the underground forces to be organized supposed to attack? The unhappy implications of Mao's statements were all too apparent, and one may readily imagine that they provoked consternation in Nationalist councils.

If the anticipated formal offer came from Tokyo, as it might at any moment, the Nationalists were in an extremely bad position. With their troops deployed in West and Southwest China, they could not hope to move rapidly to take over such key cities as Shanghai, Hankow, Nanking, Tientsin, Tsinan, or Peip'ing, to say nothing of reaching critical points in Manchuria before the Communists seized them. The principal cities of North China were islands in a vast sea of 100 million peasants under Communist control and responsive to Party direction. Organized bands of guerrillas under Party leadership had developed rapidly in the preceding two years in Manchuria and the adjacent province of Jehol. The strategic prospects in the entire area north of the Lung-Hai (Lienyunkang-Sian) railroad were thus heavily weighted to the advantage of the Communists. Each side was well aware of this fact.

Tokyo spoke on August 10; while the Allies pondered, Chu Teh, from Yenan, directed Communist forces under his command to move and called on the Japanese in North China to surrender to them in accordance with the terms of the Potsdam Agreement. Chiang issued an immediate countermanding order. *He*, as commander in chief of the China Theater, was the exclusive Allied authority to whom the Japanese commanders should render their swords. He directed the Communists to stand fast and appealed frantically for American help to redeploy his forces. This help, in the form of air and ship troop lifts to Manchuria and North China, was immediately promised. August 15, the day Hirohito directed his fighting men to lay down their arms, found Lin Piao moving across Jehol by forced marches. Destination: Manchuria.[4]

Two days before the Emperor broadcast the message that meant the end of World War II in the Far East, Mao Tse-tung addressed a gathering of Party workers in Yenan.[5] The tenor of the Chairman's discourse, more belligerent than otherwise, did not suggest that the Chinese people were soon to enjoy the benefits of the peace they so sorely needed.

First Mao made his obeisance to the Soviet government and army. The "decisive factor for Japan's surrender," he said, was "the entry of the Soviet Union into the war." In "irresistible force," the Russian Red Army was entering China's northeast.

In practically the next breath, the Chairman opened fire on Chiang Kai-shek, "the representative of China's big landlords and big bourgeoisie . . . a most brutal and treacherous fellow." Chiang's war policy, Mao declared in words he might with equal precision have used to describe his own, had been "to look on with folded arms, wait for victory, conserve his forces, and prepare for civil war." [6] Moreover, this "Generalissimo," the ungrateful "fellow" who had "knocked down" the people and "plunged them into the blood bath of ten years of civil war," wished now to begin again where he left off. But "our policy, the policy of the people," was against civil war. "Here one side does not want to fight and the other does." With "swords" in his hands, however, Chiang was about to advance on the people to "kill" them. His allies? "War lords, landlords, local bullies, bad gentry, and the imperialists." All held swords, and all were "out to kill." In the face of this imminent threat to the liberated areas, the people must seize their own swords and be prepared to return blows with blows, to "take up arms and fight . . . in self-defense to protect the lives and property, the rights and well-being, of the people of the Liberated Areas."

The Chairman prophesied many difficulties for Chiang in the struggle he anticipated. Among Communist assets, he counted a population of 100 million, "a million troops and more than 2 million people's militia." But action was required; there was much work to be done. Some misguided comrades "put their faith only in political influence, fancying that problems can be solved merely by influence. That is blind faith." Dirt must be swept with brooms; "bells don't ring till you strike them. Tables don't move till you shift them. . . . Only where the broom reaches can political influence produce its full effect. Our broom is the Communist Party, the Eighth Route Army, and the New Fourth Army." Mao exhorted his audience to "rise at dawn," grasp their brooms, and "sweep the courtyard."

"On what basis should our policy rest?" Mao asked. His answer: "It should rest on our own strength, and that means regeneration through one's own efforts. . . . Relying on the forces we ourselves organize, we can defeat all Chinese and foreign reactionaries." Chiang, the Chairman continued, relied not on himself, not on the innate appeal and strength of his policies, but "entirely on the aid of U.S. imperialism." "The trinity of dictatorship, civil war, and selling out the country" had "always been the basis of his policy." U.S. "imperialism" wanted a civil war in China and would help Chiang wage it. "But U.S. imperialism while outwardly strong is inwardly weak."

As for atomic bombs: they were not decisive; they "could not make Japan surrender." "Without the struggles waged by the people, atom bombs by themselves would be of no avail." Some comrades, Mao said, believed that the atom bomb was "all powerful . . . something miraculous." These misguided comrades showed even less judgment than "a certain British peer called Lord Mountbatten," who (according to the Chairman) had observed that it was the "worst possible mistake" to think the atom bomb could "decide a war." Such comrades were even more backward than this reactionary nobleman! They had been influenced by bourgeois thought. "The theory that 'weapons decide everything,' the purely military viewpoint," represented bourgeois influence subtly contaminating the ranks of the Party. Such influences must be swept away as one sweeps out dust.

Mao also delineated the strategy which the civil war he alleged he sought to avoid would follow:

Chiang Kai-shek will grab a lot of big peaches, such as Shanghai, Nanking, Hangchow, and other big cities. He has ganged up with U.S. imperialism, and in those places they have the upper hand, while so far the revolutionary people can by and large occupy only the rural areas. Another bunch of peaches will be contested by both sides.

These "peaches" were medium and small towns along and adjacent to the railways of North China and Manchuria. They "must be contested. They are the medium and small peaches watered by the people of the Liberated Areas with their sweat and blood." Other areas would definitely fall into the hands of the people: the vast rural areas and numerous towns in Hopeh, Chahar, and Jehol provinces; "most of Shansi, Shantung, and the northern part of Kiangsu. . . . We are sure of them, we have the strength to pick these fruits of victory."

The Chairman concluded this remarkable address by describing the present period as a "transitional stage," during which the struggle must be "to oppose Chiang Kai-shek's usurpation of the fruits of victory in the War of Resistance." Chiang's policy, Mao declared, was "set"; he wanted to launch a "country-wide civil war." The watchword was: "Prepare!"

Mao's statements made it sufficiently clear that the Party intended to create and—if it could—profit from a condition of chaos. The negotiations conducted by General Marshall must be set against this background. At the same time, the Chairman outlined distinctly and with accustomed vigor several propaganda lines to which the Party has consistently adhered. U.S. imperialism, "outwardly strong but inwardly weak," was an enemy; its atom bombs, of little account.

Mao's essentially optimistic expectations were based not only on the strategic situation in mid-August 1945 but also on careful estimates of the relative effectiveness of the leadership and the combat capabilities of his own and the Generalissimo's military forces. The Chairman, a lifelong student of the philosopher Sun Tzu's classic *Art of War*, had always paid strict attention to the Master's pithy admonition: *Chih-ti, Chih-chi; Pai-chan, Pai-sheng* ("Know the enemy and know yourself; in a hundred battles you will never be in peril").[7]

A Communist delegation headed by Chou En-lai had been in Chungking for some time during 1944 and 1945 to participate in negotiations the United States hoped would avert an armed collision between the two factions. Although these sporadic conversations, in which President Roosevelt's ambassador, Maj. Gen. Patrick Hurley, served as mediator, produced little in the way of substantive results,

Chou's sojourn in Chiang's wartime capital afforded him an opportunity to assess Nationalist infighting at firsthand. In addition, covert Communists and their sympathizers had infiltrated the Ministry of National Defense and some of its many redundant and conflicting subordinate offices. The Communists were thus well aware of the vicious feuds raging in the Nationalist military hierarchy.

Three senior generals, united only by shared ties of personal loyalty to the Generalissimo, were constantly at one another's throats. One of these, Ch'en Ch'eng, had taken over the Ministry of War from his rival Ho Ying-ch'in in 1944. In the shuffle, Ho retained the office of chief of staff, a position which enabled him to sabotage many of the reforms Ch'en tried repeatedly but in vain to apply to the Nationalist armies. The third of this ill-omened trio, Hu Tsung-nan, leader of the younger group of Whampoa officers, detested the chief of staff, who returned the sentiment. As a consequence, Hu Tsung-nan "permitted [Ho Ying-ch'in] no interference in his personal war area." Hu, moreover, "was perhaps closer to the Generalissimo's affections than any younger man in the army" and had direct access to him. Hu therefore took his troubles to Chiang, who frequently resolved them in favor of his young protégé.[8] Each of these powerful generals had, as might be expected, a personal claque in the officer corps; the shock waves generated by their encounters were quickly transmitted to lower echelons, where they had disruptive effects. It was not necessary for the Communists to try to provoke discord in the enemy's camp; the profound disunity was evident. It is safe to presume, however, that the Communists subtly did all they could to exacerbate the existing enmities.

In Yenan, the situation was precisely the opposite. A remarkable harmony prevailed in the camp of the Communists. Differences of opinion in councils of war are unavoidable, but in Yenan they were apparently amicably reconciled behind closed doors. If ill feelings between leading members of the Communist High Command existed, they were never even hinted at, much less openly expressed.

The state of Chiang's armies was not conducive to effective combat operations against an enemy as formidable as the Communists. Lieut. Gen. Albert C. Wedemeyer, the Generalissimo's American chief of staff after the departure of Stilwell, later portrayed these as he had discovered them from personal experience and observation.[9] There were "entirely too many generals in the Chinese Army, most of whom were not fitted for command in modern combat." Many senior officers of the Nationalist armies had attained high rank by means other than meritorious achievement. Officer-enlisted relationships left much to be desired. Officers were indifferent to the welfare of their men; wounded soldiers did not receive proper care and attention. Conscription was neither honest nor efficient. Peasants bore the brunt; sons of the rich, through payment of graft and bribes, evaded the obligation to serve their country.

These conditions, as evident to the Communists as to Wedemeyer, contributed to Mao's confidence that his armies would be able to gather in a handsome "harvest." He was reasonably sure that as the civil war he anticipated reached a climax, the numerical balance of 2.8 to 1 in favor of the Nationalists could gradually be reduced to parity. With parity attained, the Communists could gather in some of the larger, juicier fruits.

As August drew to a close, a massive and hastily-mustered American airlift flew Nationalist troops by thousands to Shanghai, Nanking, Hankow, Tientsin, and Peip'ing. In early October, Lieut. Gen. Keller E. Rockey's Third Amphibious Corps, Fleet Marine Force, garrisoned half-a-dozen cities in North China and in the Generalissimo's name accepted surrender of imperial Japan's North China Army. The Communists, perhaps not entirely unreasonably, saw this action as direct intervention in a problem they considered strictly Chinese. From this time on, violent expressions of anti-Americanism began to emanate from Yenan.

In this atmosphere, Gen. George Catlett Marshall, former chief of staff of the U.S. Army, flew into Chungking to assume the frustrating burden Hurley had petulantly abandoned some time before. General Marshall hoped that a truce would provide an atmosphere in which meaningful and fruitful negotiations leading to an enduring reconciliation could be conducted. This is not the place to discuss the Marshall mission, an episode exhaustively treated in other works. That it was a failure must not reflect on General Marshall's courage, tact, or perseverance. He tried honestly but in vain to discover a middle ground. There was none. When Marshall left China for the last time, two facts were clear: civil war was inevitable, and it would be war to the knife.

On July 20, 1946, a policy directive of the Party's Central Committee stated categorically that "we can defeat Chiang Kai-shek. The whole Party should be confident of this." [10] A subsequent directive of October confirmed this judgment, discussed recent operations,[11] and outlined plans for future offensives to be undertaken by the liberation armies.[12]

Mao's prudence, however, shows clearly in the directive which the Revolutionary Military Council of the Party's Central Committee issued on September 16.[13] To underrate one's enemy is "the wrong method of fighting," a bad habit which leads one to divide his forces and inevitably "lands him in a passive position." The key is concentration of vastly superior forces: "concentrate an absolutely superior force, that is to say a force six, five, four, or at least three times that of the enemy, concentrate the whole or the bulk of our artillery, select one (not two) of the weak spots in the enemy's position, attack it fiercely, and be sure to win. This accomplished, swiftly exploit the victory and destroy the enemy forces one by one."

What Mao aimed at was not just defeat of the enemy force but complete annihilation, for "only complete annihilation can deal the most telling blows to the enemy . . . [and] replenish our own forces to the greatest possible extent. It is now not only the main source of our arms and ammunition, but also the important source of manpower." Equally important, it "demoralizes the enemy's troops and depresses his followers; it raises the morale of our troops and inspires our people."

The Chairman's strategy was "step by step": "to wipe out the enemy forces one by one. . . . Using this method we shall win. Acting counter to it we shall lose." Some "military cadres" had failed to apply these correct methods. Such egregious lapses Mao ascribed to "lack of intensive education and study." To these comrades, it was obviously "necessary . . . to explain again and again the advantages of this method of fighting." This tactical adjuration no doubt recalled to erring commanders Sun Tzu's succinct advice to King Ho Lü of Wu:

If a general who heeds my strategy is employed, he is certain to win. Retain him! When one who refuses to listen to my strategy is employed, he is certain to be defeated. Dismiss him! [14]

Mao directed his commanders to coordinate operations "with vigorous activities by the regional formations, local guerrillas, and people's militia." The purpose was to mobilize all forces available to annihilate the enemy's effective strength, not to hold or seize a place. Real estate, as such, was purely a secondary consideration. Mao wanted his regular forces to hold places and areas only when they could be held. In the face of superior force, the Red Army was to abandon its positions, for "it will be possible to recover lost territory" later. This tactic the Chinese describe as "knowing when to release one thing in order to get another."

On November 15, 1946, Chiang Kai-shek addressed the first session of a National Assembly convened in Nanking to review the draft version of a constitution for the Republic of China. Two thousand hand-picked delegates listened attentively as the Generalissimo eulogized Dr. Sun Yat-sen and the Kuomintang. The Communists boycotted the gathering, and on the following day, Chou En-lai, their principal "cease-fire" negotiator, issued a strong statement attacking the "one-party" assembly summoned, he alleged, by government authorities "to whitewash their own dictatorship." The Communists would "adamantly refuse" to recognize the legality of any such assembly. "The door of negotiation," Chou concluded, had been "slammed by the single hand of the Kuomintang." [15]

During that day, Chou called on General Marshall, expressed his fears that the Nationalists were planning to attack Yenan, stated that he desired to return there, and requested air transportation for himself and his group. On November 19, Chou left Yenan in a U.S. Army plane. Although General Marshall lingered in Nanking for some weeks, Chou's abrupt departure ended what slight hope of averting a nation-wide civil war may still have existed.

The American mediator had learned a great deal in the few months he had been in China and had some sympathy for Chou En-lai's position. At the time, it appeared to General Marshall that "the Government had been using the negotiations largely for its own purposes. Following the breakdown of the negotiations in June 1946, the Government had been waging war on a constantly increasing scale. . . ." The military leaders "were in the saddle and were thoroughly convinced that the Communists would not carry out any agreement reached." [16]

The Communists, who chose to interpret the convocation of the "illegal" National Assembly as the Generalissimo's declaration of war, had also used the time gained by the "cease-fire" negotiations to good advantage. Party membership had increased by almost 150,000; reorganized and numerically stronger Red armies had acquired practically all the Japanese weapons and equipment originally surrendered to the Russians in Manchuria; peasant mass movements, particularly in Manchuria, Shantung, Hopei, and Kiangsu, had made substantial progress. Fully 70 per cent of the rural population north of the general line of the east-west Lung-Hai railway was Communist oriented. The temperature of the water was suitable for the Red Army's fish.

On November 18, 1946, the day before Chou En-lai flew out of Nanking for the last time, Mao Tse-tung composed a Central Committee directive which constituted the Party's confident declaration of war against the Generalissimo. Chiang Kai-shek was "at the end of his rope"; he had "stage-managed" the National Assembly "to split the nation." He proposed next to attack Yenan, but "even if his troops should occupy Yenan by means of a sudden thrust," their transient success "would not damage the general prospect of victory." The Red armies, Mao announced, had in the past year wiped out "thirty-five brigades" of Chiang's troops; Nationalist offensive power was "nearly exhausted." Chiang had "taken the road to ruin"; "doom" awaited him. Mao called on "the whole Party, the whole army, and the whole people" to unite to "smash Chiang Kai-shek's offensive and build a democratic China." [17]

When only tangible factors were weighed, the scales undeniably showed that victory for the Nationalists was a virtual certainty. Putting men, rifles, automatic weapons, bullets, mortars, howitzers, shells, tanks, and aircraft in these scales is, of course, a necessary step in calculations of relative strengths. But in war, as Sun Tzu had warned so many years earlier, "numbers alone confer no advantage." You first tell me, he said, "which ruler possesses moral influence, which commander is the more able, which army obtains the advantages of nature and terrain, in which regulations and instructions are better carried out, which troops are the stronger . . . which has the better-trained officers and men . . . and which administers rewards and punishments in a more enlightened manner." Then, he continued, I will tell you "which side will be victorious." [18] Many foreigners in China during this period judged the Nationalists to be incapable of making such an appraisal with any degree of objectivity.

The state structure, erected on insecure foundations, had been greatly weakened by almost eight years of war, and the Kuomintang, isolated from the people, had become a clanking political mechanism shot through with personal feuds, frustrations, petty despotism, nepotism, and corruption. China's economy was in a desperate state—a condition that could not be charged entirely against the Nationalists. The Russians had stripped Manchuria of almost $1 billion worth of industrial equipment, and the Communists had not abated, but rather increased, their campaign of wrecking the railways. Some of the major coal mines were in Communist hands; others, sabotaged earlier by the Communists, were idle. As power plants in major cities restricted the production of electricity, industrial enterprises of all kinds slowed down or suspended operations. The government, perennially short of cash, had very little to put into pressing economic and social projects, for military expenditures ate up 70 per cent of the total government budget. Inflation was already galloping; "wholesale prices had risen about seven times during one year." [19] The Communists were aware that the Nanking government was facing a financial crisis; this factor, Marshall warned the Generalissimo, certainly "entered into their calculations in forming plans." [20]

Symptoms of future trouble in the Nationalist armies matched the presentiments of economic collapse. Frictions at the highest levels of command were, as we have observed, transmitted to the lower echelons, with the result that army group, army and division commanders often refused to coordinate plans and operations. In Manchuria, where the issue was to be joined, General Tu Yu-ming, commander in chief of the Northeast Combat Command (NECC), did not speak, except officially, to General Hsiung Shih-hui, Chiang's administrator of this vast area.

Some of the troops were disaffected. In October, for instance, the 184th Nationalist Division went over to the Communists in Manchuria. Entire companies and battalions of provincial troops defected during the fighting in 1946. Lack of discipline in Nationalist ranks was reflected also in the deterioration of civil-military relationships. In this connection, Wedemeyer was later to observe that the people, who had welcomed government troops as liberators, soon experienced "a feeling of hatred and distrust because the officers and enlisted men were arrogant and rude. Also, they stole and looted freely; their general attitude was that of conquerors instead of that of deliverers." [21] In contrast, the Communists demanded impeccable behavior of their troops and so won the trust and esteem the Nationalists had fleetingly enjoyed. It soon became apparent to unprejudiced observers that the delicate and perhaps decisive balance of moral influence was swinging inexorably from the Kuomintang to the Communists.

It was ironic that the Generalissimo sought to gain control of

Manchuria before he consolidated south of the Great Wall. This was precisely what the Communists hoped he would do, for the inescapable corollary to major Nationalist deployment in the northeast was a staggering logistic problem. Supplies to Chiang's armies had to reach them over railways highly vulnerable to guerrillas operating in Honan, Hopeh, Kiangsu, and Shantung. And, as they had done before, the Nationalists again underestimated Communist generalship and the combat efficiency of the Red Army. At the same time, they overestimated their own capabilities. Since VJ-Day, most Nationalist formations had performed garrison duties in cities and along the railways. The result was a corrosion in spirit. As the troops succcumbed to "sugar bullets," their combat efficiency deteriorated; from units capable of offensive march and maneuver, Chiang's field armies were imperceptibly degenerating into "fortress troops," whose mental attitude was passive and whose physical condition left much to be desired.

On January 6, 1947, Lin Piao passed three columns across the frozen Sungari in a reconnaissance in force. Two moved against Kirin, the third against Ch'angch'un, the ancient capital of Manchuria. Sun Li-jen's New First Army responded vigorously; the Communists withdrew across the river. Again in mid-February the Communists launched probes against both cities. Again the First Army drove them back. A third attack in early March was repulsed. There was much rejoicing in Nanking.

But these operations, limited in scope, time, and strength, were designed as means of feeling out the opposition and as spoiling attacks to prevent Nationalist interference with the consolidation of Communist staging areas to the east of the Kirin–Hailung–Shenyang (Mukden) line and in the Tungliao area southwest of Ch'angch'un. On May 10, the major offensive the Nationalists awaited struck them as Communist forces of 270,000 hit in a decisive attempt to isolate the Nationalist defenders of Kirin, Ch'angch'un, and Shenyang. On May 25, Lin Piao drew the circle tight around Szeping, a rail junction halfway between the two latter cities.

In his résumé five days later to the Department of State, the American Consul General at Shenyang (which in American usage remained "Mukden") set forth some of the reasons for the catastrophe that threatened to overwhelm the Nationalists in Manchuria. Morale had deteriorated at rapidly accelerating pace. Present serious state of their demoralization . . . is reflected in jumpy nerves of military garrison. . . . Nationalists in a panicky state are feverishly building trench systems everywhere with only "Maginot" defense strategy in mind. . . . Apathy, resentment, and defeatism are spreading fast in Nationalist ranks causing surrenders and desertions. Main factors contributing to this are Communist ever-mounting numerical superiority [i.e., locally], National soldiers' discouragement over prospects getting reinforcements, better solidarity and fighting spirit of Communists, losses and exhaustion of Nationalists. . . .[22]

On June 16, Szeping fell. The Nationalists, who valued possession of cities as the Communists did possession of the countryside, reacted immediately. They hurriedly moved their 14th and 52nd armies north from the Liaotung peninsula and thus created a vacuum the Communists promptly filled. On July 2, they launched concerted drives from Ch'angch'un and Shenyang which forced the Communists to evacuate this important rail center. On maps in Nanking, at least, the situation was momentarily restored.

But this was a hollow victory. The preceding two months had witnessed a progressive decay of the Nationalist position in Manchuria, for "though the Communists were not yet strong enough to dislodge the Government from its main strongholds, the Government's units, isolated and with their lines of communication threatened, took on the aspect of beleaguered garrisons waiting for reinforcements which would never come." [23] With major government forces in the northeast contained in their urban "strongholds," the trap was set. Lin Piao now need but await the propitious time to spring it. While he waited, the Communists swung their strategic weight to Central China.

On September 1, 1947, Mao Tse-tung summarized the results achieved during the first year (July 1946–June 1947) of the "War of Liberation" and laid down the general concept of operations to be undertaken during the second year. [24] In the first year, said Mao, the Communists had "wiped out 97 1/2 brigades, or 780,000 men, and puppet troops, peace preservation corps, and others totaling 340,000—altogether 1,120,000." This "great victory" had not been gained cheaply: the Communists had given up "large tracts of territory" and suffered "more than 300,000 casualties." They had, however, held the initiative and "laid the foundation for the complete annihilation of the enemy . . . and for final victory."

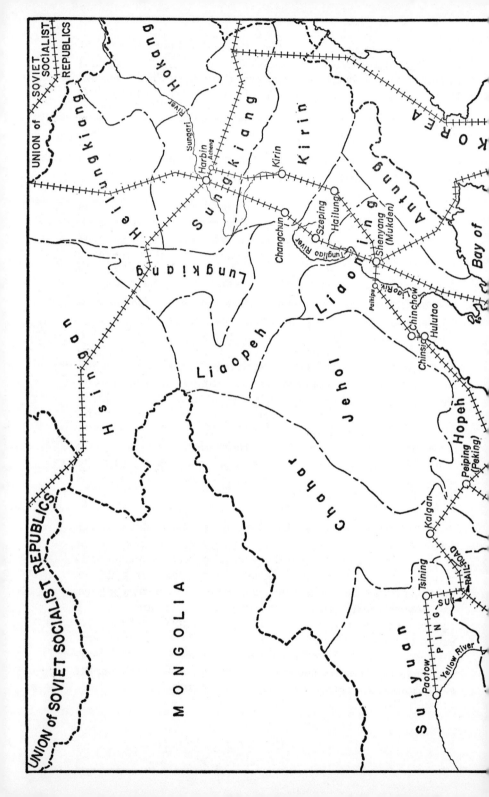

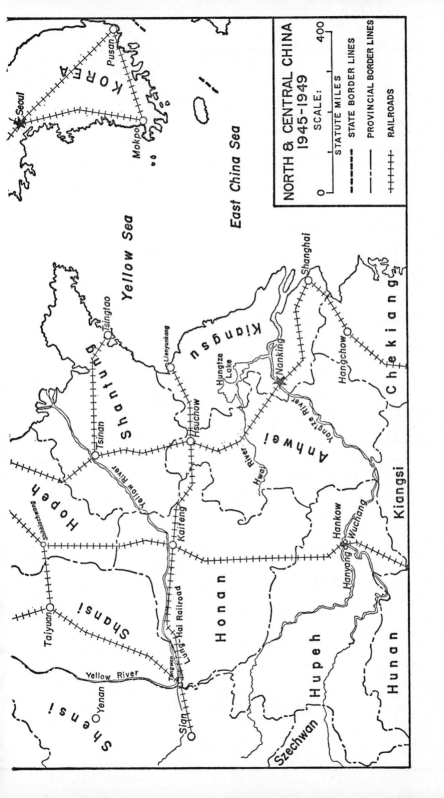

NORTH & CENTRAL CHINA
1945-1949

SCALE:

STATUTE MILES

400

STATE BORDER LINES
PROVINCIAL BORDER LINES
RAILROADS

KOREA

Seoul

Pusan

Mokpo

Yellow Sea

East China Sea

Shantung

Tsingtao

Lienyunkang

Kiangsu

Hsuchow

Hungtze Lake

Nanking

Shanghai

Hangchow

Chekiang

Tsinan

Yellow River

Hwai River

Anhwei

Yangtze River

Hopeh

Shihkiachwang

Kaifeng

Honan

Hankow

Wuchang

Hanyang

Kiangsi

Shansi

Taiyuan

Lung-Hai Railroad

Tengwan

Hupeh

Hunan

Shensi

Yenan

Yellow River

Sian

Szechwan

The mission assigned the Red armies during the second year was to launch a concerted "country-wide counteroffensive," to carry the war to Kuomintang-controlled areas. This would not be easy. Stable base areas had to be created in enemy territory. But the armies were accomplished base builders, and their formula was tested by experience: arouse the masses, distribute the land, establish Communist political power, build up the armed forces. In this connection, Mao emphasized the importance of the carrot of land reform, "the most fundamental requirement for supporting a long war and winning country-wide victory."

Mao again enunciated the operational principles to be followed:

Attack dispersed, isolated enemy forces first . . . attack concentrated, strong enemy forces later.

Take medium and small cities and extensive rural areas first; take big cities later.

Make wiping out the enemy's effective strength our main objective; do not make holding or seizing a place our main objective. . . .

In every battle, concentrate an absolutely superior force, encircle the enemy forces completely . . . do not let any escape from the net.

. . . fight no battle unprepared, fight no battle you are not sure of winning. . . . Give full play to our fine style of fighting—courage in battle, no fear of sacrifice, no fear of fatigue, and continuous fighting. . . .

Strive to draw the enemy into mobile warfare. . . .

Resolutely attack and seize all fortified points and cities which are weakly defended. Attack and seize at opportune moments all fortified points and cities defended with moderate strength, provided circumstances permit. For the time being, leave alone all fortified points and cities which are strongly defended.

Replenish our strength with all the arms and most of the soldiers captured from the enemy (80 to 90 per cent of the men and a small number of the junior officers). . . .

The Chairman's supreme confidence in himself, his program, and his People's Liberation armies can be best evaluated if we recall that at the time Mao drafted this directive, he had fled from Yenan accompanied by half-a-dozen members of the Central Committee and a small bodyguard and was living in a cave in the village of Chukuanchai in North Shensi.

Almost three weeks after Mao issued his directive of September 1, General Wedemeyer officially terminated the mission that in July had brought him again to China. On this trip, Wedemeyer was acting as a special representative of the President of the United States, who had directed him to make "an appraisal of the political, economic, psychological, and military situation." [25] In his report, dated September 19, 1947, the General projected the existing military situation against his contemporary background with commendable objectivity.[26]

In his introductory paragraphs, Wedemeyer remarked on the prevalence of corruption and incompetence, "the oppressive police measures, corrupt practices, and maladministration of National Government officials," and he noted the dangerously progressive deterioration of the economy. The General described the Kuomintang as reactionary and repressive and laid loss of popular faith in the government squarely at the KMT's doorstep.

Wedemeyer observed that while some reports ascribed peasant support of the Communists to their land-reform program, others suggested that the Party's "ruthless tactics and terrorism" had "alienated the majority" of peasants. It is apparent that the General lacked a realistic understanding of China's agrarian problem and had no real comprehension of either the nature or dimensions of the process of fermentation going on in the vast and unknown countryside. Although the party did apply ruthless tactics and terrorism to the "rich" peasants, this alienated group was not "the majority." Fully 70 per cent of China's rural population were "poor" peasants. The Party's target was this true majority, and it was this majority which responded to the Party's program and supported it. From this anonymous mass came most of the soldiers who served in the Red Army; it was the inexhaustible pool from which the Party drew man- and woman-power for the ubiquitous rural militant organizations: the Youth Corps, the Village Self-Defense Corps, and the People's Militia. The ultimate decision, as many American observers reported at the time, lay in this rural China organized and dominated by the Communists, not in the cities dominated by the Kuomintang. To this crucial fact, the President's special representative did not give the attention it demanded.

The economy, said Wedemeyer, was disintegrating. The trend would inevitably produce a "continued and creeping paralysis" with "consequent decline in the authority and power of the National Government." The financial situation was appalling. Commodity prices increased faster than new currency could be printed. While the foreign-exchange assets of the government totaled only about

$300 million, private holdings aggregated from two to five times that amount. Yet no attempt had been made to "mobilize these private resources."

The cultural scene was equally depressing. The entire educational system from primary school to university level was little better than a shambles. The Anti-Japanese War had of course disrupted the educational structure; now, inflation was inexorably destroying the intellectual class upon which the viability of the structure depended. Government officials had clamped down on academic freedom, jailed students and professors on charges of sedition without trial, and closed down periodicals because views expressed in them presumably violated "military security." The President's special representative neglected to make it clear that the immediate result of these government policies was the alienation of the intellectual class, traditionally one of the pillars of any Chinese dynasty. And in 1947, Chiang and the feckless party over which he presided stood in desperate need of this very support.

Finally, General Wedemeyer reviewed the military situation, which he found unpromising, to say the least. Although the Nationalists had a preponderance of force, the tactical initiative rested with the Communists. The Nationalists, required to protect points and lines, were in the static position; the Communists, who enjoyed "almost complete freedom of action," in the dynamic. To Wedemeyer, it appeared essential that the Nationalists "first stabilize the fronts and then regain the initiative." The General did not consider it within his purview, however, to state precisely how he would propose to stabilize evanescent "fronts" tangible only as pins and ribbons on maps in Nanking.

North of the Yangtze, the Nationalists were confined to fortified islands connected by tenuous causeways. The tides swept with increasing frequency and force against both—unexpectedly inundating an island; breaking one causeway here, another there. Islets were disappearing without trace. When chief of staff to the Generalissimo, Wedemeyer had visualized that this precise situation might develop and had urgently recommended delay of major commitment to Manchuria until the Nationalists had consolidated south of the Great Wall. As we have seen, Chiang did not accept this advice, which some years later he would admit had been sound.[27]

In December 1947, the outlook for the Nationalists was grim. In Manchuria, Ch'en Ch'eng's Northeast Combat Command, at a strength of some 400,000, still enjoyed a slight superiority in numbers and a considerable superiority in weapons and equipment over Lin Piao's Northeast PLA of 320,000. Communist columns, however, ranged unimpeded over the countryside, while the Nationalists hesitated to leave their islands—Kirin, Ch'angch'un, Szup'ing, and Shenyang—to take offensive action. At this time, mobile task forces of all arms, under able command and animated with the offensive spirit, could still have unbalanced the Communists and damaged them gravely, if not mortally. But the Nationalists, deeming themselves secure in their walled strongholds, refused to sally forth and so literally handed the initiative to Lin Piao. And this general was not one to forego opportunities offered gratuitously.

While the Nationalists sat with "their hands in their sleeves" and their morale ran down, Lin Piao held the causeways connecting their island fortresses under unceasing attack. A series of Communist drives culminating in the "Seventh Offensive" (launched on December 15, 1947) further reduced Nationalist holdings along rail lines and tightened Communist rings around the major cities of Manchuria. The crisis in the northeast was at hand.

In North China, Fu Tso-yi, with a numerical edge of 3 to 1 over the Communists commanded by Nieh Jung-chen and P'eng Teh-huai, had managed to hold his own. But in Fu's immense command area (Hopeh, Chahar, Jehol, Suiyuan, and north Shansi), mobile Communist columns found ample opportunity to cut communications, attack weak detachments, and otherwise punish isolated Nationalist forces. As in the northeastern provinces, the Communists took what they could but attacked only when certain of success. Nieh and P'eng had not yet assembled the heavy weapons necessary to push home assaults against strongly-held positions and did not attempt to do so.

Nanking could derive even less comfort from developments in the area bounded generally on the north by the Lung–Hai railroad and on the south by the Yangtze. Here, in the heartland of China, only a few hundred miles from Nanking, Liu Po-ch'eng moved at will. In Shantung, Nationalist garrisons, as yet unmolested by Ch'en Yi and Su Yü, sat in the major cities. The Communists held the countryside and had driven an east-west wedge from Shangtung into southern Hopeh which prevented overland supply of Fu Tso-yi from Central China.

The general situation was later summarized in these terms:

By the close of 1947, Communist units lay in strength along the railroads from North China to Manchuria, constantly threatening interdiction of traffic on these lines; they had occupied portions of the Tsinan-Tsingtao railroad in Shantung, had extended their holdings along the P'ing-Han [Peip'ing-Hankow] and were preparing operations which in the following months would interdict traffic on the Lung–Hai. The Communists held the rail lines in Manchuria north of Mukden [Shenyang] and as the year closed were conducting operations which cut permanently the railroad south of that city. For Government forces, which had not succeeded in developing local reserves, the supply and replacement problems were critical.[28]

The Central Committee of the CCP, still in hiding in an obscure village in North Shensi, met during the last week of 1947 and on December 25 received a report from its Chairman. In "The Present Situation and Our Tasks," [29] Mao announced that the Party was on the road to victory: "This is a turning point in history . . . a momentous event."

The Chairman poured vitriol on Chiang, "the running dog of the United States," whose "bandit gang" faced no prospect but defeat and destruction. The victory certain to come was of unique, symbolic significance. Said Mao: "The turn of the Chinese People's War of Liberation from the defensive to the offensive cannot but gladden and inspire . . . oppressed people now struggling in many countries." Mao attributed military success during the period July 1946 to November 1947 to "a correct strategy"; a strategy and tactics "based on a people's war" and on "the principles of unity between army and people, of unity between commanders and fighters, and of disintegrating the enemy troop."

In the paper, Mao developed several other theses which have become constant themes of Communist Party propaganda, both internal and external. The strength of "U.S. imperialism," he declared was illusory—"superficial and transitory." The United States, faced with "irreconcilable domestic and international contradictions," was "sitting on a volcano." This situation had forced "U.S. imperialists to draw up a plan for enslaving the world, to run amuck like wild beasts." Indeed, the United States was mustering the "dregs of humanity to prepare . . . a third world war." In this virulent diatribe, Mao assured the Central Committee that a firm grasp of the science of Marxism-Leninism would enable the Party to surmount any obstacle and infuse its ranks with invincible strength. "The dawn," he said, lay ahead; "therefore, we must exert ourselves." [30]

A week later, Chiang Kai-shek announced in a New Year's Day radio address that the "Communist bandits" would be eliminated in a year. One cannot blame the Generalissimo for greeting the new year with renewed expressions of hope that a Nationalist victory was in sight. Actually, little basis for this hope existed in fact. The prevailing disorganization of the High Command in Nanking would have been ludicrous had it not been essentially tragic. Proven field commanders—Pai Ch'ung-hsi, Hsüeh Yüeh, and Sun Lien-chung—were given positions of no importance. Chiang constantly interfered with field commanders and compounded the confusion he thus created by "pipe-lining" orders directly to subordinate headquarters with no reference to the established chain of command.

In addition, the Generalissimo was determined to hold cities regardless of their strategic importance. To him, cities were symbols of power and prestige. This fixation (which amounted, indeed, almost to a mania—as competent Americans present in China during 1947 and 1948 are well qualified to testify) played directly into the hands of the Communists.

As a strategist, Mao was much superior to the Generalissimo. He had a profound grasp of the strategist's "keys to victory." Over Mao's name, Chu Teh issued broad directives to field commanders; thereafter, they enjoyed a free hand to carry out operations as the developing situation dictated. Mao's generals never had to engage in the game of musical chairs.

On January 5, Lin Piao's Northeast Field Army picked up the Generalissimo's challenge. In its first phase, the operation he projected would eliminate the Liaosi corridor southwest of Shenyang and thus deprive the garrison of supplies except for the meager trickle that might reach the city by air. In phase two, Lin Piao proposed to seal off Shenyang completely from the north. The Communist general did not aspire to reduce this stronghold by force; he planned to isolate it and await Nationalist reaction. As the Communists attacked the corridor, the Generalissimo proceeded to Shenyang, where on January 10 he deposed Ch'en Ch'eng and replaced him with Wei Li-huang.

With Lin Piao's threat to Shenyang growing daily, Wei Li-huang began pulling troops out of Ch'angch'un and Kirin to reinforce the southern city, whereupon Lin Piao shifted the weight of his attack to the north. In early March, Communist activity slacked, and Chiang's American adviser, Maj. Gen. David Barr,

strongly urged the Generalissimo to take advantage of this opportunity to make a progressive withdrawal from Manchuria. He was aghast at this proposal, stating that no circumstances would induce him to consider such a plan. Hopeful of a compromise, I suggested the withdrawal into Mukden [Shenyang] of the Changchun, Kirin, and Ssupingchieh garrisons. To this the Generalissimo replied that political considerations precluded the abandonment of Changchun, the ancient capital of Manchuria, but that he would consider a plan for withdrawing the Kirin garrison into Changchun. The Kirin garrison was accordingly withdrawn. . . .[31]

Although the Nationalist collapse in Manchuria was delayed until October, it is not necessary here to discuss in detail the operations that led to it. General Barr's summary is, however, of interest:

The Nationalist troops, in Manchuria, were the finest soldiers the Government had. The large majority of the units were United States equipped and many soldiers and junior officers still remained who had received United States training during the war with Japan. I am convinced that had these troops had proper leadership from the top the Communists would have suffered a major defeat. The Generalissimo placed General Tu Yu-ming, an officer of little worth, in charge of field operations, properly relegating to General Wei Li-huang over-all supervision from Mukden where he could do little harm. But Tu Yu-ming also fought the battle from Mukden, placing the burden of active command in the field to General Liao Yao-hsiang, Commanding General of the 9th Army Group. Liao was a good general but was killed early in the action. Without top leadership and in the confusion that followed the Communists were able to segment the Nationalist forces and destroy them piecemeal. General Wei Li-huang and General Tu Yu-ming deserted the troops and were safely in Hulutao at the end. The efforts of the troops in the Chinsi-Hulutao area to relieve Chinchow were also futile. Instead of mounting an all-out attack with full force initially, which could have swept aside the Communists who were weakened by withdrawals sent against Wei Li-huang, the attack was developed slowly with troops being thrown in piecemeal. The attack soon bogged down with troops showing little will to fight. The loss of Manchuria and some 300,000 of its best troops was a stunning blow to the Government. To me, the loss of the troops was the most serious result. It spelled the beginning of the end. There could be no hope for North China with an additional 360,000 Communist troops now free to move against its north flank.[32]

On October 11, 1948, Mao issued to the Eastern China and Central Plains Field armies, commanded respectively by Ch'en Yi and Liu Po-ch'eng, his "Concept of Operations" for a major—and possibly decisive—campaign designed to open the approaches to the Yangtze Valley north of Nanking.[33]

In this area, the one defensible feature is the line of the eastern-flowing Hwai River, which empties in to Hung Tze Lake some 100 miles north of the Yangtze and an equal distance south of the strategic rail center of Hsuchow. In mid-August, the government had begun assembling significant forces around Hsuchow. Why Nan-king chose to accept battle here rather than along the more defensi-ble Hwai line is a mystery which can be explained only if one ac-cepts the thesis that the Generalissimo based the decision on reasons of prestige.[34] (It was in this area that Li Tsung-jen had fought the Japanese 5th and 10th divisions in the celebrated battle of T'aierh-chuang in 1938.)

The initial government deployment conduced to the "step-by-step" strategy the Communists were applying with marked success in Manchuria. Huang Po-tao's Seventh Army Group, 10 divisions dispersed along the Lung-Hai railroad from Hsuchow east to the sea, presented a lucrative target for segmentation, isolation, and annihilation. The stronger Second Army Group, commanded by Chiu Ching-chuan, was deployed to the west of the city. Mao's concept was for his forces to tie down the Second Army Group while they were at the same time annihilating Huang Po-tao's com-mand. In its first phase, the battle developed according to this plan.

Initially, reports from the Hsuchow headquarters of Liu Chih, Chiang's field commander, were optimistic. There were, however, many in Nanking who questioned the wisdom of accepting decisive battle (*chüeh-chan*) in this area. The American ambassador's analy-sis of November 8 was less than pessimistic:

. . . the isolation of Hsuchow has begun. In this situation, of all the Government there are few, if any, save the Gimo who even profess con-fidence that the tide may yet be turned. Only a few days before Mukden fell the Government had five well-equipped, supplied and trained armies in the Manchurian field, the most formidable striking force at its com-mand, and within a few days these armies were lost. They were lost not from battle casualties, but from defection, although among their com-manders were numbered officers long associated with the Gimo, and in whose loyalty he trusted implicitly. The troops at Hsuchow are far in-ferior to the Mukden garrison, and their commanders are already re-signed to defeat. There is no reason to believe in their will or ability to resist an offensive. And when they are gone, Nanking has no defenses worthy of the name.[35]

By November 15, columns of Liu Po-ch'eng's Central Plains Field Army had badly mangled two Nationalist Army groups south of Hsuchow and cut communications between the battle area and the Yangtze. General Barr recommended to the Generalissimo that the Hsuchow garrison, a force of 270,000 with the Nationalists' only re-maining artillery and armor, break out to the south and establish a battle position on the line of the Hwai. Even as these orders were being handed Liu Chih, the Seventh Army Group, after attempting in vain to break the net Ch'en Yi had woven around it, surrendered. General Huang Po-tao died of wounds received in action. The Communists took almost 90,000 officers and men; 1,000 howitzers, cannon, and mortars; and vast stores of other weapons, ammunition, and assorted matériel. With the defeat at Hwai-Hai, the central government lost the Mandate of Heaven, which in a few short months was to be formally assumed by Mao Tse-tung.

Officially, the Hwai-Hai battle ended on January 10, 1949. With it ended any fleeting hope that Nanking could re-establish the situation, even in regional terms. In his final telegram to Washington, General Barr stated: "Marked by the stigma of defeat and the loss of face resulting from the forced evacuation of China, north of the Yangtze, it is extremely doubtful if the National Government could muster the necessary popular support in this area [South China] with which to rebuild its forces even if time permitted." Only massive U.S. aid would "enable the Nationalist Government to maintain a foothold in southern China against a determined Communist advance. . . . The complete defeat of the Nationalist army . . . is inevitable." [36]

The Nationalists, General Barr subsequently wrote, were "burdened with an unsound strategy . . . conceived by a politically influenced and militarily inept high command" and "steadily lost ground against an opponent who not only shaped his strategy around available human and material resources, but also capitalized skillfully on the Government's strategic and tactical blunders and economic vulnerability." Moreover, they "seriously underestimated" the "military strength, popular support, and tactical skill" of the Communists "from the start." Through "total mobilization in the areas they control, propaganda, and the use of political commissars within their armed forces," the Communists "maintain loyalty to the established orders. Their leaders are men of proven ability who invariably out-general the Nationalist commanders. The morale and fighting spirit of the troops is very high because they are winning." [37]

They continued to win.

At midnight on April 20, 1949, in response to Mao's order for a "country-wide advance," [38] assault elements of the Second and Third Field armies (as the commands of Liu Po-ch'eng and Ch'en Yi were now designated) began crossing the Yangtze on a wide front.[39] They met token resistance: "The ridiculously easy Communist crossing of the Yangtze was made possibly by defections at key points, disagreements in the High Command, and the failure of the Air Force is to give effective support." [40]

Thus, finally facing utter disaster, the Nationalists squandered a last opportunity to heal wounds, close ranks behind Li Tsung-jen (the experienced vice-president who had taken over from the Generalissimo), rally the forces that remained, and attempt to preserve an enclave in South China. The spark was not there. Honor had been lost, and with it, hope. For the Nationalists, the sword had lost the magic of redemption. [41]

The PLA that emerged victorious from "The Third Revolutionary Civil War" was not yet a modern army in terms of organization, weapons, equipment, supply system, or communications. But from the Nationalists it had taken great stores of usable matériel. According to Communist sources, this war booty amounted to 54,400 artillery pieces of all descriptions, 319,000 light and heavy machine guns, 1,000 tanks and armored cars, 20,000 motor vehicles, "and great quantities of other arms and equipment," including 189 aircraft. [42] A good proportion of it was taken from U.S.-equipped Nationalist troops. [43]

Some immediate tasks still faced the PLA. Of these, the reduction of Hainan Island, the "liberation" of Tibet, and the final hunting down and annihilation of Nationalist remnants in the hinterlands were the most pressing. Concurrently, the Communists planned to reduce the size of the PLA, to reorganize it, and to use its available manpower in rehabilitating the nation's shattered economy.

As the industrial strength of the People's China grew, the Party planned to create new and fully modern armed forces. But even as this transition began, the People's Republic of China (P.R.C.) found itself engaged outside its borders in a new war, a war which would subject the PLA and its high command to challenges of an entirely different quality than those the Japanese and Nationalists had posed.

CHAPTER SIX

"Naked, Deliberate, Unprovoked Aggression"
President Harry S Truman [1]

At eleven o'clock on Sunday morning, June 25, 1950, a broadcast from P'yongyang, capital of Soviet puppet Kim Il Sung's Democratic People's Republic of Korea (D.P.R.K.), announced that the North Korean People's Army (NKPA) had crossed the 38th parallel and launched a "righteous invasion" of the Republic of Korea.[2] After castigating the Republic's president, Syngman Rhee, as "an American stooge," a "traitor," and a "bandit," the announcer stated that the D.P.R.K. intended to apprehend him and execute him forthwith.[3] Shortly before this broadcast, the American ambassador in Seoul, John J. Muccio, had radioed the Department of State that the aggression from the north was in force and appeared to constitute "an all-out offensive against the Republic of Korea." [4]

The crushing power of this unexpected attack was a complete surprise, not only to the great majority of the American community in Seoul but to Washington, where it was complacently believed that invasion from the north was a remote contingency and that even if an attack should come, a "well-disciplined army of 100,000 soldiers" was "prepared to meet any challenge by the North Korean forces." [5] In retrospect, however, it is impossible to reconcile this official insouciance with the intelligence picture currently available.

For some months before the North Koreans struck, there were palpable indications that an attack in the summer of 1950 was something more than a possibility. As early as December 8, 1949, Maj. Gen. Charles A. Willoughby, intelligence officer for General of the Army Douglas MacArthur, Supreme Commander, Allied Powers

Japan (SCAP); Commander in Chief, U.S. Forces, Far East (CINCFE); and Commander in Chief, U.S. Army, Far East, had reported his opinion that the North Koreans might be ready to act by April or May since "with the conclusion of the Chinese Communist campaign in China more troops and supplies could then be made available." Less than a month later, Willoughby speculated that P'yongyang had set "March and April 1950" as the time to invade South Korea. On March 10, his estimate suggested June as a likely period for an invasion from the north. He repeated his warnings in April and May intelligence summaries.[6] Perhaps Washington concluded that Willoughby was "crying wolf." But he was not alone in making this appraisal. Some members of the U.S. Military Advisory Group in Korea anticipated a full-scale attack in early summer and communicated their apprehensions to Washington, but these communications apparently generated no more concern than had the reports from Tokyo.

Actually, preliminary planning for the invasion of the southern republic probably began, under the direct supervision of the Soviet mission to P'yongyang, some time prior to March 1949. At that time, the Russians "agreed to furnish arms and equipment for six infantry divisions, three mechanized units, and eight battalions of mobile border constabulary. In addition, when North Korea had sufficient trained air force personnel available, the Soviet Union was to provide 20 reconnaissance aircraft, 100 fighter planes, and 30 light and medium bombers." [7]

While these events were in train, the Chinese Communist leadership was engrossed in bringing the civil war to a successful conclusion. Thus, it seems unlikely that Mao would have had time to devote attention to developments in North Korea. The Russians had successfully managed to exclude the "Yenan" Koreans from high positions in Kim's puppet government. There was thus small possibility that such delicate information could have been leaked at this time. Moreover, for some months after October 1949, when Mao Tse-tung proclaimed the establishment of the People's Republic of China, Peking's relations with P'yongyang were chilly: "frozen in informal channels . . . prior to the war the two nations failed to exchange ambassadors, to negotiate formal and public treaties, and to set up the usual agencies of diplomatic intercourse." [8]

Precisely when and under what circumstances the Chinese learned of Stalin's design to liquidate the Republic of Korea will possibly never be known. Probably Mao was apprised of the dictator's intent during his protracted stay in Moscow in the winter of 1949–50. Mao may not have been informed that D-Day was to be June 25; he was certainly aware that a full-scale invasion of South Korea impended. "It would be naïve to suppose," Edgar Snow has observed, "that the North Korean government began the war without China's knowledge." [9]

In the late spring of 1950, the Chinese began to redeploy major forces from South and Central China to Shantung and Manchuria. These deployments continued during May, June, and July. The Fourth Field Army, commanded by General Lin Piao, moved from South China to Manchuria in May–June. In early July, elements of the Third and First Field armies moved into training areas south and east of Shenyang. Later, in reporting these redeployments, General MacArthur correlated them with other "pertinent manifestations" and concluded that Chinese plans "for active and aggressive intervention in the Korean War were undoubtedly developed early in the summer." [10]

The course of events suggests, however, that these were contingent plans, which might or might not be implemented as circumstances dictated. In summing up available evidence on this point, Allen S. Whiting writes that there was "no agreement . . . nor . . . any direct evidence on the degree to which Communist China participated in the planning. It is possible that Stalin did not even inform Mao of the forthcoming attack during their weeks of conference in Moscow, although this is highly unlikely." But, Whiting concludes, Peking knew of the North Korean invasion "well in advance." [11]

The U.S. government acted rapidly to cope with this rupture of the peace in the Far East. When Muccio's urgent message reached the Department, Secretary of State Dean Acheson immediately telephoned the President, vacationing at his brother's farm near Independence, Missouri, and conveyed the "serious news." The following day, Truman flew to Washington and immediately convened a conference at Blair House. Those present included the Vice-President, Acheson, Secretary of Defense Louis A. Johnson, the secretaries of the Army, Navy, and Air Force, General of the Army Omar N. Bradley (chairman of the Joint Chiefs of Staff), and the three service chiefs. The result of this meeting was a decision to provide naval and air forces to evacuate U.S. civilians from Korea.

On the same day, Trygve Lie, Secretary General of the United

Nations, called the Security Council to meet in emergency session. The Council, in the absence of the Soviet delegate, Jacob Malik, who was boycotting its meetings, lost no time in declaring the North Korean aggression a breach of the peace. The Council called for the immediate cessation of hostilities and the withdrawal "forthwith" of North Korean armed forces to the 38th parallel.

On Monday, the President met again with his top advisers. By this time, it was apparent not only that P'yongyang intended to press military operations to a speedy conclusion but also that without help Rhee's badly battered army was incapable of putting up an effective resistance. To Truman the issue was clear: he directed the U.S. Navy and Air Force to render immediate assistance to the South Koreans. The following day (June 27), the Security Council, with Malik still absent, recommended that member states furnish "such assistance" to the Republic of Korea as was necessary to repel the armed attack and restore international peace and security in the peninsula.

The Party-controlled Peking press, in what might almost be described as restrained comment, charged that the Korean War had "long been prepared by the Syngman Rhee clique and the Americans, the actual instigators," and compared the "reactionary" Korean president, in unflattering terms, to Chiang Kai-shek. In Shanghai, *Ta Kung Pao*, a leading newspaper, declared that "the Syngman Rhee Government has pronounced its own death sentence by sending its puppet troops into North Korea" and noted that "this attack . . . occurred on the fourth day after American Warmonger Dulles left Seoul following his talks with Syngman Rhee." [12]

In Taipei, Generalissimo Chiang Kai-shek was considering offering "active aid" to the Republic of Korea, and the *Central Daily News* called for "an over-all Pacific alliance to resist Communist aggression in the East." [13]

Already, however, President Truman had taken an action (later to prove one of the most controversial of his career) designed to confine hostilities to the peninsula of Korea. On June 27, he directed that the U.S. Seventh Fleet interdict the Taiwan Strait. The purpose of this order was to neutralize Taiwan, where Chiang and his Kuomintang government had found refuge after the Communists expelled the Nationalists from the Chinese mainland. The mission assigned the Seventh Fleet was, in effect, to prevent either Communist attacks on the island or Nationalist forays against the mainland.

This action evoked an instantaneous response from Peking,

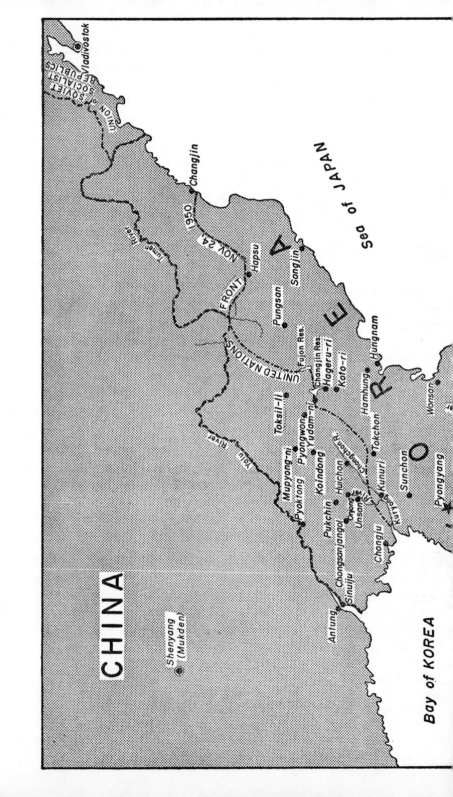

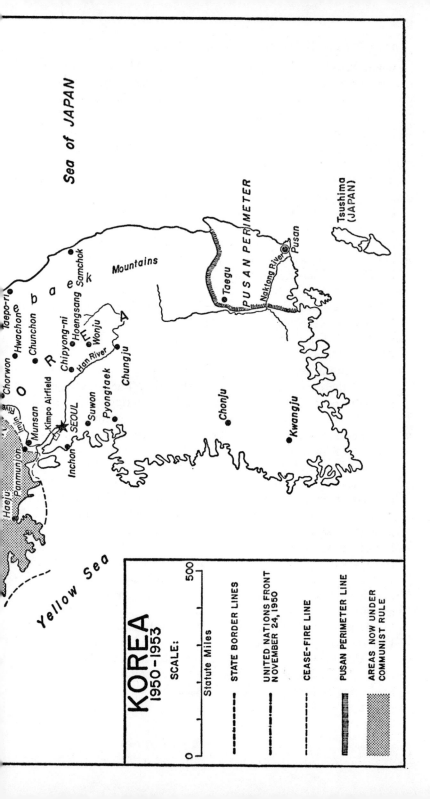

Sea of JAPAN

Tsushima
(JAPAN)

PUSAN PERIMETER

Taegu

Naktong River

Pusan

Mountains

b a e k

Samchok

Hoengsang

Chunchon

Chipyong-ni

Hwachon

Wonju

Taepo-ri

Chorwon

O

R

Han River

Chungju

Kimpo Airfield

SEOUL

Suwon

Pyongtaek

Chonju

Inchon

Munsan

Panmunjon

Kwangju

Imjin River

Haeju

Yellow Sea

KOREA
1950-1953

SCALE:

Statute Miles

0   500

———————— STATE BORDER LINES

····················· UNITED NATIONS FRONT
                       NOVEMBER 24, 1950

— — — — — CEASE-FIRE LINE

▦▦▦▦▦▦▦ PUSAN PERIMETER LINE

▨▨▨▨▨▨▨ AREAS NOW UNDER
          COMMUNIST RULE

where Premier and Foreign Minister Chou En-lai branded it "armed aggression on Chinese territory." [14] Members of the Central People's Government Council described the President's order as "a frantic act of provocation, which aroused great indignation among the Chinese people," who would "also act with firm counter blows." [15] During the next ten days, Party spokesmen, in newspapers and radio, devoted their energies to whipping up a frenetic nation-wide campaign directed against "American imperialistic aggression in Taiwan." The fighting in Korea, moving toward what Peking doubtless believed to be an ordained conclusion, received no more than routine attention in the mainland press. Presumably, this attitude reflected the government's estimate that the NKPA would not encounter any great difficulty in speedily dispatching Syngman Rhee's American-trained army.

This assessment was realistic. The Republic's armed forces were incapable of repelling a major attack. Evident military weakness was compounded by the increasing unpopularity and instability of Rhee's government. The economy of South Korea, which only American aid saved from complete collapse, staggered from one crisis to the next with predictable regularity. The government was unable to control a chronic inflation. The chaotic internal situation, exacerbated by widespread guerrilla operations and other subversive activities directed from P'yongyang, invited a *coup de main*.

But, as Kim Il Sung, his Russian advisers, and his Chinese friends no doubt realized, the key to ultimate success—or failure—lay in the hands of the administration in Washington. Obviously, the estimates made in P'yongyang, in Moscow, and in Peking were that the Americans either could not, or probably would not, intervene. At least, the risk that they might do so was deemed acceptable. A number of facts appeared to validate this conclusion. Foremost among these was the withdrawal of U.S. forces from the Far East. By mid-1948 only token forces remained in North China, where the administration was closing out its commitments as speedily as possible in an effort to avoid direct embroilment in the civil war. Occupation forces in South Korea were likewise being phased out. In Japan, the U.S. military establishment was being reduced and reorganized. All these developments were evident to the Kremlin, and the deduction obviously drawn there was that the United States was on the way to liquidating its strategic position in Asia.

If Soviet policy makers entertained any fugitive doubts as to the trend of U.S. strategic policy in this area, they must have been dispelled in early March 1949 when the London *Daily Mail* printed, under the headline "Anglo-U.S. Frontier in Japan," an interview granted its Tokyo correspondent, G. Ward Price, by General MacArthur. As Price quoted him, the General said: "Now the Pacific has become an Anglo-Saxon lake and our line of defense runs through the chain of islands fringing the coast of Asia. It starts from the Philippines and continues through the Ryukyu Archipelago, which includes its main bastion, Okinawa. Then it bends back through Japan and the Aleutian Island chain to Alaska." [16] The General failed to mention either Korea or Taiwan.

There were other indicators. In Washington, the running battle between the services, which began the moment President Truman signed the bill designed to unify them, reached a climax in October 1949 during hearings before the Armed Services Committee of the House of Representatives. Here for twelve days officers of the Army, Navy, Air Force, and Marine Corps aired irreconcilable concepts of the nature of a future war. From the welter of conflicting testimony (which ostensibly revolved around the efficacy of the B-36 bomber), several trends emerged clearly enough. One was that all eyes were fixed on Europe to the utter exclusion of Asia, an area never mentioned as a possible theater of operations during these tendentious proceedings.

Air Force witnesses stubbornly refused to conceive a war conducted on any terms except their own—that is, anywhere but in Europe, against any enemy but the Soviet Union, and without the atomic bomb as the decisive weapon. *The* strategic plan contemplated "one possible enemy" whose "industial heart" lay "not on any seashore, not on any island, but deep inside the Eurasian land mass. *It is to that type of war we must adapt all of our forces. . .*" [17] The Chief of Staff of the Air Force closed this part of his testimony with the remark that it was not "consistent with the requirements of military secrecy" to elaborate. So far as the Kremlin was concerned, no "further statement" was required.[18]

Adm. Arthur W. Radford, USN, a principal spokesman for the "balanced force" concept, was not to be distracted from his thesis by the exponents of this "all or nothing" strategy:

. . . a potential enemy can be expected to make sound estimates of our military strength. He does not depend entirely on what he reads in the papers. If the armed forces of this nation are unsoundly organized and improperly equipped, they will not be fully effective as a deterrent to aggression. They even invite it.[19]

Fleet Adm. William F. Halsey underlined the danger inherent in any exclusive strategic concept when in support of Adm. Radford he observed that a war would "be started by a foreign aggressor at the time, at the place, and in the manner that he desires. War will not commence with attacks against the continental United States. . . ." [20] In October 1949, the admirals were prophets unhonored.

The no-holds-barred infighting revealed one other matter of considerable interest to Moscow and Peking, where daily transcripts of these hearings were naturally assiduously analyzed: crippling cutbacks for the Army, Navy, and Marine Corps had already been made, and others were planned. This news tended strongly to support the justifiable assumption that the Americans were in the process of putting all their eggs in one basket.

On January 12, 1950, the American Secretary of State, in language similar to that MacArthur had used ten months previously, again defined a Far Eastern defensive perimeter which, commensurate with existing U.S. military capabilities, excluded both Korea and Taiwan.[21] As a later secretary observed, "The Communists thought, and had reason to think, that they would not be opposed, except by the then small and ill-equipped forces of the Republic of Korea." [22]

That these forces were both small and ill equipped was not entirely the result, it should be noted, of a policy which gave primary strategic consideration to Europe. Other factors influenced the administration to follow a circumspect course in supplying weapons to the Republic's armed forces. One of these was an understandable desire to restrain Syngman Rhee from disturbing the *status quo* in Korea. The arbitrary division of the peninsula along the 38th parallel was anathema to the aging President, whose personal dream was to govern a unified nation.[23] This ambition could not be satisfied without arms the Americans were unwilling, or unable, to give.

At any rate, Washington provided arms and equipment which were at best adequate to maintain internal security and repel North Korean "rice raids" across the parallel. At the time, however, even these limited missions were beyond the capabilities of the South Koreans—". . . in one week alone, March 3–10, there occurred twenty-nine guerrilla attacks in South Korea and eighteen incidents along the parallel." [24] The mountainous areas of South Korea were liberally sprinkled with guerrillas, many of them experienced and well-armed infiltrators from the north, who in sudden, vicious attacks frequently put to flight local police and small army garrison units.

The eight ROK divisions had no tanks, no artillery heavier than 105-mm. howitzers, and no anti-tank guns, rocket weapons, or even land mines capable of stopping the well-armored Russian T-34 medium tank with which the North Koreans were plentifully supplied. The rudimentary air force, equipped with a few *Harvard* (AT-10) trainers and a dozen serviceable liaison aircraft of World War II vintage, was useless. Even had the obsolete *Mustangs* (P-5 1s) authorized by the aid program been available, no South Korean pilot had yet qualified to fly combat missions. The ROK Coast Guard, which mustered 58 coastal craft, was of no consequence. Ammunition of all types and calibers was in short supply. Leadership generally left much to be desired, particularly where it mattered most: at the lower echelons. Very few of the more senior officers were professionally qualified to plan or conduct combat operations involving units larger than a battalion.

The ROK army had not yet completed a basic training cycle. Many infantry weapons crews had not attained minimum proficiency. Men qualified to serve in the technical branches—drivers, mechanics, ordnance repairmen, communicators—were few in number and inefficient. Most battalions, to say nothing of regiments and divisions, had not yet conducted field exercises.

Junior officers and soldiers were soon to prove that they—or the great majority of them—were loyal, tough, and courageous. But these qualities alone could not suffice to withstand an enemy at least equal in these respects and superior in all others.

Their adversaries were well led and equipped with about 150 aircraft; 200 thirty-five-ton T-34 medium tanks which mounted 85-mm. guns; self-propelled guns; 76-mm. and 122-mm. howitzers; anti-tank guns; and heavy (122-mm.) mortars. Almost one-third of the 135,000 officers and men in the NKPA were seasoned soldiers of Korean ethnic origin who had fought in Chinese Communist armies against the Japanese and later in the civil war the Communists waged against Chiang Kai-shek from 1945 to 1949. The North Korean 5th, 6th, and 7th (later 12th) divisions were, almost to the last man, composed of veterans of years of campaigning across North China and in Manchuria. Both the 1st and 4th divisions had a substantial proportion of Communist veterans. The total number of officers and men released by the Chinese Communists in late 1949 and early 1950 for assimilation by the NKPA was later conservatively estimated to have exceeded 38,000.[25]

The technical branches of the NKPA were largely staffed and manned by Koreans who had served in the Soviet armies or had received a military education in the Soviet Union. All political officers and lower-level cadres were Soviet-trained.

The commanders of NKPA I and II Corps, Lieut. Gen. Kim Ung and Kim Mu Chong, were graduates of Whampoa Military Academy and Eighth Route Army veterans. Their successors, Gens. Lee Kwan Mu and Kim Chan, held commissions in the Soviet Army during World War II. Several division commanders had similar backgrounds. Marshal Choe Yong Gun, Minister of Defense, was Moscow-trained, as was his immediate superior, the ex-guerrilla Premier of North Korea, Marshal Kim Il Sung. General Kim Chaek, who became Front Commander of the NKPA in August 1950, was also a tested officer and a dedicated Party veteran.

These infusions, which provided the NKPA with experienced and competent officers and noncommissioned officers at all levels, also assured the political reliability of the army.

Within twenty-four hours after crossing the parallel, two strong North Korean columns, spearheaded by eighty T-34 tanks, had reached Uijongbu, about fifteen miles north of Seoul, and on the evening of the 27th, leading elements of NKPA Third Division entered the northern suburbs of the capital. Before midnight the following day, the invaders were in possession of the city. Their rapid advance coupled with a fatal blunder, the premature blowing—probably by order of a civilian official—of bridges spanning the Han River south of the capital, produced a catastrophe. After less than one week of war, the ROK high command could account for but 54,000 officers and men. The other 44,000, caught on the north side of the Han, had simply disappeared.

This was the chaotic and apparently irretrievable situation which greeted General MacArthur, when at noon on June 29 his command plane landed at Suwon, 10 miles south of the river. Driving north in a jeep, MacArthur breasted a tide of refugees liberally sprinkled with small groups of thoroughly demoralized ROK soldiers, most of whom had cast away their arms.

The scene along the Han was enough to convince me that the defensive potential of South Korea had already been exhausted. There was nothing to stop the Communists from rushing their tank columns straight down the few good roads from Seoul to Pusan at the end of the peninsula. All Korea would then be theirs. Even with air and naval support, the South Koreans could not stop the enemy's headlong rush south. Only the immediate commitment of ground troops could possibly do so. The answer I had come to seek was there. I would throw my occupation soldiers into this breach. Completely outnumbered, I would rely upon strategic maneuver to overcome the great odds against me. It would be desperate, but it was my only chance.[26]

That evening, MacArthur cabled to Washington his urgent recommendation that U.S. ground troops be immediately committed. President Truman approved, and at 11 A.M. on July 1, a C-54 carrying the first batch of American troops to Korea landed at an airstrip a few miles north of Pusan. As Walter Millis has observed, this decision "turned the Korean Incident into the Korean War . . . until this commitment of the ground army the United States was at least technically in a position from which it could have withdrawn, recalling the air and sea forces and washing its hands of further complications. But with the Army on the ground, this would no longer be possible. Once troops were sent in, they would have to stay—until they were destroyed or driven out." [27]

Exactly a week later, the United Nations requested the U.S. government to designate a commander in chief, U.N. Forces. The President named General MacArthur, who as CINCUNC now donned a fourth hat.

MacArthur was considered by many to be the most distinguished of living American soldiers with the possible exception of George Catlett Marshall. He was an imaginative, bold, and determined general. He was also arrogant, ambitious, vain, and stubborn. His character and methods evoked in most of his immediate subordinates a blind, unreasoning, and ferocious loyalty; to others, he appeared a bombastic egocentric and a vastly overrated general. They distrusted his motives and disliked him intensely. This was the "remarkable personality" who presented what Secretary of the Navy James N. Forrestal is said to have characterized as "The MacArthur problem."

During July, General Kim Chaek's offensive moved steadily south toward Pusan, the port that was his ultimate objective. Remnants of the ROK army and U.S. formations hastily pulled out of comfortable billets and flown from Japan managed here and there to stay the tide. Piecemeal commitment of forces is not a method usually recommended by successful commanders, but in this situation, it was the one course of action suitable to the occasion. Poorly trained and inadequately equipped U.S. troops were exchanged for time—the crucial time needed to create a defensible perimeter to protect Pusan. Their sacrifice bought this. On July 19, General MacArthur felt able to report that the first phase of the campaign had ended "and with it the chance for victory by the North Korean forces." The enemy's "great opportunity depended upon the speed with which he could overrun South Korea once he had breached the Han River line and with overwhelming numbers and superior weapons temporarily shattered South Korean resistance. This chance he has now lost. . . . When he crashed the Han Line the way seemed entirely open and victory was within his grasp." [28] The Americans had mustered sufficient strength to conduct a series of planned delaying actions. These forced the enemy into repeated time-consuming deployments and costly frontal attacks. Although the situation remained fluid, the North Koreans were no longer able to dictate the operational pattern.

An incident now occurred which generated violent indignation in Peking and tended strongly to confirm her suspicions that the United States, while ostensibly attempting to restore the *status quo* in Korea, was at the same time plotting operations against the mainland. This was General MacArthur's July 31 visit to Taiwan.

Why, Peking reasoned, had MacArthur gone to Taiwan unless to concert plans with that "arch-criminal," the Generalissimo, for offensive action against the People's Republic? Nor were the Chinese Communists alone in interpreting the well-publicized meeting in this light: "In other capitals, there was great distress." Chiang's announcement, released shortly after MacArthur's departure, "was taken to mean exactly what it said—that 'Sino-American military cooperation' was in the works . . . that some kind of agreement had been reached to use Nationalist troops in Korea and perhaps for an invasion of China." [29]

MacArthur took vigorous exception to this construction. He pointed out that Taiwan had been placed within the area of his strategic responsibility by the President's order of June 27, and that he would have been derelict in his duty had he not personally ascertained Nationalist capabilities to defend the island. This sensible statement did nothing to allay the apprehensions his meetings with Chiang had aroused.

As August wore to an end, the North Koreans, despite mounting casualties and increasing logistic difficulties, pressed toward Pusan. Not until almost mid-September, after a series of desperate battles along the Naktong River had preserved the vital port, was the cutting edge of the NKPA finally blunted. It was now MacArthur's turn.

Precisely three months after tanks of Lieut. Gen. Kim Ung's NKPA I Corps rolled across the border against practically no opposition, Maj. Gen. Oliver P. Smith's 1st Marine Division, United States X Corps, which had landed at Inchon on September 15–16, fought its way down the streets of Seoul, and before darkness fell on the evening of September 25, the corps commander, Maj. Gen. Edward M. Almond, USA, who since 1946 had served as Mac-Arthur's chief of staff, announced somewhat prematurely the liberation of the ROK capital. This was news to Marines still taking casualties in bitter reduction of barricades and strong points in the battered buildings.

Until the seizure of Seoul and the breakout from the Pusan perimeter by Lieut. Gen. Walton H. Walker's 8th Army suddenly reversed the strategic situation, the government of the People's Republic of China had reason to hope that the North Koreans would succeed in their announced intention to drive United Nations forces off the tip of the peninsula into the sea. But these events, which presaged the collapse and eventual disintegration of the NKPA, required Peking to reappraise the situation.

A few hours after Almond's announcement, news of the fall of Seoul was being discussed at an informal dinner party in Peking. Among the guests of Sardar K. M. Panikkar, Indian ambassador to the Chinese People's Republic of China, was Gen. Nieh Jung-chen. After dinner, "in a quiet and unexcited manner" (the words are Panikkar's), the General told the Ambassador that the P.R.C. did not intent "to sit back with folded hands and let the Americans come to their border." General Nieh was in a position to know precisely what his government intended to do. He was acting chief of staff of the PLA.

As Panikkar relates the conversation, he asked General Nieh whether he "realized in full the implications of such an action."[30] General Nieh replied: "We know what we are in for, but at all costs American aggression has got to be stopped. The Americans can bomb us; they can destroy our industries, but they cannot defeat us on land." Panikkar then "tried to impress on him how destructive a war with America would be; how the Americans

would be able to destroy systematically all the industries of Manchuria, and put China back by half a century." General Nieh "only
laughed."

> We have calculated all that. . . . They may even drop atom bombs on
> us. What then? They may kill a few million people. Without sacrifice, a
> nation's independence cannot be upheld. . . . After all, China lives on
> the farms. What can atom bombs do there?

At a dramatic ceremony in Seoul on September 29, General Mac-
Arthur, architect of the imaginative and decisive Inchon operation,
returned the capital of the Republic of Korea to its aging but still
fiery president, Syngman Rhee. On the last day of the month, patrols of the ROK 3rd Division, advancing north along the eastern
coastal road, crossed the 38th parallel and entered the territory of
North Korea.

As U.N. forces moved forward with the confidence born of victory, the NKPA, now a defeated but not yet an entirely demoralized army, withdrew slowly toward the parallel it had violated less
than a hundred days before. Caught between X Corps and Walker's
advancing 8th Army, the enemy began to fall apart. First they surrendered in twos and threes; later by squads, platoons, companies.
Artillery pieces, trucks, ammunition, mortars, radios, machine guns,
rifles: all were abandoned. In desperation, Kim Il Sung and his
army's political officers first appealed to the troops to hold, then
threatened summary execution for those who would not stand and
fight. Appeals and threats were vain. The front was dissolving; the
NKPA had all but collapsed.

General MacArthur was justifiably jubilant, and the tenor of his
sixth report to the United Nations (covering the period September
15–20) reflected his conviction that the war in Korea was won:

> Caught between our northern and our southern forces . . . the enemy
> is thoroughly shattered. . . .

> The prompt junction of our two forces is dramatically symbolic of this
> collapse.

> Continuing operations will take full advantage of our initiative and
> unified strength to provide for the complete destruction of the enemy
> and his early capitulation.[31]

On October 1, MacArthur called upon Kim Il Sung to surrender.
Although no reply came from P'yongyang, there was immediate
and unequivocal response from Peking. There, in a speech reporting

on the achievements of the first year of Communist rule, Premier and Foreign Minister Chou En-lai assailed the United States:

The United States deliberately concocted the assault of the Syngman Rhee gang against the Korean Democratic People's Republic in order to expand its aggression in the East and the United States on the pretext of the situation in Korea, dispatched its Naval and Air Forces to invade the Taiwan Province of China, and announced that the so-called problem of Taiwan's status should be solved by the America-controlled United Nations. Moreover, time after time, it sent its Air Force, which is invading Korea, to intrude into the air over the Liaotung Province of China, strafing and bombing, and sent its Naval forces, which are invading Korea, to bombard Chinese merchant shipping on the high seas.

By these frenzied and violent acts of imperialist aggression, the U.S. Government has displayed itself as the most dangerous foe to the People's Republic of China.

The U.S. aggressive forces have invaded China's borders and may at any time expand their aggression. MacArthur, commander in chief of American aggression against Taiwan and Korea, has long ago disclosed the aggressive design of the U.S. Government and is continuing to invent new excuses for extending its aggression. The Chinese people firmly oppose the aggressive brutalities of America and are determined to liberate Taiwan and other Chinese territory from the clutches of the U.S. aggressors.

The Chinese people closely follow the situation in Korea since she was invaded by the United States. The Korean people and their People's Army are resolute and valorous. Led by Premier Kim Il Sung, they have scored remarkable achievements in resisting the American invaders and have won the sympathy and support of people throughout the world. The Korean people can surely overcome their many difficulties and obtain final victory on the principle of persistent, long-term resistance.

The Chinese are peace-loving people. One hundred and twenty million Chinese have already signed their names to the solemn Stockholm appeal and this signature movement is continuing to develop among the Chinese people. It is obvious that the Chinese people, after liberating the whole territory of their own country, want to rehabilitate and develop their industrial and agricultural production and cultural and educational work in a peaceful environment, free from threats. But if the American aggressors take this as a sign of the weakness of the Chinese people, they will commit the same fatal blunder as the Kuomintang reactionaries.

The Chinese people enthusiastically love peace, but in order to defend peace, they never have been and never will be afraid to oppose aggressive war. The Chinese people absolutely will not tolerate foreign aggression nor will they supinely tolerate seeing their neighbors being savagely invaded by imperialists.

Whoever attempts to exclude the nearly 500 million Chinese people from the United Nations and whoever sets at naught and violates the interests of this one-fourth of mankind in the world and fancies vainly to solve any Eastern problem directly concerned with China, arbitrarily, will certainly break their skulls.[32]

The next night, Chou summoned Panikkar to the Ministry of Foreign Affairs, where he told the Indian ambassador that should U.S. troops cross the 38th parallel, China would enter the war.[33] Panikkar passed this information to Prime Minister Nehru. Later, in a parliamentary speech, the Indian Prime Minister said:

The Chinese Government clearly indicated that if the 38th parallel was crossed, they would consider it a grave danger to their own security, and that they would not tolerate it. We did, as a matter of fact, convey our views to the Governments of the United Kingdom, the United States of America, as well as to some governments in Asia.[34]

The White House did not attach too much importance to the information received from New Delhi. President Truman was to write: "The problem that arose in connection with these reports was that Mr. Panikkar had in the past played the game of the Chinese Communists fairly regularly, so that his statement could not be taken as that of an impartial observer." The President viewed Chou En-lai's warning as "a bald attempt to blackmail the United Nations." [35] *Time*, the American weekly news magazine, which since the mid-1930s had compiled a singularly inconsistent record of interpretation of events in China, dismissed Chou's statement as "only propaganda." [36]

But neither the President nor his close advisers completely discounted Nehru's message. Although both he and the Joint Chiefs of Staff had always deemed Chinese intervention possible, they had never considered it probable. Nor did General MacArthur, who testified in Senate hearings in 1951 that intervention by either the Soviet Union or China "was a calculated risk from the day we landed in Korea." [37] Events were shortly to prove, however, that calculations made in June 1950 were not relevant to the situation developing during the first two weeks of October.

At this time, MacArthur was preparing to carry out a directive issued by the JCS on September 27:

Your military objective is the destruction of the North Korean Armed Forces. In attaining this objective you are authorized to conduct military operations, including amphibious and airborne landings or ground operations north of the 38th parallel in Korea, provided that at the time of such operations there has been no entry into North Korea by major Soviet or Chinese Communist forces, no announcement of intended entry, nor a threat to counter our operations militarily in North Korea. . . .[38]

Two days later Secretary of Defense George C. Marshall radioed CINCUNC that he was to feel "unhampered tactically and strategically" to proceed north of the 38th parallel. Apparently, Washington did not conceive Chou En-lai's statement to Panikkar to be either "an announcement of intended entry" or "a threat to counter our operations militarily in North Korea."

Further, on October 7, the United Nations resolved that "all appropriate steps" be taken "to insure conditions of stability *throughout Korea*" and called for "establishment of a *unified, independent, and democratic Government in the Sovereign State of Korea.*"[39] Peking's reaction to the United Nations vote was immediate and violent: the resolution "to enlarge the war of aggression" was "sanguinary" and "absolutely illegal"; its purpose was to establish "an aggressive base in Korea . . . pointing toward the People's Republic of China." In a leading editorial, the *People's Daily* announced that the Chinese people would "firmly hold the aggressors responsible for all consequences arising from their maniacal acts."[40]

By this time, leading elements of the ROK I Corps (Third and Capitol divisions), operating on the east coast, were more than 100 miles north of the parallel and closing rapidly on the defended port of Wonsan. Two days later (October 9), other ROK divisions had crossed, and all were driving toward the Manchurian border.[41] As the ROKs pushed north, MacArthur "for the last time" called on Kim Il Sung's government to surrender. The message ended with this sentence: "Unless immediate response is made by you in the name of the North Korean government, I shall at once proceed to take such military actions as may be necessary to enforce the decrees of the United Nations.[42] A few hours after this message was dispatched, Lieut. Gen. Walton Walker's victorious 8th Army began its advance toward P'yongyang.

Once again the reaction was from Peking. On October 10, Chou En-lai announced that the Chinese people could not "stand idly by" in the face of the "serious situation created by the invasion of Korea." The "war of invasion," his statement continued, "had been a serious menace to the security of China from its very start."[43] No one in Korea, Japan, New York, or Washington paid more than passing attention to this warning, which was generally considered to be but another example of Chinese bombast. Operations were progressing satisfactorily, the situation was well in hand, the enemy was on the run, the moment for a successful Chinese intervention had long since passed.

It was in this buoyant atmosphere that General MacArthur left Tokyo for a mid-Pacific meeting on October 15 with President Truman. The President's plane touched down shortly after the General's had. As the door swung open, Truman appeared, and Mac-Arthur moved toward the foot of the gangway. The General chose not to salute his commander in chief. This calculated insult to the President of the United States—which did not escape those who witnessed the historic meeting between the President and his pro-consul—did not visibly disturb Truman. He would later have reason to recall the incident.

The President's reaction to the Wake Island meeting was one of satisfaction. The purpose of the trip, he said later, was to discuss "the final phase of the U.N. action in Korea." [44] MacArthur assured Truman that the war was indeed in the final phase, that he anticipated an end to organized resistance by Thanksgiving and expected the 8th Army to celebrate Christmas in Japan. He informed the Joint Chiefs that he would soon be able to release a division for Europe.

The President asked the U.N. Commander what he thought of the possibility of Chinese intervention. MacArthur replied that this was a remote contingency. It was one, at least, which did not particularly perturb him:

Had they interfered in the first or second months it would have been decisive. We are no longer fearful of their intervention. We no longer stand hat in hand. The Chinese have 300,000 men in Manchuria. Of these, probably not more than 100 to 125,000 are distributed along the Yalu River. Only 50,000 to 60,000 could be gotten across the Yalu River. They have no Air Force. Now that we have bases for our Air Force in Korea, if the Chinese tried to get down to P'yongyang there would be the greatest slaughter. [45]

While the President and the General thus pleasantly conversed on a remote mid-Pacific atoll, the vanguards of the Chinese Fourth Field Army began to cross the Yalu and to disappear without trace in the broken mountains of North Korea.

CHAPTER SEVEN

"*An Act of International Lawlessness*"
General of the Army Douglas MacArthur[1]

Probably we will not know for years, if ever, precisely when the Peking government decided to enter the Korean War, what aid the U.S.S.R. promised the Chinese, what guarantees were exchanged, or what other mutually agreeable political and financial arrangements were made by the two powers. A realistic assessment of the situation as of early September must have indicated clearly to Peking and Moscow that Kim Chaek's faltering bid to take Pusan and push the U.N. forces into the sea was destined to fail. That Peking then made just such a judgment and a contingent decision based upon it is confirmed by the quickened flow of troops from South and Central China toward Manchuria, which in September and early October taxed Chinese rail capacities to the limit.

These and previous troop deployments do not positively establish Peking's intent, *prior to Inchon—Seoul*, to intervene on a major scale. But this unexpected and decisive operation, followed by the rapid disintegration of the NKPA, confronted Chinese and Soviet policy makers with the unpleasant reality that the Americans would inevitably soon be standing on the Yalu and Tumen unless someone used force to stop them. Obviously, Kim Il Sung's government did not have the means to do this. And without risk of a major war, in which there was a distinct possibility that atomic weapons would be used against Russian cities, Soviet troops could not directly confront the United Nations on the peninsula.

Mao was thus faced with an extremely difficult decision. But the philosophy which had sustained him through the years assured him that any government of a Korea unified under "imperialist" auspices could not possibly be friendly to his regime but must, by definition, be implacably hostile. In Peking, the press emphasized the theme that occupation of Korea had been imperial Japan's preliminary to assimilation of Manchuria, ingestion of the northern provinces, and the later attempt to subjugate China. Korea is one of China's "lips," and "when the lips are lost, the teeth are cold; when the gates are crashed, the halls are imperiled."

Moreover, certain advantages could be derived from an intervention even if it accomplished no more than forcing the United Nations back to the 38th parallel. First, even such a limited success would make it possible to re-create a viable Communist government —Chinese rather than Soviet-influenced and oriented—in P'yongyang. Second, it would unquestionably confirm Communist China's position not only as the most powerful nation in Asia but as one henceforth to be respected in the West. Finally, a war ostensibly waged in "self-defense" against the "imperialist" United States, which could be depicted as seeking a foothold on the Asian mainland, would offer the Party an untrammeled opportunity to accelerate and intensify domestic programs necessary to consolidate its position.

As the Chinese weighed the situation after Inchon-Seoul, it must have been apparent that potential gains outweighed the inherent dangers. Of these, the most critical was the possibility that the Americans might use the atomic bomb on mainland targets. This the Chinese accepted as a remote albeit existing risk. In the Chinese view, the atomic bomb was not a decisive weapon.

On October 19, the day U.N. forces entered P'yongyang, the U.S. State Department "came to the conclusion" that Chinese intervention in Korea was "unlikely." [2] This assessment was by no means confined to the department over which Acheson presided. It was shared alike by the President, the Joint Chiefs of Staff, members of the National Security Council, Gen. Walter Bedell Smith, director of Central Intelligence, prominent senators, congressmen, and political pundits of all hues. If questioned, that amorphous character, "the man in the street," would have expressed the same opinion. In Tokyo on the same day, Headquarters CINCFE issued Operation Plan 202. This provided for the withdrawal of U.N. forces from Korea when hostilities were successfully concluded. The assumption on which this plan was based was that "there would be no intervention either by Chinese or Soviet forces." [3]

Nevertheless, daily intelligence estimates issued during early October by Maj. Gen. Charles A. Willoughby, MacArthur's G-2, consistently gave high priority to the possibility of "Reinforcement by Soviet Satellite China." On October 14, Willoughby estimated with commendable accuracy that there were 9 Chinese armies totaling 38 divisions in Manchuria. Of these, 24 were disposed along the Yalu at crossing points. In this general deployment, "the grouping in the vicinity of Antung is the most immediately available Manchurian force, astride a suitable road net for deployment southward." [4]

Then, following hard upon General MacArthur's return from Wake, this capability—to deploy available forces southward—was relegated (strangely enough) to a lower position. What had happened to change the G-2's assessment? Was this revised estimate based on an analysis of indications or on hard intelligence? Or could it have been no more than a wishful reflection of the assurances CINCUNC had given his commander in chief at the island conference?

It would, however, be a perversion of historical fact to assign sole responsibility for this gross miscalculation to MacArthur or to Willoughby. The conviction that China would not intervene represented an emotional rather than an intellectual conclusion, an ascription to the enemy of *intentions* compatible with the desires of Washington and Tokyo. The assessments were subjective to a damaging degree, and events were shortly to prove once again—as they had on several occasions during World War II—that the art of divination is not one which chiefs of state, their high advisers, and their field commanders can profitably practice.

Shortly before the occupation of the abandoned North Korean capital, MacArthur had issued an order delineating a "restraining line" across the peninsula, beyond which only forces of the Republic of Korea were to advance.[5] This line ran generally from Songjin on the east coast through P'ungsan, Toksil-li, P'yongwan, Koindong, and Ch'ongsanjangol. Thence it bent southwest to meet the Bay of Korea slightly north of Chongju. The restraint imposed by CINCUNC was in accordance with the spirit of the Joint Chiefs' policy directive of September 27, which had specified that only ROK units should be employed in North Korean provinces bordering on Manchuria and the Soviet Far Eastern territories. The "restraint" held for five days: on October 24, MacArthur took it upon himself to lift the restriction and ordered all U.N. forces to advance rapidly to the Yalu. The JCS primly reminded MacArthur that his action was not in consonance with the September 27 directive. But they did not countermand his order. Significant consequences were to derive from this abdication of command responsibility.[6]

The day after MacArthur issued the order to advance to the northern frontier, amphibious ships of Vice-Adm. Arthur D. Struble's Joint Task Force 7 stood into the harbor of Wonsan, on the east coast of Korea, and on October 26, the 1st Marine Division, X Corps, began to disembark. After Inchon-Seoul, the Wonsan landing was anticlimactic. The city had been taken several weeks previously by the ROK 3rd Division, and Marines crossed the beaches standing up. Before noon the following day, Maj. Gen. Oliver P. Smith opened his command post in a dilapidated frame building a mile north of the city. The "eastern front" on the peninsula, a front MacArthur had decided to create shortly after the fall of Seoul, was now a reality.

MacArthur's subordinates had not received their commander's concept of a major amphibious landing on the east coast with much enthusiasm; indeed, the General's critics will long continue to question the wisdom of removing X Corps from western Korea. The situation created by this redeployment no doubt did—as MacArthur averred—greatly simplify the problem of logistic support, but at the same time it created one of coordinating the actions of two major groupings physically separated one from the other by some of the most forbidding terrain that can be imagined. To Gen. Walton Walker, who had expected this corps to be assigned to his command, the decision came as an unpleasant surprise. Other senior officers, who were never consulted by CINCUNC, privately questioned the move. The naval command viewed it as a wasteful and unnecessary effort; the Joint Chiefs were apprehensive. "A lot of people," General Bradley later testified, "were worried about the fact that the X Corps was isolated from the rest [sic] of the 8th Army, and that the right flank of the 8th Army was exposed." [7]

On the face of it, the redeployment of Almond's corps created a situation in which—if the Chinese should intervene in force—the possibility of total disaster was inherent, for neither Almond nor Walker could come to the aid of the other. But none dared challenge the Commander in Chief on the spot. The Inchon landing, to which almost all had strenuously objected, stood as irrefutable testimony to MacArthur's infallible tactical imagination, or, as others perhaps more accurately described it, his intuition.

Smith's orders from X Corps directed him to "advance rapidly in zone to the Korean northern border." [8] The zone prescribed was 50 miles in width; the "Korean northern border" more than 300 road miles north of Wonsan. No provision for contact liaison with the 8th Army to the west could be made, for the rugged and desolate Taebaek Range, with elevations reaching to more than 7,000 feet, intervened. The broken terrain between the left (west) flank of X Corps and the right flank of ROK II Corps (on the right [east] flank of the 8th Army) was a veritable no-man's land. Or so General Mac-Arthur then conceived it to be.

And on the basis of information derived from air reconnaissance, this conclusion was justified. For weeks, U.S. Air Force, Navy, and Marine planes had flown daily photographic missions and conducted low-level visual reconnaissance of terrain immediately south of the Yalu, in the zones of action of the 8th Army and X Corps, as well as over the Taebaek Mountains. Results of such reconnaissance were almost invariably negative. No significant activity was visible from the air, nor did patrols from the 8th Army rove more than a few miles beyond the army's right (east) flank.

A sense that all was over but the victory parades pervaded Far East Headquarters as Washington planned redeployment of the triumphant 8th Army. MacArthur recommended that ammunition ships en route to Korea be ordered to return to Hawaii or U.S. ports on the west coast for off-loading. Operation "Cutback" was in full swing.

Had American leaders been familiar with the classic works which for centuries have provided a basis for the Chinese conduct of war, the fog generated by such euphoria might to a degree have been dissipated:

All warfare is based on deception. Therefore when capable, feign incapacity; when active, inactivity. When near, make it appear that you are far away; when far away, that you are near.[9]

In midafternoon, October 24, a motorized battalion of the ROK 6th Division arrived at the village of Onjong, some 65 air miles due north of P'yongyang and fifty-odd air miles south of the Chinese border. This battalion was advance guard for the remainder of the Second Regiment, which soon closed on the deserted town. The mission of the Second Regiment was to destroy NKPA remnants and advance to Pyoktang, on the Yalu.

The following morning the Third Battalion moved out to secure Pukchin, a road-junction hamlet some ten miles north of Onjong. Two miles from the destination, leading vehicles of the battalion ran into land mines and a road block. As trucks loaded with ROKs slithered into ditches, automatic fire opened from high ground on both sides of the road. Before the troops could be organized to break out, the enemy plugged the exit. The ROKs were trapped. The battalion, overwhelmed by fire, was shattered.

When news of the disaster which had befallen his Third Battalion reached the regimental commander in Onjong, he dispatched the Second Battalion to the rescue. With combat patrols to front and ranging the high ground to both flanks, the battalion advanced warily. These patrols captured two prisoners. Both were indubitably Chinese. One stated that strong Chinese forces had crossed the Yalu on October 14 and taken up positions three days later in the mountains which surrounded Pukchin.

During late afternoon, the battalion attempted to return to Onjong. Although pocketed by a superior enemy, it managed to withdraw almost intact and returned by a circuitous route to the town. It was already apparent to the regimental commander that he was in serious trouble. He could not hope for reinforcements: the other two regiments of the division were distant.

A few minutes after three-thirty the next morning, his command, struck by at least a division of the Chinese 40th Army, was in mortal danger. For three hours, until first light on the 26th, the ROKs underwent an ordeal soon to become familiar to other U.N. troops. Chinese bugle calls, shrill whistles, and blasts on shepherds' horns rose above almost continuous explosions of mortar shells. The Chinese closed in and brought grenades and Russian "burp guns" into action.

But at dawn the fire slackened as the attackers faded away, and the regimental commander started what remained of his two battalions toward the east. Three miles from town, they ran into a road block. Now, as fierce converging fires from commanding ground on both sides poured into the column, the ROKs broke. The Second Regiment, ROK 6th Division, disintegrated. On the following day, the Chinese surrounded and severely punished the remaining elements of this division plus the Tenth Regiment of the ROK 8th Division. ROK II Corps, protecting the right flank of Walton Walker's 8th Army, was crumbling. Only two days before, in reply to a question Walker had said: "Everything is going just fine." [10]

The day following this disaster, Maj. Gen. Willoughby estimated that "the auspicious time" for Chinese intervention had "long since passed." [11] In his Eighth Report to the United Nations, which covered the period October 15–31, CINCUNC stated: "There is no positive evidence that Chinese Communist units, as such, have entered Korea."[12] The commanding general, ROK 6th Division, knew better, but it was to be some time before the news was given credence in Tokyo.

On the date Willoughby released the document that stands as one of the most egregiously wrong strategic intelligence estimates in history, there were at least four Chinese Communist armies in North Korea, three deployed west of the Taebaek range in the zone of action of the 8th Army. These, the 38th, 39th, and 40th, composed the major portion of 13th Army Group. They were reinforced by elements of the 1st Motorized Artillery Division, two regiments of the 2nd, and a cavalry regiment. The 42nd Army took position in the desolate hills surrounding the Changjin (Chosin) Reservoir, in the zone of action of Almond's X Corps. Within the week, two more armies, the 50th and 66th, together with the 8th Artillery Division and a motor transport regiment, crossed from Antung to Sinuiju. As of October 31, the Chinese High Command had deployed, in the utmost secrecy and within relatively few miles of the unsuspecting enemy they were to strike, almost 200,000 troops.[13] Some of those had crossed the Yalu before October 15.

The massive Chinese deployments of October 1950 indicate not only that a very high level of planning and executive competence was common to all staff and command echelons of the PLA but also that the troops were tough, well disciplined, and able, without faltering, to meet the demanding march schedules prescribed. Moving only at night, in units of company and battalion size, the Chinese were led to designated assembly areas by North Korean guides familiar with every inch of the ground. Relays of porters carried some of the heavier equipment along obscure paths and byways. To the Westerners the Chinese would soon meet in combat, this barren, tortured terrain was an enemy; to them, it was an indispensable ally. The officers who planned the initial deployment in Korea had not forgotten the words of their ancient master of the art of war:

Those who do not know the conditions of mountains and forests, hazardous defiles, marshes and swamps, cannot conduct the march of the army. Those who do not use local guides are unable to obtain the advantage of the ground.[14]

By day, the troops lay up, cleaned their weapons, and attended meetings called by company commanders and political officers. At these sessions, attack plans were reviewed and discussed in detail, and the soldier's determination to annihilate the "vicious imperialist enemy" whose "wanton aggression" threatened his motherland, encouraged. Throughout, the most rigid movement and camouflage discipline were enforced. Thin wisps of smoke rising from scattered North Korean hamlets suggested to U.N. observers flying pre-dusk reconnaissance missions only that the inhabitants were peacefully preparing the evening meal. But in these thousands of huts, cooks were tasting the cabbage soup and boiling the rice and noodles tough Chinese soldiers needed to sustain them during another wearying night march in the mountains. After dark, the columns silently formed and at command as silently moved on, phantoms in the light of the waning moon, toward the next day's bivouac areas.

This was essentially a semi-literate peasant army, with a hard core of experienced and dedicated veterans. Many soldiers who had fought with the Nationalists did not meet the Party's rigid standards of ideological purity, but the political officers and Party cadres spared no efforts to convert them. That he was engaged in a just war, in a wholly righteous cause, and that the enemy he was about to face was vicious, cruel, and predatory, the average Chinese soldier was convinced.

We must not, however, imagine that the cadres devoted themselves to preaching ideology from morning till night. This was but a minor function. A more important one was to nurture in the peasant soldier that deep sense of duty and confidence in himself, his comrades, and his commanders without which true courage, as distinguished from mere bravado or momentary gallantry, cannot exist. In combat, the political officer was expected to set an example—and many lost their lives doing so.

It is true that political officers had authority to punish cowards and malingerers, but the picture of Chinese soldiers advancing into battle with the Party representatives holding Mausers against the bases of their skulls is simply ridiculous. Soldiers who shirked their duties were given opportunity to redeem themselves in the eyes of their comrades by participating in particularly dangerous missions. This form of punishment—or rehabilitation—is not peculiar to Oriental armies.

Thus, whatever the demerits (and there are many) of a divided authority, it would seem that at low levels both political officers and cadres served a variety of useful purposes in the PLA as it was constituted during the Korean War. Whether they will be equally useful in a more literate and technically competent PLA than that of 1950–53 remains to be seen.

The leadership of this army was of a high quality. Practically all the senior officers had fought with the 8th Route Army against the Japanese. Most battalion, company, and platoon commanders were veterans of the civil war. Noncommissioned officers were equally experienced. All were imbued with the tactical doctrine which the Communists had applied with such success against both enemies. This was based on mobility, deception, distraction, surprise, concentration of superior force at the vital point, a "short attack," and speedy disengagement. Thorough reconnaissance, an essential preliminary to all attacks, accounts for the almost uncanny Chinese ability not only to strike along boundaries between enemy units, but to flow along neglected avenues of approach deep into the rear of enemy positions.

At this time, the firepower of a 10,000-man Chinese Communist division (three infantry regiments, a pack-artillery battalion, and engineer, transport, medical, and communications companies) was by no means comparable to that organic to a U.S. Army division. With the exception of Russian-type "burp guns," which were in ample supply, individual arms were not standardized. Many soldiers carried American rifles, carbines, or pistols; American-made submachine guns, bazookas, mortars, automatic rifles, and heavy and light machine guns had been taken from the Nationalists in wholesale quantities during the civil war; Soviet occupation forces in Manchuria had seen to it that the larger portion of Japanese weapons surrendered in Manchuria found their way into Communist hands. A Western ordnance officer would have deemed this heterogeneous collection more suitable for the junk pile than for employment in the field of battle.

The Chinese, however, found these weapons eminently satisfactory, not only because they worked but also because they would now be turned against Americans. In fact, said Kuo Mo-jo, a senior Party mouthpiece, the Chinese owed the Americans a debt of gratitude: "Since a greater part of the planes, guns, tanks, warships, and American equipment" furnished the Nationalists "got into the hands of the People's Liberation Army, Chiang Kai-shek came to be the head of the transport department of the People's Liberation Army and the United States our arsenal." [15]

The Chinese had no anti-tank weapons, but each platoon carried enough TNT to make eight to ten five-pound satchel charges, each capable of blowing the track off a tank. These charges, of course, had to be placed, but there was no lack of men willing to sacrifice themselves to immobilize U.S. tanks. Below regimental level, there were no radios and few field telephones. In action, battalion and company commanders would exercise control by colored flares, bugle calls, and horn and whistle signals. Primitive means, to be sure. Indeed, they were not essentially different from those used for centuries to control movement of Chinese troops in battle. But they proved to be effective in another respect, for these strange sounds had a most unsettling impact on their antagonists.

While the Chinese 38th and 40th armies were macerating the ROK 6th Division in the Huich'on-Onjong area, the ROK 1st Division was in serious trouble at Unsan, a strategic road junction which controls access from the north into the valley of the Kuryong. This river, a major tributary of the Ch'ongch'on, joins it a few miles west of Kunu-ri. As always, terrain was to dictate the nature of the battle.

The stakes were high, for if the Chinese could smash the 8th Army pivot at Unsan, the entire right flank would be unhinged and the way clear for the enemy to roll down the Ch'ongch'on Valley, both north and south of the river, to the Bay of Korea. Had the Chinese succeeded in doing so, they would have destroyed Walker's army as an effective fighting organization.

As early as October 27, Maj. Gen. Paik Sun Yup, commanding the ROK 1st Division engaged at Unsan, told the commanding general, U.S. I Corps, that he was facing "many, many Chinese." [16] Already, a few prisoners had been taken, and Walker, although skeptical that the Chinese had intervened in force, concluded that his right flank was seriously menaced. Accordingly, he directed ROK II Corps (7th and 8th divisions) to refuse this flank. At the same time, he pulled the U.S. 1st Cavalry Division out of P'yongyang and ordered it to proceed to Unsan, pass through Paik's division, and attack to the north. The stage was set for the first major combat action between U.S. troops and the "People's Volunteers," as Peking radio euphemistically described the Chinese army in Korea.

In late afternoon, November 1, battle was joined when the Chinese 116th Division attacked the 15th (ROK) Infantry northwest of Unsan. By midnight, this ROK regiment had been overwhelmed and annihilated. It was now the turn of the U.S. 8th Cavalry, whose three battalions held ground north, west, and south of the town.

The regiment, occupying an exposed salient and under attack by vastly superior enemy forces, received orders from the division commander to withdraw to the south. Shortly after midnight, Col. Raymond D. Palmer began to move his battalion and regimental trains, attached tanks, and supporting artillery toward Ipsok. Not all were to make it.

The Chinese surrounded and isolated the Third Battalion and in three successive nights of vicious fighting tore it apart. The remainder of the regiment fought its way through road blocks south of the town and only escaped by abandoning most of its artillery pieces, prime movers, trucks, jeeps, tanks, 4.2-inch mortars, and other heavy equipment. The proud 8th Cavalry had been shattered. It was not again to be a combat-ready unit for some time.

Unsan, however, was but the prelude to a more decisive battle for the Ch'ongch'on bridgehead. Here, from November 3 to first light on the 6th, major elements of the Communist 38th and 40th armies repeatedly threw all they had at the defenders. The 8th Army, now consolidating, punished them severely. At dawn on the 6th, Chinese bugle notes were heard along the bridgehead positions. This time the buglers were not signaling an attack but a withdrawal. All along the line, the Chinese broke contact. The "First Phase Offensive" against the 8th Army had ended, at great cost, in failure.

Or so, at the time, it seemed. But in terms of Chinese strategy, this first effort was primarily defensive: designed to slow the drive to the Yalu, to develop U.N. positions, to test U.N. capabilities, to measure U.N. command and leadership, and to try the mettle of U.N. forces. These the Chinese had apparently done to the satisfaction of the high command in Shenyang, over which P'eng Teh-huai, a soldier victorious in many battles against the Japanese and Nationalists, was then reported to preside.

The withdrawal confused the U.N. field command; senior intelligence officers, unfamiliar with Mao Tse-tung's strategic concepts, were unable to account for it. Most ascribed it to the disproportionately heavy casualties they believed the Chinese had sustained and cited the enemy's need for resupply, reorganization, and rest. Official reports did not reveal the full psychological effect of the vicious "short" surprise attacks on U.N. forces—particularly on the ROKs, many of whom were literally terror-stricken at the very mention of the word "Chinese."

From these first engagements, the Americans seemed to have learned very little; their enemy, a great deal. The tactical pattern the Chinese used with such success against the 8th Cavalry was to be repeated many times and at staggering cost to the prestige of American arms. Masterful use of terrain, deception, infiltration during darkness, and close combat in which superior numbers were applied at vital points in the deep flanks and rear, spelled disaster first to the defenders of Unsan. Other U.N. forces—British, Turkish, French —were shortly to become acquainted with this combination, so well designed to negate the Westerners' superiority in firepower and to take full advantage of their almost complete dependence on roads and wheels.

In a more profound sense, the Chinese withdrawal in early November was designed to "encourage the enemy's arrogance"; to lure the U.N. forces deeper into North Korea, where their tenuous supply lines could be interdicted and where units separated from one another by the broken terrain could be isolated and annihilated. This was the nature of the deadly trap P'eng, at his Shenyang headquarters, was setting for the overconfident general in the Dai Ichi Building in Tokyo.[17]

On the day preceding the disappearance of Chinese forces from the fronts of the 8th Army at the Ch'ongch'on and X Corps in the east, General MacArthur forwarded a Special Report to the Security Council. This contained information of matters which, said the General, "it is incumbent upon me to bring at once to the attention of the United Nations." CINCUNC set forth evidence, gathered from interrogations of 35 Chinese soldiers captured, that elements of three armies (38th, 39th, and 40th) had crossed into Korea and were "deployed for action against the forces of the United Command." [18] His estimate of total Chinese strength in Korea (not included in the report) was of the order of 40,000 to 60,000. This was wildly inaccurate; actually, about 200,000 "People's Volunteers," including 15 infantry divisions, were already south of the Yalu.

As he forwarded this report, CINCUNC directed the Far East Air Force to bomb the principal Yalu bridges over which Chinese troops were flowing from Manchuria in uninterrupted streams. According to Marine night-fighter pilots, Sinjuiju "seethed with activity" during the first week of November. On return to base, they reported "heavy," "very heavy," "tremendous," and even "gigantic" convoys moving south.[19]

The JCS, intent on restricting combat operations to the Korean peninsula, immediately countermanded MacArthur's order to bomb the bridges and instructed the General to refrain from attacking targets in a zone five miles south of the river. This message evoked a blazing protest from Tokyo. In his reply, MacArthur literally ordered the JCS to take the matter to the President for resolution, "as I believe your instructions may result in a calamity of major proportions for which, without his personal and direct understanding of the situation, I cannot accept responsibility." [20] The former West Point ballplayer was covering all the bases. If things went wrong, no one could blame him.

This message shook the Joint Chiefs, who hastily reversed themselves and authorized MacArthur to bomb the Korean ends of the bridges. They added the condition, however, that under no circumstances was Manchurian territory to be bombed, Chinese air space to be violated, or electric-power installations on the Korean side of the Yalu—from which power was transmitted to Manchuria—to be attacked. They hoped thus to demonstrate clearly to Peking that U.N. operations would be strictly limited to Korea and did not constitute a threat to the security of the People's Republic of China. These statements did not placate the Chinese, who continued to attack America with habitual virulence in the press and on the radio. Although MacArthur could not yet bring himself to believe that the Chinese intended to intervene on a major scale, his dispatches to Washington at this time indicated that he planned to resume the move north with a degree of caution not altogether characteristic. His purpose, so he informed the JCS, was to take "accurate measure" of enemy strength.[21] This "wary phase of U.N. strategy" [22] (as Marine Corps historians so aptly described it) was to be of short duration, for only two days later, MacArthur felt that his air power could deny significant reinforcement of Chinese forces "now arrayed against me in North Korea." [23]

This statement seems unwarrantably optimistic, not only in light of the volume of traffic pouring through Sinjuiju and disappearing in the mountains south of the Yalu but also because a new factor had been introduced. This was the Soviet MIG-15, a swept-wing, heavily armed, sub-sonic jet fighter which at the time was superior to the F-80 "Shooting Star." MIGs first entered Korean skies on November 1, and although for some time they would not become a peril to U.N. control of the air over North Korea, their presence presaged an inevitable challenge.

It also provoked another major controversy between the General in the Dai Ichi Building and the Joint Chiefs in the Pentagon. This arose over the question of "hot pursuit," generated by MIG opposition to the attacks on the bridges:

As American planes appeared at the Yalu, the Red airmen took off from Antung, climbed to superior altitude on their side of the river, crossed the border at about 30,000 feet, dived down in firing passes against the Americans, and then scampered back to safety beyond the Yalu, when if they desired they renewed the attack cycle.[24]

MacArthur wanted authority for "hot pursuit"—that is, for his pilots to pursue enemy planes into the Manchurian sanctuary. The request was not approved.

The restrictions under which MacArthur's air force was operating were obvious enough to Peking but did not have the restraining effect Washington anticipated. In Washington, general opinion continued to be that Chinese participation would at most be limited to contributions of "volunteers": no more than sufficient to brace the fugitive North Korean government temporarily. As Washington saw the situation, no possible advantage would accrue to the Chinese were they to intervene at a higher level.

Elsewhere in America, citizens occupied themselves with normal pursuits and indulged in customary pleasures. Football season was in full swing; Thanksgiving holidays less than three weeks in the future; "only forty-one more shopping days until Christmas." The country was prosperous. Some Americans—parents, wives, children —were vitally interested in Korea, where sons, husbands, and fathers were fighting and dying. But the war brushed lightly on America.

In China, things were a little different. Early in November, the government launched an intensive nation-wide campaign under the slogan, "Resist America, Aid Korea, Preserve Our Homes, Defend the Nation." For twenty-four hours of every day, the Chinese people were bombarded by propaganda pouring from loudspeakers, radios, and platforms. Thousands of mass meetings, attended by tens of millions, were organized daily in every city, town, factory, school, village, hospital, and university. At these, the United States, Truman, MacArthur, the "American-manipulated United Nations," and American troops were attacked with unbelievable virulence as "mad dogs," "bloodstained bandits," "robbers," "murderers," "rapists," and "savages." A nation of more than half a billion "peaceloving" people, lashed into a frenzy of hate, promised to exact due vengeance from those who had first "attempted to murder" the "people's government" of North Korea and were now threatening the sacred soil of China. This, the Chinese people were told, was to be a war *à l'outrance*, one in which no quarter was to be asked and none given until "the imperialist aggressors" were annihilated or driven into the sea by the righteous "Chinese People's Volunteers."

CHAPTER EIGHT

"The Immense Ocean of War"
Mao Tse-Tung [1]

In "On Protracted War," Mao Tse-tung, in May 1938, wrote of the strategy to be employed against the Japanese invaders of China:

Our strategy should be to employ our main forces in mobile warfare over an extended, shifting, and indefinite front, a strategy depending for success on a high degree of mobility in difficult terrain, and featured by swift attack and withdrawal, swift concentration and dispersal. It will be a large-scale war of movement rather than a positional war depending exclusively on defensive works with deep trenches, high fortresses, and successive defensive positions. . . . We must avoid great decisive battles in the early stages of the war, and must first employ mobile warfare gradually to break the morale, the fighting spirit, and the military efficiency of the living forces of the enemy. [2]

Although the pattern of the "First Phase Offensive" accorded with the precepts so succinctly expressed by Mao, its scope was limited by concrete factors, for the Chinese were confronted, both at the Ch'ongch'on and on the east coast, with equipment and other logistical shortages for which they had at the time no satisfactory solution. The basic problem was supply of food. Mao's peasant soldiers, inured to hardship and deprivation, could not march for many days on empty stomachs. Nor could they fight without ammunition. They were tough and courageous, but these qualities must be supplemented in the field with bullets and rice.

The majority of the "People's Volunteers" crossed the Yalu with 80 rounds of rifle ammunition and four or five "potato masher"-type grenades. In addition to his basic combat load, each soldier and officer carried a few extra clips for automatic rifles and "burp" guns, loaded belts for machine guns, one or two mortar shells, or TNT for satchel charges. Each carried emergency rice, tea, and salt for

138

five days, an "iron ration" to be supplemented by food requisitioned from the natives, who had little to spare. Impressed Koreans and Chinese porters carried forward heavy equipment.

The Communist divisions had practically no administrative "tail." In their experience, shortages had always been rectified on the battlefield. If this source failed them, the "People's Volunteers" could not sustain the offensive. Thus, problems of supply would dictate the ebb and flow of Chinese operations.

At the same time, American intelligence agencies continued grossly to underestimate Chinese combat capabilities. Because their arms and equipment were not what Americans considered "first class," it followed that "combat efficiency" was of a low order. The lessons of Pacific fighting against a technically inferior but determined enemy had obviously, and most unfortunately, been forgotten.

And forgotten as well had been the high quality of performance of indoctrinated Communist troops against both Japanese and Nationalists. The general tendency, which MacArthur shared, was to equate the average Communist soldier of 1951 with the average Nationalist soldier of 1948. To be blunt: the Americans did not respect this new enemy. They would soon learn, the hard way, to do so.

For almost three weeks after November 6, the two separated U.N. fronts in Korea were relatively quiet. In the west, the 8th Army prepared for the great offensive scheduled to jump off the day after Thanksgiving. On the east coast, elements of the U.S. 7th Division pushed unmolested toward the Yalu. Maj. Gen. Smith's 1st Marine Division continued its calculated desultory trek, over a narrow mountain road, now glazed with ice, toward a reservoir later to become famous as "frozen Chosin." The speed of the Marine advance—or, more exactly, the lack of it—exasperated the X Corps commander. But Smith did not intend to be hurried. With his division strung out on the road from Hamhung to Koto-ri, he could not afford to be as optimistic as was Almond in his estimate of Chinese Communist capabilities. This imperturbable Marine, a general both wise and prudent, had no intention of scattering his precious resources over the snow-mantled mountains.

Nevertheless, by Thanksgiving Day two of the division's three regimental combat teams were under orders to close Yudam-ni, from where they were to jump off in a sweep designed to terminate at Mupyong-ni, 55 miles to the west. The Marines were thus spearheading the right arm of MacArthur's "giant pincers," of which the left arm was the 8th Army.

On November 20, CINCUNC issued a directive which clearly indicates that he had discounted all reports—and there were many —of a continuing Chinese buildup in North Korea. What Mac-Arthur, and, indeed, most others, still anticipated was a peaceful occupation of Korea north to the Yalu:

Elements of minimum size only will be advanced to the immediate vicinity of the geographical boundary of Korea. No troops or vehicles will go beyond the boundary between Korea and Manchuria, or between Korea and the U.S.S.R., nor will fire be exchanged with or air strikes requested, on forces north of the northern boundary of Korea. Rigid control of troop movements in vicinity of northern boundary will be exercised.[3]

It would all be over soon, and "the boys would be home by Christmas." On Thanksgiving Day, mess sergeants and cooks were out of their bedding rolls long before dawn broke. The menu for dinner this day read: shrimp cocktail, stuffed olives, roast turkey, cranberry sauce, candied sweet potatoes, fruit salad, fruitcake, mince pie, and coffee.[4] All that was lacking was the traditional football game.

In the snow-covered hills, the Chinese cleaned and oiled weapons and ate cabbage soup and rice. That night at Yudam-ni, the temperature dropped to four degrees below zero.

On Friday, November 24, CINCUNC issued a message to his command which, because it so well reflects the prevalent mental attitude, is worth repeating in full:

The United Nations massive compression envelopment in North Korea against the new Red Armies operating there is now approaching its decisive effort. The isolating component of the pincer, our air forces of all types, have for the past three weeks, in a sustained attack of model coordination and effectiveness, successfully interdicted enemy lines of support from the north so that further reinforcement therefrom has been sharply curtailed and essential supplies markedly limited. The eastern sector of the pincer, with noteworthy and effective naval support, has now reached commanding enveloping position, cutting in two the northern reaches of the enemy's geographical potential. This morning the western sector of the pincer moves forward in general assault in an effort to complete the compression and close the vise. If successful, this should for all practical purposes end the war, restore peace and unity to Korea, enable the prompt withdrawal of United Nations military forces, and permit the complete assumption by the Korean people and nation of full sovereignty and international equality. It is that for which we fight.

Douglas MacArthur
General of the Army
United States Army
Commander in Chief [5]

On the same day, MacArthur forwarded a special communiqué to the United Nations:

The giant U.N. pincer moved according to schedule today. The air forces, in full strength, completely interdicted the rear areas, and an air reconnaissance behind the enemy line, and along the entire length of the Yalu River border, showed little sign of hostile military activity. . . . The logistic situation is fully geared to sustain offensive operations. The justice of our course and promise of early completion of our mission is reflected in the morale of troops and commanders alike.[6]

Twenty-four hours later, at Tokch'on, about 70 air miles southwest of Yudam-ni, the bubble burst. Here, on the night of November 25, the Chinese hit the ROK II Corps, which, as in October, was on the right (east) flank of the 8th Army.

Walker realized that this flank was vulnerable: ROK II Corps was by any measure the weakest element of 8th Army. But the rugged ground on the east flank was naturally strong and could be speedily developed. With mutually supporting bunkers in terrain such as this, Walker felt the ROKs could hold. And there was an added factor that predisposed him to adopt this disposition: British and U.S. forces preferred to operate on the west flank where a developed road net facilitated supply, tank operations, and deployment of artillery.

Walker had seen what the Chinese could do, and there was little reason for him to be infected with the optimism which pervaded the Dai Ichi Building in Tokyo. Unfortunately, it appears, he, too, was perhaps less objective than he should have been in his assessment of ROK capabilities to defend a night against sudden fierce attacks. One American division commander, Maj. Gen. Lawrence B. Keiser, was more realistic in his assessments. He was sure that when the Chinese struck they would hit the ROKs.

The Chinese attack in October had clearly demonstrated that the ROKs were extremely vulnerable to the type of sudden, overpowering, close-in night assault at which the "People's Volunteers" were adept. These attacks were habitually preceded by an uproar of noise raised in all quarters. This horrendous cacophony was designed to encourage the ardor of the attackers and paralyze the defenders with fear. The Chinese for centuries had considered this an essential preliminary to close combat. Marco Polo described the custom:

As soon as the order of battle was arranged an infinite number of wind instruments of various kinds were sounded, and these were succeeded by songs, according to the custom of the Tartars before they engage in fight, which commences upon the signal given by the cymbals and drums, and such singing, that it was wonderful to hear.[7]

As far as the South Koreans were concerned, this overture to battle, far from being "wonderful to hear," chilled them to the bone. Nor did other U.N. troops derive any particular pleasure from the music, although they soon learned to reply to it with an orchestration of flares and bullets.

There is an ancient Chinese military axiom to the effect that a superior general is one able to transform apparent disadvantages to advantage, and during the early period, the Chinese commanders did precisely this. By marching and operating at night, they nullified U.N. close air-support capabilities to a decisive degree, just as by using primitive means of transport, they did its aerial interdiction capabilities. The supply of U.N. forces, and hence their mobility, depended essentially on complete control of highways—a control always disputed by guerrillas, whose cut-and-run operations created interminable logistic problems only partially ameliorated by a superb system of resupply and evacuation by air.

Night attacks and close-range combat tended also to cancel U.N. superiority in heavy weapons and combined arms, for one element of the infantry-tank-artillery team, armor, was incapable of functioning (except as a static and generally ineffective artillery piece) during darkness.

The broken mountainous country (particularly on the east coast) seriously inhibited U.N. tactical radio communications, while guerrilla remnants of the NKPA and infiltrators cut rear-area wire lines almost as fast as linemen could string them. Consequent inability to communicate with adjacent units and with supporting arms in moments of crisis spelled disaster for many isolated platoons and under-strength companies and produced delay and confusion in the transmission of vital information and orders.

U.N. troops found the Korean terrain a handicap to their operations, but the Chinese, who early learned that ground is the handmaid of victory, turned the inhospitable hills and desolate valleys to good advantage. From youth, the relationship of the Chinese peasant to the land has been one of intimacy so close as to verge on identification. It is perhaps for this reason, as well as for an almost innate artistic sense the Westerner lacks, that the Oriental is an expert *camoufleur*. This quality was frequently remarked by U.S. troops, who were often taken under fire at almost point-blank range by skillfully concealed machine guns and automatic weapons.

By nightfall of November 27, the Chinese, in overwhelming force, had flowed through and around the three divisions which composed ROK II Corps, almost literally annihilated them, and threatened the right flank of the 8th Army. Everywhere, the assault pattern was the same: while "short attacks" of fierce intensity struck fronts and flanks, the Chinese in small groups seeped simultaneously into the rear, where road blocks, covered by short-range converging fires from commanding ground, turned withdrawals into bloody debacles. ROK II Corps was not the only victim; on the afternoon of November 27, the newly arrived Turkish brigade, committed east of Kunu-ri in a vain effort to stop the flood, was seriously crippled.

These attacks followed a pattern developed earlier by Lin Piao, known as the "one point-two sides method," i.e., a frontal fix at the base of the V with simultaneous double envelopment executed suddenly and precisely. The attack was characterized by its intensity, a quality the Chinese described as *san-meng kung-tso,* or "the three fierce actions," i.e., fierce fires, fierce assaults, fierce pursuit.

On the east coast, the Chinese committed Sung Shih-lun's 9th Army Group of twelve divisions (120,000 men) in an attempt to amputate the right arm of MacArthur's "giant pincers." Of these, eight were assigned to destroy the 1st Marine Division,[8] and shortly after 9 P.M. on November 27, with the temperature at an appalling twenty degrees below zero, two—the 79th and 89th—hit the Marine perimeter at Yudam-ni. "By 2100, Northwest Ridge was crawling with Chinese. . . . The enemy troops padding silently on their rubber sneakers had as yet given no hint of their presence." . . .[9]

Ordered to "annihilate the enemy at Yudam-ni," the Chinese struck repeatedly during the first night and again on the two following nights. A distinctive tactical pattern emerged. First there came a series of probes by eight- to fifteen-man groups to feel out the defensive position, determine its outline, create confusion, and draw fire, particularly from automatic weapons. A brief lull succeeded these preliminaries. When the attack came in, "superior numbers of troops" hit the front "in coordination with strong enveloping tactics designed to fold the flanks" of the defenders, "to surround, isolate, and eventually destroy [them] piecemeal." [10]

But the conclusion reached was not precisely the one Sung Shih-lun had anticipated. Simultaneous attacks on Marine positions at Hagaru and Koto-ri were repulsed after fierce fighting. Both sides suffered heavily, but the Marines held. After three nights of close combat, the Chinese were able to salvage no more than remnants of two divisions.

Official reports described the attacking troops as "well trained, well organized, well equipped, and ably led. . . . Ironically enough, it was with U.S. weapons that the Chinese were for the most [part] armed. These included the 60- and 81-mm. mortars, Thompson sub-machine guns, and heavy and light machine guns, most of which had been captured from Chinese Nationalist forces." [11]

On December 1, CINCUNC met with Walker and Almond, who at his behest had flown to Tokyo. Both subordinates were hopeful that the situation could be retrieved. Walker believed that with reinforcements he could establish tenable positions in the waist of Korea, in the general vicinity of P'yongyang. Almond, exuding the incurable optimism characteristic of those who served on Mac-Arthur's staff, proposed that his corps drive west over snow-covered mountains to relieve the pressure on the 8th Army's right flank! [12] These recommendations were consistent with the ambiance of unreality that at this time pervaded MacArthur's headquarters. Neither had the slightest relevance to the existing situation. MacArthur no longer held the initiative in his hands. The Chinese High Command had wrenched it from him.

At the time Almond flew to Tokyo, X Corps was, in his words, "scattered all over the landscape." The Corps commander has never explained why he had allowed such a situation to develop. Smith was attempting to collect the bulk of his division to attack west; elements of Barr's 7th Division, separated from the Marines by "frozen Chosin," were advancing north and out of touch with the ROK 3rd and Capitol divisions, which were pushing into the desolate waste-lands of the northeast provinces without any objective except to reach the river boundary. The U.S. 3rd Infantry Division, holding the Hungnam-Wonsan area, was not in a position to assist any of these elements, nor could any of them render, or receive, support from any of the others.

This deployment—if such a feckless dispersion of Almond's corps may be so described—apparently did not unduly worry the conferees in the Dai Ichi Building, but it did worry the Joint Chiefs of Staff, who saw that it invited a tragedy of monumental proportions. On November 29, they had summarily directed CINCUNC to halt the advance of X Corps, to extricate it from exposed positions in northeast Korea, and to redeploy it to a junction with the 8th Army. All this was to prove more easily said than done.

In the meantime, the situation in the 8th Army zone moved to a tragic climax. On the last day of November, the bulk of Keiser's 2nd Division, withdrawing from Kunu-ri toward Sunchon, was ambushed, segmented, and practically destroyed as an effective fighting unit. To the west, other U.N. forces withdrew from Ch'ongch'on bridgehead positions and retreated south. In Korea now, there was indeed "a new war." [13]

Within a week following MacArthur's sanguine pronouncements that the "massive compression envelopment in North Korea against the new Red Armies" was "approaching its decisive effort," the left arm of his "giant pincer" had been mangled; the right, bruised and bloodied. There would be no triumphant march to the Yalu, no December victory parades in Tokyo. The problem now was to save X Corps and 8th Army from the destruction that threatened to engulf them.

Had Generals MacArthur or Almond ever taken the time to read Mao Tse-tung's "On Protracted War," they might have had at least a faint conception of the ordeal that awaited the 1st Marine Division:

. . . in campaigns and battles . . . we should not only employ large forces against small and operate from exterior against interior lines, but also follow the policy of seeking quick decisions. In general, to achieve quick decision, we should attack a moving and not a stationary enemy. We should concentrate a big force under cover beforehand alongside the route which the enemy is sure to take, and while he is on the move, advance suddenly to encircle and attack him before he knows what is happening, and thus quickly conclude the battle. If we fight well, we may destroy the entire enemy force, or the greater part of it, and even if we do not fight so well, we may still inflict heavy casualties. [14]

For the Chinese, the first important problem was to get the Marines on the move. This idea happened to coincide with that of the

Marine commander, who concentrated his division in battle, faced south, and began "to advance in a new direction." [15]

The division, fighting its way down the ice-sheeted road that led to safety, was to march not just from Hageru-ri to Hungnam but into history. Behind, on naked hills and in frozen valleys, the Marines left the beaten and demoralized wreckage of what less than a month before had been Gen. Sung Shih-lun's 9th Army Group. A member of a PLA medical unit captured during the Chosin campaign estimated that 70 per cent of all Chinese combat troops suffered from frostbite and that 5 per cent of the cases required amputation. His own regiment of the 59th Division entered the Chosin area at a strength of slightly more than 2,000 and suffered about 1,000 combat casualties. Incidence of tetanus was "high," and night blindness, the direct result of vitamin deficiency, "common." [16]

Sung's divisions returned to Manchuria for reorganization. For six months, none would again appear in an enemy order of battle.

Meanwhile, questions of mortal import faced General Walker: where could 8th Army's precipitate retreat be halted, the troops rallied, defenses organized, and the front stabilized? By December 3, although Chinese pressure had relaxed, Walker sensibly concluded that to save his army, he must fall back on Seoul—perhaps to the south bank of the Han, perhaps even farther.

That U.N. forces had sustained a serious defeat and were in a grave situation may not have been apparent to MacArthur. But it was apparent to President Truman, who in a public statement described the Chinese offensive as "in great force" and the battlefield situation as "uncertain." He promised the country that although the United Nations might suffer "further reverses," they had "no intention of abandoning their mission in Korea." [17]

But even the President did not seem to realize the more profound implications of the Chinese victory at the Ch'ongch'on, described by one American historian as "one of the major decisive battles of the present century." [18] For the indirect effects of the Ch'ongch'on were felt throughout the world. There a Chinese peasant army had put to flight a modern Western force commanded by a famous, and hitherto almost ever-victorious, American general. At one bound, Communist China had become a world power—a force to be reckoned with not just in Tokyo and Washington but in London, Paris, Delhi, and Moscow—and had wrecked all hope for a united Korea.

Peking had reason to exult and did so:

The gigantic counter-offensive launched by the Korean People's Army and the Chinese volunteers is developing victoriously. . . . Korean and Chinese fighters are vigorously chasing enemy troops on the west front and encircling and eliminating others in the east. The main forces of the enemy are facing collapse and destruction.

This total stampede of the enemy has also aroused panic and confusion within the imperialist camp. But still the American imperialists are not willing to accept this lesson and are thinking of further frenzied struggles." [19]

The reasons for the Chinese victory in North Korea in 1950 are complex. But one of them is to be found in the character of Douglas MacArthur, who had frequently been acclaimed—and who believed himself to be—America's greatest living soldier. During his Pacific campaigns, MacArthur's sometimes brilliant and unexpected tactical improvisations had impelled Winston Churchill to describe him as the outstanding general of World War II. The startling success at Inchon naturally contributed to the General's supreme confidence that Nike, the Goddess of Victory, would continue in November and December 1950, as she had always in the past, to bless his banners.

In more practical terms, some of MacArthur's conceptions, developed during the Pacific war, proved almost fatally wrong in Korea. Principal among these was his reliance on air power. In his message of November 24, it will be noted, he said:

The isolating component of the pincer, our air forces of all types, have for the past three weeks, in a sustained attack of model coordination and effectiveness, successfully interdicted enemy lines of support from the north so *that further reinforcement therefrom has been sharply curtailed and essential supplies markedly limited.*[20]

Here, the General unfortunately overlooked an important geographic fact: North Korea was not an island. During the first three weeks of November, more than 100,000 Chinese troops had crossed the Yalu. By Thanksgiving, almost a quarter of a million Chinese "Volunteers" were lying in the hills of North Korea.

General MacArthur could not bring himself to accept even a minor share of the responsibility for a strategic defeat which cost U.N. forces (exclusive of ROK units) 12,965 battle casualties, and, in the west, very heavy losses of weapons and equipment of all types:

The withdrawal of both our forces was made with great skill. I regarded the professional part of the operation with the greatest satisfaction. I felt that the hard decisions I had been forced to make, and the skill displayed by my field commanders had saved the army. The movement north had upset the enemy's timetable, causing him to move prematurely, and to reveal the surreptitious massing of his armies. He had hoped quietly to assemble a massive force till spring and destroy us with one mighty blow. Had I not acted when I did, we would have been a "sitting duck" doomed to eventual annihilation.[21]

This theme has been echoed by MacArthur's supporters ever since November 1950. MacArthur was not surprised; *he* surprised the Chinese, who had the unconscionable temerity to engage his forces, to drive them out of North Korea, and in the process to destroy an image almost half a century in the making. "MacArthur," wrote his aide-de-camp, Maj. Gen. Courtney Whitney, "was greatly saddened as well as angered at this despicably surreptitious attack, a piece of treachery which he regarded as worse even than Pearl Harbor." [22] One is justified in wondering precisely what MacArthur had expected the Chinese to do when presented with such a golden opportunity. P'eng Teh-huai deliberately encouraged MacArthur's evident arrogance; he blundered into the trap.

This, naturally, is not the way things appeared to Whitney, whose effort to revise the history of later November 1950 would excite the admiration of the most dedicated Russian historian of the Stalin era. MacArthur was ready, Whitney avers:

. . . he was *not* taken by surprise. His troops did *not* rush blindly north into a massive ambush as claimed by some detractors. The big push north had been carefully designed to be effective either as a mopping-up operation or as a reconnaissance in force and now it had unhappily become the latter. But the plans were already made for this development and Walker at once ordered them executed.

There followed a series of delaying actions.[23]
There also followed the longest retreat in the history of American arms.

And obviously there was treachery somewhere. MacArthur would later write

that there was some leak in intelligence was evident to everyone. Walker continually complained to me that his operations were known to the enemy in advance through sources in Washington. . . . Information must have been relayed to them, assuring that the Yalu bridges would continue to enjoy sanctuary and that their bases would be left intact.[24]

The administration, too, had tied his hands. Washington had placed upon him "a welter of restrictions . . . American forces were compelled to face odds never before encountered in the military history of the nation." Although as one result of his visit to Taiwan in the previous July, he had strongly recommended against the use of Nationalist troops in Korea, he now urged that "the eager, fresh troops" offered by Chiang K'ai-shek be made available to him, but "United Nations member governments refused to consent to this." [25]

From his Tokyo command post, General MacArthur now began to bombard the Joint Chiefs with cables prophesying that unless they acceded to his demands to extend the war, he would have to consider evacuation from Korea. At the front north of Seoul, the troops momentarily expected a Chinese attack—worse, many of them, still in a state of mental and emotional shock, expected to be beaten!

In this crisis, on December 23, 1950, Walton Walker was killed in an accident when his jeep was run off the road by a truck. Three days later, Lieut. Gen. Matthew B. Ridgway flew into Taegu and assumed command of U.N. forces. In him, the defeated 8th Army found the general it so badly needed, one both "bold and courageous" and "able to swim with measured strokes in the immense ocean of war."

CHAPTER NINE

"They Are Not Invincible"
General of the Army
Omar N. Bradley

On December 14 the General Assembly of the United Nations, fearful that the "new war" might burst from the restricted confines of the Korean peninsula, had passed a resolution sponsored by an Arab-Asian bloc of 13 nations, which expressed the anxious hopes of the members that some basis for a "cease fire" could be found. Accordingly, Nasrollah Entezam of Iran, currently president of the Assembly; Lester B. Pearson, the Canadian delegate; and Sir Benegal Rau of India undertook to develop a formula which they "felt constituted a reasonable basis for discussion." [1]

Some time previously, a delegation which the United Nations had invited Peking to send to Lake Success had arrived there. The leader of this group, Gen. Wu Hsiu-ch'üan, presented the position of his government at a press conference called on December 16, 1950. Here, Wu announced that he and his colleagues had come "to strive for peace"—but he soon made it clear that peace could be bought only at the price set by Peking. The solution to the Korean problem, he insisted, lay only in unqualified acceptance by the United Nations of the "rightful proposal for peace of the Central People's Government of the People's Republic of China." [2]

There could be no "cease fire" in Korea, said Wu, until the U.S. government agreed to withdraw "its armed forces of aggression against China's territory, Taiwan," to cease its intervention in Korea, and to remove all its armed forces from the peninsula. The "real intention" of a "cease fire first," as advocated by the United Nations, was, he revealed, to demand that the Korean People's Army and the Chinese Volunteers tie their own hands so that the United States armed forces of aggression may continue their aggression in Korea . . . to demand that Taiwan be kept under the invasion and occupation of the United States armed forces . . . to demand that Japanese militarism be revived again by Mac-Arthur . . . to demand that the American people be driven at will by the United States ruling circle into the abyss of war.

Five days later, Premier Chou En-lai again stated Peking's terms for peace.[3] He reiterated his delegate's assertion that the "cease fire first" formula was "a trap," and to General Wu's proposals added a new ultimatum—a seat in the United Nations for his government. The Premier closed his broadcast on an ominous note:

Invading troops of the United States arrogantly crossed the 38th parallel at the beginning of October. The U.S. government, recklessly ignoring warnings from all quarters and following the provocative crossings of the border by Syngman Rhee in June, thoroughly destroyed and hence obliterated forever this demarcation line of political geography.

At first light on New Year's Day, a major offensive cracked with irresistible impact against the 8th Army. Twenty-one Chinese and four North Korean divisions—a total of 237,000 men—were thrown into assault on a front of almost 100 miles. Behind the assault troops, 15 Chinese and three NKPA divisions were grouped in reserve for exploitation of the strategic breakthrough the high command anticipated.

A few short hours later on this New Year's morning, it looked very much as if the Chinese might succeed in their attempt to destroy the U.N. forces. Even before the sun rose in frozen skies, Ridgway—who only a week before had taken command of an army on the brink of defeat—started north from Seoul in a jeep toward the ROK sector, where the front had collapsed:

Only a few miles north of Seoul, I ran head on into that fleeing army. I'd never had such an experience before, and I pray to God I never witness such a spectacle again. They were coming down the road in trucks, the men standing, packed so close together in those big carriers another small boy could not have found space among them. They had abandoned their heavy artillery, their machine guns—all their crew-served weapons. Only a few had kept their rifles. Their only thought was to get away, to put miles between them and the fearful army that was at their heels.

I jumped from my jeep and stood in the middle of the road, waving them to a halt. I might as well have tried to stop the flow of the Han. . . . The only solution was to let them run—and to set up road blocks far enough back where they could be stopped, channeled into bivouac areas, calmed down, refitted, and turned to face the enemy again. . . .[4]

Ridgway, calm in the face of impending disaster, halted the "bug-out." "We came back fast, but as a fighting army, not as a running mob. We brought our dead and wounded with us, and our guns, and our will to fight." [5] On January 3, Seoul was evacuated; the next afternoon, after the British Centurion tanks crossed, the pontoon bridges over the Han were blown. The army fell back unmolested to prepared positions along the general line Pyongtaek–Wonju–Samchok, some 70 miles south of the 38th parallel. According to General MacArthur:

> I stabilized the lines of the Eighth Army at a position midway in South Korea. . . . Walker's skillful withdrawal had been accomplished with such speed that it led to many comments by ignorant correspondents that the troops were in flight. Nothing could have been further from the truth.
>
> The troops moved in good order and with unbroken cohesion among the various components. . . .
>
> I myself felt we had reached up, sprung the Red trap, and escaped it. To have saved so many thousands of lives entrusted to my care gave me a sense of comfort that, in comparison, made all the honors I had ever received pale into insignificance. [6]

In a similar desperate situation during his defense of Petrograd against the army of the White General Yudenitch in 1918 Leon Trotsky, People's Commissar for War, reacted in a refreshingly different manner. Trotsky ordered his subordinates "not to send in false reports of hard fights when the actual truth was bitter panic. Lies will be punished as treason. Military work admits errors, but not lies, deception, and self-deception." [7] And, if credit for saving "thousands of lives" is to be accorded any commander, surely Matthew Ridgway deserves it.

But something more than Ridgway's inspired leadership was required to retrieve a situation that verged on disaster. Here, two factors operated. The first of these was the intervention of the Fifth Air Force, whose unopposed fighter bombers ranged over the battle zone from dawn to dusk. The second was the inability of the Chinese to maintain offensive momentum. P'eng Teh-huai's Army groups did not have the capacity to support assault formations in a rapidly moving situation. The Chinese logistic organization could not cope with the demands laid upon it. Although tactical mobility was excellent at divisional and lower levels, higher commands were unable to exploit local success. And so, in early January, the Chinese advance reached its terminal point, and a calculated withdrawal, the third such since October, began. General MacArthur later aptly compared these almost rhythmic movements to the alternating extension and compression of an accordion.

Now Ridgway, "with characteristic directness,"

began facing the army's eyes to the front. Step by step, in deliberate and carefully conceived actions and orders, he bore down on his new command. By example and by exhortation, he began shaking his staff, commanders, and men out of their defeatist mood. Where toughness was required, he was tough. Where persuasion was indicated, he persuaded. And where personal example was needed he set the example.[8]

Eighth Army patrols in increasing strength began to probe north "to find, fix, and fight" the enemy. At first, platoons went forward, with close-support air on station or immediately available; then reinforced companies; then battalions. Each day the fingers probed north; each day they probed more deeply. These practical manifestations of the offensive spirit gradually rebuilt the Army's confidence and restored its morale.

But in the meantime, MacArthur's lugubrious cables had disturbed the President and his military advisers, the Joint Chiefs, who ordered two of their members, Gen. J. Lawton Collins, Chief of Staff of the Army, and General Hoyt S. Vandenberg, Chief of Staff of the Air Force, to Korea for an on-the-spot appraisal. Simultaneously, Truman addressed a personal telegram to the General in Tokyo.

In this message, the President told MacArthur that successful resistance to Chinese aggression in Korea would serve important political purposes, not only in the peninsula or even in the Far East but elsewhere. Among other effects, determined resistance would serve "to deflate the dangerously exaggerated political and military prestige of Communist China which now threatens to undermine the resistance of non-Communist Asia and to consolidate the hold of Communism on China itself." Should the Chinese force U.N. troops to withdraw from Korea, the world would be told that "that course was forced upon us by military necessity, and that we shall not accept the result politically or militarily until the aggression has been rectified."[9]

Truman's message and the simultaneous sudden trip to Korea of two members of the Joint Chiefs clearly indicate to some students of the Truman-MacArthur controversy "an administration belief that perhaps MacArthur had deliberately exaggerated the desperateness of the military situation in order to win approval of his own strategic program"—an extension of the war by aerial bombardment of mainland China combined with a tight naval blockade of her coast.[10]

To ascertain the situation for themselves, Collins and Vandenberg arrived in Tokyo en route to Korea on January 14 and were briefed by General MacArthur and his staff the following morning. CINCUNC conveyed to them a dismal picture which they accepted with customary deference. (In the context of JCS relations with General MacArthur it must be remembered that he was chief of staff of the United States Army when Collins was a first lieutenant in the Army, Vandenberg a lieutenant in the Army Air Corps, and Sherman a junior lieutenant commander in the Navy.)

The two chiefs then flew to Korea. Collins visited front-line units, saw Ridgway's operation WOLFHOUND—a combat reconnaissance by a heavily reinforced infantry regiment—jump off, and talked with corps and division commanders, junior officers, and enlisted men. The Chief of Staff of the Army was heartened by what he saw. And what he saw convinced him that MacArthur had painted the situation in too somber a hue. On his return to Tokyo on January 19, he again called on MacArthur. Later, at Senate hearings, the following colloquy ensued:

SENATOR JOHNSON: Had your opinion of the situation changed as a result of your visit to the front?

GENERAL COLLINS: Yes, sir; I felt much reassured after having gone over to the front itself, and having talked with General Ridgway.[11]

Vandenberg was equally confident that the revitalized 8th Army would shortly again prove itself an effective battle instrument. Within the month, the army would justify these expectations.

Although the front was stabilized, near chaos reigned each night in the deep rear of the U.N. Command as well-armed guerrillas increased the tempo of their operations.

Shortly after the Chinese entered the war, General MacArthur had reported:

Communist guerrilla units varying from a few hundred to several thousand men operating in isolated areas throughout the United Nations occupied portion of Korea. *At present, nearly thirty per cent of the United Nations troops in Korea are employed against them in the essential task of protecting supply lines and the more vital urban centers.* From 1 to 21 November, for example, there were nearly two hundred guerrilla raids and attacks, most of which required the immediate attention of United Nations anti-guerrilla forces. These units are primarily composed of former North Korean soldiers, and are led by professional leaders, many of whom have had extensive prewar guerrilla experience. Guerrilla forces now total thirty thousand to thirty-five thousand in strength. *There is growing evidence that guerrilla activities are being controlled and coordinated by the enemy high command* and that this menace to United Nations operations will necessitate continued anti-guerrilla measures. Of these, the most successful to date has been the destruction of many major guerrilla supply caches.[12]

Locating odd caches of supplies was one thing, but netting the fish—in Mao Tse-tung's descriptive word—was something else again. For they were almost an intangible force, as impossible to pin down as shadows. The guerrillas terrorized the villagers, who had no choice but passive cooperation. And so they continued with success to attack police stations, raid supply dumps, blow tracks and switch junctions, derail trains, mine roads, and ambush convoys. In large areas of South Korea, it was impossible to operate motor vehicles or trains after dusk. The casualties the guerrillas inflicted in each isolated attack were not serious, but the toll mounted inexorably—as did strain on the supply system. And the psychological effects of the sudden, vicious onslaughts eroded the morale of the local police.

By mid-January, the scope of guerrilla operations had reached a high-water mark considerably above the average of twenty incidents a day cited in MacArthur's report. The attacks, which invariably surprised the defenders, were based on detailed target information, meticulously planned, and executed with split-second timing. Decisive superiority both in numbers and firepower were always applied to most vulnerable points.

G-2, Far East Command, in his report of January 30, concluded that guerrilla operations were coordinated with those of orthodox forces at a common headquarters.[13] Such operations were frequently noted in the rear of the most active sectors of the U.N. front.

Analysis of ninety attacks during the period January 1–5 indicated a switch of major effort from attacks on regular U.N. detachments to concentration on less costly operations against South Korean police and inadequately guarded lines of communication. This shift in emphasis clearly reflected the influence of Chinese guerrilla doctrine.

U.N. efforts to suppress these operations met with only a fair degree of success. Heavy and constant infiltration of personnel and supplies from North Korea as well as skillful use of refugees indicated "long and intelligent planning for the use of guerrilla elements." This planning had included establishment of two training centers in North Korea where prospective guerrillas were thoroughly indoctrinated prior to infiltration through U.N. lines.

As in China, these guerrillas did not exist "merely to fight." Indeed, fighting was a secondary mission; political tasks, primary. These included organization of cells, agitation, and dissemination of propaganda designed both to create dissatisfaction against the government and resentment against the presence of U.N. troops.[14]

But in South Korea the one ingredient necessary to assure something more than local tactical success was lacking. This was the active participation of the population, upon which partisans depend for their security and from which they derive information, food, shelter, and recruits. The North Korean infiltrators were never able to gain this positive support or to communicate Mao Tse-tung's brand of revolutionary fervor to their countrymen south of the U.N. front lines. In the long run, it was not so much active "guerrilla hunting" as the silent, stubborn passivity of the South Korean peasant which proved to be the decisive factor in the gradual wasting away of the movement directed from P'yongyang.

To achieve the same effect in the rear of the Chinese as the guerrillas were attempting to achieve in the rear of the U.N. forces, the Far East Air Force in January inaugurated an interdiction campaign directed against rail and road targets in North Korea. During daylight hours, anything that moved on the roads was attacked with napalm, bombs, and machine guns. Animals were not immune. Horses, camels, mules, donkeys, burros, and Mongol ponies were slaughtered by the thousands.

Other aircraft with suitable armament attacked roads, bridges, yards, stations, tracks, and—where they could find them—locomotives, trains, truck convoys, and isolated vehicles. Photo reconnaissance revealed scores of traffic "choke points" that were held under almost daily attack. Expert photo interpretation brought to light imperfectly camouflaged supply depots and repair facilities. Critical bridges—hundreds eventually—were dropped, and tunnel entrances bombed to produce cave-ins. Thousands of miles of tracks were torn up, abutments and piers wrecked, marshaling yards mangled.

This effort, which involved the loss of scores of aircraft and hundreds of air crewmen, did not produce the decisive effect anticipated. The flow of supplies to Chinese front-line troops was, however, diminished and their capability for sustained offensive action thus seriously curtailed.

In assessing the air interdiction campaign, Gen. Mark Clark later wrote:

The Air Force and the Navy carriers may have kept us from losing the war, but they were denied the opportunity of influencing the outcome decisively in our favor. They gained complete mastery of the skies, gave magnificent support to the infantry, destroyed every worth-while target in North Korea, and took a costly toll of enemy personnel and supplies.

But as in Italy, where we learned the same bitter lesson in the same kind of rugged country, our air power could not keep a *steady stream of enemy supplies and reinforcements from reaching the battle line.* Air could not isolate the front.[15]

In view of the circumstances which prevailed, it is difficult to perceive how air could have been expected to "isolate the front." In sustained combat, a Chinese front-line division consumed 40 to 50 short tons (80,000 to 100,000 pounds) of supplies a day. (This is but 8 to 10 pounds a man as compared to almost 60 pounds a man required to sustain a U.S. division. Needless to say, the Chinese did not provide their troops with the amenities their U.S. counterparts seem to require.) As broken down, this basic tonnage included:

19.2 tons Class I (rations, water)
8.8 tons Class II (clothing, equipment)
4.0 tons Class III (fuels, lubricants)
8.0 tons Class IV (ammunition)
———
40.0 tons

When 50 tons could be delivered to division dumps, the 10-ton excess was dispersed in dozens of dug-in, camouflaged supply points behind the front.

To supply a maximum of 50 front-line and local-reserve divisions, and to build forward stockpiles, the Chinese needed to move up no more than an average of 2,500 short tons a day. In contrast to this low level of supply, the reinforced 1st Marine Division, at an effective strength of almost 22,000, consumed more than 700 tons per day in sustained combat; a smaller U.S. Army division required almost 600. Thus, on a man-for-man basis the U.N. command had to move to the front almost seven and a half tons to each ton the Chinese moved.

As the intensity of combat constantly fluctuates, the consumption of supplies fluctuates also. In a stable, low-intensity situation, supplies are not consumed, destroyed, or wasted as they are in fluid situations. Relatively quiet periods permit rapid build-up of ammunition, food, and equipment inventories. For the interdiction campaign to be effective, therefore, it would have been necessary to force the Chinese to expend combat consumables at a more rapid rate than they could acquire them from the rear.

Those enthusiasts who conceived the interdiction operation in absolute terms overlooked the fact that the Chinese had available an unlimited pool of manpower to repair wrecked rail facilities. While the unremitting, methodical air attack appeared to be thoroughly destructive, analysts soon discovered that U.N. fliers could not completely deny the Chinese the use of railroads, for in the speedy rehabilitation of bridges and tracks, they proved to be as ingenious as they were industrious. Well-disciplined, efficiently directed labor groups of 40 to 50 men were dispersed at intervals of two to three miles along all rail routes. Hand tools, baskets, rails, switches, and ties were stocked in hidden dumps, in ditches, and under culverts, and rails were relaid as fast as U.N. fliers broke them. And as locomotives were destroyed and freight cars reduced to twisted junk, they were replaced from a seemingly inexhaustible storehouse in the inviolate sanctuary of Manchuria.

At the height of STRANGLE, careful estimates showed that the Chinese could still move between 1,000 and 2,000 tons a day from Manchuria over eastern and western rail nets. They "could supply approximately half their needs by rail alone." [16] Optimistic reports and evaluations to the contrary, this aspect of the interdiction campaign was thus a failure—one FEAF was reluctant to admit.

Another major supply network available to the Communists was the highway system.

While none of the Korean roads could have been rated good by Western standards (none being hard surfaced, and all being either rough gravel or dirt) the network was to prove an even more difficult target system than the rail network. *In fact, the very primitiveness of the roads was an advantage to the enemy and made them unprofitable targets to air assault.*[17]

Here again, the Chinese turned apparent disadvantage to advantage. Tens of thousands of Chinese and Korean carriers—no one knows, or will know, how many—were mobilized and organized to move supplies from rear dumps to forward areas. At night, roads, trails, and bypaths swarmed with battalions of impressed peasants, moving south in relays at a subdued, tireless trot. Each carried 80 to 100 pounds in two balanced bamboo baskets suspended from the ends of a flexible shoulder pole or packed on an A-frame. At night and during inclement weather, the carriers moved with impunity, their laden baskets swaying rhythmically. In these hordes of silent, shuffling coolies, the machine met its match.

In justice to FEAF and Navy and Marine Corps fliers who participated in STRANGLE, we must repeat that an air-interdiction campaign such as STRANGLE can be decisive *only if constant ground pressure is simultaneously maintained.* The enemy must be *forced* to consume or expend all classes of supply *at more than a normal rate.* The moment pressure is relaxed, he will again build up. This is precisely what happened in Korea after stabilization of the battle front.

Of STRANGLE, the Marine Corps historian has written:

There can be no doubt that it added enormously to the Communists' logistical problem. It is equally certain that they solved these problems to such an extent that their combat units were never at a decisive handicap for lack of ammunition and other supplies. Operation STRANGLE, in short, merely added to the evidence that interdictory air alone was not enough to knock a determined adversary out of the war. . . .[18]

On January 25, Ridgway launched two divisions, one from I Corps and one from IX Corps, in Operation THUNDERBOLT. Objective: the line of the Han, defended by the 38th and 50th Chinese armies. Ridgway's tactics, careful and methodical, were designed to inflict maximum casualties with minimum loss. Infantry, air, armor, artillery, in almost perfectly coordinated actions, took a frightful toll. The G.I.'s aptly described the step-by-step operations, characterized by accurate application of murderous firepower, as "the meat grinder." Slowly, but with relentless determination, Ridgway turned the handle.

A subsidiary, but critical local operation, PUNCH, mounted on February 5 to seize a dominating hill complex seven miles north of Suwon, followed the same pattern. The convoluted terrain was held by a reinforced regiment of the 50th Army; its capture would open the way to the Han. "It was reckoned that when the Chinese became dislodged from the Hill 400 mass, their tactical forces in the subordinate ridges between that bastion and the Han would then be in flux." [19] Armor could then slash into the enemy to further disrupt, disorganize, and—with the other three integrated elements—inflict maximum casualties.

By the morning of February 9, the Americans had dislodged the

"Volunteers" from the last of many heavily-timbered and camouflaged bunkers on Hill 400; 4,251 Chinese corpses were counted on
the rocky ridges. The attacking battalions, one each from the 25th
and 27th regiments, 2nd Division, lost 70. Two days later, I Corps
overran Kimpo Airfield, recaptured thoroughly gutted Inchon, and
stood on the south bank of the frozen Han, looking toward the capital of the Republic of Korea. U.N guns neutralized the desolate
city.

On the night of February 10–11, the Chinese 40th and 66th
armies and the NKPA V Corps, in an attempt to break the lock imposed by these punishing tactics, began to drive down the Hoengsang–Wonju corridor. Forty-eight hours later, three divisions, attacking from the north and northeast, hit the U.S. 23rd Regimental
Combat Team (2nd Division), to which a French battalion was attached, at Chipyong-ni. This village, a strategic road junction, lay
on the boundary between U.S. IX and X Corps. Although Chinese
strength was of the order of 10 men to each defender and the command was surrounded and isolated without hope of immediate reinforcement—indeed, in imminent danger of annihilation—the man at
the top had galvanized the army. This time there was to be no fall
back, no retreat, no "bug-out" in the face of overwhelming numerical superiority. Ridgway ordered the 23rd RCT to stand and fight,
and the 27th Commonwealth Brigade (Brigadier B. A. Coad, DSO)
to move to reinforce.[20]

In his Fifteenth Report to the United Nations, CINCUNC characterized this period as one of maneuver "with the object of inflict-
ing as heavy a punishment upon the enemy as possible, striving constantly to keep him off balance, to prevent his obtaining and holding
the tactical initiative, while at the same time avoiding the hazards
inherent in his numerical superiority." [21] Ridgway, not one to delay
when the opportune moment presented itself, immediately pushed
his advantage and launched KILLER on February 21. Objective:
to kill as many Chinese as possible.

As March drew to a close, U.N. forces once more stood generally
along the parallel they had first crossed almost six months before. In
terms of military geography, the situation of June 24, 1950, again
prevailed; the artificial boundary of the Republic of Korea had been
restored. The larger strategic picture had, however, been radically
altered, not by the Chinese successes of November and early December or the compensating defeats Ridgway had later inflicted on

them but by political developments of which the soldiers fighting in the cold mud of the inhospitable peninsula were largely ignorant.

In one way or another, the Korean War had placed the Truman administration in a series of critical predicaments. The President's first problem was that his appointed commander in chief in the Far East was completely unsympathetic to the announced desire of the U.S. government to confine hostilities to Korea and when possible to seek an honorable "cease fire." MacArthur, on the contrary, wanted to expand the war into China, and in the U.S. Senate particularly, he found vociferous adherents. Neither the General nor his supporters made any effort to conceal his views, which were widely circulated in the press on both sides of the Atlantic and were a source of endless embarrassment to the administration in its dealing with Allied governments and the United Nations.

Additionally, MacArthur's plans to bomb and blockade the mainland and to employ Nationalist forces in Korea provided Peking with ready-made propaganda material of inestimable value to the regime. MacArthur's object, Mao's government announced, was to enslave the Chinese people. To the Chinese, the threatening pronouncements of the General in Tokyo came in loud and clear. Conflicting statements of administration spokesmen, who repeatedly disavowed these views and asserted that the United States had no intention of carrying the war to China, were either disbelieved or ignored in Peking. America was speaking with two voices, and the Chinese listened to the one it best suited their purposes to hear.

It is not particularly relevant to this narrative to describe in detail the events which brought the situation to a head in early April. MacArthur's attempts to force the administration to adopt his views finally became intolerable to his commander in chief, and on April 11, 1951, the President dismissed him from all his commands and assigned these responsibilities to Ridgway. Three days later, Lieut. Gen. James A. Van Fleet, USA, assumed command of U.N. forces in Korea with concurrent operational control of the ROK Army.

Van Fleet assumed command of a battle-tested army. In Ridgway's words, it was an army proud and tough: "a magnificent fighting organization, supremely confident that it would take any objective assigned. . . ."[22] this multinational army now held a general line from Munsan in the west, through Chorwon (at the base of the

"Iron Triangle") to Hwachon, thence along the south shore of the Hwachon reservoir to Taepo-ri on the east coast. North of the front, intensive air reconnaissance developed a clear pattern of heavy Chinese reinforcement and continuous logistic build-up. Obviously, a massive "end-the-war" offensive impended. This enemy intent was confirmed by prisoner interrogation.

Chinese and NKPA order of battle as of April 18 indicated that the weight of the expected attack would fall in the west. Here the 19th Army Group, 1st Field Army, had disposed 10 to 12 divisions (63rd, 64th, and 65th armies). To its east, on the central front, 3rd Army Group, 2nd Field Army, deployed in equivalent strength the 10th, 12th, and 15th armies. Still farther to the east, the 9th Army Group, reconstituted since the debacle of the previous November–December, held poised the 20th and 27th armies. The "First Impulse" striking force thus comprised approximately 30 divisions at a strength of more than 250,000. Another 40 divisions were held in reserve to the north.

Before midnight on April 22, under a full moon and after massive and effective artillery and heavy mortar preparation they had not previously enjoyed, the Chinese launched the "First Impulse, Fifth Phase Offensive." This offensive, which Peking radio announced was designed to drive the United Nations from Korea, struck 8th Army positions in the sectors held by I and IX Corps. Again, the Chinese found a vulnerable point, the ROK 6th Division, attached to IX Corps; and as before, in the face of a sudden, numerically overwhelming night attack, the ROKs collapsed. On their right, the 1st Marine Division refused its western flank; on the left, the 24th Division folded its right back to protect Seoul. The Chinese drove into this gap and destroyed the ROK 6th Division in the process. By April 26, U.N. counterattacks from both flanks had effectively sealed the penetration.

During April 23, Chinese pressure in the west built up. Under partial cover of smudge from thousands of brush fires set to neutralize U.N. air intervention, two Chinese divisions (the 118th and 187th) crossed the Imjin River near Choksong and threw themselves upon the 27th British Brigade. Fighting here was vicious, as it was along the entire front north and northeast of Seoul, which P'eng Teh-huai had promised as a May Day gift to Mao Tse-tung. Although smoke and haze obscured the field from time to time, fighter bombers of the Far East Air Force mounted more than 1,100 sorties, 340 of which were in close support of the ground troops. On each of the following three days, Stratemeyer's aircraft flew more than 1,000 sorties.[23]

By April 29, the "First Impulse," after gains in some places of about 35 miles, had spent its force. Chinese casualties were of the order of 70,000; U.N. losses less than one-tenth that number. Two Communist Army groups had been shredded in the U.N. meat grinder, and the U.N. flag still flew over Seoul. The Chinese, not yet ready to give up, fell back to reorganize and re-equip.

The same basic factor which had limited previous Communist advances operated again in the "First Impulse." Although able in the preparatory stages gradually to build up overwhelming strength, the Chinese again were unable to sustain initial momentum or to switch forces rapidly to exploit local breakthroughs. Stubborn U.N. resistance in well-coordinated delaying actions was aided decisively by the Far East Air Force, which flew more than 7,000 close-support, armed reconnaissance, and interdiction sorties in seven days.[24]

The type of resistance the Chinese encountered was exemplified by the 29th British Brigade's stand north of Seoul, which "completely frustrated the Chinese plan to break the 8th Army front." For three days, the brigade "blocked all attempts to cut the road to Seoul and inflicted casualties on the enemy which brought his offensive to a halt and resulted in his withdrawal. All had fought bravely and well." [25]

In the early hours of May 16, after tentative probes and under cover of fog and rain, 21 Chinese divisions, the "Second Impulse, Fifth Phase Offensive," rolled down the Chunchon–Inje corridor in an attempt to outflank Seoul. Successive waves of assault infantry smashed in tremendous strength against ROK III Corps and the two ROK divisions on its right.

Five days and nights of heavy attacks wrecked ROK III Corps, which ceased to exist as a fighting unit and was deactivated. Demoralized remnants were reassigned. Van Fleet, a worthy successor to the imperturbable Ridgway, switched U.S. 3rd Division from reserve in the Seoul area to the threatened sector, and by the evening of May 21, these fresh troops had stabilized the east-central front and inflicted very heavy casualties on the Chinese. On the following day, the "People's Volunteers," screened by stubbornly-conducted delaying actions, began to withdraw slowly to the north.

The second installment of the [Chinese Communist Forces] Fifth Phase offensive had failed even more conclusively than the first. The enemy had only a narrow penetration on a secondary front to show for ruinous casualties. Worse yet, from the Chinese viewpoint, the UN forces were in a position to retaliate before the attackers recovered their tactical balance. The Eighth Army had come through with relatively light losses and it was now about to seize the initiative.[26]

Both "Impulses" of the "Fifth Phase Offensive" planned by P'eng Teh-huai clearly revealed that the Chinese High Command had, in desperation, decided to seek an answer to U.N. weapons superiority in the most elementary terms. If—they appeared to reason—enough men, in wave after calculated wave, could be thrown against a chosen defensive position, the opponent's fires—no matter how intense, how flexible, or how well directed—would eventually be saturated by sheer humanity. *Some* attackers would live to make the final short-range assault; *some* would manage to survive to reach U.N. positions and to disrupt the defensive organization. These tactics were momentarily successful, but, as in the past, momentum could not be sustained in the face of the defender's fires and blasting air attacks.

The collapse of the spring "win the war" offensives, after staggering losses had achieved no more than transitory local successes, made it clear to the Chinese High Command that Mao's "strategy of annihilation" had failed and that they must perforce accommodate to one of attrition. In the final analysis, it is apparent that P'eng Teh-huai and his staff in Shenyang egregiously discounted the firepower, command flexibility, and mobility of Van Fleet's army. More importantly, they had imprudently failed to assess the high morale and battle competence of the U.N. command. The Chinese were now fighting a veteran and professional army: "The Eighth Army . . . had been welded by fire into one of the finest military instruments" in American history.[27]

The extent of the casualties inflicted on the "People's Volunteers" during the "Fifth Phase Offensive" is reflected in what happened to one Chinese assault battalion. As the battalion's medical officer, captured after the collapse of the "Second Impulse," later related, the battalion jumped off on May 18, continued the attack the following day, and was stalled on the 20th. That evening, the commander received orders to defend in successive delaying positions. On the 25th, the battalion was ordered to "break contact" and withdraw from its last delaying position. "Breaking contact" in an orderly manner under enemy pressure is more easily planned than executed.

During these seven days, the battalion, which had entered action with 530 officers and men, suffered exactly 400 combat casualties: 235 killed and wounded in action; 165 missing. Examination of bodies recovered and of the wounded in dressing stations showed that 92 per cent of the casualties were inflicted by ground weapons; 8 per cent by air-delivered weapons.[28]

Sickness added its toll. The medical officer testified that most survivors in his battalion suffered from malaria, dysentery, and scabies. Another captured medical officer stated that during the same period at least 30 per cent of the troops suffered from constant diarrhea and another 10 per cent from malnutrition.[29]

General Van Fleet had prepared plans to launch a counterattack as soon as the "Second Impulse" ran out of steam, and on the morning of May 23, the U.N. offensive, with massive close air support, jumped off. Hundreds of tons of napalm and proximity (VT)-fused fragmentation bombs spread panic among the Chinese. In the five days that followed, almost 12,000 "Volunteers" and North Koreans surrendered. This increased the total U.N. bag of prisoners of war to 163,130. At the same time, U.S. intelligence estimated that since the war began the enemy had suffered more than 800,000 battle casualties.[30]

On June 11, armored tank forces of U.S. I Corps occupied Chorwan and Kumhwa (at the southwest and southeast corners of the "Iron Triangle"), and against scattered resistance, two armored columns pushed into its apex, P'yongyang, shot up the wrecked city, and withdrew unmolested. The Chinese were beginning to break. This was no longer a well-ordered withdrawal. It was turning into a rout, "a flight of beaten troops" scourged from the air "with bullets, rockets, and napalm . . . where it had been rare for a single Chinese soldier to surrender voluntarily, remnants of platoons, companies, and even battalions were now giving up after throwing down their arms. . . . The enemy was on the run!" [31] General Van Fleet later wrote: "We met and routed the enemy. We had him beaten and would have destroyed his armies. . . . In those days in Korea we reached the heights." [32]

On June 23, Jacob Malik, Russia's representative on the Security Council, proposed "cease-fire" talks as a preliminary to "peaceful settlement of the Korean problem."

In stragetic terms, the Korean War had reached a stalemate. But although future ground operations would be confined to localized bloody actions, the air battle assumed a radically new character. The costly defeats inflicted on the Chinese during the Fifth Phase Offensive, defeats to which Allied air power had made signal, if not decisive, contributions, convinced the Soviet government that major commitment of fighters to the theater was mandatory. In early June the build-up began.

As of June 1, no more than 300 MIG-15s were based on the Antung airfield complex. By the end of that month, the count was 445; two months later (September 1), it had increased to 525. Heavy air fighting now took place daily in the skies from P'yongyang north to the Yalu as the Russian-made jets, alerted by an efficient early-warning net, tangled with U.N. fighters and fighter bombers in "MIG Alley." The interdiction campaign was seriously threatened:

The Soviet Jet MIG 15s, supplied in large numbers to the Chinese Communist Air Force, owed the tactical height advantage which they frequently enjoyed in the air combats near the Yalu River to the adequate and consistent early warning of the approach of United Nations bombers and fighters supplied by Soviet-manned early warning radar units. These often enabled the Chinese-flown MIG 15s to be airborne in time to gain a height advantage and to dive out of the sun on their U.S. and British air opponents.[33]

This well-engineered aircraft was roughly comparable to the U.S. F-86 Sabre. Although faster than the U.S. interceptor at altitudes above 35,000 feet, the MIG was less stable at high speeds. It also lacked radar gun sights and was "an inferior piece of shooting equipment." [34]

Nor were MIG pilots so experienced as U.N. fliers, many of whom had established fine records in World War II. It was not uncommon for inexperienced Chinese pilots to lose control during high-speed maneuver and spin in. Aerial cameras mounted in Sabres occasionally even showed that nervous Chinese pilots ejected before the Sabre attacked.

It would be incorrect, however, to assume that Sabre pilots had an easy time against the MIGs. Certainly, they did not after mid-June 1951, when General Liu Ya-lou, the Chinese Air Force commander, initiated a comprehensive program to improve air combat and operational capabilities. The most significant measure was organization of an "International Communist Volunteer Air Force." [35] This, General Liu unveiled on the morning of June 17, when Sabres on patrol in "MIG Alley" south of Antung met 25 "unusually aggressive" MIGs. That engagement marked the first appearance of obviously experienced enemy pilots. Americans dubbed these more capable fliers *"honchos"*—Japanese for "boss"—to distinguish them from the less adept. The assumption at the time that the *"honchos"* were Russians was later proved correct.

Naturally, Chinese historians of the Korean War report the air battles in somewhat different terms than those recorded by the cameras.[36]

The very day when the young air force of the Chinese People's Volunteers first appeared in the skies over Korea, it came to grips with the Air Force of the No. 1 imperialism in the world. The atrocious U.S. air bandits included large numbers of veteran fliers who had participated in the Second World War, each with nearly 1,000 hours of flying time to his credit. On the other hand, their opponents were all young fliers. However, technical training and equipment were not the determining factors in air battles. Members of the People's Air Force had courage and righteousness which the U.S. flying bandits did not have.

Although the "celestial eagles" took a beating practically every time they encountered "Sabrejets," they levied an increasingly heavy toll on allied piston bombers, and in October, General Vandenberg announced that the Chinese Communist Air Force must be reckoned one of the most powerful in the world. Still, at no time did the Chinese effectively challenge U.N. control of the air south of the "Iron Triangle." This situation was due in part to their inability to operate from fields south of the Yalu. As fast as they rehabilitated air installations in North Korea, FEAF bombers took the fields out.

As the Chinese Air Force built up in the Manchurian "sanctuary," defense of crucial bridge and marshaling yard targets improved. Radar-controlled, heavy anti-aircraft guns and automatic weapons batteries blossomed all over North Korea. Daylight attacks on the transportation system required increasingly intensive flak suppression efforts, and night-bombing missions suffered severely.

In the final analysis, Chinese air operations in the Korean War were not effective, although ultimately they had available 1,300 jet fighters backed by efficient Soviet-operated early-warning radar and radar-controlled anti-aircraft fire: [37]

At the time the MIG 15, apart from the lack of a radar gunsight, was roughly the technical equal of the best jet fighter planes in the world and was in fact clearly superior to many of the machines in United Nations air squadrons. More than that, the Chinese Communist MIG 15 regiments had relatively speaking a simple tactical task. They had no escorting of bomber formations to carry out. By and large, they had to defend the same airfields, power stations, bridges and other targets near the Yalu River. But despite the tactical advantage of defending the same limited area day after day and the enjoyment of strong local numerical fighter superiority, they failed to do their job of local air defence. The main reasons were the inferior training and quality of the Chinese pilots and the fact that without a radar gunsight or air-to-air guided missiles the MIG 15 was a poor gun platform from which to shoot down bombers.[38]

The official historian of the air war in Korea maintains that the Communist failure to produce a better showing resulted largely from lack of experience:

The Communist air leaders never adequately or consistently exploited the advantageous characteristics of their aircraft. The Reds consistently misused the available power by failing to exploit their numerical advantage and the superior high-altitude performance of their equipment. By a skilled application of sound and aggressive tactics the Communists might have enjoyed a certain degree of air superiority over North Korea. . . . Lack of knowledge of air warfare prevented the Reds from making the most of their capabilities. . . . What was true of air leadership was also true of the calibre of the men who flew the MIGs. As a group, the Communist pilots ranged in skill from the very few "honcho" pilots down to a predominant mass of "recruit" pilots. . . . Sabre pilots believed that most of the "honcho" pilots were Russian and that the "recruits" were Chinese and North Koreans. When the Communist "trainee" pilots could be brought under attack they were apt to display utter confusion. Some forgot to drop their external tanks, others fired their guns wildly and many ejected from their aircraft without particular provocation.[39]

The historian adds this epitaph on the Chinese Communist Air Force in Korea: "In the last months of the war—when the *'honchos'* had apparently gone home—many MIG pilots refused to break into an attacking Sabre . . . by acting the coward [i.e., ejecting] these MIG pilots lost their aircraft." [40]

While the war in the skies raged without intermission, fighting on the ground was sporadic as both sides devoted major energies to improvement of static defenses.[41] Each patrolled vigorously, and every night fierce, short-range fire fights erupted along the front. Occasionally, local attacks, which rarely involved more than a regiment, were launched to gain ground tactically advantageous or to ease a salient. Invariably, these attacks were extremely costly.

As the negotiations at P'anmunjom dragged through early 1952, a vast amount of digging went on in the battle zone. The Chinese literally honeycombed the hills they occupied with tunnels. Usually, they selected reverse slopes and built the defensive organization around a pattern of mutually supporting, heavily bunkered positions, with connecting tunnels or covered and camouflaged trench systems to protect personnel against air attack and insure mobility and flexibility in defense. The Chinese were alert, their patrols were aggressive, and they offered determined opposition to local attacks. Their artillery and mortar fires were well directed and frequently delivered in great volume. They were, indeed, "a formidable enemy, well prepared for operations in a ground war of position and attrition." [42]

The tempo of this deadly but inconclusive fighting on naked ridges remained unchanged until the end. Chinese techniques, however, constantly improved. This improvement was particularly apparent in their increasing ability to mass and shift artillery fires in support of intermittent local attacks. Although usually unsuccessful, these gave evidence of excellent discipline and a high quality of small unit leadership:

The enemy makes good use of terrain during an attack . . . he habitually attacks [U.N. strong points] from more than one direction. The Chinese follow-up preparatory artillery and mortar fires closely. This is done to the extent of accepting some casualties from their own fires . . . the Chinese are well and courageously led at the small unit level . . . [The Chinese soldier] is thoroughly disciplined . . . an industrious digger. His conduct of the defense is accomplished in spite of UN superiority in the air, his inferior communications, and his hodge-podge of weapons and equipment.[43]

Thousands of men died in Korea, and tens of thousands were wounded there before the armistice which silenced the guns was signed at P'anmunjom at 10 A.M. on July 27, 1953. The "skirmish," the "bloody, costly skirmish, fought on the perimeter of the free world," was at last ended.[44] Neither side had "won."

Could the United Nations have gained a clear-cut victory? Could Van Fleet's army, rampaging north in pursuit in the early summer of 1951, have gone on to the border? And what then? These questions cannot be answered. Even Matthew Ridgway found it useless to speculate on what might have been:

Military men, and statesmen, too, will long debate the wisdom of stopping that proud Army in its tracks at the first whisper that the Reds might be ready to sue for peace. To my mind it is fruitless to speculate on what might have been. If we had been ordered to fight our way to the

Yalu, we could have done it—if our government had been willing to pay the price in dead and wounded that action would have cost. From the purely military standpoint the effort, to my mind, would have not been worth the cost. A drive to the line of the Yalu and the Tumen would have cleared Korea of the Chinese enemy. But he would have still been facing us in great strength beyond those rivers. The seizure of the land between the truce line and the Yalu would have merely meant the seizure of more real estate. It would have greatly shortened the enemy's supply lines by pushing him right up against his main supply bases in Manchuria. It would have greatly lengthened our own supply routes, and widened our battlefront from 110 miles to 420. Would the American people have been willing to support the great army that would have been required to hold that line? Would they have approved our attacking on into Manchuria? On into the heart of the great mainland of Asia, a bottomless pit into which all the armies of the whole free world could be drawn to bits and destroyed? I doubt it.[45]

The United States had, indeed, no intention of allowing itself to become deeply involved in Asia. The "critical strategic prize," as both the Truman and Eisenhower administrations evaluated the global picture, lay not in Asia but in Europe. To have engaged a disproportionate share of U.S. power in Asia would (so the Joint Chiefs of Staff believed) have uncovered Europe and thus increased, rather than (as General MacArthur asserted) diminished, the risk of general war. "Red China," General Bradley testified at Senate hearings during May 1951, "is not the powerful nation seeking to dominate the world. Frankly, in the opinion of the Joint Chiefs of Staff, this strategy [that recommended by General MacArthur] would involve us in the wrong war, at the wrong place, at the wrong time, and with the wrong enemy." [46]

The announced purposes of both U.N. and U. S. policies in Korea were thus to contain the Chinese Communists, to punish them as severely as possible in the process, and to bring them to the conference table. These aims were achieved: in Korea, the Chinese were taught that they were "not invincible." [47]

But from the Korean War, China emerged as the most powerful nation in Asia. That she had fought technically superior forces to a stalemate greatly enhanced her prestige abroad as well as that of her newly-established government at home. Resistance to American "aggression" provided the unifying theme the Party needed to gain the unqualified support of 500 million Chinese. Nor did the fact that Peking failed to realize announced ambitions in Korea diminish Chinese arrogance.

The Korean War was an experience of inestimable value to the

People's Liberation Army. In terms of weaponry and techniques, the PLA which crossed the Yalu was almost a primitive horde. In two and a half years, that army suffered terrible casualties. But at the same time, under conditions of rigorous and testing combat, the PLA vaulted into the twentieth century. And as it did so, it destroyed the long-cherished Western myth that the Chinese was an inferior fighting man.

General Ridgway, the American officer uniquely qualified to assess the competence of the Chinese command, writes:

[In Korea the Chinese] leadership achieved results of a very high order in organizing, training, indoctrinating, and supplying its forces, and in their tactical handling from initial concentration and forward movement to contact, and through subsequent offensive, defensive and retrograde operations.

In doing so, this leadership overcame the handicaps of a largely illiterate peasantry which constituted much of the front-line strength of its armies. It took full advantage of the individual soldier's docility, of the simplicity of his wants, of his ability to endure extremes of temperature and great physical exertion with a minimum of food, clothing, shelter and medical care. It inculcated an excellent acceptance of rigid discipline with unflinching response to orders and apparent loyalty to superiors under the severest demands of campaign and combat.

Its use of terrain, cover, concealment and deception were of a high order. Its tactical handling of troops accorded full consideration to inferiority in weaponry, communications, transport and supply, and a complete lack of air power in the zone of ground combat.

Considering the conditions under which it operated in Korea during the period described, the PLA must be rated highly. With good leadership, time for training, and first-class equipment, Chinese ground forces, with their huge reservoir of manpower, must be reckoned a formidable foe.[48]

A major share of credit for sustaining the morale which contributed signally to this impressive performance must be given the Communist Party. It is true that thousands of Chinese soldiers surrendered, but the anticipated major break in morale never occurred. At all levels, dedicated political officers, cadres, and activists worked unceasingly to inject into the peasant soldier hatred of the Americans, to imbue him with ideals of loyalty and obedience, and to nurture in him the willingness to endure and, if necessary, to sacrifice his life. Their efforts were not in vain.

CHAPTER TEN

"A Great Victory"
P'eng Teh-huai

A month before the tortured negotiations at P'anmunjom finally dragged to a conclusion, General P'eng Teh-huai sent a congratulatory telegram to Marshal Kim Il Sung, Supreme Commander of the North Korean People's Army. In this message, P'eng struck the major chords of the Chinese Communist themes respecting the Korean War. In concert with their friends and allies, the "peace-loving" Chinese, the Korean people, P'eng averred, had scored "a great victory" over "the common enemy." Together, they had successfully defended the "cause of peace in Asia and the rest of the world"; "forged with blood" an unbreakable friendship; frustrated "the mad ambitions of American imperialism to dominate the world," and gained the support of all "lovers of peace." [1]

P'eng returned to Peking on August 12, 1953, where a conqueror's welcome awaited him. A feature of these festivities was an address by Kuo Mo-jo, then the Party's verbose and ubiquitous cultural watchdog and Chairman of the Chinese People's Committee for Defense of World Peace and against U.S. Aggression. In this characteristically vicious effusion, Kuo reiterated the line that the Korean War had not only resulted in a "victory" for China "and all peace-loving people" but had "upset the timetable of American imperialism for aggressive war" and "exposed its inner weaknesses." In marked contrast, Kuo concluded, "construction in the People's Republic had progressed by leaps and bounds." [2]

During August, the "Hate America" campaign, also progressing by leaps and bounds, reached literally lunatic proportions. Daily, the American "monsters" were accused of committing every conceivable atrocity. This unceasing cascade of mendacity and slander would have aroused the jealous admiration of Hitler's degenerate Reich Minister for Propaganda. The watchword in the People's Republic was: "Despise America, Condemn America, Hate America."

Almost exactly a month after his triumphant reception, P'eng appeared at the twenty-fourth meeting of the Central People's Government Council to render to Chairman Mao and the assembled hierarchy his "Report on the Work of Resisting U.S. Aggression and Aiding Korea." [3] If the public version of the "Report" coincides with what P'eng told the delegates, they learned nothing at all about the conduct of the Korean War. The address, as released to the press, was entirely devoid of factual content and sheds no light whatever on such enigmas as the background of the original North Korean aggression, the degree of Chinese participation in pre-invasion planning, the factors which impelled the Chinese to intervene when and as they did, the material and other aid received from the Russians, the casualties suffered, or the real reasons the Sino-Soviet side sought to terminate the costly Korean adventure. Possibly it is too much to expect that the General should have adverted, even indirectly, to any of these embarrassing subjects.

P'eng declared that "the war against aggression was won" despite "conditions in which our military equipment could not compare with that of the enemy." Although the Americans had used Korea "as a testing ground for new weapons of wholesale murder," the "People's Volunteers" had triumphed because they were a "true people's force possessing high political consciousness and great nobility of character." On the field of battle, more than 300,000 Chinese soldiers, inspired by the "righteousness" of their cause, distinguished themselves by "heroic exploits, bravery, fortitude, and stubbornness." All this would have been impossible, said the General, without the wise leadership of Mao Tse-tung, the firm ideological basis created by the Party, and the support rendered the "Volunteers" by the great mass of the Chinese people.

P'eng made it clear that the experience of the Korean War marked a transition for the PLA, for both Chinese and Korean forces "not only rapidly improved and raised the level of their equipment, added new formations and various new types of arms, but also acquired rich experience in modern warfare, thus daily increasing their fighting power." [4] However, P'eng gave no figures in terms of either lives or money to indicate what the Chinese people had paid to enable the PLA to acquire this "rich experience."

The price in human terms was staggering: an estimated 900,000 battle casualties. Other thousands of Chinese—no one will ever know how many—froze to death; uncounted thousands died of cholera, dysentery, typhus, and smallpox. These epidemic diseases, which existing medical facilities could not control, more than decimated the PLA and gave rise to the fabrication that the United States was using bacteriological warfare in Korea. Primitive hospital and surgical facilities were unable to care for the seriously ill and gravely wounded, a large proportion of whom died from lack of attention.

Naturally, P'eng did not discuss matters of such serious import. Nor were they revealed to the Chinese people. But they could not be concealed from the "Volunteers," thousands of whom threw down their arms in May and June 1951. Significantly, most of those who gave up came over in groups rather than as individuals. This certain sign that a morale crisis was incipient was obvious to the Party and was possibly the principal reason the Chinese sought negotiations at the time they did.

Although morale in the PLA reached a low point in mid-June 1951, the process had been cumulative. Casualties in previous offensives had taken a very heavy toll of lower-level cadres and political officers. Party members, indoctrinated to set a combat example and obligated by solemn oath to do so, had absorbed a percentage of casualties out of all proportion to their relative number in the army. The Party's hold on the troops was thus progressively weakening; its organization in battalions, companies, platoons, and squads, steadily eroding, and at an alarming rate.

Another factor operated in the context of surrender. This was the innate common sense of the Chinese peasant soldiers, some of whom had concluded that the only escape from a situation beginning to strike them as hopeless was to run away. In reaching this decision, they were acting in accord with Chinese tradition which teaches that when defeat is inevitable, surrender or flight is morally justified. But they could not run backward: there certain death on the charge of cowardice awaited. They had, perforce, to reach U.N. lines. And this, increasing members had done.

"Construction" was the euphemism Kuo Mo-jo used to describe the government's activities in the People's Republic of China while the "Volunteers" were dying in Korea. Under the slogans "Resist America, Aid Korea," and "Support the Government; Love the

People," the Party mobilized the urban and rural masses and mounted a series of campaigns to register "reactionaries" and to apprehend "secret agents," "notorious criminals," "betrayers of the revolution," grafters, profiteers, and anyone else branded as a "people's enemy."

We cannot even guess how many Chinese opposed the Party's policies or resisted its programs and thus automatically qualified as "people's enemies," but since the government found it necessary to mount large-scale "bandit suppression" campaigns in Hunan, Chekiang, Fukien, and Kiangsi during 1951, a considerable number obviously did. At the same time, the entire population was required to register, and each household to sign a pledge of loyalty. This measure armed the internal-security organs with a weapon they could use arbitrarily to render harmless those who did not actively demonstrate enthusiastic support of the government and love for the people.

On February 21, 1951, the Party found it necessary to promulgate a "Law for the Punishment of Counter Revolutionaries." In May, Lo Jui-ch'ing, then director of Public Security in Peking, announced that 505 "counterrevolutionaries" had been brought before the Tribunal of the Military Control Commission of Peking. Of them, 211 were executed. In Tientsin, 600 "counterrevolutionaries" were brought to trial and on November 11, 1951, 277 were executed. In the month of May 1951, more than 11,400 persons were brought before the Shanghai "people's court" and during May, June, and July, at least 909 persons were executed in that city alone. Shanghai was obviously a hotbed of "counterrevolutionary" activity, for the Party announced that during the four-month period April 27 to August 27, 1951, more than 38,000 cases were prosecuted in "people's courts" there.[5]

In connection with agrarian reform, peasants "spontaneously" held thousands of "accusation meetings." The result of this program was the physical elimination of many landlords and the occupational liquidation of others fortunate enough to save their heads. The campaign extended to the near-extirpation of "reactionary" Buddhists and Taoists and nationalization of their temples and temple properties.

The nation-wide "Three-Anti" Movement, inspired by Mao Tsetung's speech of October 23, 1951, to the People's Political Consultative Conference, was directed against corruption, waste, and "bureaucratism" in the Party and in government. Undoubtedly, the campaign touched the rear-echelon bureaucracy of the PLA, but under existing conditions this fact would not have been made public.

The operation to cleanse the Party and government of bribers, embezzlers, forgers, miscellaneous crooks and wastrels was entrusted to Po I-p'o, Minister of Finance and concurrently chairman of the Production and Thrift Supervisory Committee. Almost immediately, Po's investigators and informers uncovered such spectacular evidence of criminal graft and bureaucratic maladministration that he called on the entire populace to join in a "tiger hunt."

How many Party members, government officials, and army officials lost heads or jobs during this safari is not known. But the publicity which attended the campaign suggests that the figure exceeded the Party's most pessimistic expectations and ran well over 10,000: "Mayors, department heads, bureau chiefs, Party executives, and high regional and provincial officers were accused and dismissed from office. Party members of more than twenty years' standing were expelled from the Party and severely punished." [6] But no senior Party members were implicated.

Nevertheless, it was obviously necessary to remove the stigma of corruption from the Party. The "Five-Anti" Movement, launched while the "Three-Anti" campaign was in its last violent paroxysms, was designed, in part, to shift the blame for this widespread corruption to another easily identifiable group: the petty bourgeoisie, whose members, it was alleged, had "seduced" Party members found guilty of corrupt practices from the paths of righteousness. But there was another more important reason for the "Five-Anti" operation: the Party needed money, and the relatively small bourgeois community, not as yet systematically expropriated, had it.

The "Five-Anti" campaign was thus directed against merchants, petty capitalists, managers, and entrepreneurs suspected of tax evasion, bribery, fraud, embezzlement of state assets, and theft of "economic secrets." These "five evils" were defined in terms sufficiently elastic "to permit charges to be leveled against any merchant or industrialist whom the regime wished to persecute. It was possible to accuse any businessman of fraud on the ground that he had made excessive profit. Once a merchant had been accused of profiteering it was easy to charge him with tax evasion. . . ." [7]

To exploit patriotic sentiment, the "treacherous acts" of small merchants, suppliers, and industrialists "were held responsible for misfortunes in the Korean War. 'Fraudulent merchants' were

177 of its equipment

accused of selling 'ineffective medicines' to the PLA, and 'unscrupulous manufacturers' with providing the fighting men 'inferior raincoats which could not withstand inclement weather.' " [8]

The government abruptly terminated partnerships with private enterprise and confiscated small businesses, whose owners were incontinently reduced to the status of employees. Some few of the dispossessed capitalists were nominally recompensed with long-term, low-interest-bearing bonds.

To help pay the mounting costs of the war, the government also withheld a significant portion of all wages and salaries and extracted considerable sums from the people by intensive bond drives coupled with nation-wide campaigns for "voluntary" contributions to purchase aircraft for "protection" of the homeland. Thus, the war in Korea was financed by the most comprehensive and effective "squeeze" operation in Chinese history.

It is difficult to estimate how much hard cash the Party extracted from the people during these various campaigns. One source gives a figure of U.S. $1,250 million.[9] Many merchants heavily fined by people's courts for alleged tax evasion were in addition forced to surrender family jewelry and other negotiable assets.[10]

In sum, the "Three-Anti" and "Five-Anti" campaigns "provided the exchequer with far more actual cash than had the bond sales and private donations"; they also "increased the power of the state not only over private business but, through general 'mobilization,' over the population as a whole. The executions, jail sentences, property confiscations, imposition of fines, and public humiliation suffered by victims of the purge offered vivid examples of the treatment awaiting whoever dared to deviate from the path prescribed. . . ." [11]

Such was the nature of "construction" in the People's Republic during the years 1951 and 1952.

P'eng's claim that the PLA had "rapidly improved and raised the level" of its equipment was not idle braggadocio, as U.N. forces could attest. The improvements became spectacularly evident during 1952, when despite heavy cumulative losses of aircraft, the Chinese built "an air order of battle on Manchurian soil which became powerful enough to threaten the survival of U.N. forces in Korea." [12] By June 1952, the Chinese Communist Air Force reached an estimated strength of about 1,800 aircraft, including more than 1,000 jet fighters, the majority based on fields in the Antung complex. Back of the Chinese stood a Soviet Far East air order of battle of about 5,300 combat aircraft. "The Communist air order of battle in the Far East not only dwarfed the U.N. air forces, but the Reds also possessed more modern planes. . . ." [13]

In addition to aircraft, the U.S.S.R. provided airfield construction and maintenance equipment, jet fuel, ammunition, ground-control intercept radars, almost 800 heavy (85-mm.) antiaircraft guns, and twice that number of automatic weapons of smaller caliber. Flak defenses, fully integrated with a well-designed early-warning system, gun-laying radar, and radar-controlled searchlights protected important installations in North Korea.

The equipment the Russians provided was generally excellent; indeed, they gave their Chinese allies the best they had available. U.S. electronic experts in late 1952 assessed ground-control intercept radars positioned near the Antung complex to be "as good as any possessed by the U.N. command." [14] Russian technicians trained Chinese to operate this new equipment effectively. Thus, after June 1952, Chinese air-defense capability was of a high order.

Concurrently, Chinese ground forces were rearmed and re-equipped. Artillery, particularly, was increased and calibers standardized. The PLA received new prime movers and other modern vehicles which considerably improved capabilities both for rapid deployment of artillery and reserves and more effective logistic support.

During late 1951 and 1952, infantry battalions, regiments, and divisions were reorganized and re-equipped. Most changes reflected the influence of Soviet experience and doctrines. Divisional firepower was drastically increased as Heavy Weapons and Heavy Mortar (120-mm.) battalions were added to Tables of Organization and Equipment. At this time, separate tank, anti-aircraft, armored car, and truck regiments were identified.

The PLA infantry divisions of late 1952 bore little resemblance to their primitive predecessors which crossed the Yalu in October and November 1950. As Chu Teh said, "the great historic transition of the PLA from its lower stage to its higher stage" had begun.

As we have seen, the Party quickly took advantage of the situation created by the Korean War to expand and deepen its control of every aspect of Chinese life and to consolidate the "democratic dictatorship." Nor was the PLA to escape attention. Although the apparatus which insured Party control in the army was not funda-

mentally altered during the Korean War, it was constantly strengthened and refined. The basic structure—still in effect—is shown in
the following chart.

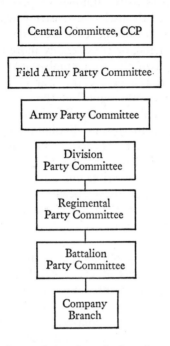

Commissars (regimental level and above) and political officers
(battalion and company level) were necessarily competent and experienced Party members of proven loyalty. They were *direct representatives* of the supreme power: the Party.

At every level, these representatives were provided with a trained
staff. In the infantry division headquarters (1951–52), the section
assigned the Commissar numbered 65 political officers and 132 enlisted men. The section consisted of six functional groups:

	Officers	*Enlisted Men*
Organizations	12	36
Youth	12	36
Security	6	12
Investigation	6	12
Liaison	6	12
Propaganda	24	24

(It is interesting to note that the Division Staff Section, responsible for intelligence, operations, training, personnel, and cryptography, totaled only 42 officers and 107 enlisted men.[15]

Exact information as to the number of personnel in an infantry division who occupied themselves exclusively with political work is not available. But a reasonable estimate indicates that the figure would approximate 1,200, or considerably more than 10 per cent of the effective strength of the 1951 combat infantry divisions. This percentage was increased before the war in Korea ended. These political personnel were the "guts" of the Chinese army in Korea.

The functional organization of political sections in regiments and battalions was similar to that in divisions. At the lowest level—company—there appears to have been no specific compartmentation. There, the political officer, assisted by a small Party Branch Committee, was held responsible for all Party activities. Political work in the company had always been emphasized, and during the Korean War the Party devoted particular attention to strengthening the "ideological fortress" at this echelon, which it correctly deemed the most sensitive.

In addition to those who functioned in the official structure, there were Party members at every echelon in the army. "The power of the army," a captured political officer stated, "derives from one source: the Party's organization." The Party had made of the army "a fully developed political machine"; the cogs in this "machine" were Party members who comprised about 20 per cent of the fighting forces of the PLA in Korea.[16] All senior officers belonged to the Party, as did most company commanders and a high proportion (about two-thirds) of the platoon leaders.[17] Another 50 to 60 per cent of all personnel were enrolled either as "probationers" or as expectant candidates who hoped to "establish merit and enter the Party": *li kung, ju tang.*

Party control was thus assured not simply by the machine but by group organization of Party members and "progressives" at every echelon. Party members were expected "to work hard and set high standards," to encourage emulation. Although they enjoyed "no special privileges," they had "better opportunities for promotion and education."

Interference by political officers in processes of tactical planning and decision making was common, and at lower levels, i.e., battalion and company—frequently produced indecision, delay in execution of plans, vacillation, and confusion. Only in "a combat emergency," for example, was a company commander permitted to make a tactical decision without reference to the Political Officer and the Party branch. Naturally, many battalion and company commanders hesitated to act when tactical opportunities presented themselves.

Prisoners frequently mentioned the pervasive controls in the PLA, and one political officer concluded a detailed statement to his U.S. interrogators with the observation that he sensed a "feeling of revulsion in the army" to the activities for which he was responsible. "The atmosphere in the army makes one feel soulless—no matter what one thinks or feels in his heart, one has to apply a Communist formula in speaking or doing things." This "feeling of revulsion," he continued, "is hidden deep in the hearts of the troops—nobody as yet dares express it openly." To have done so would have invited personal disaster.

There is no doubt that the Party members, "probationers," and candidates fought courageously in Korea. Prisoners of war unanimously agreed that morale of this committed group was very high and that Party members would not desert or surrender "under any circumstances." This is substantiated to a degree by interrogation records. Almost a hundred such records examined in detail by the author showed very few prisoners who admitted Party membership. But naturally, Party members would not be disposed to admit the fact to enemy interrogators.

The oath taken by "probationer" members on their admission to the Party bound them to dedicated service. They literally "gave their hearts"—and their bodies—to the Party:

With the approval of the Branch Party Committee and the Selected Review Board . . . is hereby admitted to the Chinese Communist Party. Said member will devote himself sincerely and faithfully to the revolution; he will demonstrate perseverance and be unafraid of any sacrifice before and after battle; he will advance in combat and remain in the rear in retreat; he will sacrifice all personal privileges and obey the Party.[18]

As we have observed, the Party derived considerable political profit from the Korean adventure. The war confirmed its legitimacy and enabled it to expand, deepen, and consolidate its domestic power position. The fact that China had dared to challenge mighty modern armies fielded by the United Nations and had fought them to a stalemate also won grudging admiration from many in the non-aligned and newly emerging nations. In the eyes of some Asian and African peoples, the Korean War enhanced the image of a new and strong China.

In crude terms, the casualties the PLA suffered on Korean battle-fields were more than offset by Soviet technical and material aid. Close and apparently entirely friendly relations with the Soviet Union implied that Chu Teh's hope for a "great, historic transition" of the PLA to a fully modernized military establishment would soon be realized. As events were to prove, this expectation was ill founded.

But in the summer of 1953, the Chinese High Command had reason to be optimistic. Within the limitations imposed by equipment, training, and experience, the air force had performed reasonably well, if not with uniform distinction. Heavy toll had been exacted of junior leaders and political cadres, but the younger men who survived provided a pool of tested combat veterans to leaven the new army the Party hoped to construct. Supporting arms and services and technical branches had been created and staffed, and their personnel trained under emergency conditions. Field operations against a technically first-class army had forced the senior commanders of the PLA to learn something of staff organization, functions, and procedures and in all to adopt a more workmanlike and professional orientation than had been required of them in the anti-Japanese and civil wars.

At the same time, a capacity—albeit on a small scale—to manufacture rifles, sub-machine guns, mortars, automatics, small-arms ammunition, grenades, and explosives had been created. Limited sectors of the Manchurian industrial base looted and destroyed by the Soviets in 1945–46 had with Russian help been rehabilitated.

Thus, although the Korean episode may have set back the Party's plans for the rapid development of a heavy-industry base, the war was by no means an unmitigated disaster, at least in the eyes of the leadership.

But in the general international context, China's intervention, her consistently virulent and obviously mendacious propaganda, her treatment of allied prisoners, and her intransigence at P'anmunjom combined to tarnish the image she had hoped to project. China depicted herself as a crusader in Korea. Most others did not see her in this role but condemned her in a formal U.N. resolution as an aggressor nation. The Chinese protested loudly and at length that the action of the United Nations was wholly illegal and inspired by U.S. hostility. Peking's vociferous propaganda against the United Nations served only to confirm for the majority of member states their estimate of Communist China's irreconcilable bellicosity.

We have no way of knowing precisely what conclusions the High Command of the PLA drew from the Korean War. Obviously, one was the need for a well-schooled, professional officer corps, and for trained technicians to maintain and operate modern weapons and equipment. With Soviet assistance, these projects had been put in train as early as 1951.

What role the Soviet Army played in succeeding years in the steady professionalization of the PLA is unknown. Certainly by 1957–58, the uniformed Russian "elder brothers" had exerted a powerful cumulative influence to this end. Estimates as to the number of Russian military advisers assigned the People's Republic during the post-Korea period are necessarily speculative. Figures ranging from 5,000 to 10,000 have been suggested as representative. Nor is it possible to make any realistic assessment of how many Chinese officers and military technicians went to Russia for schooling and training during the six-year period from 1953 to 1958. Certainly, the number ran into the thousands.

Therefore, although the Chinese People's Volunteers were badly battered in Korea, the ultimate results of the war conduced measurably to improve the quality and technical capacity of the PLA.

Still, any objective evaluation of the Korean War will reveal that the PLA was on the verge of disaster at the time Jacob Malik proposed a "cease fire." General Van Fleet's succinct summary perhaps bears repetition here: "We met and routed the enemy. We had him beaten and we would have destroyed his armies. . . . In those days in Korea we reached the heights."

Book II

Book II

CHAPTER ELEVEN

"We Have Stood Up"
Mao Tse-tung

China's bellicose posturings and her unrelenting thrust to achieve status and power in the contemporary world are usually ascribed to Mao Tse-tung's combatively messianic ideology. But to some extent, at least, they derive from China's historical experience. The People's Republic may be Maoist, but it is also inescapably Chinese. And whether at any given moment it is more one than the other is not always easy to determine. Some of the attitudes and policies for which the Chinese Communist regime is condemned are consistent with a heritage Mao and his colleagues could not completely disavow even if they wished to do so.

We frequently forget that for more than two thousand years China lived in isolation. This state was ordained by her geographic environment. The terrain bounding her to the north, west, and south is by any measure as inhospitable as may be found in the world. The Swiss can live in their mountainous country, but man has not yet learned to cope with the savage Himalayas, Kun Lun, T'ien Shan, and Pamirs, the uncompromising deserts, and the freezing steppes. To the east, the Pacific stretches for thousands of miles. Thus it happened that for centuries China was locked out of the world community and left to develop a culture wholly indigenous, coherent, and comprehensive.

Her geographic position also decreed that for centuries China would remain unchallenged by other advanced powers. Those peoples with whom the Chinese had relationships were usually weaker and manifestly culturally inferior. Chinese ethnocentrism—a conviction of racial and cultural superiority—thus developed naturally. The behavior of the "sea barbarians" who in the mid-nineteenth century began shooting their way into the "Celestial Kingdom" did nothing to modify this attitude but only served to confirm it.

During most of these hundreds of years, China exercised a benevolent hegemony over the weaker states along her borders. From time to time, Peking used force to assert what she considered to be her rightful prerogatives. "Sinification" of the peripheral countries of Southeast Asia and Korea and of Japan was a long and gradual process. But ultimately, almost all of them were brought within the Chinese culture area. She was less successful with the nomadic peoples of the steppes and deserts, who, although subjugated from time to time, did not readily assimilate to the Chinese cultural pattern.

In the context of this imperial heritage, it may be instructive to compare the irredentist claims of the Communist government with those of the rival Nationalists. There is no fundamental difference. No self-respecting Chinese government in Peking could conceivably consider the Soviet puppet "Mongolian People's Republic" to be anything but a fictive and transient phenomenon. Nor would any central government sufficiently powerful to bring Tibet under direct control have failed to do so. This attempt was made repeatedly during the Ch'ing dynasty, but it was not until 1951 that Peking had in hand the power to impose what all Chinese consider a rightful jurisdiction over that desolate region. We may recall that the Nationalists applauded the formal incorporation of Tibet as an integral part of the People's Republic of China.

Nationalist and Communist cartographers alike invariably include a huge chunk of India's Northeast Frontier Agency (NEFA) within Chinese borders. The same maps incorporate as well the disputed Aksai Chin area. Although Prime Minister Nehru objected to this situation on numerous occasions, Chou En-lai fobbed him off with the excuse that Communist map makers had not yet had opportunity "to correct" the old editions prepared under the Nationalists. For some time, Nehru publicly professed to see nothing ominous in this consistent cartographic aggression.

Maps produced in both Taiwan and Peking have shown the Ryukyu Islands—which include Okinawa—as Chinese territory, and until relatively recently, some versions indicated a large part of the Southeast Asian peninsula, once known as Annam or "The Pacified South," as within the area over which Peking should again exercise "rightful" hegemony. The competing governments agree, too, that Taiwan is an inalienable part of China.

At one time or another, the Russians have appropriated millions of acres of Siberian real estate, not a square inch of which the Chinese consider, and with some reason, as anything other than *terra irredenta*. The Chinese have made it clear that they have "some"—the number is several thousand—border claims to settle with Moscow. Even were the Soviets inclined to discuss these territorial questions—and they are not—the Chinese ability to drag out a negotiation suggests that no substantial number could possibly be amicably adjusted in the course of the next several centuries. Nevertheless, one may be certain that so far as these and other dormant claims are concerned, Chiang and Mao see eye to eye.

Nor would one discover significant differences of opinion between Taipei and Peking as to other peripheral areas in which Chinese hegemony should rightfully be asserted and dutifully and humbly acknowledged. Korea, Nepal, Bhutan, Sikkim, and Burma all fall within this category, as do several Asian states now questionably rejoicing in the status of "Soviet republics" or "autonomous regions."

No strong central government in Peking would view with complaisance either the progressive development of a powerful state—and particularly one which inclines to the West—based on the Indian subcontinent or the establishment in Southeast Asia of regimes both friendly to China's Number-One enemy, the United States, and willing to cooperate with her.

In the context of China's Asian goals, Japan presents a special case, one which must be handled with a degree of delicacy. Logically, it appears that Chinese diplomacy would be directed toward nurturing mutually beneficial relations in both the political and economic spheres. At the same time, Peking will use both overt and clandestine means to gain Japanese support for her Asian policies and to erode the American position in Japan.

Obviously, China cannot realize her ambitions in Asia unless she can gradually attain a position of power parity with the United States there. This is a necessary preliminary toward her ultimate goal of ejecting the United States from that part of the world. For years to come, however, she cannot achieve this limited capability even in local areas.

Moreover, her vociferous enmity toward the United States, her quarrel with the Soviet Union, and her intransigent attitude toward India combine to compromise her ambition to extend her influence in the Asian borderlands. Nevertheless, the inherent instability of the Southeast Asian countries and the small Himalayan states exercises a

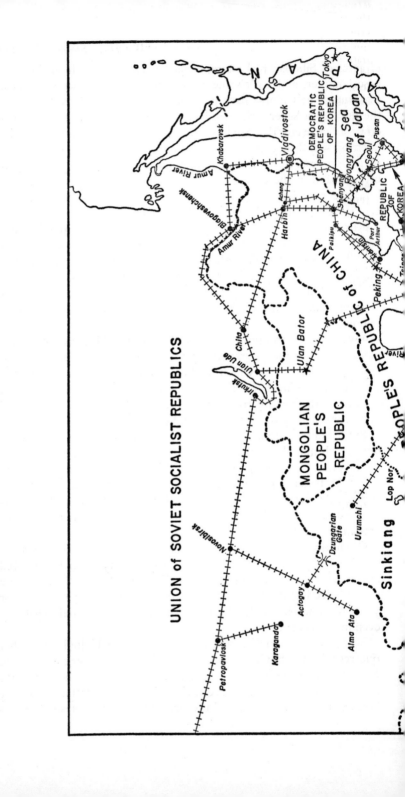

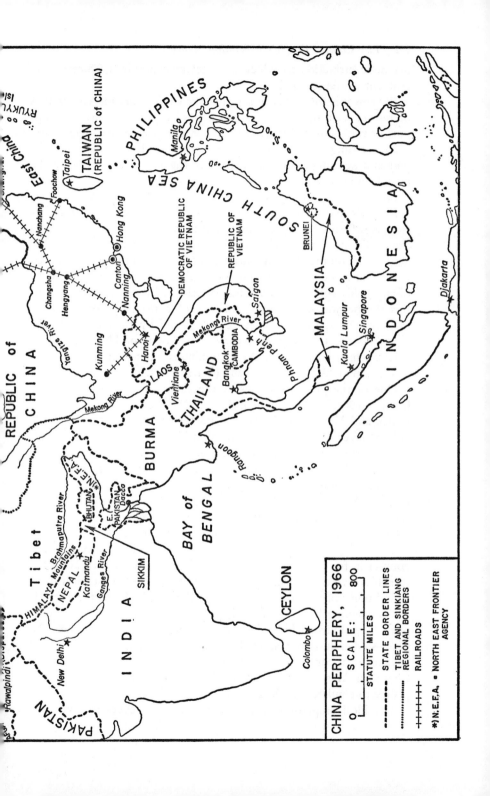

CHINA PERIPHERY, 1966

SCALE:

0   800

STATUTE MILES

- - - - - STATE BORDER LINES
············ TIBET AND SINKIANG REGIONAL BORDERS
+++++++ RAILROADS

*N.E.F.A. = NORTH EAST FRONTIER AGENCY

magnetic attraction to which any strong centralized Chinese government would respond.

Perhaps it is too much to say that the Chinese are more conscious of history than other peoples, but a good case can be made in support of the thesis. Whether true or not, the government over which Mao Tse-tung and his Party preside is mindful of China's imperial past and determined to regain for her the position of primacy she once held in Asia.

Peking's doctrinal pretensions, which first amused, then exasperated, and finally infuriated the Russians, derive at least in part from the traditional Chinese view of the world and their place in it. Mao may not sit on the Dragon Throne, but he lives in the golden-roofed palaces once occupied by those who did, a fact not calculated to diminish his egocentricity. The accession of dynastic emperors to this throne was confirmed by virtue of a mandate conferred by Heaven, and the emperors were recognized by their Chinese subjects and the tributary peoples alike as "Sons of Heaven." Their edicts, which concluded with the ominous injunction "tremble and obey," ran in "All under Heaven" (*T'ien Hsia*).

One of the principal duties of the Emperor was to nurture the harmonious relationship which should ideally exist between Heaven, Earth, and Man. (The Chinese character *wang*, which means "ruler" or "sovereign," depicts this relationship graphically. The character is formed of three horizontal strokes ≡, depicting Heaven, Earth, and Man, connected by a vertical stroke, 王 to signify the essential link: the Emperor.) The Chinese have always realized that this happy state of affairs was best achieved by moral suasion rather than by coercion. The ruler and the elite set an example which lesser men were dutifully expected to follow.

This attitude is very much alive in Chinese society today. We encounter it, for example, in the PLA, where ceaseless efforts are made to achieve vertical harmony within the ranks and to establish horizontal unity of the armed forces with the people. Here, the Party is the connecting link. The PLA is presented to the people as a model of dedicated virtue: loyal, industrious, frugal, and self-denying. The good soldier lusts not after the pleasures of the flesh, professional advancement, or material gain. His sole desire should be to serve Chairman Mao and the Party. The Party ceaselessly exhorts the people to emulate the Chairman's "good soldiers."

The ideal emperor emanated beneficent influences to "the four quarters," to "darkened countries," and "unenlightened peoples" who did not enjoy the manifold benefits of Chinese culture. The Chairman's "glorious thought," so we are constantly informed, has similar transcendent qualities. Traditionally, it was held that these imperial radiations were sufficiently persuasive to cause "barbarians" to submit of their own volition, "to come and be transformed" (*lai hua*), and we should not be surprised that the transformation of man's nature is a very important part of the Chinese Communist ecclesiastical rubric.

Some, who perversely preferred their own way of life, remained oblivious to these benign influences. It then became the obligation of a virtuous ruler to correct such wayward attitudes. This could be—and frequently was—accomplished by bribery, by an engineered palace coup, or by threat of "military persuasion." Those who persisted in their recalcitrant ways qualified for merited and "righteous" chastisement. No opprobrium attached to a sovereign who conducted a "moral" war to further China's civilizing mission. Thus, the concept of "just" war, albeit an aggressive one, is by no means a Maoist "enrichment" of the science of Marxism-Leninism.

The peculiar syndrome described in the West as "the cult of Mao" germinated during the latter years of the "Yenan era" and has been assiduously cultivated since. Efforts to identify "Great Chairman Mao" as the source of all benefits enjoyed by the people are unceasing. These, too, are in the tradition. Writing centuries ago on "The Threefold Obligations of the Ruler," Tung Chung-shu described the ruler as "the basis of the state":

In administering the state, nothing is more effective for educating the people than reverence for the basis. If the basis is revered then the ruler may transform the people as though by supernatural power, but if the basis is not revered then the ruler will have nothing by which to lead his people. Then though he employ harsh penalties and severe punishments the people will not follow him. This is to drive the state to ruin, and there is no greater disaster.[1]

Today, it is essential to display active "reverence for the basis": to study the "thought of Mao Tse-tung." To be conversant with the writings of Marx, Engels, Lenin, and Stalin is of course most desirable, but as these (according to several Party spokesmen) are somewhat "complex" and "complicated" and "not always easy to understand," familiarity with Mao's thought becomes obligatory.

The Party beatifies those who dedicate themselves to studying

Mao, serving Mao, and obeying Mao; for the past several years, Communist hagiographers have been absorbed in the sanctification of model soldiers. There was, for instance, Lei Feng, a lowly member of the PLA who was killed in a vehicle accident. Lei Feng, so we are told, studied the thoughts of "Great Chairman Mao" from morning till night. Indeed, he frequently deprived himself of both food and sleep to peruse the sacred books. Lei Feng had no ambition other than to be a submissive tool of Mao Tse-tung and of the Party. He gave all his money to worthy causes; after his untimely demise, cadres discovered that his estate consisted only of a dog-eared, annotated copy of *The Selected Writings of Mao Tse-tung*. Lei Feng was never tempted by "sugar-coated bullets," he was celibate, humble, studious, submissive, industrious, and frugal. He helped those who needed help, but not—as Party biographers take care to explain—because he was motivated by "bourgeois sentimentality." Lei Feng was not impelled to perform his countless worthy deeds by any sense of tenderness, humanity, compassion, or common decency. On the contrary: Lei Feng acted because he was politically motivated.

According to the authorized biography, Lei Feng's poor peasant family had "eaten bitterness" under the Nationalists and sustained indescribable humiliations inflicted by the "imperialists." In the PLA, he learned to read and for the first time to appreciate the "sweetness" of the new life brought by Chairman Mao and the Party. In the process, he learned that "individualism" constitutes a mortal sin. This revelation impelled him to devote all his energies toward learning how to sublimate human instincts and to submerge himself utterly in "collective life." If Lei Fengs do not exist, the Party can and does invent them.

The Party's determination to transform the Chinese people into a nation of Lei Fengs reflects the traditional concept that the proper function of the masses is to serve their masters with unquestioning loyalty and unflagging zeal. In this endeavor as in others, the Party will apply received values selectively to further its purposes. In sum, where tradition is found to be a useful tool, it will be used; where inapplicable, it will be either rejected or warped to serve the Party's requirements.

Many Westerners find it difficult to conceive that the Chinese Communists are really serious when they announce, as they have repeatedly and stridently, their intention to destroy the existing world order and to replace it with one designed and handicrafted in Peking. Accordingly, the verbose and bellicose speeches of Chinese Party leaders are often described as essentially harmless manifestations of a growing frustration deriving from their impotence to influence events on the international stage. Others hold that Peking would begin to behave in a more civilized manner if she were brought into the United Nations, invited to participate in "summit" conferences, recognized by the United States, enabled to trade freely in world markets, and so on. Still others perhaps more realistically attribute Chinese virulence to the need for an external "hate object" to maintain revolutionary fervor and justify repressive policies on the home front.

Undoubtedly, native arrogance, traditional chauvinism and xenophobia, a frustrated impotence which appears to have reached the psychotic stage, and domestic tensions all contribute to the CCP's syndrome. But the messianic motivation to remold the world in a Maoist image provides a primary urge. Only thirty years ago, complacent Europeans described the announced intentions of a strutting rabble rouser—who made no secret of his grandiose schemes—as "lunatic," "preposterous," "ridiculous," and "mad." The world has not yet recovered.

In his *Nuclear Weapons and Foreign Policy*, Henry L. Kissinger examines what he describes as "this strange phenomenon":

Time and again states appear which boldly proclaim that their purpose is to destroy the existing structure and recast it completely. And time and again the powers that are the declared victims stand by indifferent or inactive, while the balance of power is overturned. Indeed, they tend to explain away the efforts of the revolutionary power to upset the equilibrium as the expression of limited aims or specific grievances until they discover—sometimes too late and always at excessive cost—that the revolutionary power was perfectly sincere all along, that its call for a new order expressed its real aspirations.[2]

Mao has repeatedly called upon the people of the whole world to "unite to defeat the U.S. aggressors and all their running dogs." Several years ago, for example, the Chairman exhorted his world-wide audience to "be courageous, dare to fight, defy difficulties, and advance wave upon wave. Then the whole world will belong to the people. Monsters of all kinds shall be destroyed."[3]

In December 1964, Chou En-lai issued a declaration of war couched in more explicit terms than his master's. In his report to the Third National People's Congress, the Premier described the United

States as "the most arrogant aggressor ever known in history, the most ferocious enemy of world peace, and the main prop of all the forces of reaction in the world" and urged the people of the world to "direct the sharp edge of their struggle against U.S. imperialism." [4] The Premier promised nebulous Chinese support for the world-wide anti-U.S. crusade he clearly implied would be directed from Peking, whose "international prestige has been enhanced" as her "revolutionary influence has become wider."

Several months after Chou raised "the militant banner of struggle against U.S. imperialism," Lo Jui-ch'ing, former chief of the PLA's General Staff Department, declared that since the end of World War II, "two great historical currents, the socialist revolution and the national liberation movement," had merged. [5] The merger, he said, produced "a magnificent spectacle. . . . The four seas are raging, the five continents are rocking." This chaotic vista filled Lo with "boundless confidence in victory."

After consigning Khrushchev and other "revisionists" to history's dustbin, Comrade Lo turned on the United States, which since World War II had played "a role more ferocious than that of Hitler," and had become "the sworn enemy of the people of the world." He then restated the Chinese thesis on the inevitability of war:

The danger of war exists as long as imperialism exists. Until imperialism is eliminated, and socialism has won victory throughout the world the victory of socialism in one or a number of countries cannot be regarded as final.

In adjuring the socialist countries to heighten their vigilance and continue their preparations for inevitable violent struggle, Lo warned that the "wars of aggression" precipitated by the imperialists might be "small scale," "medium," or "large scale." In any of these, he said, the enemy might use nuclear, as well as conventional, weapons.

Lo assured his audience that nuclear weapons are of no practical use in "small-scale" and "medium" wars. They are myths "used to intimidate the revolutionary people; to disarm the targets of their aggression morally." But they are not "decisive":

Victory in war does not depend on new weapons of one kind or another, or on a particular technical arm. It depends on the close integration of the armed forces and the civilian masses, the joint effort of the people at the front and in the rear, the coordination of the battlefield at the front and the battlefield in the enemy rear, and close cooperation among the different armed services of which the ground forces, and particularly the infantry, are primary.

Without heroic fighting by the ground forces, no new weapons, however powerful, can determine the outcome of battles or achieve the political aim of a war. This is another law or truth governing war.

Hitler's fate, Lo went on, testified to the "objective truth" of this theory. Stalin, he said, had compensated for initial weapons inferiority by the brilliant strategy of trading space for time. Lo did not bother to explain the irrelevance of space-time strategy to a conflict in which, in just a few minutes, nuclear weapons could destroy the fabric of an entire society, create contaminated deserts where major cities had stood only an hour before, and render impossible "close integration of the armed forces" with demoralized civilian masses.

It is impossible to say whether the Chinese leadership really believes that the pattern of a future major war would duplicate that of World War II as it was fought in the Soviet Union and in China or whether this line is consistently emphasized primarily for domestic consumption. Whatever the reason, the constant derogation of nuclear weapons has produced in the West a feeling the Chinese do not appreciate their destructive power and, when they acquire a modest inventory, may be tempted to embark on adventures. This seems to have been one of the factors which motivated Khrushchev first to deny China a prototype bomb and soon thereafter to terminate Soviet aid to Peking.

Chinese doctrine has fairly recently begun to project a "zonal" picture of the world. Between the two "camps" of socialism and imperialism, the Chinese posit two "intermediate zones." The first of these is Asia, Africa, and Latin America; the second includes Western Europe, Oceania, Canada, and "other capitalist countries." (Presumably, "Oceania" includes the Philippines, Australia, and New Zealand.) It is in the "first intermediate zone"—"the storm centers of world revolution"—that the Chinese propose to instigate, nurture, and support by what means they can revolutions and "wars of liberation" and thus neutralize the nuclear superiority of the "imperialists."

In the opus cited above, Lo Jui-ch'ing advanced the theory, later to be elaborated in more specific terms by Lin Piao, that socialist countries should serve as "base areas" for these activities and should act as the "main force in combating imperialist aggression." He anathematized "socialist countries" which did not "dare" to aid "people's revolutions in other countries." China, at least, would "dare"; China, he promised, would support revolutionary struggles everywhere—morally, politically, and materially to the limit of her capabilities.

Specifically, China was prepared to send her men to fight in Vietnam. China would continue to support the Vietnamese people whether or not the United States "enlarged" the war. The Chinese people, Lo proclaimed, were not afraid of such threats. Finally, Lo announced that the Chinese would not attack unless first attacked but promised that China and the PLA were "fully prepared for war" and would respond to a U.S. attack "on the same scale."

Apparently, the Politburo devoted June, July, and August 1965 to assessment of the "balance of forces" and reached the conclusion that the United States, "in danger of being swamped in Vietnam," was "deeply worried" and had no recourse but to escalate the war there. The U.S. decision to bomb military targets in the north required Peking to respond with words if not deeds, and on September 2, 1965, the New China News Agency released the text of a 20,000-word article entitled "Long Live the Victory of the People's War." [6]

This inflammatory essay, ascribed to Minister of Defense Lin Piao, must be presumed to reflect Mao Tse-tung's views with authority and accuracy. After habitual obeisances to the leading role played by the Chairman's thought, Comrade Lin developed the thesis that people's revolutionary wars and national liberation movements on the Chinese model are the most suitable weapons to apply against "U.S. imperialism" and its "lackeys."

Mao's theories of uniting all forces that can be united—primarily by promoting the spirit of nationalism, mobilizing the masses, and conducting protracted war from secure base areas—were once again elaborated. The Party's revolutionary experience in China, Lin asserted, validated Mao's concept of people's war, which has universal application and constitutes "a great contribution to the revolutionary struggles of the oppressed nations and peoples throughout the world."

In the global context, Lin Piao compared North America and Western Europe to cities and Asia, Africa, and Latin America to rural areas. It is these rural areas which, he said, must encircle the cities precisely as the Chinese Communists, from their bases in the countryside, encircled the points held by the Japanese.

China stands ready, the Minister promised, to "firmly" support and "actively" aid any and all such struggles: "It has been so in the past, it remains so in the present and, when we grow in strength as time goes on, we will give them still more support and aid in the future." But, Lin added, the struggles of the revolutionary peoples must be essentially "self-reliant." (This cautionary note, although not particularly emphasized, tends to detract somewhat from the effect of the Minister's broadside. In fact, despite its generous but nebulous promises of "help" to practically any group dedicated to following an anti-U.S. policy, Lin's article leaves the over-all impression that China is frantically searching for any means to establish her position as a power to be reckoned with.)

The rationale of this strategy appeals to the Chinese for a number of reasons. First, it is a reversion to the traditional method of "using barbarians to control barbarians." Second, it promises disproportionate returns for small investments. From a situation of sustained international turmoil in which she invests little, Peking sees herself certain to collect a lucrative political dividend. At the very least, she would, so she may reason, be in a position to mediate and to demand a fee for doing so. Third, as Lin Piao points out, these wars, by draining American power, will in the long term produce a profound effect on the balance of forces. Finally, a prolonged condition of tension increases the chances that the "imperialists" and the "modern revisionists" will destroy each other. In sum, China conceives this indirect strategy to be the safest, cheapest, and most rewarding method consistent with Mao Tse-tung's first principle of war: "Preserve one's self; destroy the enemy."

Nature and geography have endowed China with the essential attributes of world power: a vast continental expanse; a varied climate; adequate if not abundant natural resources, a homogeneous culture; and an intelligent, industrious, and amenable population. An authoritarian government avid for power, and possessed of what its leadership is convinced is an infallible doctrine for attaining it, is dedicated to the proposition that China must and will assume her "rightful" position in the modern world.

But for some years at least a variety of constraints will operate to prevent the consummation of this ambition and to limit the strategic options available to Peking. (This statement presumes that the two major powers will continue to conceive that their national interests are best served by preservation of a peace, however uneasy, between themselves.) During this time, the Chinese will manage progressively to reduce the vulnerabilities which at present circumscribe their strategic horizons.

But certain incorrigible facts must be faced. Of these, the ratio of mouths to food supply is by all odds the most important. China's population, which by 1980 may reach almost 900 million, is not a source of strength, as the Party maintains, but a serious source of weakness. As the situation is now and for some time will remain, it is clear that a grossly disproportionate share of total national effort must be devoted entirely to providing this enormous population with the basic necessities of life. Given an estimated rate of increase of some 15 million a year, the Chinese are going to have to run very fast indeed to stay in the same place. In the past few years, the regime has been forced to commit hundreds of millions of dollars in scarce foreign exchange to purchase grain abroad, and in late October 1965 and again in 1966, negotiated contracts for deliveries of foreign cereals over a five-year period.

Chronic food shortages—which are likely to bedevil the Chinese economy for many years—thus set up a vicious circle, for in order to ameliorate them, the government must cut back other critical sectors of the economy. Only when we recall that the $403 million allocated in October 1965 to purchase Canadian wheat represents eight complete refineries and eight complete chemical fertilizer plants, or three or four good-sized hydro projects together with power distribution systems, or two major steel complexes, can we appreciate what effect this diversion of scarce funds produces on a primitive and struggling industrial economy.

This economy is now, and for at least a decade must remain, one of hard choices. The vaunted Chinese ability to deploy resources to critical sectors in accordance with Mao's "chessboard" theory will help relieve unanticipated pressures. But there remains the problem of capital accumulation. Barring massive aid from external sources—an unlikely prospect—this accumulation can only be hastened by "squeezing" the consumer, a ploy at which the Chinese are adept. The "squeeze" can be applied in a variety of ways or by a judicious combination of them. These would include such measures as strict control of consumer goods, imposition of heavier taxes, curtailment of mass purchasing power by control of salaries and wages, and forced subscription to low-interest-bearing government bonds. Of one thing we may be sure: the Chinese are determined to expand their industrial base as rapidly as possible and will take what measures they deem necessary to do so. For in the final analysis, China's position as an international power depends not on bombastic pronouncements from Peking but primarily on her success, or lack of it, in the drive to broaden her agricultural base and to industrialize.

However much the Party may publicly derogate modern weapons, it obviously intends to have them and to have, as well, a plant that will enable Peking to conduct warfare on the world's economic battle fronts.

According to Premier Chou En-lai's report to the Third National People's Congress, the Chinese economy during 1961–64 had been going through a "period of readjustment, consolidation, filling out and raising standards." [7] Reduced to plain language, this jargon meant that the economy was only gradually recovering from the disastrous effects of the Great Leap Forward and the "perfidious" withdrawal of Soviet aid and technical assistance. Chou's statement confirmed in general the observations of visitors to the mainland during the period.

But, the Premier said, "sound foundations for the future development of China's socialist construction" had been laid. Even as of mid-1966, however, the economy had not fully recovered from the recession of the early 1960s. For example, one unprejudiced Canadian traveler who visited China's largest motor-vehicle factory in 1965 estimated production at only 25,000 units a year and remarked that there seemed "great scope for improvement." The particular plant he visited had a rated capacity of 100,000 units a year. This report is particularly revealing because rapid development of the automotive and transportation system would normally be assigned a high priority—especially in China, which is not yet well endowed with an integrated rail net. Still, there seems little point in turning out motor vehicles if sufficient fuel is not available to insure their productive use and if the roads are as poorly maintained as the Minister of Transport has on occasion admitted they are.

The situation in the automotive transport industry prevails in general across the board. Although there has been some improvement in China's capacity to produce synthetics, textiles, refined fuels, and fertilizers, great gaps remain, as is clear from the lists of items with which the Chinese government from time to time provides prospective exhibitors and vendors. Principal among these requirements have been road-building equipment; machine tools of all types; mining and drilling equipment; special steels; electric motors; generators, transformers, and allied apparatus.

The fact that the People's Republic exploded a nuclear device in late 1964, another in May 1965, and three in 1966 should not lead to the fallacious conclusion that her progress in this field is representative. In many important areas—particularly in aircraft, chemicals, electronics, and computer technology, China lags far behind the West—so far, indeed, that Vice-Premier and Foreign Minister Ch'en Yi observed in September 1965 that it would take her "thirty to fifty years" to catch up.[8]

What priorities she proposes to accord modernization of her armed forces is debatable. Certain statements made by prominent spokesmen suggest that she will proceed relatively slowly in this direction. Modern weapons systems are expensive and difficult to design, and the construction of prototypes absorbs funds and scientific and engineering skills urgently needed elsewhere. The creation of a defense industry capable of mass production of a variety of modern aircraft, tanks, cross-country vehicles, artillery, prime movers, construction machinery, computers, anti-aircraft missiles, and electronic control equipment will be beyond China's capabilities for some time unless she is willing to forego more basic requirements.

Thus, while it would be imprudent to presume that the unsatisfactory equipment situation reflected in the 1961 *Bulletin of Activities*[9] still prevails in the PLA, we may doubt that major shortages indicated in these papers have been rectified to any significant degree. Until they can be, possibly in a decade, the obvious imbalance in PLA force structure cannot be corrected, and the PLA must remain what it is today: essentially an infantry force equipped primarily for close combat, with a relatively small number of elite formations such as mountain troops and parachutists capable of performing limited missions in particular environments in the contexts of special situations.

No one doubts any longer that China has "stood up," and even if she does not yet stand very tall when measured in terms of world power, she casts menacing shadows. In 1962, with an arrogant insouciance, she humiliated and chastised India. She publicly taunts and insults her erstwhile "elder brother," the Soviet Union. She conducts a vicious and unrelenting world-wide propaganda campaign against a second great power, the United States. She constantly asserts, and usually in offensive language, her determination to assume her "rightful place" in the world and in the process to overthrow the established order and replace it with one conceived by Mao Tse-tung. She is making every effort to create in the underdeveloped countries of Africa, Asia, and Latin America an image of revolutionary invincibility, confirmed by what she asserts is an unchallengeable doctrine of which she is the exclusive custodian. She is publicly dedicated to the extirpation of the American presence and liquidation of American "imperialist" influence in these areas. Nor are "modern revisionists" to be welcomed there. We, the Russians, and other countries distant from China may not feel immediately threatened, but to her weaker Asian neighbors—not excluding Japan—she is something more than a "bean-curd tiger."

For the foreseeable future, however, China will probably pursue an indirect strategy consistent with her power position vis-à-vis both the United States and the U.S.S.R. Although Peking's language will continue to be provocative, her actions will be dictated by a prudent appreciation of her vulnerability.

CHAPTER TWELVE

The Martial Tradition in People's China

The Korean War conclusively destroyed the myth that the Chinese were deficient in the martial qualities elsewhere deemed virtues. In the West it had been generally believed for many years that the Chinese were inherently a pacific people who detested war, and who either could not, or would not, fight. Chinese generals were represented as incompetent and venal nepotists who smoked opium, carried parasols, padded the payrolls, and won their battles with "silver bullets." In the Western press, the peasant soldier fared no better than his commanders.

There was just enough truth in this superficial characterization to mislead American intelligence officers whose duties in the fall of 1950 required them to assess Chinese combat capabilities. Their mistaken judgments, soon rectified by harsh experience, were to some extent excusable, for they appeared to be confirmed by Chinese history.

During the many centuries when Confucian thought dictated the distinctive values of their civilization, the Chinese habitually displayed a curiously ambivalent attitude toward the warrior. While their literature—particularly the classical drama—perpetuated the exploits of martial heroes of antiquity, the people at the same time consistently repudiated the professional soldier and denied him a respectable position in contemporary society. In the social hierarchy, he ranked fifth, below the scholar, the farmer, the artisan, and the merchant, all of whom held him and his vocation in contempt. "Good iron," they said, "is not wrought into nails, good men do not become soldiers."

In the catalogue of unavoidable natural calamities, that inflicted upon the people by cruel generals and their rapacious retainers was more to be feared than the droughts, floods, and plagues of locusts which periodically ravaged the countryside. (These were the four *tsai*—the catastrophic visitations of elemental forces which the peasants were born to suffer, and from which there was no escape.) The pacific philosopher Lao Tzu had said: "Where soldiers are, there thorns and brambles grow." Through long centuries the Chinese people had ample opportunity to confirm the truth of this laconic observation.

The Confucian scholars who administered the empire considered war a calamity:

The very necessity of war was proof of inferior virtue in the Son of Heaven, for Confucians had always contended that a truly virtuous prince would have no enemies. The force of his moral qualities would in itself suffice to keep peace within the Empire and pacify the barbarous peoples beyond the frontiers. Rebellion was an indication of bad government, and foreign wars a confirming of inferior virtue.[1]

The peasants feared and hated the soldiery; the intellectuals—the *literati* indoctrinated with Confucian precepts—scorned and despised them as members of the lower orders. In the administrative and social hierarchies of the dynastic state, the soldier's place was with the menials and the slaves:

When the nation was at peace, if a military man who had risen to a high command called upon a civil official, even though the latter was greatly inferior to him in rank, he had to wear the traditional uniform, with a sword hanging at his left side, a bow and quiver at his right, and with warrior's cap, trousers, and boots on. When he entered the hall to make obeisance, he had to identify himself on a calling card as "Your Honor's Running Dog." And when he withdrew, he had to go along with the civil official's slaves or servants.[2]

While this low status may seem to carry subordination of the military to their civilian masters to a degree undesirable in a contemporary democracy, it was not so considered in China during the Ming dynasty. And with reason, as Huang Tsung-hsi, a critic who in 1663 wrote *A Plan for the Prince*, makes abundantly clear. Describing the Imperial Army, which in 1644 abandoned Peking in panic at the approach of the rebel bandit Li Tzu-ch'eng, Huang wrote that its commanders and officers were of inferior caliber: "mere upstarts, who had not in the past dared to strike a blow against the enemy." When the crisis arrived, "they rode with the tide, changing flags and using their sharp swords on nothing but the carcasses of the helpless."[3] He described these generals as "brutish rascals who profit from the world's misfortunes and pervert the natural order."[4]

Huang's solution to the perennial problem of civilian-military relationship finds contemporary echo. Huang wrote:

If the soldier and scholar are brought together in one profession, the scholar would realize that military classics and battle tactics do not lie outside his province; studying them, he would learn that they are not completely impractical subjects. The military man would learn that loyalty to the throne and love of the people are not to be mistaken for ability. If this is done, all men would be revolt-proof.[5]

Almost three hundred years were to pass before a dynasty capable of creating a "revolt-proof" army appeared on the historical scene. In the meantime, the quality both of the military art and of its practitioners continued steadily to deteriorate. During the last decade of the nineteenth century, some efforts were made to reform the army. But even then, officers were generally selected for no better reasons than that they were related to noblemen, bureaucrats, or wealthy landowners, or were accomplished horsemen, expert archers, and physically imposing. These young men, usually semi-literate wastrels, were motivated to serve not by "loyalty to the throne" or "love of the people" but by the prospects of personal gain which an army career promised.

The soldiers they commanded were no better: peasants conscripted at sword's point; vagrants and riffraff; escaped criminals and ex-bandits who sought anonymity, an unbreakable rice bowl, and a chance to rape and rob at will. The concept of sacrifice expressed in the maxim *Dulce et decorum est pro patria mori* inspired Roman citizen-soldiers to perform prodigies of valor in battle. But this idea would have struck a Chinese peasant reluctantly impressed into military service as utterly impractical, if not indeed idiotic. When such sacrifice was demanded, armies had a remarkable tendency to melt away. Generals and their undisciplined soldiers were then, as during the warlord period of this century, commodities which could be bought and sold.

The generation of foreigners who lived in China during the twenty-five chaotic years from the downfall of the Ch'ing in 1912 to the beginning of the Anti-Japanese War in 1937 held the Chinese armies in contempt. The ragged soldiers were underfed, harshly treated, poorly disciplined; their officers, more often than not, were uneducated, brutal, and corrupt. Most foreigners were convinced that an under-strength battalion of Western troops could have disposed of a Chinese warlord division before breakfast.

In April 1931, Col. John Magruder, U.S. Army, who had served as military attaché in Peking, wrote in *Foreign Affairs* of the Chinese as a fighting man. In this analysis, Magruder observed:

A glance at Chinese history is proof of the characteristic flavor of Chinese pacifism. The early wars of China were practically all defensive, and passively defensive at that. The few aggressive wars filled in political vacuums created in neighboring countries by internal dissension. Those aggressions followed intrigues started by the Chinese and the military feature of the conquest consisted only of an expedition of occupation. *Such wars required no great military skill, and developed none. Thus the Chinese have no military history worthy of scientific study. The only military traditions which have grown up are those which surrounded legendary characters whose glory lay in miraculous performance rather than human martial accomplishment.*[6]

It is not my intent to contest Colonel Magruder's interpretation of the nature of China's many aggressions against her neighbors, but that he is demonstrably incorrect the Tibetans, Indians, Turki peoples of Central Asia, Indo-Chinese, Mongols, Burmese, and Koreans, are competent to testify. And since Colonel Magruder wrote, we have learned at great cost in blood and treasure that the Chinese *do* have a military history, literature, and traditions "worthy of scientific study."

China's martial tradition was born in remote antiquity and has been enriched during almost three thousand years of history. For hundreds of years before the philosopher Confucius appeared in the fifth century B.C., poets and musicians had celebrated the exploits of warrior-rulers and their generals in verse and song. Many examples are found in the ancient *Book of Odes*. Here one general is described as a "stalwart, martial man . . . a shield and wall . . . a head and heart to his prince"; another as "grandly martial and strong . . . an ornament of his country." [7] A wife bids her warrior husband farewell: he is "tranquil and serene"; his "virtuous fame spreading near and far." [8]

The "awe-inspiring" general Nan Chung assembles his army and leads it to subdue the barbarians. The scene is impressive: "How splendid his dragon, his tortoise and serpent flags." Chieh Fu, a great officer apt in both war and peace—"a pattern to all the states"— prepares an expedition to the distant borderlands, there "to achieve merit by his valor and martial exploits." [9] The next ode celebrates the arrival of Fang Shu, a commander both intelligent and true, whose majesty awes the enemy. His plans are "vigorous"; he exhorts the troops to "valorous deeds."

The swift, silent march of these ancient hosts is "inscrutable; invincible" (*pu ts'e; pu k'o*); their advance like water flowing. Led by its "tiger-like" officers, the army in orderly array is "firm as the mountains"; its march as "irresistible as the current of the mighty rivers" (*ju shan chih pao; ju ch'uan chih liu*).[10]

The period of the Warring States, which began in 453 B.C. and lasted until the founding of the Ch'in dynasty slightly more than two hundred years later, is particularly notable, not for the long-forgotten wars that regularly engulfed and desolated the entire country, but because it was an age of intellectual ferment. Itinerant philosophers, political advisers, and strategists traveled from court to court peddling advice to rulers ambitious to "roll up All-under-Heaven like a mat, and put the four seas in a bag." This was the age of Sun Tzu and Wu Ch'i, who composed essays on the art of war; of the famous strategist Sun Pin, whose covered baggage cart was the first mobile operations office in history, and of Han Hsin, whose troops, standing in defense, broke their pots and pans in sight of the enemy to indicate their determination to fight to the death.

The masters of the art of war were adept at espionage, subversion, and infiltration; they devised and practiced stratagems of every sort. They laid great store by surprise. "Go forth when the enemy does not expect you," Sun Tzu counseled. "Take him unaware." Had we studied the ancient Chinese masters with an assiduity equal to that of their apt pupils, the Japanese, we might have avoided the debacles at Pearl Harbor, at Savo, and in the Philippines.

During the later "Three Kingdoms" (A.D. 220–265), the Chinese developed generals who by any measure of skill and accomplishment were equals of their contemporaries in the Western world. Of Western commanders who flourished in the nine centuries after A.D. 100, only Belisarius deserves to be ranked with Ts'ao Ts'ao, Chu-ko Liang, or T'ai Tsung (A.D. 627–650), the great warrior emperor of the T'ang.

Of these, Ts'ao Ts'ao (A.D. 155–220), founder of the short-lived Wei dynasty, was the most celebrated. His name and martial achievements, perpetuated for centuries in the classical drama, are familiar to every Chinese. He was a master of mobile war; the incredible swiftness of his moves is best illustrated by a common proverb: *Shuo Ts'ao Ts'ao, Ts'ao Ts'ao chiu lai* (As you say the name of Ts'ao Ts'ao, Ts'ao Ts'ao is upon you). The *Wei Dynastic History* describes this "Renaissance Man" in the following biography, which, even when allowance is made for exaggeration, depicts clearly the amazing versatility of a cultivated warrior-ruler:

T'ai Tsu [Ts'ao Ts'ao], since he governed the whole empire, mowed down numerous scoundrels. In his military operations, he followed in the main the tactics laid down in the Sun-tzu and Wu-tzu. In accordance with different situations, he took extraordinary stratagems; by deceiving the enemy, he won victory; he varied his tactics in demonic fashion. He himself wrote a book on war, consisting of a hundred thousand and several tens of thousands of characters, and when his generals undertook any campaign they all followed this new book. Furthermore, on each occasion he gave them personal directions; those who obeyed them won victory, and those who did not were defeated. In the face of the enemy on the battlefield, he remained unperturbed, as if he had no intention whatever of fighting; but seizing his opportunity, he would strike for victory in the highest spirits. This is why he always won victory whenever he fought, not a single instance of his successes being attributed to mere good luck.

He knew men well and was adept in judging them; it was difficult to dazzle him by false display. He picked YÜ CHIN and YÜEH CHIN out from the rank and file, and CHANG LIAO and HSÜ HUANG from among the surrendered forces; all of them became his supporters and achieved merit, becoming famous generals. Furthermore, the number of those whom he picked up from mean and insignificant positions, and who eventually rose to be governors of provinces and prefects, cannot be counted. It was thus that he laid the foundations of his great work.

He cultivated both the art of peace and the art of war: during the thirty-odd years when he commanded troops, books never left his hand. During the day he attended to military matters, during the night he applied his mind to the Classics and their commentaries. When he climbed a height, he would always compose verses. When he made new poems, he would set them to pipe and string, and they all turned out to be excellent songs. His talents and strength were unsurpassed; with his own hands he could shoot down flying birds and capture ferocious beasts alive. Once he shot down sixty-three pheasants in a single day at Nan-p'i. When palaces were constructed and machines repaired, he always laid down rules which proved to work to the utmost satisfaction.

By nature he was temperate and frugal, not given to pomp and adornment. Ladies of his harem did not wear any embroidered garments, his attendants did not have two pairs of footgear. When his coloured curtains and wind-screens were damaged, he had them patched; he had his bedding only for keeping warm, devoid of border ornament. All things of beauty and elegance which he obtained as booty from captured cities and towns, he would distribute among those who had shown merit. In acknowledging and rewarding services, he was not one to consider a thousand gold pieces too much; but to those without merit who sought to profit from his largess, he would not give a single cash. Gifts presented to him from the four quarters, he shared with his subordinates. He was of the opinion that the funeral service of the time was too extravagant and useless, the vulgar carrying it to excess; he therefore made a stipulation as to his own funeral, that no more than four basketfuls of clothing were to be buried with him.[11]

The mine of Chinese literature devoted to the art of war, to generalship, strategy, tactics, and techniques is almost inexhaustible. Many of the techniques are, of course, dated. But the theories of strategy and the doctrines of tactical combat developed by the ancient masters are in the main timeless, and on the whole as relevant to war in this age as when they were first conceived.

Although for centuries the Chinese have accorded Sun Tzu's *Art of War* pre-eminent position in their martial canon, he is by no means the only strategist whose works they esteem. As early as the eleventh century A.D., the Sung emperor Sheng-tsung (1068–85) designated seven "Martial Classics" as required study for all aspirants to commission in the army. These works, largely neglected during the alien Ch'ing dynasty (1644–1911), were rescued from temporary oblivion by Chiang Kai-shek when he became first commandant of Whampoa Military Academy in 1924. There, all cadets were required to study Sun Tzu, as they are today in the military schools of the People's Republic.

Sun Tzu saw war not as a transient aberration of society but as a constant factor in state relations. Because war was "the province of life and death, the road to survival or ruin," it was of vital importance to the state. "It is mandatory," he wrote, "that it be intensively investigated."

This ancient master considered morale of the people and of the army the basic factor in war and in his celebrated "Thirteen Chapters" repeatedly reverts to this point. He antedated Clausewitz by centuries in the view that war was a continuation of state policy by violent means. But these means were not to be employed unless all others had failed. To capture all intact, to attain one's aims without recourse to arms, was to him the acme of political skill. Violence was to be applied to deliver the coup to an enemy already defeated. Creation of a "victorious situation" was thus the first obligation of the ruler whose state was threatened by predatory neighbors. This situation was to be achieved by isolating the potential enemy through destroying his alliances; alienating his people from a hostile ruler; "driving wedges" between competing factions; subverting officials and sowing disagreement and dissension. It is obvious that these courses of action have continuing relevance to interstate relationships. And it will become apparent, in our survey of Chinese military doctrine, that contemporary leaders consider the strategic and tactical concepts expressed by Sun Tzu to be as valid today as when the Master first wrote them.

Of Sun Tzu's essays, B. H. Liddell Hart has observed: "[they] have never been surpassed in comprehensiveness and depth of understanding. They might well be termed the concentrated essence of wisdom on the conduct of war. Among all the military thinkers of the past, only Clausewitz is comparable, and even he is more dated than Sun Tzu, and in part antiquated, although he was writing more than two thousand years later. Sun Tzu has clearer vision, more profound insight, and eternal freshness." [12]

During recent years, the Chinese Communist Party has ransacked a vast literature in search of material suitable to encourage the bellicose attitudes which Chinese society had for centuries consistently rejected. Stories, essays, drama, poetry, opera, music, the dance must all reflect "struggle." Prerevolutionary works which do not, or which, even worse, tend to reflect favorably on "bourgeois" or "feudal" attitudes, are of course banned. Some of the classical dramas have been rewritten and redesigned to provide the desired content. Art in all forms is expected to be purposely militant and revolutionary.[13]

The martial quality of *Shui Hu Chuan* (*Water Margins*—translated by Pearl Buck as *All Men Are Brothers*) explains its particular appeal to Mao Tse-tung during his formative years. These fascinating stories relate the martial exploits of outlaw heroes who dedicated themselves to aiding the peasants of medieval China in the perennial struggle against oppressive landlords and repressive governments. Another of Mao's early favorites was *The History of the Three Kingdoms* (*San Kuo Chih*). From this absorbing account of Ts'ao Ts'ao's campaigns against the generals of the kingdoms of Wu and Shu (where Chu-ko Liang was prime minister and commander in chief), Mao painlessly assimilated a sound fundamental education in the arts of generalship and strategy and the science of tactics.

These and other heroic tales are widely circulated today in cheap paperback editions, as well as in colorfully illustrated booklets designed to appeal specifically to children. Great warriors of antiquity, including Wu Ch'i, Sun Pin, Han Hsin, Chu-ko Liang, Liu Pei, and Li Ching have been restored to deserved positions in

China's military pantheon. With many lesser figures, they have lived excitingly for centuries in the popular drama known as "Peking opera."

Ever since the trying days on Chingkangshan, the Party has also made consistent efforts to encourage the drama as a revolutionary art form; and as the Red Army began to create a martial tradition of its own, young writers cast the stories of its "heroes" and "martyrs" into simple plays. These dramas, specifically designed to win support for the Party and its army, were primitive and tendentious. But they got the Party's messages to illiterate peasant audiences.

One of the first groups to take the new plays to the people was the Workers and Peasants Dramatic Society, formed in Juichin, Kiangsi province, in 1932. Its leader, Ts'ao Ping-san, later recounted his history to the American correspondent, Nym Wales:

> I stayed in Kiangsi . . . after the army had left on the Long March. We divided into three mobile sections: The Red Bell Players (the name meaning to awaken the people . . .); the Five Star Players (meaning the sign of the revolution); and the Trumpet Players (meaning the call to arms). We were ordered by the Party to do this work to keep up popular morale. Dramatics had an important influence in Kiangsi—the Society took its plays to the villages with spectacular success.[14]

Old plays were also adapted, with music retained but content changed. These, another director informed Miss Wales, made "effective propaganda." [15]

On May 23, 1942, Mao Tse-tung delivered the concluding address to a forum of artists and writers in Yenan. In this discourse, he elaborated the policy which has governed the development of "revolutionary art and literature" in the People's Republic ever since the Party took power.[16] Several weeks earlier, at the opening of the forum, the Chairman had made it unmistakably clear to the assembled members of the "cultural army" that they were expected to "adopt the standpoint of the Party and adhere to Party spirit and Party policies." But he now cautioned them that in doing so they were not to jettison the rich legacy of the past. This legacy was to be "remoulded and filled with new content." [17]

Now, the content is explicitly revolutionary, militant, and habitually anti-American.[18] Both the contemporary drama and the rapidly expanding motion-picture industry are exclusively devoted to producing "effective propaganda" designed to further regiment and martialize Chinese society. This is even the function of poetry in the People's Republic.

Chairman Mao is certainly the most widely read Chinese poet. The Chairman is addicted to martial verse; his poetry is elliptical, vigorous, and replete with martial symbols and allusions. Mao sees the wind whipping the army's "scarlet banners" and unfurling its "crimson flags"; he hears the ringing of horses' hoofs, the clear notes of distant bugles, the rolling of drums. He sees "a thousand stallions rearing and plunging in the thick of battle"; "a forest of rifles." The "matchless troops" and their "flying generals" will "at one step" cross over a pass "defended with iron." Mountains, snows, icy winds, wide rivers challenge the army. But it will conquer all hazards. Mao speaks of the "unnumbered heroes" of the past; "the great emperors of Ch'in and Han . . . T'ang and Sung"; "the prodigious Genghis Khan." The Chairman may not rank with the great poets of the T'ang—the "golden age" of poetry in China—but his martial poems in praise of the "heroic Red Army" are evocative and powerful.[19]

Party literary hacks are now busily engaged in the fantastic industry of "hero production," for it is the principal function of "comrade writers" to produce "more wholesome, brilliant, and even greater heroes."[20] The authors have had considerable practice. Reams of poems have been written extolling the virtues of Communist fighters and martyrs who faced Chiang Kai-shek in the "Bandit Extermination" campaigns, undertook the Long March, triumphed in the civil war, "liberated" the "exploited" Tibetans, defeated the American "aggressors" in Korea, and successfully "defended" Chinese soil against Indian encroachment. The crop generated by the alleged deeds of the "People's Volunteers" in the Korean War would fill several bookshelves. Few, if any, of these outpourings have even the slightest artistic merit, but this is not the criterion.

The Party is well aware that tradition, whether handed down from antiquity or manufactured to order the day before yesterday, is a powerful spiritual cement.[21] The modern "hero industry" adds new characters: devoted cadres who sacrifice all for the Party and for Chairman Mao.[22] Tradition is thus manipulated or created to encourage a strident militarism, xenophobia, and chauvinism. When a messianic ideology is added to these, the inevitable result is the development of a bellicose national character and an aggressive national policy.

CHAPTER THIRTEEN

"The Gun": The People's Liberation Army

As in classical China the army was a ruler's "talons and teeth," so today the People's Liberation Army (*chieh fang chün*) is the Party's "gun." This gun has been the Party's indispensable tool; the Party's power, as Mao said in 1938, grew "out of the barrel of a gun."

> Our principle is that the Party commands the gun, and the gun will never be allowed to command the Party. But it is also true that with guns at our disposal we can really build up the Party organizations, and the Eighth Route Army has built up a powerful Party organization in North China. We can also rear cadres, create schools, culture and mass movements. Every thing in Yenan has been built up by means of the gun. Anything can grow out of the barrel of a gun. According to the Marxist theory of the state, the army is the chief component of the political power of a state. Whoever wants to seize the political power of the state and to maintain it must have a strong army.[1]

Article 20 of the Constitution of the People's Republic of China, ratified by the First National People's Congress on September 20, 1954, legally established the PLA as the "chief component" of state power. This article states that the armed forces "belong to the people" and that their mission is "to safeguard the gains of the people's revolution and the achievements of national construction, and to defend the sovereignty, territorial integrity, and security of the country." [2]

Article 42 vests command of the armed forces in the Chairman of the People's Republic, who sits as the Chairman of the Council of National Defense (CND).[3] "In pursuance of decisions of the National People's Congress, or the Standing Committee of the National

People's Congress," the Chairman of the Republic is empowered to proclaim martial law, a state of war, and to order mobilization. The same article confers on him the prerogative of appointing and removing the vice-chairman and other members of the Council of National Defense.[4]

As will become apparent, the CND is not analogous to the National Security Council in the United States. The CND as now constituted is a body of 119 members. Of these, one (Liu Shao-ch'i) is chairman and 13 are vice-chairmen. Of these 13, nine are former marshals and senior generals of the PLA and four are ex-Nationalist generals.[5] The cast of characters is familiar enough: Lin Piao, Liu Po-ch'eng, Ch'en Yi, Ho Lung, Teng Hsiao-p'ing, Hsü Hsiang-ch'ien, Nieh Jung-chen, Yeh Chien-ying, and, until he was purged, Lo Jui-ch'ing. (As late as 1964, P'eng Teh-huai, dismissed as defense minister in 1959, was still carried as senior vice-chairman of the CND.) The former Nationalist generals, all once trusted friends and subordinates of Chiang Kai-shek, are Fu Tso-yi, Ch'eng Ch'ien, Wei Li-huang, and Chang Chih-chung.

It is difficult to conceive that a body of this size could be other than unwieldy or that it could act quickly and decisively on matters of vital importance to the state. The functons of the Council are not defined in the Constitution, and available copies of the authoritative *Bulletin of Activities* issued by the General Political Department, Headquarters, PLA, never mention it. The press does so rarely, and then usually only to report that its members assembled "to hear a speech" or that several of them had welcomed distinguished military visitors from Cambodia, North Korea, or a friendly African state. Although it may have minor coordinative functions, the CND seems primarily to be another governmental façade and a device to provide prestige and official perquisites to senior military officers and Party hierarchs who have "established merit." If the aging ex-marshals and generals are no longer particularly useful, they are no doubt ornamental—or were, until a 1965 edict deprived officers of distinctive uniforms, caps, and insignia of rank.[6]

Article 31 of the Constitution assigns a number of functions and powers to the Standing Committee of the National People's Congress. Several of these relate specifically to national defense. For instance, when the NPC is not in session—which is most of the time—its Standing Committee can remove from office any minister, can proclaim "a state of war in the event of armed attack on the country or in fulfillment of international treaty obligations concerning common defense against aggression, "and can decide on general or partial mobilization. This committee consists of a chairman (Chu Teh), fourteen vice-chairmen, a secretary-general (at this writing still formally P'eng Chen despite his fall from official grace), and 62 other members. (Again we encounter many familiar names.) Aside from its power to remove the minister of defense, the NPC Standing Committee has apparently no constitutional authority to develop or deal with military policy.

There is still another major governmental organ which ostensibly has a finger in the defense pie. This is the State Council, chaired by Premier Chou En-lai. Articles 47, 48, and 49 of the Constitution describe the State Council as "the executive organ of the highest state authority." As such, its responsibility is "to guide the building up of the defense forces." [7] This body has a membership of about 55, including 16 vice-premiers, a secretary-general, and an assortment of ministers and chairmen of commissions. The Ministry of National Defense is one of a number of ministries and commissions organizationally subordinate to the State Council. The Constitution does not define the relationship between the State Council and these subordinate organs, nor does it delineate either their responsibilities or their authority.

But in Communist states, substantive power does not inhere to the bureaucracies established by their constitutions, and thus there was for some time considerable uncertainty as to just where the locus of power in matters military was to be found in the People's Republic. The *Bulletin of Activities* resolved this problem. Substantive power resides in the Military Affairs Committee (MAC), the organ of the Central Committee and its Politburo (the "Central Authorities") which deals with military policy. The MAC, routinely chaired by Lin Piao, generates policy directives affecting the armed forces on all but the most sensitive and important matters, which are handled by the Politburo and its Standing Committee. Mao, who is chairman of the MAC, is kept currently informed of its deliberations and reads and occasionally comments on its papers.

This offspring of the Revolutionary Military Council of guerrilla and civil war days is undoubtedly the smallest and most exclusive military club in the world. Only top members of the Party's hierarchy assemble at the call of "Chief" Lin. No precise information is available as to MAC membership, the membership of its Standing Committee, or to its defined functions. The *Bulletin* shows that the MAC's interests in the armed forces are indeed catholic and not confined (as one might hastily conclude) strictly to ideological problems. These are, to be sure, one of the major concerns. But the entire spectrum of military affairs falls within its purview.

For example, the *Bulletin* reveals the Committee's lively interest in morale; training; equipment; officer procurement; professional and technical education; rations; dispersal of military installations; rectification, emulation, and other types of campaigns; health; the militia; the state of all-weather flying proficiency in the air force; relations of the army with the people; anti-aircraft defense; marksmanship; night marching; current standards attained by the PLA in its campaigns to raise cereals, hogs, chickens, and ducks; treatment of soldiers' families; literacy in the army; the unfortunate prevalence of superstition (soldiers afraid to lay communication wire near graveyards at night); the problem (which exists in all armies) of prevailing upon trained technicians to continue their military careers; the arrogant behavior of officers' wives; frugality; licentious liaisons of junior officers with women of questionable character; and the deplorable laxity in routine handling of classified material. Literally no aspect of life in the armed forces is immune from the searching attention of this vigilant and powerful Party committee.

When Lin Piao leaves a MAC meeting, he puts on another hat, that of minister of National Defense. In this capacity, he is the direct, day-to-day overseer of the PLA and, under the chairman of the People's Republic, commands its field forces. Nine Deputy Ministers assist him, and four department chiefs report to him. These are the chiefs of the General Staff Department (Yang Cheng-wu); the General Political Department (Hsiao Hua); the General Rear Services Department (Ch'iu Hui-tso), and the General Administrative Department (Hsiao Hsing-jung).[8] The commanders of the air force, navy, air defense command, armored force, artillery, military academy, engineers, signal, technical services, and railway troops have access to the Minister. (Leading personnel of the Ministry of Defense of the People's Republic are listed in Appendix B.)

"Chief" Lin, his deputies, and the heads of the staff departments command and administer the PLA through 13 regional headquarters. Of these, three strategically critical border areas—Sinkiang, Tibet, and Inner Mongolia—are designated "Direct Control Military Regions." The other 10, which are further subdivided into 22 provincial districts and sub-districts, presumably enjoy a greater degree of autonomy than do the "Direct Control Regions." Elements of the PLA appear to be assigned to the various regions on a semi-permanent basis. This system, compatible with the army's important production and construction missions, likewise tends to nurture that close relationship between the army and the people which is one of the Party's principal objectives.

Regional headquarters are organized along the same pattern as is the Ministry in Peking, and close liaison is maintained between corresponding departments and sections of the staff. Similarly, commanders of the arms and services deal directly with their subordinates at regional level in matters of administrative and technical nature. Operational control, however, is centralized in the MND. It may be imagined that this system would inevitably produce conflicts of interest, as for example between the regional representatives of the GPD and the GSD in questions relating to allocation of time for political and military training. Apparently, these did develop frequently in the past, but such matters are now settled at MND level.

Generally, regional commanders command all PLA ground, naval, air, and Public Security units (which include Border Guards) assigned to their regions and are responsible for recruiting, organizing, arming, and training the People's Militia. The PLA is custodian of arms and ammunition allocated to the militia. Commanders render administrative support to specialized elements such as Air Defense, Railway, Airborne, and Amphibious troops training or operating in their geographical areas. They operate local military schools and training centers and handle induction and separation from the service. They are responsible for the maintenance of law and order and for apprehending "counterrevolutionary elements," "bandits," and enemy agents. On the whole, they appear to enjoy a considerable degree of local autonomy in routine matters.

But in the sphere of policy they are kept on a very tight rein, and there is no doubt they are carefully watched for incipient tendencies which might develop into dangerous regionalism. Members of the Politburo are not likely to forget Kao Kang's attempt to create a semi-independent satrapy in Manchuria between 1946 and 1953. Nor are either regional military or political commanders likely to forget his fate: in 1954, Kao Kang's "crimes" were discovered, and he was arrested, deprived of all his posts, expelled from the Party, and—so it was said—committed suicide.[9]

The dual command system is designed to check such developments. At the side of every regional commander stands a political commissar of equal rank. With him, and the Regional Party Committee, the regional commander must discuss every decision he desires to take and every order he wishes to issue. Should a deadlock be reached, the question is referred to the Ministry for decision. Only in three of the thirteen regions are the posts of military commander and commissar combined in one individual. These three—Foochow, Inner Mongolia, and Sinkiang—are strategically critical.

The armed forces of the Chinese People's Republic stand today at an over-all strength of some 2.3 million. The vast majority of men wearing the uniform of the PLA serve in infantry divisions. Estimates as to the number of these vary from a low of 105 to a high of about 120. If a figure of 110 be presumed, there are about 1.3 million men now serving in the infantry arm.

The personnel strength of the air force can perhaps best be estimated by using crewing levels as a measure. If we assume that 60/70 officers and men are required to crew one aircraft, we arrive at a figure (based on 2,500 combat aircraft) of 150,000 to 175,000.

The latest figure for naval strength—135,000—may be somewhat low. The navy supports a small air arm. Presumably, this component would be employed in short- and medium-range over-water reconnaissance and coastal mine laying. There is also a small landing force. From the Nationalists, the Communists inherited a heterogeneous collection of U.S. landing ships and craft.

In estimating the strength of specialized troops in the ground forces and in supporting arms and services, we are again in the cloudy realm of uncertainty and speculation. There are, we know, a small number on lightly-equipped mountain divisions at a manning level of 8,000 to 10,000, Border Guard formations, and People's Armed Police.

Well-equipped mountain troops demonstrated superior high-altitude abilities in October and November 1962 in India's North East Frontier Agency. The Chinese were appropriately armed, warmly clad, thoroughly acclimatized, moved rapidly, and executed demanding combat maneuvers with skill and precision.

The number of Security troops and People's Armed Police is believed to exceed 300,000. These are select troops and we must presume them well armed, mobile, loyal, and proficient.

In addition, the PLA has two or three cavalry divisions which are particularly useful in Northwest and West China, two or three airborne divisions, and some separate brigades and regiments. Some of these are probably specially trained in guerrilla operations.

The Chinese armies assigned to military regions equate roughly with a U.S. corps of three divisions. Each army is basically composed of headquarters military and political command and staff personnel; headquarters troops; reconnaissance, signal, security, transport, and engineer battalions, and three infantry divisions. The 1955 T/O for a PLA infantry division provided for a strength of 17,600. The established strength of the 1965 infantry division was about 10,000. Well balanced in terms of organic weapons, the division as yet lacks sufficient motor transport to assure strategic mobility. For motive power, the PLA's infantry must still rely on the legs of its tough soldiers. As marching standards are far more rigorous than in Western armies, shortage of motor transport is a matter of less concern. Still, despite their remarkable march capability, Chinese infantry formations would be at a grave disadvantage in rapidly moving situations in reasonably open terrain where cross-country mobility or tracked-vehicle task forces would greatly exceed theirs. On the other hand, in tropical jungles or mountainous country they could exploit proven cross-country march capability against a road-bound enemy.

Divisional organization is triangular, which permits ready formation of all-arms task groups appropriate to specific missions. The Chinese press has shown pictures of infantry-tank maneuvers supported by attack aircraft (and presumably artillery). There is no way to tell how frequently such maneuvers are held or how well they are executed. However, as in more than one issue of *The Bulletin of Activities* the authorities indicated marked concern with standards of technical proficiency (particularly in respect to armor, motor transport, and communication personnel), it is evident that as of 1961 at least, performance left much to be desired.

The PLA's Armored Command is small, but each of its four or five armored divisions is formidably equipped with 80 to 100 Soviet Model T-34 and T-54 tanks (or Chinese copies) plus a number of JS-2 heavies. The World War II T-34 (85-mm. gun) is still a combat-effective tank. The T-54, a well-designed, high-performance medium tank, mounts a high-velocity 100-mm. gun and has excellent cross-country capability. The JS-2, a 50-ton low-silhouette, wide-track tank, carries a 122-mm. high-velocity gun, is well armored, and has good cross-country performance. The assault gun company of the armored division is provided with four to six Soviet Model

SU-109 self-propelled assault guns. Separate tank regiments are equipped with the larger Soviet Model JSU-122 and JSU-152 self-propelled assault guns. These weapons are considered obsolescent in the West but are rugged and reliable.

The two-battalion infantry regiment organic to the armored division is transported by Soviet supplied six-wheel-drive armored personnel carriers. Tracked vehicles are also used for this purpose. A truck or tractor-drawn artillery regiment, engineers, and an anti-aircraft artillery battalion, together with security, maintenance, signal, and reconnaissance companies, complete the PLA armored division. As now organized, the division can break into two self-contained armored task groups to conduct independent operations or to reinforce an army or an infantry division. The Chinese have had no experience with armored warfare, and whether or not their communication techniques would permit efficient independent employment of armored formations is at least arguable.

Following the Soviet model, the PLA has organized separate Artillery, Anti-Aircraft Artillery (AAA), Anti-tank, and Cavalry divisions. The last are few in number and are stationed in Kansu, Mongolia, and Sinkiang, where remounts are easily had, where forage is plentiful, and where the terrain is suitable.

There are currently two distinct types of artillery division: gun and howitzer. The gun division comprises six battalions of direct support artillery, each equipped with 12 122-mm. guns, and three battalions of general support artillery, each equipped with 12 152-mm. guns. The howitzer division packs a tremendous high-explosive punch: 36 122-mm. howitzers; 36 152-mm. howitzers; 24 132-mm. rocket launchers, an AAA battalion (dual-purpose guns), and a heavy mortar regiment. One thing the Chinese learned from the Americans in Korea was that there is no substitute in battle for high-explosive firepower when combined with good artillery technique. By 1952, the Americans had discovered that the Chinese were apt pupils.

Problems of replacement and maintenance of this Soviet-supplied equipment plagued the PLA during 1960 and 1961. Whether or not Chinese industry can replace obsolescing tanks or even provide sufficient spare parts to keep what the PLA has in operable condition is a hard question to answer. The spare-parts problem can be solved, but only temporarily, by cannibalizing. To this the Chinese, who hate to destroy anything that could possibly be put to any conceivable use in an indeterminate future, would by nature be averse.

In 1961, the MAC directed the PLA to establish and operate its own spare parts program. This would work if facilities were central, properly organized and equipped, suitably manned, and directed by competent managerial and technical personnel, of whom there is a decided shortage. The spare parts problem cannot be solved by traditional handicraft methods and "back-yard" operations. The necessity to replace and maintain armor, self-propelled artillery, and other heavy and complicated equipment of Soviet origin will obviously put a very serious strain on Chinese industry, which must also simultaneously satisfy other equally important requirements.

It is now clear that six of the eight Ministries of Machine Building (Second to Seventh) are responsible for design and production of military matériel. The First and Eighth are apparently devoted to the heavy industrial sector. Liu Chieh, chief of the Second Ministry, has been associated with the nuclear program since 1956. Sun Chin-yuan, who heads the Third Ministry, is a former officer in the PLA. His specialty is not known, but it seems probable that his ministry is in charge of development and production of heavy infantry weapons. Wang Cheng, head of the Fourth Ministry, is an electronics expert. Ch'iu Ch'uang-ch'eng, who directs the Fifth Ministry, was a lieutenant general in the PLA and is an artillery specialist. Fang Chiang, at the Sixth Ministry, was formerly deputy commander of the navy. Wang Ping-chang, chief of the Seventh Ministry, is a former lieutenant general of the air force. A reasonable presumption is that Nieh Jung-chen, chairman of the Scientific and Technological Commission, is responsible for coordinating the activities of these armaments ministries.

One may conjecture that purchase abroad of heavy equipment such as locomotives, road machinery (one list of equipment wanted named excavators; rock crushers, small, medium, and heavy tractors; and bulldozers) is in part designed to release plant for the manufacture of armored vehicles, artillery, and military prime movers.

The PLA's Railway Corps is a distinctive organization charged with strategic railway construction in the People's Republic. Its responsibilities include engineering planning, technical services, construction of major bridges and tunnels, maintenance, and operation of repair facilities. Although Railway Corps personnel serve in the six Railway Engineering Bureaus under the Ministry of Railways, the corps' link with the Ministry is technical. Command is exercised through headquarters, PLA.

During the Korean War, the Railway Corps operated with great effect to ameliorate the logistic deficiencies resulting from the U.N. air interdiction campaign (STRANGLE). Only a very well-directed, highly organized, efficiently-controlled railway corps could have kept traffic moving through North Korea at the height of STRANGLE. American analysts frequently remarked on the ingenuity and industry with which bridges in North Korea were repaired and rebuilt or dropped spans replaced to receive nightly rail traffic. Underwater bridges were sometimes used. Elsewhere, bridging elements with rails laid were towed from camouflaged hiding places after dusk, installed, and towed again to their hidden shelters before the following dawn.

Between 1953 and 1962 the Railway Corps constructed a number of strategic links in the existing mainland system and built major extensions. Principal among the latter were:

1. The Lanchow-Urumchi (Sinkiang) line (more than 1,000 km.), designed to connect with a Russian-built line at Ala-Shankou. As far as is known, work ceased on the Chinese side in 1960; the line has not yet been driven west of Urumchi.
2. The south-north Tatung-Ulan Bator line (otherwise known as the Suiyuan-Mongolia line). The purpose of this particular line seems to be primarily military. Unlike the Sinkiang line, it does not open territories rich in mineral resources. The link was designed originally to provide a short, reasonably secure route from North and Central China to Central Siberia.

In 1960 the Railway Corps completed the Paotow–Lanchow line which links the two major strategic lines described above. Other strategic construction has been noted in South and Southwest China.

Although the chief of the Railway Corps has engineering and construction responsibilities, his branch is organized along military lines and appears to have devoted its major efforts to strategic building. In a war situation the Railway Corps would be assigned to operate and maintain the railways. Recent reports indicate that a number of Railway Corps units have been deployed to North Vietnam. Personnel employed there may aggregate 50,000. There are also credible rumors that the Railway Corps is now paralleling certain particularly vulnerable sections of the K'unming-Hanoi and Nanning–Hanoi lines. This branch of the PLA is experienced and extremely versatile and has coped with construction and rehabilitation emergencies in North Vietnam as expeditiously as previously in Korea.

The status of the PLA's Air Force is a major enigma at the present time. The air force General Hoyt Vandenberg described in 1952 as "formidable" has since largely become obsolete. During the Korean War, MIG-15s formed the bulk of the Chinese Air Force. During the mid-1950s MIG-17s were phased in. Some— possibly as many as 100—MIG-19s were acquired from the Russians prior to 1960. There have been unconfirmed reports that PLA inter- ceptors similar to MIG-21s have been sighted by Nationalist air patrols south of Shantung province and in American/South Vietnam- ese reconnaissance missions over North Vietnam. If these reports are correct, at least a limited capability to produce air frames, jet engines, weapons, and control and guidance systems has been devel- oped. One must not underestimate the Chinese determination to create a modern jet air force. An important step toward this goal was taken in December 1964 when the Seventh Ministry of Machine Building was established. The appointment of a very senior officer, Wang P'ing-chang, former deputy commander of the air force, as minister, is significant. But how deeply the Chinese will commit themselves to an expensive manned interceptor program cannot now be estimated.

To date, surface-to-air missiles (SAM) deployed in North Viet- nam have not proved particularly effective. (According to a good source—Premier Khrushchev—the Russians "gave" the Chinese "some rockets" prior to 1960. It is reasonable to speculate that these "rockets" were SAM and air-to-air types and that working-model guidance systems were provided.) As early as 1951, the Chinese were operating excellent Soviet-made radar-controlled anti-aircraft equipment in Korea, and heavy concentrations of AAA are now in North Vietnam. It is a reasonable assumption, therefore, that the present early warning and air-defense system designed to protect critical target areas in China is reasonably effective and that its con- tinuing development is receiving a very high priority.

The air force is generally credited with about 300 to 400 IL-28 (*Beagle*) twin-jet light bombers. This must still be considered a very good aircraft. The Chinese have also a few TU-4 (*Bull*) four- engined propeller bombers. (Some of these are reported to be con- figured for long-range reconnaissance.) This Soviet copy of the

U.S. B-29 of World War II has long been obsolete in Western air forces. It must now be considered no better than a slow and highly vulnerable aircraft with little strategic value except for long-range reconnaissance, as a possible launching platform for short-range missiles, or a fueling plane.

Despite Chinese assertions that they have attained "basic self-sufficiency" in petroleum, we may suspect that jet fuel supply will be a continuing problem for the air force. In 1961 and 1962, the Soviets drastically cut deliveries of petroleum products to China, and she is in the market for refineries at the present time. There are many technical difficulties involved in refining, rectifying, transporting, storing, and routine handling of volatile jet fuels. Thus, "basic self-sufficiency" in petroleum at the source does not by any means solve the problem of adequate jet fuel for the air force.

Some reliable analysts have asserted that Communist pilots averaged no better than ten hours a month in 1963–65. This figure is probably derived from observed sortie rates and may be misleadingly low. Nevertheless, Nationalist sources stated in 1964 that they believed the figure of ten hours a month representative. If so, Communist pilots were then averaging one-half the time considered minimum in the U.S., Japanese, and Nationalist air forces to maintain all-weather pilot proficiency. As of 1961, training standards were poor and caused the MAC much concern.

Since 1962, the Party has evinced a notable interest in parachute training; during the 1964 "summer-camping" jamboree, parachuting (apparently from towers) was a featured exercise and a popular attraction. This was part of an over-all physical training program which stressed swimming, river crossing, climbing, grenade throwing, bayonet exercise, and night marching.

However, other than in the capacity of elite ground troops, parachute formations are not much use without the lift required to get them to the target. The PLA could conceivably muster sufficient lift to put two battalions simultaneously on related targets, but in nearby areas only. Terrain, distance, weather and transport vulnerability severely limit air lift capabilities against Indian targets, except in the North East Frontier Agency (NEFA). This area is not only vulnerable but inviting, and such an operation there in coordination with ground thrusts could rapidly produce decisive local results.

Shortly after the Korean War, the People's Republic began to pay some attention to naval requirements, and with Soviet assistance and advice, a rudimentary naval force was established. From the first, emphasis was laid on submarines and coastal-defense craft.

How many long-range diesel-powered "G"- and "W"-class submarines the U.S.S.R. sold the Chinese is unknown; estimates are in the range of 20 to 30, of which only one "G"-class boat has been identified. This submarine is equipped with three missile-launching tubes and has transoceanic capability. A second "G"-class boat is reportedly being built. Some sources credit the Chinese with as many as 30 "W"-class boats. Of these, a few are equipped with deck ramps for launching short-range missiles. A submarine force of this size could pose a substantial threat to traffic in the far Pacific from Korea to Indonesia and, with boats modified for the purpose, would constitute a respectable Chinese variant of the French *force de frappe*. Further development of China's submarine fleet must be counted a distinct probability.

For defense of coastal waters, the Chinese rely on high-speed patrol boats, motor-torpedo boats and defensive mining. The Chinese are known to have some Soviet Komar-class patrol boats equipped to fire the *Styx* anti-shipping missile. The U.S. Navy discovered to its dismay in the fall of 1950 at Wonsan that Soviet mines and mining techniques were extremely good, and a prudent assumption must be that the Chinese learned both how to manufacture mines of various types and how to sow them in effective patterns.

The Navy's landing force is relatively small (28,000), and details of its organization and equipment are not available. The Communists inherited a heterogeneous collection of landing ships and craft from the Nationalists and have evinced some interest in amphibious operations. Press photographs have shown LST's disgorging tanks and trucks in exercises. Other photographs have shown Landing Craft Tank (LCT) and Landing Craft Vehicle and Personnel (LCVP). Amphibious ships and craft of these types are relatively simple to produce in quantity and could be augmented by motor-junk and towed barges. Taiwan is the obvious target for an amphibious operation, but air superiority over the Strait and the landing areas would have to be guaranteed. In view of the present state of the PLA's air force, such a capability seems remote.

Beyond what is made public by the Chinese themselves, very little is known of their progress toward creation of nuclear weapons systems. But the mushroom clouds that rose above the desert in Sinkiang in October 1964, May 1965, and in 1966 symbolized the determination of those who govern the People's Republic to make their country a member of the exclusive group of nuclear-armed powers. There can no longer be the slightest question that the Chinese have the scientific, engineering, and industrial capacity to achieve their goal, and within a relatively short period.

Doubtless, the Chinese nuclear weapons program includes development of delivery systems. The "G"-class submarine and the "W"-class boats, as modified for ramp launchings, may provide the basis for a "first phase" delivery system. But one may conjecture that the Chinese will not be content until they have intercontinental ballistic missiles in their nuclear inventory. This would necessarily be a long-range project which would require diversion of resources from more productive sectors. Nevertheless, it must be anticipated that the Chinese will pursue this course with their demonstrated vigor, skill, and determination.

Since the fall of 1959—when Marshal P'eng Teh-huai was removed from office for alleged "anti-Party activities"—Chairman Mao, "Chief" Lin, and their colleagues of the MAC have devoted considerable time and energy to devising programs to enhance the political consciousness of the PLA, to improve ideological work, and to eradicate remnants of "nonproletarian thought." The pace, scope, and intensity of these relentless campaigns testify both to the constant apprehension of the leadership that the PLA is not so Red as it should be and to their determination to make it so.

The first of these operations (announced in September 1958) was the *Hsia-Lien Tang-Ping Yun-Tung:* "Go down to the companies and soldier movement." The essential purpose of this was to chasten the officer corps. Officers (and some of their wives, too, it appeared) were becoming too "arrogant," too "caste conscious," too "bureaucratic," too "self-important." Some seniors, exposed to the luxuries and temptations of the cities, had succumbed to "sugar bullets"; not a few juniors had taken advantage of their positions to get more than their share of meat, wine, and other scarce items.

To demonstrate clearly that no military man had an "iron rice bowl," the Party decreed that all senior officers must serve for at least a month in the ranks. Thus, they "could learn from the masses." One may assume that colonels and generals were not too happy when directed to perform police duties, clean spittoons, wash pots and pans, and peel potatoes. Nevertheless, they "went down" as ordered.

A corollary of this campaign was one designed to take the "thought" of Chairman Mao to the galleys and mess halls. All problems which might conceivably arise in these important areas could be solved if the cooks and their officer assistants devoted more time to reading the Chairman's works.

When in 1960 the Party deemed that the officer corps had been put in its place, the persecution—for the *hsia lien* movement cannot be otherwise correctly described—slacked off. Officers continued to "go down" but were no longer required to perform menial tasks under the eyes of semi-literate privates. On the whole, the experience undoubtedly had a traumatic effect on the officer corps, one which many of its members are not likely to forget—or forgive.

Before the *hsia lien* movement had died down, General Hsiao Hua launched one designed to cultivate "a fine traditional working style" in the army. This "style" had been described by none other than Mao Tse-tung himself as the "three-eight working style" and was epitomized by the Chairman in three phrases and eight characters. The hortatory phrases called upon each individual in the PLA to achieve "a correct political orientation"; to cultivate "an industrious and thrifty working style," and to develop "flexible and mobile" strategy and tactics. The characters were those meaning unity, earnestness, seriousness, and liveliness.

Armed with this invincible "working style," the PLA would "be able to crush all enemies in wartime."

It will not be defeated under attack or worn out in a war of attrition. On the other hand, it will conquer all positions in offensive action and hold its own position firmly in defensive action. It will be able to achieve a great victory at little cost.[10]

As the PLA's soldiers, sailors, and airmen labored to perfect "a fine working style" Lin Piao generated a campaign described as the "Four Firsts." The "Four Firsts" established the basic context for political work in the PLA. These principles had long been familiar to every political and military cadre, Party member, and aspirant in the armed forces; the fact that the high command found it necessary to enunciate them again indicates that some cadres had (even if only temporarily) succumbed to a surfeit of the Chairman's "glorious thought" and as a consequence had neglected to elucidate it to the rank and file with sufficient force and clarity.

In paraphrase of his master, Lin used the phrase "Four Firsts" to describe what he considers four fundamental "relationships." These are:

1. The relation between weapons and men. "Human and politico-ideological factors are primary factors affecting fighting strength."
2. The relation between political work and other work. "Politics is the soul and the supreme command. Political work is the lifeline of the army. . . ."
3. The relation between routine political work and ideological work. ". . . special emphasis should be placed on ideological work . . . to establish proletarian thinking and wipe out non-proletarian thought."
4. The relation between theory and practice. "Education from books must be combined with reality." [11]

These campaigns were barely under way when the MAC launched yet another. The purpose of this one was to develop "Five-Good" soldiers. A "Five-Good" soldier, as described by the MAC, should be "good"

1. In political thought. He should "study politics hard, study Chairman Mao's writings, obey Chairman Mao's words, carry out Chairman Mao's directives," and so become Chairman Mao's "good soldier."
2. In military training.
3. In the "Three-Eight" work style.
4. In accomplishing tasks.
5. In physical training.[12]

Having taken care of the "Four Firsts," the "Three-Eight," and the "Five-Good," the MAC suspended its mathematical ratiocinating for a few weeks. This no doubt welcome hiatus was short; early in 1961, the numbers game was resumed with a "Four-Good Movement." The object of this exercise (aside from keeping cadres more fully occupied) was to raise the fighting strength of PLA companies. This movement, said the MAC, was an application of Chairman Mao's thinking "with regard to army building in the new historic era, the most comprehensive and the greatest work." The "Four-Good Movement" would play "a decisive role in war preparations" and was a task "of great strategic significance." As might be expected, the first goal of a company which aspired to the "Four-Good" category was to be "good" in political thought. Then it was to be "good" in the "Three-Eight" work style, "good" in military training, and "good" in management of living.

Simultaneously, the MAC announced "Five Principles in Carrying Out Management and Education Work" and followed this with a summary outline of how best to grasp "Ten Experiences of Living Thought." The first, naturally, was to grasp the thinking of Mao Tse-tung. We need not here list the other nine, but all were designed to raise the class and political consciousness of the soldiers and to "cause them to feel from the bottom of their hearts the care shown by the Party and the warmth of the revolutionary big family."

About a year passed before the GPD issued another numerical directive. This (April 1962) was entitled "Seven Measures for Improving the Leadership of Armed Forces Organization over Companies" and was apparently designed to take pressure off the lower echelons. The only practical "measures" prescribed relieved the companies of excessive paper work and permitted them some slight initiative in the use of "spare time," a commodity which during the mathematical blitz they had obviously enjoyed very little if at all.

Although the Party insistently adjures the Chinese people to love the PLA, to emulate its dedicated devotion to Mao, and to practice the virtues of obedience and frugality which distinguish the "Five-Good" soldier and the "Four-Good" company, one may suspect that the repeated campaigns the Party conducts in the armed forces are inspired by a deep feeling of insecurity which derives at least in part from traditional distrust of the military.

This apprehension was reflected in the proceedings of the 1966 PLA conference on Political Work, over which Hsiao Hua presided. The official report on the proceedings of this conference made it clear that the Party is very much concerned that the PLA is still not sufficiently "politically conscious," that it may be susceptible to the taint of "modern revisionism." The conferees agreed that only by "putting politics first" could it be ensured "that the army never disintegrates."

"Putting politics first" means putting Mao Tse-tung's thinking first, said the conference. It means regarding Chairman Mao Tse-tung's works as the highest instruction on all aspects of the work of the whole army, and putting Mao Tse-tung's thinking in command of everything. Chairman Mao Tse-tung's instructions are the criterion for all work. All his instructions must be resolutely supported and carried out, even if their accomplishment involves "climbing a mountain of swords and crossing an ocean of flames." [13]

The Chairman's platitudes appear in the Chinese press with monotonous regularity, but few more frequently than his pronouncement that man is the factor of most importance in war. "Man," he said, "decides everything." To accord to weapons what Mao believes to be an undue emphasis is by implication to depreciate the place of man. Those who hold such beliefs, or make the mistake of voicing them, cannot aspire to high position in the PLA. It is often said that P'eng Teh-huai and his hand-picked chief of the General Staff Department, Huang K'o-ch'eng, were dismissed from office in 1959 in part because they subscribed to this "mechanistic" heresy and connived with the Soviets to implement it.

It follows that the Party is expressly concerned with qualitative values in the annual selection of young men to serve in the armed forces. This is a luxury the Party can well afford, for the problem of finding bodies has never been an acute one in China. But until the Communists came to power there had never been an effective conscription system. If the ingenious Chinese peasant could possibly conceive a plan to avoid serving in the armed forces without incurring a penalty, he was quick to embrace it.

General Wedemeyer remarked that the conscription system under the Nationalists was administered in a scandalous fashion. Actually, the "system" he (and others) observed in operation was one of impressment rather than conscription. But, whatever the reasons may have been, the Chinese Communists did not seem to experience the difficulties the Nationalists encountered in collecting men. There is little doubt that during the Anti-Japanese War and (particularly) the civil war, they occasionally resorted to impressment. But until 1947, when wholesale integration of surrendered Nationalist formations began, the Red Army was essentially composed of volunteers or at least of men who had not been rounded up at the point of the bayonet and roped together by press gangs.

The voluntary enlistment system did not, however, satisfy the Party's requirements for a revolutionary "class-conscious" army, and in 1955, the People's Republic abandoned the voluntary system in favor of national conscription. This obviously gave the Party better quality control than was possible under a voluntary program. As some 7 million males reach the age of eighteen every year, the PLA can afford to be selective and to apply very rigid standards in respect to the mental, physical, psychological, and political attributes of prospective service men. As a matter of principle, the

PLA prefers to induct young men only from families with poor peasant and proletarian backgrounds. The Party presumes, probably correctly, that this will preserve the ideological purity of its armed forces.

The same family background criterion is applied to aspirants to "leader" (officer) status. Young men with bourgeois or landlord parents are systematically excluded from opportunity to become "leaders." In this manner, the Party hopes to create a leadership corps which is "class conscious," animated with revolutionary zeal, dedicated, obedient, and of unquestioned loyalty.

A totally militarized life program enables the Party to observe an individual's career in its children's and youth organizations and in lower and middle schools and to spot those who tend to be too individualistic or too skeptical or who do not otherwise enthusiastically conform to its conceptual and behavioral norms. With equal facility, the Party can distinguish "progressives" at an early age. Thus, the entire organizational structure may be seen as consisting of a series of built-in "filters." By the time a young man reaches his eighteenth year, the Party has formed a very good idea of his leadership potential. Those who have consistently displayed the characteristics wanted of "leaders" in the armed forces are encouraged to make the service a career.

As a "leader" moves up the ladder in the armed forces, he discovers again and again that intellectual "individualism" is treated as an even more grievous deviation than "bureaucratism" or "commandism." A "leader" may exercise technical initiative—indeed, is distinctly encouraged to do so—but his thoughts must be the thoughts of Mao Tse-tung. Mao's thoughts are the focus around which all life and all activity must revolve. In some effusions, these thoughts are described as "guideposts," in others, as "compasses," "arrows," or "lighthouses."

This leads us again to the perplexing question implicit in the slogan "Be Red and Expert." Is there an inherent contradiction in these terms? Are they, indeed, even—or sometimes—mutually exclusive? The Party obviously considers them compatible. But the Party finds it difficult to assess the degree of a person's "Redness." Is he a "beet" or a "radish" or somewhere in between? If P'eng Teh-huai, Huang K'o-ch'eng and Lo Jui-ch'ing were "radishes," how many others are there? Who are they? These questions must frequently plague the PLA's General Political Department and its representatives in the armed forces.

Ostensibly, at least, they bothered Senior Gen. Lo Jui-ch'ing at the time he addressed a special message to the PLA on New Year's Day 1965. Lo found it necessary to warn that the "overthrown exploiter class" in China had not yet been "wiped out." The PLA, he said, must be constantly vigilant and with sober mind and open eyes continue to raise its class consciousness, "master the skills of class struggle, resolutely support and carry out the policies of the Party," and continue to develop its "hard-fighting traditions." He added that the "enemy" within the gate was secretly distributing "sugarcoated pills" and urged the PLA to be on its guard against "complacency."

The Party has admitted that about 5 per cent of the population follows its lead only with the greatest reluctance and that another unnamed but significant percentage consists of "wavering elements." Selective induction and promotion processes will, it obviously hopes, exclude these unreliable elements from ever attaining a dangerous foothold in the PLA. But some termites are already in the woodwork, according to General Lo, who warned that they were infiltrating the PLA "trying to grab the official seats from us [the staunch Party men] in certain fields."

It is statements such as this one which lead some people to question the loyalty of the PLA. On Taiwan, it is one of the articles of faith that the PLA is only superficially loyal. But facts lend little support to this view. In the great exodus during the spring of 1962, more than 125,000 mainlanders came into the Crown Colony of Hong Kong (including the "New Territories"). As far as is known, not one of these was a serving officer or soldier. Some few were demobilized ex-officers or noncommissioned officers, several of whom had, so their questioners discovered, been dismissed from the PLA. Surely, had dissatisfaction been as rampant in the armed forces as Taiwan sources insist it is, a great many serving soldiers would have thrown away their rifles, put on peasants' clothing, and crossed over. The brief Sino-Indian border war also refutes the claim advanced in Taiwan. There, no Chinese soldier "turned his hat around." The Indians took one prisoner. He was lost and blundered into an Indian outpost.

Despite huge offers of money, coupled with promises of complete immunity and good treatment, the Nationalists have induced only two or three Communist fliers to desert to them. It is true, as the Nationalists never tire of pointing out, that desertion with a jet aircraft is not so simple as it may seem. Pilots are under a surveillance which would naturally be more strict than that exercised over their colleagues in the ground or naval forces. And—although there are no figures to confirm this—one may suspect that the great majority of air force leaders and senior enlisted men are Party members. Nevertheless, if a trusted pilot planned to desert with his aircraft, he would find means of doing so.

The Party consistently emphasizes, in its patriotic propaganda, that the primary mission of the PLA is to repel "imperialist aggressors" and to foil the "nefarious plots" of the "Chiang bandits." The theme of "defense of the Motherland" is repeated in every speech made by a member of the military hierarchy. There is no reason to believe that the PLA would not loyally respond to any challenge directed against the Chinese mainland.

Its behavior in a frustrating and prolonged combat situation outside China's borders would depend on a variety of material and psychological factors. Of the latter, the most important would be the Party's ability to maintain its control, for until this control can be eroded, the PLA can be expected to perform as creditably as it did in the Korean War.

CHAPTER FOURTEEN

The Magnificent Military Theories
of Chairman Mao Tse-tung

That the Communist Party of China was able, under extremely difficult conditions to create and build up the PLA and victoriously lead China's revolutionary war was principally due to the fact that it had the guidance of the magnificent teachings of Mao Tse-tung. With the integration of the universal truth of Marxism-Leninism with the concrete practice of the Chinese revolution as the guiding principle, Chairman Mao eminently solved the strategic problem of China's revolutionary war and created magnificent military theories, and the PLA was armed with this ideological weapon.

—Hsiao Hua

The creation of the Chinese people's armed force is entirely due to Chairman Mao's genius in Marxist-Leninist political ideology and strategic thinking.

—Ch'en Yi

The precise nature and importance of Mao Tse-tung's original contribution to the "science" of Marxism-Leninism has been widely debated—but not in the People's Republic, where no one dares question the abiding significance of the Chairman's thought. And regardless of what the outcome of the "national liberation war" in South Vietnam may be, there is small likelihood, until Mao departs from the scene, that anyone in Peking could successfully challenge the essential features of a doctrine now held to be infallible, if not, indeed, sacrosanct.

In Peking, there is no diminution in the volume of verbose essays and tiresome discourses devoted to establishing the universal applicability of Mao's "magnificent military theories." Elsewhere, critics have for some time questioned the degree to which the Chairman has "enriched," "refined," and "developed" Communist thought and practice. A recent entrant in these lists is Arthur A. Cohen.[1]

As Cohen observes, the Chairman is not a philosopher. His life and writings attest that he is not essentially an intellectual but a man of action, a good analyst, and a logical thinker. Above all, Mao is a realistic politician interested in the manipulation of power. Thus, his really original contributions pertain "primarily to the pragmatic policies [he] devised for attaining power and consolidating that power." [2] As we have seen—and as Cohen remarks—Mao's principal claim to be a revolutionary innovator rests in his formulation of a systematic strategy of "protracted guerrilla warfare waged from . . . rural base areas." [3]

In the West, disporportionate emphasis has been given the strictly military aspects of this strategy, and other features of equal, if not more, importance have been occluded or at least obscured. Mao did not make this error. He comprehended the inherent unity of revolutionary struggle and saw clearly that it embraced a great deal more than simple violence. He sought and found a formula for fusing military action with political, economic, social, cultural, and psychological ingredients and produced a model with a cogent appeal and a special dynamism.

Mao is a student of Chinese history. This history taught him that he could achieve success only by organized, disciplined effort. He early rejected any idea that pure "guerrillaism," as exemplified by "roving insurgents," could contribute to the permanent conquest of power which was his aim. Thus, his policy from the beginning was to expand the Red Army on a selective basis rather than by "hiring men and buying horses" and "recruiting deserters and accepting mutineers." The correct line was systematic expansion of local Red Guards and militia in order gradually to develop the main forces of the Red Army, the Party's "gun."

Mao's devotion to disciplined organization is evident in the program he designed for the revolution to be led by the Chinese Communist Party. Mao presented this program to the First Party Congress of the Hunan-Kiangsi Border District on May 20, 1928. As far as can be determined, it was at this local congress, held in a remote town near the base on Chingkangshan, that Mao boldly sketched a concept of revolutionary strategy radically opposed to that dictated by the Comintern and promoted slavishly by its puppets on the

Central Committee of the CCP. Mao's enforced sojourn in the mountains had apparently afforded him some time for reflection; when he descended, he brought with him the tablets.

According to Ho Chung-jen,[4] "Great Chairman Mao . . . arrived at the conclusion that the economic and political development in China showed great unevenness which determined the great unevenness in revolutionary development, the possibility of the revolution to win victory first in rural districts by exploiting enemy weakness, and the possibility of establishing bases of long-term revolution." The revolution in China "could neither take the form of starting with uprisings in urban areas nor that of a repetition of the Northern Expedition. Revolutionary victory in China could be achieved only by a protracted wave-by-wave struggle carried out with the rural areas as bases." [5] Mao thus emphatically rejected the Comintern line that the Chinese revolution must follow the Russian pattern.

The formula he conceived was simple and logically progressive:

1. Create local power in a chosen sector.
2. Introduce land reforms and other measures designed to win the loyalty of the peasants.
3. Use the Party organization of the armed forces to develop local Party organization.
4. Use the armed forces to develop militia and local self-defense forces.
5. Prepare the populace for protracted struggle.
6. Concentrate the armed forces to fight; disperse them to mobilize the masses.
7. Defeat enemy forces one by one.
8. Adopt a "wave-like" expansion policy.
9. Oppose "adventurism" in all forms.[6]

Here we have the essential features of all Mao's subsequent theorizing on this subject. Revolutionary bases are established in chosen sectors, i.e., in naturally defensible areas remote from the incumbent government's centers of power. A formula which gains the sympathy and support of the rural masses is devised. A Party base is formed. The army conducts propaganda, agitates and mobilizes the people, and creates militant mass organizations. The armed forces engage the enemy only under propitious circumstances, i.e., when victory is certain. Movement is "wave-like": where the enemy is weak, the wave advances; where strong, the wave recedes. Finally, calculated prudence must govern action. This formula presupposes a prolonged struggle during which the weaker side slowly and patiently consolidates a local political authority welded to a firm military position, accumulates strength, expands its holdings, gradually attains parity, and ultimately gains superiority.

Mao clung to his model with unwavering and dedicated persistence. In 1937, he prophesied its successful application elsewhere. Others would learn from China's historical experience, an experience "written in iron and blood . . . a page in history that has no precedent." In fact, the influence of this experience would not be confined "solely to China in her present Anti-Japanese War, but will be world-wide." [7] In those days, few people paid any attention to prophecies emanating from Yenan. One who did was Truong Chinh, a Vietnamese Communist.

In September 1947, a full decade after the appearance of Mao's principal works on the strategy of protracted guerrilla war, Truong wrote an essay that quickly became the bible for the Vietnamese resistance movement.[8] Whether Truong visited Yenan (as some have claimed) or whether he did not make a pilgrimage to that shrine is irrelevant. The fact remains that his essay reflects Mao's ideas almost exactly. Indeed, were it not for Truong's more forceful and felicitous style, one might imagine he was reading the Chairman's work.

In his preface, Truong sketched the basic outlines of the war the Vietnamese Communists led by Ho Chi Minh were to wage against the French:

At present the Vietnamese armed forces are still weaker than those of the enemy; therefore it is necessary to prolong the Resistance war. In the course of the fighting we shall develop our forces, gradually wearing down the enemy's strength, awaiting the day when we can crush him completely. This Resistance war must be waged by the entire people in every field—military, political, economic, and cultural—so that, wherever the enemy goes, he meets our fierce resistance, which encircles and chokes him, making it impossible for him to live in peace in our country. . . .

Vietnam's armed resistance is a just war. A just war generally receives much support and derives immense strength from the people. . . .

To win final victory in this long and hard struggle is not an easy task. Success can only be achieved on the following fundamental conditions: the correctness of our political line, the achievement of close national unity, the consolidation of our rear, the heroism of our army and people and the competence of our command.

As Mao had muted the theme of class struggle in his calls for national resistance to the Japanese, so Truong, defining the Communist-led revolution in Vietnam in terms of a people's patriotic war, invoked legendary and historical figures whose victories in the remote past had been based on stratagems and ruses, perseverance and endurance, speed and ferocity in attack. If their heroic examples were followed and if all Vietnamese sacrificed and put forth strenuous efforts, "the long resistance of our people will certainly be victorious."

With Mao, Truong saw protracted war as the key to victory. *"The guiding principle of our strategy must be to prolong the war."* But (again echoing Mao) "in every individual campaign and from a tactical viewpoint we must achieve rapid settlements." The enemy must be annihilated in a methodical, sector-by-sector process, in which superior forces suddenly strike him when he is unprepared, weary, eating, or sleeping. The guerrillas strike at the less mobile enemy's communication lines, harass him constantly, "render his forces lame, lost, hungry, thirsty. . . ." As the enemy's strength and morale are sapped, guerrilla strength increases, and morale improves. And as the war drags on, the guerrilla army will gain experience, will acquire recruits and arms "so that mobile warfare will be applied more extensively, until, finally, in the stage of general counteroffensive, positional warfare will play the paramount role."

Truong summoned the people to unite with the armed forces; ". . . . we must mobilize the people to support our armed forces enthusiastically and to fight the enemy together with them. The people are the eyes and ears of the army, they feed and keep our soldiers. It is they who help the army in sabotage and in battle. The people are the water and our army the fish." The united people are an ever-present and inexhaustible source of strength. Again following his preceptor, Truong stresses the importance of political, economic, and cultural factors of the resistance war.

Drawing a balance as between the resistance and the French, Truong writes that the strong points of the former were fundamental, while those of the French were auxiliary. He allowed the French superiority in modern arms and granted them numerous and well-trained officers and troops, a high standard of organization, and excellent facilities for foreign propaganda, but he cast on the scales the countervailing factors: the French were waging an aggressive (and hence unjust) war; they had few friends and many enemies; they suffered from internal divisions; they were not supported by the people; and their effective strength was constantly diminishing. Thus "their strong points are rendered useless."

"In a word," Truong concluded, "after comparing our forces with the enemy's *we will certainly win.*" He based this unequivocal prophecy partly on his conviction that the Vietnamese were fighting a "people's war," "progressive" and "just," against an aggressive colonialism and that they would be able to capitalize on French mistakes, difficulties, and inherent weaknesses. But success, he wrote, would be *"chiefly due to our close unity, our self-reliance, our strenuous efforts to strengthen and develop our forces. Long-term resistance and self-reliance are our guiding principles in this war for national liberation."* Here he echoes Mao's theme of self-reliance.

But the resistance must overcome many obstacles before this victory could be achieved. One—the most important one, perhaps—was to settle the relationship between military affairs and politics. Here Truong excoriated (as Mao had) those who failed to comprehend that military affairs could not possibly prosper unless the political line was correct. Others, who placed primary reliance on politics to settle matters, sought "reconciliation contrary to principle" and had tendencies to make concessions or even to surrender. The militarists, on the other hand, were inclined to believe that everything could be settled by force. They failed to apply political mobilization, neglected political work, relied on coercion rather than persuasion, failed to achieve unity of the army and the people and within the army, and neglected propaganda designed to disintegrate the enemy. Such people, Truong concluded in another paraphrase of Mao, knew "only how to fight."

Essentially, Truong's structure was almost a stereotype of Mao's. There are, it is true, minor differences in emphasis: Truong devotes more attention to economic and cultural factors and perhaps less to the political aspects of protracted war than had Mao. The important point, however, is that Mao's revolutionary package, with minor modifications to suit specific conditions, was found to be eminently exportable, to a semi-feudal, agriculture-based society.

In other respects, Mao's strategic thinking, largely underpinned by familiar Marxist-Leninist dogmas, is less original. Basic to it is Clausewitz' concept that war is a continuation of politics by other means. Lenin, much impressed by this thought, which struck him with the force of revelation, conceived war as a "violent" expression of political relationships. So it also appears to Mao, who in a pungent restatement of Lenin's dictum described war as "politics with bloodshed" and politics as "war without bloodshed." Only the most vulgar and mediocre bourgeois chauvinists, Lenin remarked, are incapable of recognizing such an obvious fact.[9] In this integral context, peace becomes "a respite from another war," and war "a method of obtaining a somewhat worse or better peace." [10]

Mao did not, however, have to appropriate this particular concept from Lenin's ideological ragbag. The Chinese have traditionally considered war a part of political life and have always believed that those who govern not only must study and know war but also must be able to conduct it successfully. Great officers of the dynastic state were expected to be as competent in campaign as they were adept in negotiation. Warrior statesmen were by no means the rare phenomena in imperial China they have been in the Western world. (The Japanese, incidentally, inherited this view from the Chinese. Tokugawa Ieyasu, founder of the shogunate which bore his name, would describe the arts of war and the arts of peace as the two "wings" or "wheels" of statecraft.) The men who today comprise the top leadership of the CCP are in this tradition.

Another basic tenet (one recently disavowed by the Russians) is equally familiar. As long as "class society" exists, war is "inevitable": "When human society advances to the point where classes and states are eliminated, there will be no more wars, counterrevolutionary or revolutionary, just or unjust; that will be the era of perpetual peace for mankind. Our study of the laws of revolutionary war springs from the desire to eliminate all wars; herein lies the distinction between us Communists and all the exploiting classes." [11] But mankind cannot enjoy the happy era of "perpetual peace" until the "exploiters" are crushed: "War will disappear only when this private ownership and the antagonistic classes are destroyed forever." [12] Since "wars for the emancipation of the world from capitalism *will necessarily arise* . . . the primary duty of the proletariat . . . is to make all the necessary political, economic, and military preparations for these wars, to strengthen its Red Army—that mighty weapon of the proletariat—and to train the masses of the toilers in the art of war. . . . Revolutionary war of the proletarian dictatorship is but a continuation of revolutionary peace 'by other means.' " [13]

As it is axiomatic that the "imperialists" will not voluntarily surrender, they must be isolated from friends and allies; attacked both directly and indirectly everywhere and by every means; and, when circumstances promise victory, subdued by "just" war. "The banner of mankind's just war is the banner of mankind's salvation." [14]

Mao did not borrow this article of his creed from Marxism-Leninism. It is embedded in Chinese history. Since ancient times, the Chinese have justified attacks on their neighbors by the pretense that an enlightened sovereign was morally obligated to impose superior culture on barbarians who refused to accept the higher values of Chinese civilization.

So today, any measures that might conceivably hasten the demise of capitalism and imperialism are in Chinese eyes morally justified. This thesis provides a built-in rationale for the conduct of propaganda, agitation, and subversion and the generation and support of movements the Chinese choose to classify as "struggles for national liberation." The Chinese comrades have again and again made it unmistakably clear that this is and will continue to be their policy in Asia, Africa, and Latin America—"the most vulnerable areas under imperialist rule and the storm centers of the world revolution." [15]

When during his visit to Moscow in late 1957 Mao Tse-tung announced that the "East Wind" prevailed over the "West Wind," he conveyed in allegorical language the CCP's estimate that in the "new historical stage" the world balance of forces favored the Communist bloc. As events were shortly to prove, his Russian hosts, who weighed the situation more objectively, had not arrived at a similar conclusion. They did indeed appreciate the fact that the Sputniks ushered in a new era, one in which the Soviet state would no longer occupy a position of absolute inferiority vis-à-vis the West. But as they must have seen the situation, the accretion of power promised by their missile and space programs was not such as to warrant nuclear confrontation with the United States. To them, Mao's confident assertion indicated a Chinese inclination to pursue "left adventurist" policies which involved gambles the Soviets were not prepared to take. It is in the context of the radically differing estimates of the world power situation then made by Moscow and Peking that we find the genesis of the Sino-Soviet split.

While it is not necessary to discuss in detail the issues involved in this seemingly endless and tendentious dispute, it is desirable to summarize the Chinese position on the question of war and peace in the nuclear age.[16] During their polemic with the Russian comrades, the Chinese vigorously rejected the Soviet charge that they were recklessly propagating the thesis that war between the capitalist and socialist systems is "inevitable." After protracted semantic labor, Peking produced a statement, that when judged by the standards of her doctrinaire lexicon, is mild indeed: "So long as capitalist imperialism remains in the world, the source and possibility of war will remain." [17] After all, the Chinese no doubt realized that espousal of a bellicose and fatalistic doctrine which left them no room for diplomatic maneuver was scarcely consistent with the "peace-loving" image they wished to project to emerging nations.

The unrelenting attacks on Khrushchev, which appeared regularly in the Chinese Party press and in pamphlet form and resounded daily on the air waves, were inspired by the Soviet Premier's attempts to seek some sort of tolerable accommodation with the "criminal system of imperialism." In *Two Different Lines on the Question of War and Peace*, the Chinese castigated Khrushchev as a revisionist and a promoter of the insidious line of "the renegade" Kautsky, an early Marxist theoretician, a member of the Second Communist International, and one of Peking's favorite whipping boys. This tract alleges that Khrushchev followed Kautsky in "prettifying" imperialism, turning "the minds of the people away from their struggle," and blunting "the fighting will of the people." To Mao, who holds that "struggle" in both domestic and external contexts is a constant, this was blatant heresy. (Whether the necessity for unremitting struggle is actually relevant to given conditions in China is not the point. It is, simply because the Party *says* it is. Thus anything that tends to diminish mass militancy becomes "a road extremely dangerous to world peace.")

The Soviet Premier put several other holes in "The Great Red Banner" of Chairman Mao's "glorious military thought." He propagated the "modern revisionist" view that in the nuclear age "weapons decide everything"; he failed to distinguish between "just" and "unjust" wars; he stated that world peace "could be achieved through disarmament." Finally, Khrushchev took occasion to remind Peking that while Chinese "paper dragons" might "melt in the rain," imperialist paper dragons had "nuclear teeth."

Whether eventual possession of a modest stock of nuclear weapons and a delivery system of some sort will modify either the Chairman's strong anti-mechanistic views on the nature of modern war or Peking's verbal bellicosity remains to be seen. One may, however, hope that Mao and the aging "Long Marchers" who surround him still retain sufficient intellectual elasticity to enable them discreetly and gradually to de-emphasize a dogma which has survived from guerrilla days and which so dangerously underrates nuclear arms. And, as Ellis Joffe recently observed, continuing emphasis on the

244 The Chinese People's Liberation Army

superiority of human over material resources is at least in part the Party's rationalization for China's lack of atomic weapons, "a smoke screen" to hide "the painful reality of military and technological inferiority." [18]

There is nothing esoteric in Chinese Communist operational doctrine. It derives in large measure from traditional sources, as those familiar with Chinese history and literature—and particularly with the *Seven Martial Classics*—can attest. The Party has adapted the received canon but, in a strictly military sense, has contributed very little original to it. To be sure, battle experiences in the Chingkang period, during the Extermination Campaigns, on the Long March, and during both the Anti-Japanese and "Third Revolutionary" wars produced some modifications, refinements, and changes in emphasis. But the heritage provided a basis both inclusive and sound.

A disciple once asked Confucius to comment on generalship. The Master is alleged to have replied that while he knew nothing of such matters, he would prefer not a general "who rushes a river" but one "who succeeds by strategy." Here, Confucius was conveying his belief that impetuous direct action is to be avoided if there are other means to achieve the end. Later, Sun Tzu wrote that the best policy in war was "to take a state intact. . . . To capture the enemy's army is better than to destroy it . . . to subdue the enemy without fighting is the acme of skill." [19]

In the following verses, Sun Tzu writes that what is of supreme importance is "to attack the enemy's strategy" and "disrupt his alliances." Then the enemy, weakened and isolated, can be subdued at little cost. What is implied, as in the remark attributed to Confucius, is a patient and prudent process. Mao's thesis of "protracted war" and the "step-by-step" strategy which the Communists applied to disintegrate and defeat Chiang's armies during the "Third Revolutionary War" fit this context. So also does the Chairman's statement that the Red Army had no use for "impetuous hotheads" who would butt their heads against stone walls. Mao asked for generals calm and prudent, able to swim with measured strokes in the immense ocean of war.

Chinese doctrine might be described—to use B. H. Liddell Hart's words—as one which relies primarily on methods of "indirect approach":

. . . throughout the ages, effective results in war have rarely been attained unless the approach has had such indirectness as to ensure the opponent's unreadiness to meet it. The indirectness usually has been physical and always psychological. In strategy, the longest way round is often the shortest way home.

This observation naturally holds true, as well, on both operational and tactical levels. Captain Liddell Hart continues:

More and more clearly has the lesson emerged that a direct approach to one's mental object of physical objective along the "line of natural expectation" for the opponent, tends to produce negative results.

For to move on this line

consolidates the opponent's balance and thus increases his resisting power. . . . Success by such a method only becomes possible through an immense margin of superior strength in some form—and, even so, tends to lose decisiveness. In most campaigns the dislocation of the enemy's psychological and physical balance has been the vital prelude to a successful attempt at his overthrow.[20]

For most of its life, the Red Army found itself facing successive antagonists endowed with an "immense margin of superior strength." This disparity created an operational imperative. Some compensators had to be devised to rectify the obvious imbalance in relative combat power. The Red Army found such compensators in imaginative and bold command, high morale, indirection, deception, distraction, and surprise. But to deceive and surprise a reasonably well-informed and vigilant enemy, one must have superior information of both him and the ground, as well as the ability to draw correct conclusions from that information. Mao has repeatedly emphasized the necessity for proper assessment and correlation of the objective and subjective conditions peculiar to each "struggle" situation.

It is a key point of Chinese Communist doctrine to fight only when the situation promises victory. There are, of course, ways of creating such situations, provided one is sufficiently imaginative and will take the time to do so. Thus, battles are decided before they are fought. If the flux of combat produces a disadvantageous situation, the Reds normally retire or "run away." "Running away," according to Mao, is an offensive tactic to buy time for consolidation in advantageous ground and sucks the enemy into terrain where he can be handled. This very tactic—"luring deep"—was used frequently in Kiangsi, in the "Third Revolutionary War" against Chiang's armies, and later against an unwary U.N. command in Korea.

Mao's constant stress on unity of the army and the people and unity within the army reflects a traditional Chinese concern with harmonious relationships. It is the business of a ruler to assure harmony among the people, and of a general to assure "the harmony of his host." This is the quality we define as morale. In Sun Tzu's words, it is "that which causes the people to be in harmony with their leaders so that they will accompany them through life and unto death without fear of mortal peril." The morale of the people is high when the government is humane, benevolent, just, and righteous. The morale of the army is high when the general is wise, sincere, humane, courageous, and strict; when his orders are sensible and consistent; when his rewards and punishments are honest and equable. The good general treats his soldiers as "his children," as "his own beloved sons"; they share every peril and every hardship and march together "into the deepest valleys." Morale is the foundation of national life and the fundamental requisite to victory. Only when the people and the army are in harmonious accord will "superiors and subordinates go forward with united purpose."

Other characteristics of Chinese operational doctrine, summarized below, are not to be considered as "principles of war" but rather as guides to action:

Freedom of Action. Mao has repeatedly emphasized the imperative importance of freedom of action. He who is free to act holds the initiative. To Mao, passivity is anathema. If freedom of action is lost, it must be regained. In this context we may once again observe that withdrawals from advanced or exposed positions either political or military are often necessary—as was the Long March—to regain freedom of action.

Deception. "All warfare is based on deception," is one of Sun Tzu's most-quoted apothegms. Deception is always legitimate in the promotion of national self-interest or national defense. Deception requires active measures of simulation and dissimulation so that the enemy will be deceived, deluded, and mystified. He must be led to believe what one wants him to believe so that his action will contribute to the attainment of one's own aims.

During the Sung dynasty, a student of the military art wrote: "Create an uproar in the east, decoy him to the west, distract him to the front, strike him in the rear." Even Mao has not been able to improve on this succinct advice.

Dislocation. Centuries before Liddell Hart propounded his thesis on dislocation of the enemy's balance, the Chinese had perfected the technique. This may be accomplished by an entirely unexpected strategic or tactical maneuver which the enemy is too inflexible mentally or too ponderous physically to counter successfully. The enemy is to be worn out, plagued, bothered, harassed, irritated, and given no rest. Thus, there is initiated a chain reaction which produces cumulative effects on the enemy's state of mind, on his morale, and on his ability to plan.

The creation of cleavages between allies, between segments of the people, between a ruler and his counselors, between a general and his advisers, between officers and their men is a technique of dislocation the Chinese describe as "wedging" or "wedge driving."

Surprise. Sun Tzu exhorted the general to "go forth when the enemy does not expect you; take him unaware." To achieve surprise, it is usually necessary to proceed by a devious route or "to make the indirect the most direct." Deception and distraction contribute decisively to the attainment of surprise and multiply its effects.

Surprise is most frequently achieved on the tactical level but should be sought on all levels of action in terms of time, place, doctrine, and technology.

Mobility. No matter how successfully the enemy may be deluded and deceived as to one's true intentions, surprise can not be gained unless forces are mobile. An ancient Chinese military maxim says: "At the lightning flash, there is no time to shield the eyes; at the thunderclap, no time to cover the ears."

Rapid maneuver on political, strategic, operational, and tactical levels is essential to make the enemy react. By observing the enemy's reactions, one can establish his "pattern." This concept is sometimes expressed as follows: "If no maneuver, no reaction. If no reaction, no pattern establishing."

Timing. The Chinese say that the hawk breaks the back of its prey "because of its timing." Timing is essential to achieve surprise. To time action in relation to ever-changing circumstances requires the ability to recognize the fleeting opportunity and the will to grasp it. Timing is obviously as important in terms of political action as it is in combat.

Flexibility. As used by the Chinese, this term refers to a quality of mind and will—that is to say, to adaptability and the expedient use of available resources under changing circumstances. The less subtle Western concept relates primarily to the ability to shift forces.

Concentration. Sun Tzu said: "In war, numbers alone confer no advantage." The enemy must be divided; "many must strike few."

He who cannot divide his enemy is no master of the art of distraction. We distract; the enemy responds by dispersal of his forces to meet our threats; we then direct overwhelming power against selected weak points.

Power embraces superior intelligence, superior planning, superior generalship, superior troops, better use of weather and of the ground. "Concentration" thus consists of intellectual, physical, and psychic elements and has a more comprehensive meaning than the same word does as used in the West, where it is ordinarily equated with "mass."

Momentum. In writing of momentum, Sun Tzu compared it to "a cataract plunging into a bottomless abyss." Momentum must be sustained, or the effects of disruption will be dissipated. In Korea, the PLA was not able to sustain the momentum necessary to attain more than tactical success.

Chinese doctrine has always accorded less weight to the material factors than does our own. It is more devious, more indirect, more subtle. But not necessarily less effective. The Chinese leadership, now in the process of creating a modern military establishment, has a viable and tested doctrine with which to endow it.

It is one function of military theory to design roles, missions, and operational procedures for the armed forces that will enable them to gain victory in a future war. It is therefore necessary to postulate correctly the nature of such a war. Here the Chinese seem to have accepted an exclusive concept. This is apparent from a secret report made by Yeh Chien-ying at a training conference convened by the Military Affairs Committee in January 1961. On this occasion, Yeh developed his concept of a war that might take place "in the next few years":

If a war should come upon us in the next few years, what kind of weapons can we primarily rely on to overcome the enemy? Here arises the problem of the relationship between conventional weapons and super weapons. At present, some foreign military theoreticians, including some American military theoreticians, maintain that in future war the final solution will still lie in conventional weapons. Though the power of atomic weapons is great, they can only attack the other party's centers in strategic air raids and destroy its economic potentialities. Afterward they can only be used primarily, according to their power, as firing preparation before an attack. To resolve the battle, to cut down the enemy's living strength, to capture positions, and to achieve victory, it will still rely upon the ground force, the army, and conventional weapons. Reliance upon the army and conventional weapons is reliance upon men. Thus, in the last analysis, it is men upon whom we are relying. We are relying upon men, and we are emphasizing the importance of political factors. We want to raise men's political awareness and to display men's power. Though some military experts of American imperialism have reached this conclusion, in theory, they have never been able to act accordingly. They maintain that the mere reliance on men cannot overcome China and the Soviet Union, and therefore they still have to rely on weapons. Since China is a country with extensive territories and a vast population and complex terrains, they also maintain that the mere reliance upon nuclear weapons cannot solve the China problem. They thus intend to use biological weapons, which can do the greatest harm to agricultural crops, so that China will have no food and consequently will suffer from internal dissension and insurrections. Now they are secretly preparing biological warfare.

In the light of conditions prevailing in our country, if war breaks out in the next three or five years, we shall still have to rely upon the weapons [now] in our hands. Chief Lin has found the answer to the question of how to use the weapons in our hands to overcome the enemy, i.e., the question of long-distance warfare and close combat. By long distance is meant any distance beyond several scores, hundreds or thousands of kilometers; by close combat is meant a distance ranging from two hundred meters to several meters, from face to face. In the case of long-distance warfare, the enemy is stronger than we. However, in the case of close combat, especially in face-to-face combat, we are in a superior position. We should thus avoid running into a situation where the enemy is stronger and should attack where the enemy is weak. In face-to-face combat, what can be counted on is nothing more than hand grenades, bayonets, and flame throwers. We should use close combat, night combat, and mining warfare to overcome the enemy. For this reason, we must pay special attention to training in close combat, to increasing the soldiers' courage, and to emphasize the importance of fighting with maximum individual courage. In future warfare our Army units will still be able to continue the fight even if they suffer organizational breakdown.

On the other side, we should make great efforts toward developing super [weapons]. This is to walk on two legs. The Air Force should study high-altitude as well as low-altitude operations. The Navy should study not only battles in distant oceans, but also along the coastal lines. All this is to walk on two legs. In the event that war breaks out in the next few years, we shall be able to destroy the enemy in close combat, even if we still do not have super weapons. Therefore, the key lies in getting familiar with the weapons in our hands. We must use this sort of thinking to train our Army units.[21]

Other information tends to substantiate the conclusion that, at least for the present period, the MAC and the high command of the PLA are primarily concerned with a war in which the ultimate phase would be fought with conventional arms, at "close range," and on the Chinese mainland. In other words, they contemplate (for the short term) a repetition of the Japanese invasion by a new generation of "imperialists" immune to the lessons of historical experience. Apparently, little consideration has been given the obvious fact that a nation which attacks China may sensibly decide to use other combat methods than those on which the Chinese place ultimate reliance.

Ground and air-forces training programs for 1961 clearly indicated Chinese preoccupation with the type of war described by Yeh. The *Bulletin of Activities* prescribed that training was to be focused on the company and its subordinate elements. Particular emphasis was to be given night marching, small-unit tactics, and night combat.[22] All training was to be conducted "under the most difficult and complicated conditions . . . under circumstances of severe cold, great heat, and stormy weather so that [the troops] can resist attack, continue fighting, and complete their mission under whatever adverse conditions." [23] This is a sound program as far as it goes and is, moreover, distinctly relevant to "Volunteer" operations in "national liberation" wars.

The arms and equipment situation as of 1961 clearly did not permit extensive large-unit training or training of high-level commanders and staffs in the use of combined arms (an infantry-tank-air-artillery team). One must presume that as modern equipment is acquired and standards of professional and technical competence raised, more advanced training, particularly in combined arms, airborne, and amphibious operations will receive due attention.

Although the essential spirit of traditional Chinese doctrine (and of Mao's as well) is offensive, the present capabilities of the PLA are so severely restricted that conventional roles and missions for the short-range future are necessarily primarily defensive in nature. It would be prudent, however, to regard this as a temporary phenomenon enjoined by circumstances. With the improvement of the PLA's offensive capabilities, we shall see corresponding changes in Chinese strategic and doctrinal concepts.

CHAPTER FIFTEEN

"The Army Can Not Be Neutral"
V. I. Lenin

While the Anglo-American tradition has tended to isolate serving soldiers from politics, things are otherwise ordered under Communist dispensations, where every effort is exerted to make them politically motivated animals. The Bolsheviks called upon their revolutionary soldiers to be "Expert and Red," the Chinese today exhort theirs to be "Red and Expert." In 1918, the Soviet government established an elaborate bureaucracy charged with assuring proper coloration of its armed forces. In the People's Republic, the General Political Department of the People's Liberation Army has a similar mission: to raise the political consciousness of the armed forces to even higher levels. A politically conscious army was what Liu Shao-ch'i was talking about when he said: "We have the spiritual atomic bomb." It was also what Lenin was talking about forty years earlier when he declared: "The army can not and must not be neutral." [1]

This concept was part of the intellectual baggage the Russians brought to Canton in 1924, when they arrived there at Dr. Sun Yat-sen's invitation to help him organize a revolutionary army. It cannot, therefore, be numbered among Comrade Mao Tse-tung's more "glorious" contributions to "military thought." What Mao did here, as he as done in other contexts, was to draw upon historical experience, refine it, and adapt it—"assimilating what is useful, rejecting what is useless, and adding what is specifically our own." [2]

A brief review of the Soviet experience may thus be germane to discussion of the role of the CCP in the People's Liberation Army today.

How to create a reliable and motivated army was the crucial question which faced Lenin in the spring and summer of 1918.

Without such an army, the Bolsheviks could not possibly retain the power they so tentatively held. The dimensions of the problem were staggering: remnants of the Imperial Army continued to disintegrate as ragged, war-weary, and half-starved peasant soldiers threw away their rifles, deserted in droves, and headed for the countryside to claim the land the Party promised them. Entire units simply evaporated. Soon, White "counterrevolutionary" armies threatened the very existence of the shaky government over which Lenin presided.

Assimilation of more than 30,000 former Czarist officers by the new Red Army compounded the difficulty of insuring its loyalty to the regime. Many of these officers were politically suspect. Still, they had to be used: as commanders and staff, in the services of supply, in the technical branches. For only they had professional knowledge and experience. But could they be trusted? A system of surveillance—the commissar system—provided an answer, a key to "the secret of making proper use of our enemy . . . of how to build communism out of the bricks that the capitalists had gathered to use against us." [3]

On April 6, 1918, the People's Commissariat for War, headed by Leon Trotsky, issued an order formally establishing the institution of military commissars in the Red Army. Three months later, the Fifth Congress of Soviets defined their functions as "guardians of the close and inviolable internal bond between the Red Army and the workers' and peasants' regime as a whole. Only irreproachable revolutionaries, stanch champions of the cause of the proletariat and the village poor, should be appointed to the posts of military commissars, to whom is handed over the fate of the army." [4]

Although commissars in Red Army units participated in all planning and validated all operations orders, their authority to intervene in a combat situation was limited. In the context of a campaign or in battle, the "military specialists"—as the Communists described former officers of the Imperial Army—made the operational decisions. Under such circumstances, "commanding personnel" were required to seek the advice of the political officers; they were not, however, required to accept it. Only if the commissar had good reason to suspect the loyalty and motives of the "specialist" was he authorized to relieve the commander, to replace him, or to assume command himself. This happened rarely.

In all matters of discipline, administration, and supply, the commissar and the commander shared authority and responsibility. But political work was the sole responsibility of the commissar. This extensive domain included agitation, propaganda, education, cultural affairs, recreation, activities of Party organizations, and compilation of dossiers on all personnel. In addition, the commissar functioned as a personal counselor, welfare officer, and "thought detective."

The commissar was expected to set an example to the soldier at all times, and particularly during combat "in those parts of the battlefield where the fighting was most severe." The Party did not temporize with those who failed to set this example. At least once, Trotsky ordered a regimental commissar before a firing squad on the charge of cowardice. He made his policy perfectly clear: "I issue this warning: if any detachment retreats without orders, the first to be shot will be the commissar, the next the commander. . . . Cowards, scoundrels, and traitors will not escape the bullet— for this I vouch before the whole Red Army.[5]

This system of dual command satisfied neither the "military specialist" nor the commissar. The former often resented what he considered gross meddling in matters he conceived to lie strictly within his purview; the latter, a dedicated revolutionary and Party member, resented having to share authority with a "class enemy." Not for this, many commissars must have thought, had a revolution been made. Nevertheless, however reluctant he might be to cooperate, the commissar had to make the relationship viable.

The commissar, whose person was by decree inviolable, embodied the ultimate authority of the Party in the Red Army. But the Party's presence was elsewhere manifest in the pervasive network of committees and cells which existed at all echelons. These quasi-official groups were the mechanisms the Party used to maintain intimate contact with the common soldiers. One may readily imagine the pressures for obedience and conformity these cohesive groups could exert on the inchoate mass of semi-literate, predominantly peasant soldiery.

Despite the contradictions inherent in the dual-command structure, the system the Bolsheviks imposed on the army was effective. There is plenty of testimony to this fact—some of which comes from former Whites. M. V. Frunze, who later replaced Trotsky and became a leading Soviet authority on the theory of war, considered that the system had played a decisive part in the winning of the civil war. "Political activity," Frunze wrote, became "a new weapon . . . which at times . . . proved more powerful than rifles or guns, and . . . effectively increased the army's fighting efficiency."[6]

The pattern of Party organization in the Chu-Mao Army was established during 1928, when the Communists based on Chingkang-shan astride the Hunan–Kiangsi borders. In some respects, the situation in the embryonic Red Army was similar to that of the Soviet Army in 1918. At least one-third of all squad leaders and platoon, company, and battalion commanders were former Nationalists and war lord soldiers who had "changed hats" and whose loyalties were naturally suspect. These men, unindoctrinated themselves, could not possibly inject "proletarian ideology" into those serving under them, nor could they be expected to be sympathetic to the emphasis placed on political work to the detriment of military training.

In these early days, commissars (or, more exactly, political officers) were installed at four levels: company, battalion, regiment, and army. At each of these levels, a Party Committee functioned. This system was a departure from that which Chiang Kai-shek had established on the recommendation of his Soviet advisers, for in the Revolutionary Army, the Kuomintang assigned political officers only to regimental and higher echelons. On the face of things, Mao's political organization was no more than a logical extension downward to the structure the CCP had inherited. Actually, however, it was a modification of prime importance, for, as we have already noted, it enabled the Party to keep an up-to-date ideological temperature chart on every officer and man in its army, indoctrinate recruits, and apprehend dissatisfaction and incipient deviations.

A typical Party Branch Committee was composed of four or five Party members: the political officer, the unit commander, the deputy commander, and one or two Communists (usually officers) who had been elected at a unit meeting of Party members and confirmed in office by the Party Committee at the next higher echelon. The Party Committee received all orders, discussed ways of implementing them, and provided "collective leadership." Literally nothing could be undertaken in any unit without explicit approval of the Party Committee. And this usually meant the explicit approval of the political officer, who, as the Committee's permanent secretary, was the key man.

Party organs naturally devoted serious attention to selection of these cadres, who were expected to manifest all conceivable virtues, both political and military. This man was the single most important man in the unit. "Facts have shown," Mao wrote, "that the better the party representative, the sounder the company." Mao rejected the idea that political and military functions could successfully be combined: "The company commander," he said, "can hardly play this important [political] role." [7]

Until the Chinese intervened in the Korean War, prisoners had been interrogated, and captured documents translated and analyzed, interested Westerners had little positive information relating either to the structure of the Party's *apparat* in the army or to the crucial role assigned it. Of the few "foreign devils" who reached Communist areas in Northwest China between 1936 and 1944, only Edgar Snow and Evans Carlson devoted even superficial attention to this matter.

In reading today what they wrote almost thirty years ago about the primitive Red Army they knew, one is able to appreciate their enthusiasm. Both men saw a new and different army. Both praised the idealism, the evident spirit of egalitarianism, the obvious ardor and dedication of the soldiers. Both remarked on an ill-disguised contempt for the Nationalists as fighters and a common confidence in the ability of the 8th Route Army to defeat the Japanese.

Both were profoundly impressed with the crusading spirit that animated this puritan army. Both commented on the monastic lives of the soldiers, who did not swear, drink, smoke, or gamble and who admitted no interest whatever in the opposite sex. To be sure, Northwest China was some distance from the Shanghai fleshpots, and a degree of sublimation was enforced by the environment. But as we know, emotional relations have always been discouraged by the Party, which demands unqualified commitment. The soldiers were expected to "give their hearts to the Party," and they did. Carlson, a Bible-reading New Englander in the Puritan tradition, was greatly impressed with this spirit of abnegation and compared the Red Army to Cromwell's.

Superficially, there was no indication that pressure was applied, but there was an iron hand in the velvet glove. The Communists had already learned a great deal about mass psychology, and the docile material was easily molded. One journalist who visited Yenan in 1937 commented on the "organic precision," "the single mass mind," of the 8th Route Army and decided that "the whole Red Army seemed to have developed that mass instinct which guides a flock of birds . . . they took action together spontaneously without any apparent signal. Their discipline was automatic. . . . I suppose they all think exactly alike . . . a kind of self-mesmerizing and self-educating body." [8]

The robotlike, "automatic" discipline this writer described is purposefully designed not to encourage expression of individual initiative by the soldier—a specific aim of training in our army—but to discourage it. Western observers never asked themselves whether it was possible for an army to be too well disciplined. This paradox was to plague the Chinese in Korea, particularly during the earlier phases when the situation was fluid. Was unremitting pressure to conform compatible with exercise of initiative at lower levels in kaleidoscopic combat situations? And there is a complementary question. What effect did political officers exert on processes of decision making and on battlefield behavior?

Indirect evidence is provided in Chinese action reports, which generally place the blame for tactical rigidity in Korea on poor communications. In a critique of operations against the 1st Marine Division, the 20th Army had this to say:

> . . . it took more than two days to receive instructions from higher level units. Rapid changes of the enemy's situation and the slow motion of our signals communication caused us to lose our opportunities in combat. . . .[9]

Opportunities were there, but no one dared exercise the initiative to grasp them. Nor, after suffering a check, could lower commanders select a possibly more rewarding course of action. They had been told by "higher levels" exactly what they must do. They did that and no more. They rationalized failure to exploit tactical success by laying the blame on unspecified "higher levels" and on the breakdown of communications.

One student who has analyzed the Chosin Reservoir campaign in detail reaches the conclusion that at lower levels the Chinese suffered from "command paralysis."

It is highly probable that the political officer and his committee again deserve much of the blame. War is not an exact science and the correct solution to unanticipated opportunities and unpredictable situations can only be determined as these arise. This being so, an important task of orthodox military training will remain the encouragement and development of command initiatives on the basis of sound tactical principles. But except in emergency the major source of initiative in the Chinese Communist Forces was intended to be the party committee which exercised collective leadership under the guidance of the political officer. Consequently, initiative had been neither encouraged nor properly developed in the military commander, and because this was true he was unprepared for the exigencies of modern combat.[10]

Both Matthew Ridgway and Mark Clark commented on the apparent inability of the Chinese to react with speed and flexibility when fleeting opportunities existed. Many nettles were not grasped.

While extreme centralization, inefficient communications, and a propensity to adhere rigidly to detailed plans all operated to constrain the exercise of initiative on the battlefield, there is no doubt that the contradiction inherent in the system of command also made its contribution. The official U.S. history of the Chosin campaign, citing captured Chinese Communist documents, clearly establishes this fact.

The story of an unsuccessful counterattack mounted by the 1st Battalion, 235th Infantry, on November 28, 1950, is revealing. In this fight, the battalion was destroyed—or, to be more precise, was forced to commit suicide. Again and again, the Chinese assaulted a position strongly held by elements of three marine companies. Finally, only one platoon remained intact. But Liu Sheng-hsi, the 2nd Company's political officer, was determined to make the worst of a bad situation. He ordered the platoon to attack. (One wonders where the company commander was at the time.)

The assault began with two squads forward, led by the platoon leader and his assistant. They charged uphill into Charlie Company's position. Like all the others, they were ground into a mat of corpses on the blood-soaked snow. To complete the suicide of the 1st Battalion, 235th Regiment, the reserve squad of this last platoon was committed. A few minutes later "there were only six men left." [11]

But the records also suggest that political officers often exercised a more productive influence, and if they are to be blamed for overreaching their prerogatives in combat, they must be given credit for helping prevent a paralysis of morale. The prescription was a nicely balanced one—its ingredients: uncomplaining fortitude, persuasion, personal courage, unflagging zeal, promise of reward, hints of punishment. The threat of the gun, impalpable, was always there. And the soldiers knew that the political officer had authority to use it.

It is indeed amazing that Sung Shih-lun's forces held together and fought as well as they did. Consider the situation: ". . . our soldiers frequently starve. . . . They ate cold food . . . some had only a few potatoes in two days. . . . They were unable to maintain physical strength for combat . . . wounded personnel could not be evacuated." [12] Ninety per cent of the men in the 26th Army suffered from frostbite. Things were no better in the 27th Army. "The troops did not have enough food . . . enough houses to sleep in . . . the bitter cold . . . snow covered the ground . . . feet, socks, and hands frozen together in one ice ball . . . they could not unscrew caps on hand grenades . . . fuses would not ignite . . . skin from the hands stuck on the shells and mortar tubes." [13]

Nevertheless, the Chinese fought. The soldiers showed slight inclination to surrender. Fewer than 400 did so. Many of these met a ghastly end between Hagaru and Koto-ri when the Chinese ambushed a U.S. Marine column in which there were 160 prisoners. The attackers paid no attention to the Marines but blasted the prisoners, most of whom they killed. This brutal episode no doubt suggested to the PLA that surrender was not a good idea.

Chinese tales of that winter campaign, from which the horrors, frustrations, and defeats are naturally omitted, describe it as a "glorious victory." The plot is always the same; the protagonists: political officers, Youth League activists, and aspirants to Party membership, always heroes.

Stories of the Chinese People's Volunteers,[14] a collection devoted almost exclusively to the deeds of Party members, provides interesting information on how the Party Committee system functioned in Korea. One tale describes the storming of a terrain feature known to the Chinese as Old Baldy. There is a preliminary planning meeting, "an enlarged meeting of the Regimental Party Committee," during which the 1st Battalion is selected by the Party Committee —not by the regimental commander in conference with his staff—to assault the mountain. As Regimental C. O. Liang explains the scheme of maneuver, the regimental commissar silently nods his approval.

The scene shifts. Hou Yung-chun, the assault battalion commander, confers with Political Instructor Ho Shu-lin. Colonel Hou is worried that his men are disposed to take the enemy too lightly. Instructor Ho sees this as a serious ideological problem. Has not Chairman Mao repeatedly warned of the danger of underestimating one's enemy on the battlefield? True, the enemy is to be despised strategically, but he must be taken seriously tactically. A nasty deviation has been uncovered. Perhaps the officers and men of Colonel Hou's battalion have not been studying the thought of Chairman Mao. There is much preparatory work ahead for Instructor Ho.

The 3rd Company is to lead the attack. A "Victory Flag" to be planted on "Old Baldy" is sent to the company political officer—*not* to the company commander. And so on. Throughout this and other stories, the point is made clearly enough that political officers are in ultimate control.

In another story, there is some discussion as to how to assign credit for victory. "This is to our company commander's credit," Kao Yung-ho, a young Communist fighter, says. Kao is promptly squelched by Li Han-yu, the company political officer.

"The credit goes to our Party," Li gravely states. "The Party Branch made the correct decision, and we on our part faithfully carried out the directions of the Regimental Party Committee." Party Representative Li looks at his watch, yawns, and bids everyone good night.

In 1956, P'eng Teh-huai, speaking before the Eighth National Congress of the CCP, described in general terms "the basic system of leadership in the Chinese People's Liberation Army." This speech suggested that no important structural changes had been made in the Party's apparatus in the army since before the Korean War.

The system of individual responsibility by the commanders under collective leadership of the Party committee is the basic system of leadership of the PLA. . . .

. . . All important matters in the army, such as important directives and orders issued by the higher organizations, the plan and arrangement of military, political and logistic tasks, the transfer and readjustment of working personnel, etc., except in emergency circumstances, should be discussed by Party committees' meetings. Clear-cut decisions should be made through the wisdom of all and then transmitted to the commanders of the army for implementation.

Both military commanders and political commissars in our army are leaders of the armed units, and both are responsible for the leadership of the army. However, there is a division of labor between them: military commanders should be responsible for the implementation of orders and directives so far as they concern military affairs, while political commissars should be responsible for the implementation of those concerning political work.[15]

Interrogation and other reports enable us to construct a fairly detailed picture of how the machinery General P'eng described was put together and how it operated in combat at the lowest level.[16]

At the time the Chinese intervened in Korea, Company "Branch Committees" (*chih pu*)—the Party's "ideological fortresses"—consisted usually of from four to six members, two of whom were the political officer and the company commander.[17] Ostensibly, the three or four other Party members who sat with these two on the

"Branch Committee" were elected by a democratic voting process in which all Party members in the company participated. But actually, the election was rigged even before ballots were distributed since the candidates were hand-picked by the Party Committee at Battalion. After each Party member had duly deliberated and marked and sealed his ballot, the political officer collected them and took them to Battalion, where votes were tabulated. However, there was a final "gimmick" even in this quasi-democratic process: voting continued until the man the Battalion political officer wanted was "elected." Thus, in reality, "election" of majority blocs within Party Branch Committees in the Battalion lay entirely in his hands. (Presumably, he would have been amenable to recommendations made by his colleagues at company level.) In emergencies when Party members could not be assembled to vote, the Battalion political officer simply filled vacancies in Company Branch Committees by appointment.[18]

The Party cells (*hsiao tsu* or "small organisms"), which existed in every company, consisted of three to five Party members who elected one of their number "leader." The "leader's" normal tenure was one year. His election had to be approved by the political officer, who could also remove him at will. In a typical company of the 118th Division, 40th Army, in which there were twenty-four Party members, there were seven such groups.[19] Additionally, in each company as many as half-a-dozen "Little Youth Groups" participated in Party work. Membership in these was restricted to candidates for Party membership enrolled in the New Democracy Youth Corps. In one company of 130 officers and men, there were 75 such aspirants. This appears to be an abnormally high proportion, for screening routings were rigorous. Background was a determining factor; those who could not establish a proper "class" origin were rejected. "It was very difficult for a former Chinese Nationalist Army man to join these groups. Approval of the Regimental Party Committee was required in each [specific] case." [20] It is not surprising that this discrimination tended to create its own contradictions: some soldiers definitely "belonged"; others were as definitely "outsiders."

The political officer exercised total supervision over Party activities in the company, and his manifold responsibilities allowed him little time to relax. Principal among his duties were:

1. Investigation of the loyalty, efficiency, and thought of all individuals in the unit

2. Propaganda
3. Political education
4. Supervision of administration (personnel; logistics)
5. Organization of Party members
6. Supervision of all Party activities
7. Approval of promotion, transfer, and demotion of all enlisted men.

"Political education" absorbed a considerable amount of the political officer's time and energy. He was held responsible for "unification of thought" in the company; encouragement of "progressives," elimination of antiquated family concepts; extirpation of "individualism"; promotion of friendly ties between Party members and "followers," control of mass psychology, and raising morale. These duties required his attendance at a variety of meetings regularly scheduled for squads, platoons, and the company. Moreover, he presided over a weekly meeting of all Party members in the company and attended another of all unit-level political officers in the regiment. Once a month, the regimental commissar convened a meeting of all political officers in the regiment. These meetings were routine. There were others, including frequent "general assemblies," as well as "special meetings" held to publish punishments adjudged for commission of serious offenses or to witness liquidation of soldiers sentenced to death.[21]

During combat operations, some routine meetings were necessarily canceled or postponed in favor of others more relevant. Before battle, the political officer and company commander jointly chaired a "popular channel" assembly where they in turn briefed the company on the political and military aspects of the general and local situations. They then described the company's mission and assigned tasks to platoons and squads. Soldiers were encouraged to participate freely in the ensuing open discussion of how best to accomplish these tasks. Prisoners testified that these meetings elicited many constructive ideas and that soldiers' recommendations were often accepted and embodied in the orders issued. Immediately before battle, officers and soldiers signed a common pledge to fight bravely. These mechanisms were exceedingly helpful in promoting group solidarity.

After battle, the company—or what was left of it—assembled for "summing up" of experiences. Here mistakes were freely admitted and openly discussed, and objective conclusions apparently drawn. Prisoners agreed that the pre-combat assemblies and post-combat gatherings were valuable. Many, however, professed to have developed a positive aversion to routine meetings held primarily for criticism and self-criticism.

Over the years, senior members of the Party's hierarchy have repeatedly and emphatically stated the official position on the correlation of political and military work in the PLA. No useful purpose could therefore be served by verbose rehash and tiresome documentation of scores of statements which repeat a refrain unchanged since the Kutien Conference. This position was again summarized in a *Red Flag* editorial of March 31, 1964, entitled "Political Work Is the Lifeline of All Work."

For a very long period of time, the Chinese revolution has been primarily a military struggle and all work of the Party has been directly or indirectly geared to military struggle. Therefore, treatment of the relations between political and military affairs has been an outstanding problem. Shall politics lead the military or shall the military lead politics? Is it the Party which directs the gun or is it the gun which directs the Party? This question concerns the direction to be taken in building the army and also the success or failure of the revolutionary task.

Far back in the days of the founding of the Workers and Peasants Red Army, Comrade Mao Tse-tung had already concentrated his energies on the solution of this problem. In the resolution of the Ninth CCP Congress of the Fourth Red Army, also known as the resolution of the Kutien Conference, which was drafted by Comrade Mao Tse-tung himself in 1929, the general principle of placing the armed forces under the leadership and supervision of the Party was laid down. Comrade Mao Tse-tung criticized the purely military viewpoint which hindered the execution of the Party's correct line. Those who held that viewpoint refused to recognize that the army was only one of the instruments for the fulfillment of political tasks, opposed military affairs to politics, even maintained that military affairs should lead politics, saying that "as long as the military situation is good, the political situation will also be good, and if the military situation is bad, the political situation will also be bad," and so advocated that organizationally the political work organs of the armed forces should be placed under the military work organs. Emphatically pointing out the dangers of such a viewpoint, Comrade Mao Tse-tung said, "If such thinking is allowed to develop, there will be the danger of [our] being divorced from the masses, putting political power in the hands of the army and departing from proletarian leadership, just like the armed forces of the Kuomintang who are going the way of war lordism." Subsequently, Comrade Mao Tse-tung pointed out repeatedly: "Our principle is that the Party should direct the gun and the gun shall never be allowed to direct the Party."

It is necessary to put political work in first place in armed forces' work and to stress the Party's role of political leadership because our armed forces belong to the people and to the proletariat. This army must submit itself absolutely to the Party's leadership, arm all its personnel with Marxism-Leninism and the thought which combines the universal truth of Marxism-Leninism with the concrete practice of the Chinese revolution—the thought of Mao Tse-tung, carry out thoroughly the Party's programmes, lines, and policies and the Government's laws and decrees, foster among its personnel a voluntary sense of discipline and the "three-eight" style of work, strictly carry out the principles of unanimity between officers and men, unanimity between the military and civilian population and disintegration of enemy forces, strengthen unity within the army and between the army and others, etc. It is only in this way that the army can have proletarian consciousness and strong fighting power, can stand firmly and closely together with the people, may not fear any difficulty or hardship and can defeat any enemy. All this is possible only by relying on the Party's systematic political work in the army. Without political work none of this will be possible.

In order to do political work within the army and carry out the principle of making politics lead military affairs and the Party direct the army, the Chinese Communist Party has established [Party] committees at different levels in all regimental and higher units of the army as the core of centralized leadership and unity in the armed forces, and instituted the system of divided responsibility for commanding officers under the centralized, collective leadership of the Party committees as the basic system of Party leadership over the army. This system is a concrete application in the army of the Party's principle of democratic centralism. Except under emergency conditions, when commanding officers may take decisions and act according to their discretion, all important matters concerning the army must first be fully discussed by the Party committees, which will make clear and definite resolutions to be carried out at separate levels. To ensure the political leadership of the proletarian party over the army, a system of political commissars and political organs has also been instituted in the army. These political organs are the working apparatus of the Party. Meanwhile, a system of dual leadership over the army by the military system under the unified leadership of the Party Central Committee in conjunction with local Party committees is also enforced, so that the local Party committees may also exercise leadership and supervision over the army.

Such systems ensure for our army complete, systematic, regular and effective political work. They also ensure that our army will be a truly proletarian revolutionary army under the absolute leadership of the Party, a responsive and obedient tool which will fight to fulfil the Party's political tasks at any time, in any place and under any circumstances.

After the victory of the revolutionary war, the People's Liberation Army has become a principal part of the state power of the proletariat. Undoubtedly, to continue promoting the glorious tradition of the political work of the PLA and to constantly revolutionize and modernize the army is one of the important and essential conditions for strengthening the proletarian dictatorship.

Politics leads and commands everything else, and to regard political

264 The Chinese People's Liberation Army

work as the soul of all other work is a general principle of Marxism-Leninism. Of course, it is applicable not only in the military domain but also in other respects.[22]

The mere fact that the Party felt it necessary to publish this lengthy statement in its official theoretical journal suggests that some reactionary termites were still lurking in the woodwork. Certainly, all senior military cadres have lived with the system for years and are well aware of the nature and purposes of the Party's structure in the armed forces. Presumably, then, this statement (and a number of more recent reiterations of long-established and well-known policy) was designed as a reminder and a warning: the Party does not propose to allow military cliques which could conceivably challenge its authority to arise. What the Party wants and is determined to have is "a responsive and obedient tool which will fight to fulfill the Party's political tasks at any time, in any place, and under any circumstances."

In light of the intensity of surveillance, it is difficult to see how dissident groups could long exist undiscovered. No senior or junior officers could possibly gather, even for a social dinner, without their political colleagues. And, in the unlikely circumstance that no watchdog happened to be present, what senior commander or junior officer who harbored "deviationist thoughts" would dare express them, even "in the wine cups"? For mutual trust cannot exist in a system specifically designed to inhibit the germination and fruition of those truly close and comradely associations which form spontaneously and mature naturally in any environment where toil, hardship, danger, and suffering are a lot common to all.

CHAPTER SIXTEEN

The People's Militia:
"A Magic Sword Which Never Rusts"

On March 24, 1917, V. I. Lenin living in exile in Switzerland wrote to revolutionary comrades in Petrograd a "Third Letter from Afar." In this epistle, Lenin discussed his program for the creation of a proletarian militia, a project he described as "the task of the day—the slogan of the present hour." [1] This "really universal militia" would assume all police functions and "guarantee absolute order and a comradely discipline." Even more important, it would take the place of "the army separated from the people," that counterrevolutionary tool which the ruling class used for purposes of "domestic suppression and foreign adventure."

Lenin planned a People's Militia to embrace practically the entire population: "all adult citizens of both sexes" between the ages of eighteen and sixty-five. Officers and noncommissioned officers were to be elected by direct vote. As the mass militia grew and gained experience, its members would arm, train, and educate the illiterate masses, assure them an opportunity to participate "in affairs of state . . . ; draw the youngsters into political life," and tear adult women "away from the stupefying domestic and kitchen atmosphere." Unless such a militia were organized, Lenin continued, it would be "impossible to secure real freedom . . . impossible to build a democracy, let alone socialism."

Mao Tse-tung was familiar with Lenin's thesis, but by 1928 he had seen enough of revolution and counterrevolution to be convinced that no such quasi-military organization could possibly play a decisive role in the China of that time. What was required was a regular army, an army under the leadership and discipline of the Party:

. . . the existence of a regular Red Army of adequate strength is a nec-essary condition for the existence of a Red political power. If we have only Red Guards [Militia] of a local character but no regular Red Army, then we can only deal with the house-to-house militia [the local forces of the landlords], but not the regular White troops. Therefore, unless we have regular armed forces of adequate strength, even though we have won the mass support of the workers and peasants, we certainly cannot create an independent regime, let alone an independent regime that lasts long and develops daily.[2]

Mao thus clearly distinguished between the purpose of a "regu-lar" Red Army and that of Red "Guards." The army's mission was "to deal with . . . the regular White troops" and make it possible for an independent regime to exist and expand; the "Guards" were subsidiary, local organizations with local functions. This was to be the pattern in every part of China that fell under Communist con-trol.

The first thing the Reds did when they established themselves in the Hunan–Kiangsi borderlands in 1928 was to organize Red Guard detachments to fight "the house-to-house militia forces . . . and to safeguard the political power of the border area."[3] The Red Guards (*chi'ih wei tui*), equipped with rifles and trained by the army, had limited combat capability. They were assisted locally by so-called Insurrection Detachments (*pao tung tui*), clandestine groups assigned to identify and dispose of "counterrevolutionary" elements, "evil landlords," and "local bullies." (Not all these "class enemies" were liquidated, however. Kidnaping prosperous landlords and rich peasants and holding them for ransom was a lucrative busi-ness in Communist areas.) Finally, there were the Self-Defense Armies (*tzu wei chün*): peasants armed with hoes, spears, pikes, homemade swords, daggers, scythes, and bird guns. These various organizations were supplemented by women's auxiliaries, Young Pioneers (*shao sheng tui*), and a children's corps of "small devils" (*hsiao kuei*). The militia thus embraced practically the entire popu-lation in every area under Red control; its covert tendrils ran into adjacent counties where control was nominally exercised by the Whites.

This pervasive system provided the Red Army and its guerrilla groups with a loyal, versatile, readily available auxiliary. The militia's loyalty was ensured by its class composition and the con-stant, close supervision which Party cadres and reliable Red Army men exercised. Two complementary functions common to all its echelons were collection of information for the Reds and denial of information to the Whites. Then, as later, the militia provided porters to carry supplies and evacuate wounded. From the "Pioneers," the Reds drew partially trained and indoctrinated young men into the army. Militia detachments assigned to cooperate with the Red Army performed many missions of a quasi-combat nature. They conducted deception and distraction operations designed to mystify and confuse Nationalist commanders; they also guarded prisoners, hid and cared for wounded Red Soldiers, and conducted routine reconnaissance patrols.

The general pattern developed during this early period was to prevail, with minor modifications, for many years. Mao Tse-tung's faith in the system was fully justified during the resistance to Japan and the later civil war. An official Party historian has written: "The experience of the Chinese people in the revolutionary wars showed that the militia was an indispensable, important instrument. . . . This popular armed force . . . played an inestimably great role in winning victory." [4]

Against the Japanese, the militia waged what the Communists described as "tunnel war," "demolition war," and "sparrow war." Complex and extensive tunnel systems, literally hundreds of miles in length, provided safe underground highways for guerrillas and militiamen. "Demolition war" was mine warfare on a huge scale. Primitive "box mines" (not the less effective because they were homemade) blew hundreds of Japanese trucks into small pieces on North China highways. "Sparrow war" was essentially harassment carried out by small groups. One tactic was for three or four men to lie hidden in fields of standing kaoliang or sorghum and await the passage of small Japanese patrols, which were never particularly security conscious. A murderous fusillade was followed by immediate swift dispersal. Sniping was another favorite method, particularly in towns. These activities inevitably provoked brutal Japanese reprisals.

But killing Japanese was the least important of many tasks. The principal one was to feed Communist guerrillas with information of Japanese movements. Thanks to its network of spies, the Red command was able "to see a distance of 1,000 *li*" and "to hear voices far away." At the same time, the militia helped turn the Japanese commanders into men both "blind and deaf." ". . . they [the militia] helped our regular forces to create favorable opportunities, seize upon the weaknesses of the enemy, and concentrate superior forces for annihilating groups of enemy forces." [5]

The nocturnal activities of militiamen in villages adjacent to railway lines kept them busy. When they were not lifting sections of track, stealing tools required for maintenance, robbing and setting fire to warehouses in which Japanese materials and supplies were stored, and ditching roads, they were otherwise causing the Imperial Army's widely dispersed garrison detachments the maximum amount of inconvenience. The militia kidnaped and secretly executed collaborators, accumulated and cached grain and flour for the guerrillas, spread rumors designed to deceive Japanese Intelligence, subverted puppet troops, hid 8th Route Army spies, passed messages, escorted agents, and conducted anti-Japanese and anti-Nationalist propaganda.

In the civil war, Nationalist strategy—identical to that of the Japanese earlier—called for holding "points" (*tien*)—the cities and principal towns—and "lines" (*hsien*)—railways and important highways. The countryside (*mien*), abandoned to the Communists, literally boiled with revolutionary activities in which the Party assigned a leading role to the militia, whose principal targets were landlords, rich peasants, and members of the small-town bourgeoisie suspected of Nationalist sympathies. The militia effectively isolated the cities garrisoned by Chiang's troops and wrecked hundreds of miles of railway and roads in the process. For example, in 1947 the right of way from Tsinan to Tsingtao in Shantung province was utterly destroyed. The revolutionary waters began to lap ever closer to the cities of North China.

After the seizure of power, the militia functioned as a police force responsible for establishing order in rural areas. In October 1950, more than 5 million men, an almost inexhaustible reservoir of manpower for the PLA, were carried on militia rolls.[6] During the Korean War, the Party relied on the militia to preserve peace in the countryside, and the militia apparently acquitted itself well. At the same time, the militia took over routine security assignments in coastal areas.

After the Korean War, the principal duties of the militia continued to be those of a rural police force. An article in the *Liberation Army Daily* indicates the general nature of activities in mid-1957: ". . . among the cases of murder, arson, poison, and burglary in a certain place last year, the militia participated in 80 per cent of the cases in which the criminals were apprehended. The militia has also assisted the public security organizations in arresting counterrevolutionaries, . . . in watching over warehouses, . . . in protecting . . . means of communications." [7]

Early in August 1958, Party Chairman Mao Tse-tung left Peking to visit a model rural project established about a month previously in Honan province. This was the Hsiliying People's Commune, a "progressive" experiment in communal living, in which the Chairman was profoundly interested. Mao arrived at Hsiliying on August 4, toured the pilot commune, and talked to some of the peasants. Before he left, he remarked that the country needed more such enterprises. Mao repeated this remark on August 9 during his inspection of a large agricultural cooperative in Shantung. There he said that rural communes, which combined industry, agriculture, commerce, education, and military work, were suitable for China as such an organization was uniquely adaptable to effective "guidance." [8]

A few days after the Chairman returned to Peking, members of the Politburo gathered at the seaside resort of Peitaiho. In this salubrious atmosphere, enjoyed exclusively by foreign "imperialists" in prerevolutionary days, the Politburo designed drastic changes in the traditional economic and social fabric of China's rural society and some time before August 25 passed to the Party's Central Committee the basic decision to establish rural communes. On August 29, the Central Committee approved a "Resolution on the Establishment of People's Communes in Rural Areas" setting forth the details of the plan. [9]

After blandly observing that "an upsurge in setting up communes" would probably soon develop, that the people had spontaneously "taken to organizing themselves along military lines," were "working with militancy," and were beginning "to lead a collective life," the resolution outlined in specific terms the Party's concept of the rural Utopia it proposed to create:

In the present circumstances the establishment of people's communes with all-round management of agriculture, forestry, animal husbandry, side occupations and fishing, where industry (the worker), agriculture (the peasant), exchange (the trader), culture and education (the student), and military affairs (the militiamen) merge into one, is the fundamental policy to guide the peasants to accelerate socialist construction, complete the building of socialism ahead of time and carry out the gradual transition to communism.

Two days later, the campaign went into high gear when a *Red Flag* editorial exhorted the people to "get organized along military lines," to "do things the way battle duties are done," and to "live collective lives." Only this type of militant organization, *Red Flag* continued, would enable the Party to deploy the people "with greater freedom and on a large scale." [10]

In the context of the commune program, a large-scale militia seems to have been viewed as an instrument the Party could use to impose its line, to control the masses, and to stimulate production. The military function, which was not stressed, was apparently considered subsidiary. [11]

At this juncture, however, there was a development—one perhaps not entirely fortuitous—which enabled the Party "to accelerate socialist construction" and to endow the militia movement with the most compelling of all emotional appeals: defense of the homeland. During the latter part of August, tensions had been building up in the area of the Nationalist-held islands of Quemoy and Matsu off the shores of the mainland, and at the beginning of September, the situation turned into a full-fledged crisis. According to Peking, "imperialist aggressive forces" posed an imminent threat to the security of China. During the first week of September, under the slogan of "Everyone a Soldier," the Party launched a movement to enroll practically all able-bodied adults in a universal people's militia, deluged the country with floods of xenophobic anti-American propaganda, and once again worked the population into a state bordering on hysteria. [12]

By the middle of the month, in response to the Party's "clarion calls," peasants were "rushing joyously" to join communes, and the militia movement had gathered the momentum of a tidal wave. Not only peasants but workers, students, traders, government officials, miners, teachers, and fishermen "spontaneously" flocked to shoulder arms. According to Communist sources, tens of millions put themselves under martial discipline during the first three weeks of this spasm as militia units "sprouted like bamboo shoots after the rain." Shantung province reported 15 million in training, Fukien, "several million"; Amoy University, "a division"; Foochow, "a hundred regiments"; Canton, "over a hundred units"; Peking, "fifty divisions." [13]

In early October, Szechwan province claimed that 30 million inhabitants were drilling daily; Shantung, 25 million; Kiangsu, 14 million; Honan, 20 million; Liaoning, 8 million. [14] Even if one makes the usual allowance for habitual gross exaggeration of Chinese Communist statistics, the movement represented a stupendous achievement—"a wonder of proletarian organization," as Lenin once described the universal militia he wished to see develop in Russia.

In January 1959, General Fu Ch'iu-tao, director of the Mobilization Department, PLA, and commander in chief of the militia, proudly announced that the Party's objective had been achieved:

> Over the past months, under the care of the Party Center and Chairman Mao, a powerful movement to turn the whole nation into soldiers has spread to all parts of our country simultaneous with the establishment of people's communes. The movement has been launched by our people for the purpose of defending their fatherland and crushing the imperialist military provocations. Tens of millions of people are organized and armed; they are majestically marching forward to conquer nature in a communist spirit of cooperation so as to accelerate the pace of socialist construction in our country. Should the imperialist brigands dare to invade our country, the whole nation will be mobilized to wipe out the enemy resolutely and completely. This is an important development and a great victory of Chairman Mao Tse-tung's military thinking in the people's war and is a fundamental measure of our people to defend our socialist fatherland and cope with imperialism.[15]

At about the same time, Peking claimed a staggering total of 225 million militiamen ready to repel any "mad aggressors" who would "be drowned in an ocean of a whole nation turned into soldiers."

To hasten the pace of this movement, the Party mounted a remarkable psychological operation that has received very little attention. This was the use of martial and bellicose terminology to stimulate the peasants who were suddenly transformed into "fighters" on the "agricultural front." Rural areas became "battlefields"; the forces of nature "enemies" to be conquered. "Shock troops" "stormed the heavens," led "assaults" to collect manure, ditch fields, plow, sow, weed, and harvest. The tenor of the language used was consistently militant. Workers in the fields did not work, they "fought" (*chan tou*). After "estimates of the enemy situation" were made and "battle plans" drawn, "shock troops" conducted "storm attacks." Red flags planted after a successful manure foray indicated another "rampart" successfully "stormed," another "enemy position" carried, another "tactical battle" won.[16]

Military duties were not, however, entirely neglected. Occasional items in the mainland press reported activities in Kwangtung and Fukien provinces, where militiamen assisted the PLA in patrolling the coast; acted as members of air-warning units; guarded railway bridges and factories; tracked down "counterrevolutionary elements," Chiang Kai-shek agents, assorted spies, saboteurs, and disturbers of the peace.

In 1960, rumors originating in Taiwan suggested that perhaps all was not well with the People's Militia. These rumors were well founded. Investigation disclosed that the Party's "magic sword" was both blunted and rusty. Just how serious the situation was is fully revealed in the "Report by Comrade Fu Ch'iu-tao on the Inspection of Work of the Honan Militia" and in the accompanying endorsement by the Party's Military Affairs Committee (MAC). These appeared in the classified *Bulletin of Activities*.[17]

Comrade Fu visited Honan province from November 12 to December 21, 1960, at the behest of the MAC. This was at a time when the communes had collapsed and severe food shortages existed in the countryside. A large part of Honan province, traditionally a rich farming land, had become a "seriously affected disaster area." Fu's honest picture of the state of the militia—of which, be it remembered, he was commander in chief—bears no resemblance whatever to that created by Party propagandists for domestic and external consumption.

General Fu's report indicated that 19,980,000 men and women, almost 40 per cent of the population of the province, were enrolled in the militia but that "the . . . organization was very impractical." Expansion in 1958 had been too rapid, and "practical work" had lagged. Many young people interviewed said they had joined the militia in 1958 but were no longer members. Of one "paper battalion" of 620 members, Comrade Fu could discover no more than 16 active militiamen, and these did not even know to what squad, platoon, or company they were supposed to belong.

Many "bad elements . . . descended from ruffians and bandits" had sneaked into the militia, as had "middle peasants," members of the landlord class, counterrevolutionaries, and other "rightists." Comrade Fu attributed this "heterogeneous situation" to the fact that those in charge locally "did not realize that the militia was the instrument of the proletarian dictatorship." Alas, very poor judgment had been exhibited in selection of cadres. Thus, many "evil" spirits had infiltrated the militia and were using their offices "to rob, beat up, and push around people, rape women, and practice seriously unlawful acts." In one county, 11 of 13 militia commanders had committed such acts. Three of every four militia regimental and battalion commanders in the entire province were guilty of these and other unspecified crimes.

In one county, the people referred to the militiamen as "mad dogs," in another as "gangsters," in another as "bandit kings." Elsewhere, the peasants described the militia as "tiger bands" and "living bandits." As Comrade Fu ruefully observed, this sort of thing reflected seriously on the Party and harmed "the glorious tradition" of the militia.

Care of weapons—or, more correctly, the lack of care—also distressed General Fu. Of the more than 3,500 rifles that were inspected in one county, his investigators found almost half unusable. Hundreds of rifles had been sold to bandits, who used them to carry out "cruel and evil deeds." Militiamen dissatisfied with obsolete weapons refused to care for them, abandoned them, or sold the barrels as scrap. But, Comrade Fu observed, "in future warfare we must not only employ the present weapons, but also in the militia we must use long-handled swords and red-tasseled spears."

The cadres, almost uniformly careless and lackadaisical, had failed to exercise close supervision. Falsification of reports was common. Militiamen carried on rolls in one county frequently fled to another to escape drill. Depraved and decadent cadres, interested only in self-advancement, "paid no attention to the masses," misunderstood the Party's policy, and revealed an unfortunate tendency toward "evil and lawless deeds."

In concluding this otherwise interesting and admirably factual secret report, Comrade Fu departed from the standards of objectivity supposed to distinguish Marxist-Leninist analyses. The Party, as usual, was not to blame for the sorry situation he described. "Class enemies" were still powerful and rampant. They "had grasped the instrument of leadership and dictatorship, had practiced class revenge on the masses, and carried out the most inhuman cruelties." His recommendation was that the militia be completely reorganized.

In endorsing this report, the Military Affairs Committee directed that:

1. Special attention be paid to the ideological purity of the militia.
2. Leadership be exercised by reliable Party cadres.
3. Weapons (that is, rifles) be handled only by reliable persons.
4. The political and ideological education of the militia be improved, and its revolutionary alertness increased.

In 1962, as the nation recovered from the trauma of the "Great Leap," Mao Tse-tung called upon the nation to "put the people's militia work on a solid political, organizational, and military footing." [18] Once again, after a lapse of almost three years, articles on the subject appeared in the general press. However, during 1963 militia work was not particularly emphasized.

In the spring of 1964, the Party laid plans for intensified summer training of urban militia units, and in June, a "Joint Notification for Military Camping Activities" appeared in the press. Summer camping, it was announced, would be conducted under the auspices of headquarters, PLA; the General Political Department, PLA; the National Sports Commission; the Ministry of Education; the All-Chinese Federation of Trade Unions; the Young Communist League; and the National Federation of Women. The sponsors of the mass camping scheme made it perfectly clear that the purpose of this temporary migration from schools, factories, mines, industrial plants, and government offices was not recreation but "to spread military knowledge universally among young people and children." [19]

The summer program concentrated on political and ideological training, swimming, rifle marksmanship, grenade throwing, bayonet drill, signal communications, parachuting, study of Chairman Mao's thought, mountaineering, anti-aircraft defense, and reconnaissance. Under the slogan, "Conquer Great Nature, Conquer All Difficulties, Conquer All Enemies," hundreds of thousands of city dwellers betook themselves on signal to the countryside for periods ranging from several days to a month. On July 26, Peking's *People's Daily* reported that camping "with a rich and diversified content was carried out over extensive areas and in various forms." [20]

Press reports reflected the importance Party authorities attached to the movement, which was apparently designed to arouse the more sophisticated city dwellers from a dangerous state of ideological apathy. From Peking, more than 120,000 went to the country; from Shanghai, 300,000. More than 10,000 Peking University students deserted classrooms for training under PLA supervision. Figures from other cities were not given, but Canton, Hangchow, K'unming, Tsinan, Chengtu, and the Wuhan area (Hankow-Wuch'ang-Hanyang) reported enthusiastic response. Militiamen in Fukien province kept their eyes on the offshore islands, Quemoy and Matsu, "occupied by the Chiang bandits." They "carried out political studies and trained themselves hard in coastal defense, cherishing class hatred." [21]

Hatred is a dominant theme in Chinese Communist propaganda, and it was emphasized during the 1964 "camping movement." Old militiamen were held responsible for "arming the minds of the younger generation." The slogan for the summer was "You must have a gun in your heart before we [the Party] can put a gun in your hand." [22] On August 20, *Nan-fang Jih-pao* warned against lethargy and exhorted those in training to develop their work vigorously, as "class struggle in China is still very sharp and complex; domestically, the overthrown reactionaries are not yet reconciled to their defeat." [23]

During October, the PLA convened a national "Militia Work Conference" in Peking. Mao attended some sessions of the conference and personally signified the importance he attached to a renaissance of militia work by holding a reception for the delegates. Numerous Party dignitaries, marshals, and senior generals addressed sessions and emphasized the necessity for "down-to-earth efforts" to get the militia reorganized on a solid basis both "politically and militarily" in order to "strengthen its combat might for the fight against imperialist aggression, and to augment the armed forces of the people." [24] Those present expressed their unanimous determination "to raise the great Red banner of Chairman Mao Tse-tung's ideas still higher, to bring into fuller play a thoroughgoing spirit of revolution, to work with boundless devotion and improve the work of the People's Militia in accordance with Chairman Mao Tse-tung's instructions." [25]

The Chairman's instructions, said Party leaders, constituted a "major strategic measure" to cope with enemies both internal and external.[26] Apparently, they also included a new purge directive for the militia, which hereafter is to be limited exclusively to workers and poor and middle peasants who are politically reliable and competent to care for counterrevolutionaries at home as well as "imperialist aggressors" and "reactionaries of various nations."

The militia work conference also ratified the decision to strengthen the militia movement through "socialist education," i.e., intensified ideological indoctrination, "hate" sessions, and so forth. In the future, the PLA is to be more intimately associated with the militia through transfer of armed forces cadres to militia units as instructors on a permanent basis.

Renewed emphasis on the militia does not necessarily mean that the Party intends a reprise of the "Every Man a Soldier Movement." What emerges from the press indicates that the Party is primarily interested in creating a manageable, reliable, and effective production "shock force" which is politically clean and can be trusted and used by the PLA for auxiliary purposes. There is some evidence that the PLA did not cooperate as fully as it might have in the 1958 campaign to make everyone a soldier. However, the information available at present makes it clear that the armed forces are fully participating in the current campaign to reorganize, rebuild, and train the militia.

According to Party doctrine, the militia must be "under the firm and strong leadership of the Communist Party." [27] Leadership is entrusted to relatively few Party cadres, activists, and demobilized soldiers enrolled in basic or "core" militia groups or detachments (*chi kan min ping*). This "core" militia is composed of young men between sixteen and thirty and women between seventeen and twenty-two. Aspirants must establish "untainted" backgrounds—i.e., they must come from proletarian or "poor peasant" families. None other is eligible. Although reports are not so specific as they might be, it appears that the desirable ratio of "backbone" militiamen to "ordinary" militiamen is of the order of 1 to 3 or perhaps 1 to 4. This ratio would suggest one squad of "backbone" militia per platoon, with the other three or four squads being "ordinary" militia. The "backbone" militia is said to be of the order of 20 million. This indicates an "ordinary" militia of, say, 80 million. Very little information on organization or equipment is available.

A Party spokesman has described the militia as "an armed force of the masses of the people." [28] Actually it is nothing of the kind, for only members of the "core" militia are trusted with arms, and they only when on duty and supervised.

Also, the militia is "an armed producer." [29] That is to say, the militia is a docile, readily maneuverable labor force which local authorities deploy in accordance with the "chessboard" theory. In spring and fall, project priorities for plowing, gathering manure, sowing, weeding, cultivating, and harvesting are established. In off seasons, the peasants, now no longer left to their own devices, are put to work on levees, dam building, clearing and ballasting railroad rights of way, grading airfields, afforestation, ditching, road building, drainage, housing, and other projects. The massive labor power of these countless peasant battalions is gradually changing the face of China.

"The militia is organized under voluntary and democratic principles."[30] Or so the Party insists. This statement is too patently absurd to require refutation. One may imagine the fate of a Chinese peasant who obstinately refused to join the local militia unit.

The militia is still commanded by Fu Ch'iu-t'ao. The PLA provides military command, guidance, and weapons and with the Public Security Forces is jointly responsible for training and ideological indoctrination.[31] The administration of the militia, and its employment in collective enterprises are the responsibility of civil *hsien* (county) officials, who are invariably Party members.

Since 1961 public disclosure of matters affecting the militia has been punishable as a crime against the state. One must, however, presume that the conditions brought to light by General Fu taught the Party a lesson and that the "backbone" militia as redesigned is supposed to be an instrument of some quality and of at least limited military usefulness.

Recent organizational trends and recent training activities confirm this hypothesis. In the countryside, the militia is equipped as infantry and receives basic infantry training; in the cities, specialized functional units are formed. For example, railway workers and truck drivers are enrolled in transport units, electrical engineering students in telecommunications companies, medical students in sanitary platoons, chemistry students in chemical and biological warfare companies, and so on.[32]

In a recent article on the present role of the militia, Liu Yün-cheng writes that work is now on "a solid political organizational and military footing," which, he continues,

has clarified the direction in which militia building should develop and raised concrete demands on militia work. The carrying out of Comrade Mao Tse-tung's directive on militia work throughout the nation has greatly strengthened the masses of the militia politically, and put the organization and arms of the militia more firmly in the hands of the most reliable class brothers loyal to the people, the revolution, and the socialist cause. The political consciousness of the people's militia has been greatly enhanced, its ranks made purer and sounder, and its organization and discipline strengthened. The fighting power of the militia has been greatly improved.[33]

We have heard similar assertions before, but the new policy is more temperately stated. Certainly, as the militia system is an integral and necessary mechanism in the Party's indoctrination and control apparatus, as well as in the incessant battle of production, it will be continuously "purified" and strengthened at the same time as its training, and hence its combat efficiency, improves. In 1960, the Party discovered that this is not an endeavor in which "more" is necessarily synonomous with "better," and it is unlikely that the most recent upsurge in "militia building" will be carried to the extremes that characterized the movement in 1958. But the People's Militia—"the magic sword which never rusts"—will remain one of the unique features of the mainland scene.

CHAPTER SEVENTEEN

"The Five Continents Are Shaken"
Mao Tse-tung

Peking's regional foreign policy goals vis-à-vis the United States have not changed since the Korean War. Her primary objective continues to be the elimination of American influence from her Asian rimlands and ultimate liquidation of the American presence in Southeast Asia, South Korea, Japan, Okinawa, Taiwan, and the Philippines. China sees herself today as ringed to the east and south by an American power which she deems hostile and menacing. The pressure of this power frustrates the attainment of what she considers her legitimate aspirations. Asia, she insists, is for the Asians, and "Asian problems must be settled by Asians." Americans are unwanted, alien meddlers.

China is determined by one means or another to break out of this encirclement. But for some time to come, she will not be able to deploy the combination of political, economic, psychological, and military means that will enable her to do so. Accumulation of resources sufficient to achieve this end will absorb her attention and energies for many years.

When China decided to enter the Korean War, she boasted that she would "throw the imperialist aggressors into the sea." She discovered that her capabilities did not match her ambitions. For some time, she has been stridently prophesying that the Americans will be driven from South Vietnam. "This war," Foreign Minister Ch'en Yi said on September 29, 1965, "will definitely end in victory for Vietnam and defeat for U.S. imperialism." [1] Ch'en Yi added that the Chinese would stand "unreservedly" at the side of the "Vietnamese people" until this objective is attained. Peking has consistently promised aid and comfort to the Viet Cong and has delivered arms, equipment, and ammunition to them via Laos, Cambodia, and Hanoi. And although no well-defined picture of the extent of her commitment has yet emerged, it is clear that the primary thrust of her foreign policy is directed to victory—if only by proxy—in Vietnam.

The Korean experience is not a valid criterion for assessment of China's capabilities or intent to intervene in South Vietnam. In the first place, the presence of American ground forces there, although most undesirable, does not constitute an immediate threat to Chinese territory or to her national security. Even if China wished to intervene forcefully—and as of September 1966 there was no indication that she did—a variety of constraints would operate unfavorably.

The Chinese would find it extremely difficult to deploy and sustain a force of more than six to eight "light" divisions south of the 17th parallel. The area of operations is distant from China's borders. Unlike Manchuria, her southwest provinces are poorly developed, and existing transport nets primitive. The terrain is rugged, and the tenuous K'unming–Hanoi and Nanning–Hanoi rail links extremely vulnerable to aerial interdiction. Compared to the logistic situation that would face the Chinese here, the Korean problem can be described as elementary.

U.S. government spokesmen have clearly intimated to Peking that direct intervention will invite retaliatory action against the Chinese homeland. Although targeting is naturally ultra-secret, it is not secret that the United States would consider the "sanctuary" concept inapplicable and would probably attack selected military installations with conventional weapons. In this context, identified Chinese nuclear plants and installations would naturally be primary targets.

Precisely what the Kremlin's reaction would be should the Chinese overtly intervene south of the 17th parallel is a question which no doubt is causing a number of people in both Washington and Peking to lose sleep. In Korea, Soviet might stood openly behind the Chinese. But in September 1958, during the Quemoy-Matsu crisis, the Chinese tested their fraternal allies and found them wanting. Nor did Peking receive from the Soviet Union the moral support she expected in October–November 1962, when she launched her "righteous self-defense counterattack" against India. It is reasonable to suppose that the Russians have made no binding commitment to back the Chinese should they intervene in South Vietnam.

Possibly some North Vietnamese Party leaders favor Chinese intervention. It has been reported that Le Duan, Secretary of the Lao Dong, enjoys Peking's support and is amenable to this policy.[2] But in their public pronouncements, the North Vietnamese have consistently refused to commit themselves. On balance, available evidence supports the conclusion that Ho Chi Minh would not be at all eager to have PLA "Volunteers" base in, transit, or be supplied through North Vietnam, unless the security of his country was directly threatened by an invading force.

What we should anticipate, however, is an accelerated infusion of material aid in terms of individual and team weapons such as medium and heavy mortars, recoilless rifles, pack artillery, automatic arms, explosives, flame throwers, land mines, and so forth. All these items are now manufactured in PLA arsenals. At the same time, the Chinese can provide radios and other communication equipment and engineer and medical supplies on an increasing scale. China can also furnish competent advisers, engineers, technicians, and skilled labor in all categories. She can provide and man modern aircraft-warning and fire-control radars, anti-aircraft artillery, and probably a limited number of crewed surface-to-air missile batteries.

Indefinite protraction of hostilities on the guerrilla pattern in Vietnam is altogether favorable to Peking's interests. As she sees it, a long war will sap American energies, focus American attention on this area to the exclusion of others, drain American strength, impair American morale, damage American prestige, undermine American alliances, and so concretely alter "the balance of forces" to China's benefit. We may thus conclude that China will exert every pressure and take every measure short of direct intervention on the ground to prolong the fighting in South Vietnam and to prevent negotiation of a settlement.

China's ability to sustain PLA formations in Laos or in northeast Thailand along the valley of the Mekong is limited by geography, communications, and calculation of acceptable risk. She can, however, aid "national liberation" groups with the same type of support she renders North Vietnam. At present, the most effective help she can give the Thai National Liberation Front and the Pathet Lao is probably to provide personnel and facilities, arms, and equipment for training and indoctrination of military and political cadres. Undoubtedly she is doing this now, but the scale of such activities is unknown, as is the scale of arms supply.

In Tibet, the PLA is deploying the equivalent of three armies. Some sources estimate a total of six to nine 8,000-man "light" divisions plus a number of separate regiments and Border Guard formations. With special support units (principally transport and engineer), total commitment to this strategic region may be of the order of 140,000. Terrain, weather, and communications present severe problems. Logistic constraints thus put a lid on the number and type of formations that can be supported north of the western Yunnan–Himalayan arc or that could operate south of it for sustained periods.

Whether China will again choose to exercise her option in this area is doubtful. Soviet, British, and American reaction to her most recent attempt to bully India obviously deflated Peking's bellicosity vis-à-vis Delhi to some degree. Nevertheless, Ch'en Yi, on September 29, 1965, warned Delhi that there was "a limit" to China's "forbearance," that India "must cease its intrusions and harassments," and that the question of the "92,000 square kilometers" of "Chinese territory" illegally occupied by the Indians would have to be "thoroughly settled." [3] Obviously, the Indians are not going to be persuaded to give up these areas at a conference table.

To Peking, the vulnerable North East Frontier Agency must appear as a tempting target. The upper reaches of the Brahmaputra are said to offer tremendous potential for development of hydroelectric power. The famous tea gardens in this area are also inviting, as are the Digboi oil fields, which now produce 50,000 metric tons of high-grade petroleum annually. This production could be significantly increased.

Maj. Gen. D. Som Dutt, former commandant of the Indian Defense Services Staff College, in a recent assessment of the Chinese threat to NEFA, wrote:

The lessons of 1962, however, as regards logistics difficulties are bound to be remembered when considering operations in this area especially since roads to the border do not exist. It therefore seems fair to assume that, for the time being at least, major attacks into India, though possible, would be difficult to mount and are not likely to succeed. Smaller but decisive attacks with limited objectives, at moments when India was politically or diplomatically weak, or involved elsewhere, combined with a continuous undermining of Bhutan and Nepal by political means, might well be the pattern of China's future operations in the Himalayas.[4]

We may observe that "logistic difficulties" were not the sole—or even necessarily the most important—factor which limited Chinese operations in NEFA in 1962. There is every reason to believe that the Chinese visualized this campaign primarily in the context of the political objectives they sought to attain. The 1962 drive almost to the Brahmaputra was carefully controlled in terms of force committed, time, and space, as any future actions in this area are likely to be.

Peking's present relationship with the Democratic People's Republic of Korea is ambiguous, and will probably remain so for some time. In early 1966, P'yongyang announced that she proposed to follow an "independent policy," i.e., that she would no longer act as a compliant client either of the USSR or of her other powerful neighbor. Obviously, P'yongyang does not relish the idea of again finding herself no more than a counter in an Asian power struggle in which she stands to gain nothing and to lose much.

Although Peking no longer enjoys her once dominant influence over the North Koreans, she certainly views with approval their efforts to keep the pot simmering along the 38th Parallel, and to infiltrate the south. She would not, however, particularly welcome overt North Korean moves that might bring the pot to a boil. In this Asian power equation, as in others Peking must one day attempt realistically to solve, the unknown factor is the USSR.

Active hostilities between China and the Soviet Union are no more than a remote possibility, but one that planners in both Peking and Moscow must take into account. Here, China's geographic situation lays vital areas in both Sinkiang and Manchuria open to converging attacks which the Russians could mount in security and push home vigorously. Avenues of approach to critical targets are good, terrain generally suitable for tanks, and Soviet air bases relatively close to targets. In short, the Soviets hold both areas as hostages of sufficient value to deter the Chinese from provocative actions along the Sino-Soviet frontiers.

For almost twenty years, Chiang Kai-shek has been sustained by the dwindling hope that he will personally lead a return to the mainland. Only the passage of time will exorcise this chimera. Meanwhile, the existence on Taiwan of a viable government will continue to present a potential threat, if only in the psychological sense, to the Peking regime. For so long as the government of the Republic of China (G.R.C.) can maintain political and economic stability and its position on the international stage, it offers to the mainlanders at least the chance, in some indeterminate future, of opting for an alternative. It is (and will obviously remain) a major goal of Peking's foreign policy to eliminate this alternative. It should remain a major objective of U.S. foreign policy to preserve it.

Peking is well aware that in the foreseeable future she cannot take Taiwan by force. Even should the United States stand aside—which it would not—the PLA could not cope with well-trained and maneuverable G.R.C. forces standing on the defensive. The Nationalist air force is small but modern; its pilots, experienced and competent. Decisive air superiority is a prerequisite to transit of the Taiwan Strait. To establish and maintain this degree of air superiority is now, and for some years will remain, beyond the capabilities of the PLA's air force.

It is equally difficult to visualize a successful G.R.C. assault on the South China coast. There can be little doubt that the PLA would put up a vigorous defense against invasion of the mainland. Some 40 to 50 divisions are estimated to be deployed in South China, with about half in coastal defense. While coordinated air-and-sea-borne landing forces might capture one or more ports and establish beachhead enclaves in the coastal area between Foochow and Swatow (for example), such local operations could not possibly be supported without U.S. assistance and in the long term would not be decisive.

No evidence can be adduced to substantiate the G.R.C. presumptions that should the Nationalists land in force, major units of the PLA would "turn their hats around" and the People's Militia would come over. But only if defections were to occur on a large scale would an invader have any chance to convert tactical gains into more than a temporary regional victory. The possibility of such defections appears to be remote, but would increase in an unstable internal climate.

In terms of sustained offensive action in the conventional context, the PLA's capabilities are, as we have shown, circumscribed by a variety of factors. Over most of these, the Chinese have no control. Until some can be altered to China's advantage, the PLA will probably not be committed to offensive action outside her borders, except possibly in the context of the Himalayan arc. Even there, the scope of operations would be compatible with limited political objectives or confined to the seizure of economically desirable areas in NEFA for use as bargaining counters.

On October 16, 1964, near the shore of Lop Nor, a lake in the remote Takla Makan desert of Sinkiang, Chinese scientists ushered the People's Republic into the nuclear age. The U.S. Atomic Energy Commission estimated the yield of the device they designed, constructed, and fired that day to be of the order of 20 kilotons (approximately 20,000 tons of TNT) or about that of the bomb exploded over Nagasaki in August 1945.[5]

The explosion came as no surprise to Western analysts, who had been expecting a test shot for some time. What was a surprise, and a rather disturbing one, was that the Chinese fired not the plutonium device practically all the experts anticipated but a device fueled with uranium-235 (U-235). The significance of this important fact was at the time not generally comprehended.

But as Philip H. Abelson, editor of *Science,* the journal of the American Association for the Advancement of Science, wrote shortly after:

Production of weapons-grade uranium-235 is an impressive technological achievement indicative of considerable industrial capability. Successful construction and operation of a gaseous diffusion plant capable of producing substantial quantities of weapons-grade U-235 require both matériel and skill. Such a plant contains more than a thousand individual units connected in series. Each unit must be constructed with precision —small imperfections can destroy their effectiveness. Moreover, special metallurgical techniques must be available. After the units are assembled their performance must be monitored, controlled, and integrated. This requires a great deal of electronic instrumentation.

A technically incompetent people could not have succeeded in producing weapons-grade U-235 without massive help; the French, after six years, have not yet announced production of highly enriched uranium. Nevertheless, the new accomplishment was not surprising to many United States scientists who have had contact with individuals of Chinese extraction and have known of their first-class aptitude for science and technology.[6]

Abelson then pointed out that the ability to produce weapons-grade U-235 confers a very high degree of flexibility, not only in respect to uranium content of ores used but in reactor construction. "With enriched uranium, reactors may be smaller, and a wider variety of construction materials can be used."

More serious is a greatly enhanced capability of producing tritium, a key constituent of thermonuclear bombs. Tritium is often produced by the reaction of neutrons with lithium-6. Introduction of lithium into an ordinary reactor tends to stop the chain reaction. This tendency can be overcome by introducing enriched uranium. If the Chinese do not now possess quantities of tritium, they can obtain it. In view of the Chinese achievement thus far, there is no basis for hoping that they will not achieve a hydrogen bomb—perhaps in the latter part of this decade.

Another member has joined the nuclear club. He already has impressive credentials, and his long-term potentialities should not be underestimated.[7]

The day after the first Chinese explosion, President Johnson told the American people that "many years and great efforts separate the testing of a first nuclear device from having a stockpile of reliable weapons with effective delivery systems." This reassurance posed more questions than it answered. How many years is "many"? What, exactly, did the President have in mind when he used the term "effective delivery systems"? And how does one measure "a stockpile"? In American, Soviet, British, French, or Chinese arithmetic?

These ambiguities were but partially clarified by unidentified "officials" who estimated that the Chinese needed "two to three" years to produce a bomb and "five to ten" years to produce a "significant" stock of war heads and the vehicles to deliver them. But the fundamental questions abide. Of one thing only we may be certain: the CCP has accorded the highest priority to rapid acquisition of a nuclear capability which in the first stage of development will pose a credible threat to China's Asian neighbors and in a later stage to her enemy, the United States.

In late 1965, press reports indicated current assessments considerably more realistic than those originally made in Washington. At a meeting of the NATO Council of Ministers in Paris in December 1965 the American Secretary of Defense stated that China would become a major nuclear power within a decade. Several weeks later, a Japanese expert, Junno-suke Kishida, predicted even more rapid progress.

Kishida speculated that the People's Republic would test an H-bomb before midsummer 1966, and by mid-1967 would have a stockpile of 150 to 200 nuclear weapons. He reported that development of missile-delivery systems was keeping pace with weapons production and that the Chinese were also concentrating on constructing submarines of "advanced design."[8] One such submarine is known to be in commission and a second on the stocks.

In the regional context, it may be observed that approximately 25/30 weapons each of 20-kiloton yield would suffice to pose a devastating threat to India, Japan, South Korea, Taiwan, South

Vietnam, Thailand, Burma, the Philippines, Malaysia, Singapore, or Indonesia. This potential threat need not depend on expensive and elaborate delivery and guidance systems. Slight modifications to existing aircraft would enable the Chinese to deliver the bomb described to any city, industrial complex, or major military installation in the countries named. Submarines equipped to deck launch missiles with a range of 200–300 miles would provide a more secure but less accurate means of delivery.

This regional "threat scenario" is compatible with the reasonable supposition that in the first phase of her nuclear arms program, China will opt for a "counter-value" weapons system rather than for a much more costly and technologically more complex "counter-force" system. It is safe to assume that China will attain a capability of the order described not later than mid-1967.

This conclusion is based on an average of various estimates of Chinese capacity to produce U–235 of the quality required to manufacture bombs. The arithmetic indicates a capability, as of mid-1966, to produce at least two 20-kiloton bombs per month. As it is reasonable to expect the rate of bomb production to increase progressively, we should anticipate that by the end of 1967 China will have a stockpile of 80/100 weapons. We may expect China's program to proceed behind a smoke screen of propaganda designed to convince her smaller Asian neighbors that her nuclear arsenal is designed solely to protect her territorial integrity—and theirs—against the threat of U.S. "imperialist aggression." At the same time, it gives her an opportunity to use "nuclear blackmail."

In official statements, the People's Republic has made it explicitly clear that she favors proliferation as a means to break the "nuclear monopoly" enjoyed by the Western powers. It follows that having what she considers a reasonable stockpile in her possession, China might well secretly offer nuclear technology or plant components to other "peace-loving" peoples, who wish to make their own bombs.

Foreign Minister Ch'en Yi spoke to this question in October 1965 when he described as "not realistic" the suggestion that China might help other nations "manufacture atom bombs." But he expressed China's hope that "Afro-Asian countries will be able to make atom bombs themselves" as "it would be better for a greater number of countries to come into possession of atom bombs." [9]

The Chinese have consistently maintained that nuclear weapons in the hands of "socialist" nations are intruments of peace, whereas in "imperialist" armories they are weapons of war. These attitudes suggest that for some years the People's Republic is not likely to be amenable to propositions relating to nuclear arms control, especially if these propositions are sponsored by the United States.

China has publicly pledged that she will "never be the first to use nuclear weapons." She is acquiring them, she maintains, because of the aggressive attitude of the United States. In this context, she has undertaken some passive measures. Critical military installations have been removed from population centers, dug into hillsides, and concealed under forest cover where possible. An aircraft dispersal program has been in effect for some time.

During the past four to five years, the authorities in the People's Republic have obviously attached a considerable importance to training the PLA and the People's Militia in "anti-chemical warfare" measures. The mainland press frequently mentions exercises and demonstrations by specially trained groups. Apparently (although this is never expressly stated) the emphasis is on decontaminating critical installations which may survive the heat and blast effects of atomic-nuclear explosions; rendering first aid to human beings who are not within the killing radius, and constructing fall-out shelters.

Although the latest available MND organization chart does not show an "anti-chemical warfare" command, one certainly exists. Obviously, there is some central authority responsible for formulating doctrine and providing standard equipment. In this context, the militia's training in fire fighting is relevant.

In sum, China's "nuclear doctrine" has to date publicly been expressed only in defensive terms. These are motivated to some extent by counsels of prudence, but are also designed to enable the Party to extend its control. In keeping to the fore the constant "threats" of the "U.S. nuclear maniacs," the Party can for its own purposes convince the average Chinese that he lives under the imminent danger of nuclear attack. This propaganda naturally contributes to the credibility of the Party's ceaseless "Hate America" campaigns.

With a conventional establishment unable to exert any decisive pressure except in the local context and with no more than an embryonic nuclear potential, the Chinese have been forced to devise some other means to make their presence felt on the international stage. They think they have found the solution to their dilemma in Mao's thesis of "national liberation war." As we have seen, this has recently been dusted off, amplified, and enunciated with considerable fanfare.

The contemporary model casts North America and Western Europe in the role of "cities" to be surrounded, isolated, and ultimately reduced by the nations of Asia, Africa, and Latin America, in Peking's revolutionary scenario equated with "the countryside" of the Anti-Japanese War. As described by Lin Piao in September 1965, China's purpose is to generate, support, expand, and exploit "national liberation wars" in susceptible areas of this "first intermediate zone."

This strategy did succeed in China and in North Vietnam, and Peking has staked her international prestige on the hope that it will succeed in South Vietnam. For some years, at least, this pattern of indirect attack will be China's only means of debilitating vastly superior U.S. economic, nuclear, and conventional power and undermining U.S. prestige and political influence.

As far as Peking is concerned, evident Soviet reluctance to get deeply involved in such ambiguous situations—which might lead to escalation and an ultimate nuclear confrontation with the United States—is no less than unforgivable ideological apostasy. For although imperialists are "paper tigers" and their ultimate doom is assured by definition, it is the "sacred duty" of "true Marxists-Leninists" to hasten the demise, particularly when the tides of revolution are flowing—as the CCP conceives them to be—in a favorable direction. The obligation is clear enough to Peking, if not to the "timid mice" cowering in the Kremlin.

Existence in the same world order of "decadent" imperialist states and "progressive" socialist states constitutes a contradiction that the Chinese profess to believe must inevitably lead to armed conflict. But from chaos—or from radioactive ashes—there will emerge, according to Mao's thesis, "a beautiful new world," one "a thousand times better" than the world of today. This simplistic prescription for universal salvation justifies subversive and aggressive behavior by the only "true lovers of peace": the Chinese Communists.

But Mao's Utopia cannot be achieved until U.S. imperialism is overthrown. This is to be accomplished by struggles waged simultaneously "by the different peoples." These struggles, according to Lin Piao,

reinforce each other and merge into a torrential world-wide tide of opposition to U.S. imperialism. The more successful the development of people's wars in a given region, the larger the number of U.S. imperialist forces that can be pinned down and depleted there. When the U.S. aggressors are hard pressed in one place, they have no alternative but to loosen their grip on others. Therefore, the conditions become more favorable for the people elsewhere to wage struggles against U.S. imperialism and its lackeys.[10]

"Everything," Lin added, "is divisible, and so is this colossus of U.S. imperialism. It can be split up and defeated. The peoples of Asia, Africa, Latin America, and other regions can destroy it piece by piece, some striking at its head and others at its feet." [11]

Obviously, what we must anticipate is that China will attempt to promote and will nurture by both overt and clandestine means the development of xenophobic nationalism directed against the United States. How successful she will be remains to be seen. But in the cold terms of *realpolitik*, the concept has something to commend it.

Mao teaches that both subjective and objective aspects of every situation must be continuously assessed and reassessed. In subjective terms, Peking estimates that the strategy outlined by her defense minister will permit her, from a position of relative weakness, to retain the initiative in target selection. Objectively, she sees the American government unable to respond effectively to indirect manipulation of situations designed to divert, annoy, embarrass, humiliate, and harass the United States. Hopefully, in "weak-link" target areas, she will be able progressively to erode American positions. At the same time, she calculates that she can avoid the direct confrontation with implications that for her would be catastrophic. Thus, by application of Mao's "step-by-step" formula, she expects to preserve herself while others destroy her enemy.

Mao's writings on guerrilla warfare are widely recognized as masterful expositions of the subject. Both Vo Nguyen Giap in Vietnam and Ernesto (Che) Guevara in Cuba based their works on Mao's earlier discourses and essays, which comprise the first comprehensive analytical treatment of this method of warfare. The Chairman's unique contribution to military literature will continue to exercise a profound influence over the organization and conduct of revolutionary guerrilla operations.[12]

Undoubtedly, revolutionary possibilities exist in some countries of the "first intermediate zone," where economic and social conditions often combine with political instability to guarantee fragile governments short life expectancy. The CCP anticipates opportunities to act as the catalytic agent in such situations, to manipulate nationalistic and anti-American sentiments to her advantage, and, when conditions are favorable, to invoke Mao's guerrilla pattern. In this minimum-risk strategy, "atomic bombs are paper tigers."

But we may ask how realistic this strategy is. Are the Chinese, North Vietnamese, and Algerian experiences transferable? In the first place, in all three countries there was an alien presence. It was the evident Japanese purpose to conquer China, to destroy the state structure, and to reduce the people to subservience. The French returned to Vietnam to reimpose a repressive colonial rule and fought in Algeria to preserve one. Thus, in all three places, Communist parties were able to make legitimate and popular appeal to patriotism and nationalism. Anyone who opposed the Communist line in such circumstances would rightly have been branded a traitor or a collaborator. But it seems unlikely that Mao's scenario will work unless there is a truly dictatorial and oppressive local government (such as Batista's was) or an alien presence dedicated to aggression and exploitation.

Second, Peking has made her disruptive intentions perfectly clear. But there is no reason to believe that emerging nations will view Mao's plans to induce chaos with unqualified enthusiasm. They are in search of stability and the opportunity to evolve peacefully. Third, Peking's foreign adherents, who covertly plot violence, are relatively few in number and do not, at least at the present time, command either the organized strength or the weapons necessary to seize and maintain political power. And the chances that they will be able to command them are not improving but shrinking. In many countries of the "first intermediate zone," opportunities for revolutions on the Maoist pattern no longer exist. And where the armed forces are loyal to the incumbent government and will stand firm, the possibility of a successful coup under the auspices of a pro-Chinese splinter group seems remote.

One detects a note of querulous urgency in Peking's declamations on the subject of "wars of national liberation," a note that prompts one to speculate that Mao and his aging comrades may sometimes furtively ask themselves whether history has not outrun the revolutionary model which, almost a full generation ago, carried them, under circumstances scarcely to be duplicated elsewhere and in other times, to the seats of power.

On January 1, 1966, China launched a Third "Five-Year Plan." A primary—albeit unannounced—goal of this plan is to expand and diversify the defense industry base prerequisite to selective modernization and restructuring of her conventional forces and simultaneously to achieve as rapidly as possible the substantial nuclear capability that the American Secretary of Defense has described as "a most disturbing . . . prospect." [13]

As the People's Republic publishes no statistical data, it is impossible to conjecture what the national budget is, much less what proportion of it is to be devoted to national defense under the current plan. But we may presume that a good share of defense effort is programmed to rectify obvious imbalances in force structure.

It would appear that a "crash" priority will be given to the aircraft and air-defense industries. China's current air-defense capabilities are extremely poor but are being selectively improved. Repeatedly, China has delivered "serious warnings" to India for alleged violations of Chinese air space. Possibly these complaints are pure fabrications. But if they are true, interceptor and gun and missile-defense systems of key localities along the Tibet–Sinkiang highway, in eastern Tibet, and in West Szechwan can only be described as totally ineffective.[14] Air defenses of the southern "invasion coast" are reported to be improving as additional early-warning radars are installed.

Undoubtedly, a very high priority has been assigned to improving the jet fuel situation. As we have noted, refining, rectification, transport, storage, and handling of volatile jet fuels present interrelated technological, chemical, and industrial problems. Fortunately for China, in this field (as in others) she enjoys what Lenin once described as "the advantages of backwardness," and her progress may be much more rapid than we anticipate, particularly as she continues to negotiate in the European market to acquire complete refinery installations.

A third priority might well be the expansion of her submarine fleet, modification of existing boats for deck-launching short-range missiles, and construction of new long-range boats specifically designed for carrying and launching missiles capable of attaining an intermediate range (1,500 miles).

Finally, some resources are probably being directed toward equipping a limited number of PLA divisions with modern armor, self-propelled guns, and cross-country vehicles. Although public emphasis is given to close combat by the infantry, we should expect the PLA gradually to improve its capability for operations of combined arms. If Indian sources are to be believed, the armaments industry in the People's Republic is considerably more advanced than was generally thought to be the case. Reports from New Delhi in December 1965 "confirmed" the rumor that China had undertaken to reequip an unstated number of Pakistani divisions. One division was said to have already been provided with new arms and stocks of ammunition entirely of Chinese manufacture.[15] Such reports may be inspired or planted for ulterior motives but should not be arbitrarily discounted.

The PLA is making continuing efforts to improve levels of professional and technical proficiency. One straw in the wind was a decree signed in January 1965 by President Liu Shao-ch'i. This provided for increasing the length of time conscripts are obligated to serve in the armed forces. Periods of service now prescribed are:

Ground forces (infantry)	4 years
Ground force (special branches)	5 years
Public security	5 years
Air force	5 years
Navy	6 years

The extension of service in the navy to six years lends credence to the hypothesis that the People's Republic intends to emphasize the submarine program. As we are aware, very high-skill levels are mandatory in the subamarine service.[16]

Paradoxically, the requirement to orient the PLA toward improvement in modern techniques makes it necessary to emphasize the "man-over-weapons" theme with increasing vigor. The primacy of politics is constantly stressed. This fact has led some Western analysts to conjecture that a basic and unsolvable split exists between Party political types and career professionals. It is difficult to believe that this struggle threatens the primacy of the Party. Nevertheless during 1966 it became increasingly apparent that the PLA is not animated with the degree of revolutionary élan the Party wishes to see.[17]

The apprehensions of the "Long Marchers" were reflected in a January 1966 report by Hsiao Hua, director of the General Political Department, PLA, to the annual PLA Political Work Conference held in Peking.[18] This verbose and tendentious monologue contained little new. The record has been played countless times. Those participating in the conference

deeply recognized that to give prominence to politics means to stress Mao Tse-tung's thinking. This means Mao Tse-tung's books should be taken as a guideline of the highest order in all fields of work in the whole army—using Mao Tse-tung's thinking with unswervingly firm confidence, resolutely supporting and carrying out all things in harmony with Chairman Mao's instructions even if one has to scale serried mountains or sail in seas of fire to do so, resolutely rejecting and opposing all things in

contradiction with Chairman Mao's instructions and studying and applying Chairman Mao's works creatively with greater emphasis on their
application.

The true mastery of Mao Tse-tung thinking is determined, first of all,
by whether one can apply it, whether one applies it truthfully or fraudu-
lently, and whether this application can withstand challenge. In dealing
with other persons we should hear their words and observe their deeds,
with greater emphasis on their deeds. The requirement to study Chairman Mao's works, obey Chairman Mao, follow Chairman Mao's instructions, and become Chairman Mao's good soldiers is applicable not only to
the fighters and basic-level cadres, but even more so to cadres at higher
levels. If we are to devote our whole lives to revolution, we must spend
our whole lives studying Chairman Mao's works and reforming our
ideology.[19]

Hsiao Hua's choice of words is interesting. Who were the
"cadres at higher levels" who had *not* been studying Chairman Mao's
works, obeying Chairman Mao, following Chairman Mao's instructions, and attempting zealously to "become Chairman Mao's good
soldiers"? Some people had obviously not been devoting their "whole
lives" to revolution and the reformation of their ideology.

Those "cadres at higher levels" who had failed to use Mao Tse-
tung's thinking with unswervingly firm confidence were not confined to the high command of the PLA. True, the internecine
struggle between "modernists" and "traditionalists" in the Party was
most clearly reflected in the three schisms that between 1958 and
1966 rent the military hierarchy. But this struggle involved, as well,
members of the Politburo and its Standing Committee, the MAC,
other leading Party organs, and even the Chairman himself.

It would be superficial to conceive that these disputes related only
to questions of "guerrillaism" versus "professionalism" in the armed
forces. It seems clear enough that the factional contention—of which
"The Great Proletarian Cultural Revolution" of 1966 was a mani-
festation transcended this parochial issue, and sprang from profound disagreement over such basic problems as foreign and domestic policy and strategic theory and doctrine in the nuclear age.

Essentially it appears that a "modernist" alignment in the Party
challenged Mao's policies, as Su Yü, P'eng Teh-huai and Huang
K'o-ch'eng had unsuccessfully done some years previously. Apparently, this group hoped to force their more traditionally minded
colleagues to re-examine the entire spectrum of policy based on
the "thought" of Chairman Mao. The "traditionalists," led by Mao
and his Defense Minister, Lin Piao, were equally determined to

preserve the heritage of Yenan and to pursue relentlessly the revolutionary course charted by the Party's "great teacher, great leader, great supreme commander, and great helmsman." As of September, 1966, the issue was still in doubt.

The shadow cast by the P.R.C.'s relations with the Soviet Union provides a sombre background to this running disputation. We know now that P'eng's fall from grace was the direct result of his attempt to forge a closer strategic engagement with the USSR than Mao was prepared to accept. It may be surmised that Lo Jui-ch'ing, the latest military leader to lose his job, became a convert to P'eng's policy.

How deeply "The Great Proletarian Cultural Revolution" has affected, or will affect, the PLA remains to be seen. If there have been any signs of profound disaffection in the ranks, they are not evident. It is all too simple to conclude that the purge of a few military hierarchs will necessarily generate disaffection at lower levels of the armed forces, or would impel an anti-Mao clique to attempt a coup.

In October 1949, Mao Tse-tung, in proclaiming the establishment of the Chinese People's Republic, promised a vast audience in Peking that the new China over which his Party would preside would in time create a strong, modern military establishment. That goal has not yet been attained. But it is reasonable to predict that by October 1975, when the Party will celebrate the fortieth anniversary of the completion of the Long March, China will have become a power to be reckoned with on the international scene.

By that time, the processes of nature will have removed most of the veterans who now hold high position in the People's Liberation Army. Their places will be taken by men who were platoon and company officers during the Third Revolutionary War and who commanded battalions and regiments in Korea. This younger group, about which we know next to nothing, is designated "The Successors to Revolution."

The Party is alert to the succession problems in the PLA and is obviously much concerned with it. Chairman Mao has evinced personal interest and has enunciated "five qualifications" he expects "Successors to Revolution" to satisfy. These criteria are being used by Party secretaries at army, divisional, and regimental levels as "weapons" in continuous assessment and screening processes applied to all leadership cadres in the PLA.

We may hope that this second-generation leadership will not consider it necessary to display the degree of revolutionary bellicosity characteristic of the "Long Marchers" they will displace. But when they attain comparable positions, they will have vast power at their disposal—power, in truth, to shake "the five continents."

The People's Liberation Army (PLA) and the Great Proletarian Cultural Revolution (GPCR)

As of mid-January 1967, there were no indications that the Great Proletarian Cultural Revolution (GPCR) "started and led by Chairman Mao Tse-tung himself" had run its course. Rather, each day continued to bring its own quota of disturbing news from Peking, where the alleged crimes of assorted "monsters, freaks and demons" accused of "frenzied attacks on the proletariat in a vain attempt to stage a capitalist restoration" continued to be "exposed." There seems to be little prospect for any early resolution of this chaotic situation. Indeed on New Year's Day a *People's Daily–Red Flag* editorial promised that 1967 would be a year of "all-round development of class struggle throughout China." [1]

"The raging flames" of this mass movement which has swept the entire country were "personally" kindled by the Chairman on June 1, 1966. As we now know, the decision to extend the cultural revolution beyond a limited circle comprised principally of educators, playwrights and journalists had been taken in April. But it was not until May 8, 1966, when *The Liberation Army Daily* made an indirect attack on the Peking Municipal Party Committee, that this intention became manifest. Even at that time the targets were obscure. The situation was clarified shortly thereafter, when it became known that P'eng Chen, Secretary of the Peking Party Committee, had been fired. At the same time the presidents of Peking and Nanking Universities were summarily dismissed. From this point the movement progressively gained in both scope and momentum. Whether those who initiated it can bring it under control before it inflicts irreparable damage on Chinese society, the Party and the State, remains to be seen.

The conflagration has already destroyed scores—if not hundreds —of men who for many years had held respected and responsible positions in Chinese intellectual life, in the government of the People's Republic, and in the Party. Those being assailed have been accused of "stubbornly clinging to the bourgeois reactionary line," of "taking the capitalist road," of voicing "revisionist" ideas, or of traitorously impeding production. Actually, their guilt lies in having, in one form or another, opposed the policies advocated by Mao Tse-tung.

The charges brought against them are deliberately couched in terms sufficiently vague to provide the Chairman ample room for maneuver. But despite their calculated ambiguity, it has been apparent for some time that they are aimed at at least two identifiable groups: those who seek (among other policy changes) a reasonable accommodation with the Soviet Union; i.e., the "revisionists," and some who desire a more effective approach to production problems; i.e., those "taking the capitalist road." A possible third grouping might include a few who are willing to settle the war in Vietnam by negotiation, i.e., "bourgeois reactionaries" ready to appease imperialism.

As of this writing (mid-January 1967) one cannot with any precision either delineate the policies advocated by the several contending factions, or identify their members. It is of course entirely possible that an individual could support, for example, some amelioration of Mao's bellicose policy toward the USSR and at the same time favor a less dogmatic approach to problems of agriculture and industrial production.

Nor is the full extent of the involvement of the People's Liberation Army as yet clear. For some years the PLA has been held up to the Chinese as a model of virtue, loyalty, zeal and frugality. Nor could there be serious question of its ideological purity. After all, Lin Piao has been in office for more than seven years and has repeatedly grasped the broom and swept the courtyard. It thus seems most improbable that any considerable numbers of "monsters and ghosts" are still lurking in positions of responsibility in the armed forces.

Until January 12, 1967, when a *Red Flag* editorial signaled the extension of the Cultural Revolution to the armed forces, the PLA had not been obviously involved in the convulsion. During late summer and early fall, Lin Piao discreetly held the armed forces in the background. But the editors of his house organ, *The Liberation Army Daily*, were not similarly restrained. Their support for the movement and for the Red Guards was unqualified.

But the PLA was apparently untouchable. At a time when individuals long associated with cultural and educational institutions and higher Party organs were under heavy attack, the PLA was spared. Nor, with the single exception of Lo Jui-ch'ing, were any members of the military hierarchy publicly assailed. No PLA units participated in the series of gigantic and frenetic rallies staged during August and September in the great "East Is Red" square before the Gate of Heavenly Peace. Here, Mao and Defense Minister Lin Piao, the Chairman's "close comrade in arms" and heir designate, repeatedly reviewed massive formations of Red Guards who had converged on the capital from all parts of China by train, bus, and on foot, ostensibly to render homage to their "great teacher, great leader, great commander-in-chief, and great helmsman." At these dramatic spectacles the army was conspicuous by its absence.

Some have described the Red Guard crusade as "spontaneous" and others have likened it to a "grass-roots" movement. This is to misread the nature and purpose of the Great Proletarian Cultural Revolution and the function of the Red Guards in it. Widespread mass movements do not occur in People's China by chance, and the GPCR is no exception to this rule. To push China's "socialist revolution forward to a new stage," to inaugurate "a new era in the history of the international Communist movement," Mao needed a pliable instrument to act as the dynamic vanguard. He found this instrument in the mobilized youth of China—the Red Defense Guards.

An original speculation was that the Chairman had created the Guards as a counterweight to the PLA. But any doubts as to the relationship between the two were soon dispelled. By mid-September it was clear that the PLA had planned, organized and unobtrusively stage-managed the monster Red Guard rallies in Peking. Every incoming unit of young Guards was met by a select group of "army men" who greeted the demonstrators, oriented and instructed them, equipped them with lapel buttons, arm bands, slogans, and red-bound copies of excerpts from the Chairman's works, and arranged for their housing, feeding and general welfare until, on order, they paraded, and then left the capital to make way for other hundreds of thousands equally eager to "defend" Mao from the "demons" who menaced him.

Thus, from the first, the Red Guards were closely identified with the PLA. They were described in the press and in radio broadcasts as "an extension of the PLA"; its "reliable reserve." PLA units handled the Guards with kid gloves. Apparently the army was not used to control Red Guard hooliganism, which in a number of instances the police were either unable or unwilling to restrain.

In late December 1966, *The Liberation Army Daily* ran the first of a series of special columns devoted to "Talks with the Red Guards." The editor's note introducing this feature read:

Red Guard fighters, our army was personally founded by our great leader Chairman Mao and grew up under the invincible thought of Mao Tse-tung. Let us hold high the great red banner of Mao Tse-tung's thought, inherit and carry forward the revolutionary tradition of the PLA, forever read Chairman Mao's books, listen to Chairman Mao, act upon Chairman Mao's instructions, and become good fighters of Chairman Mao.

The history of the PLA–Red Guard association thus disposes of the thesis that Mao and Lin Piao created the Guards to act as a balance to the PLA. Rather, as the GPCR has developed, the PLA has taken a firm position in support, a loyal and ready reserve alert to be deployed if necessary on signal from "Chief" Lin.

Since August 1966, countless columns in the western press have been devoted to analyses of the GPCR. These reflect a wide variety of opinion. Statements and comments in the Chinese press have done nothing to clarify the real nature of the questions at issue. Very few facts emerge. Thus, observers of the Chinese scene are forced again to indulge in generally unsupported speculation.

The intensity of continuing Chinese attacks on the leadership of the Communist Party of the Soviet Union indicates clearly that the nature of the relationship between Peking and Moscow, particularly in the context of the Vietnam war, has been one of the important subjects of debate in higher Party organs. Mao's views are well known: he has always—and with some cause—been suspicious of Soviet motives, and is consequently adamantly opposed to any appeasement of the Kremlin, or to an accommodation which, as he sees it, would inevitably relegate China again to position of junior partner in a Moscow-Peking axis. He therefore rejects out of hand any policy suggestions that might conduce to ameliorate Moscow-Peking tensions, and has turned viciously on those in his own Party who have presumably advocated a united front with the Soviet Union.

In Vietnam, the interests of Peking and Moscow do not coincide. While the Chairman, assured by the doctrine that victory is inevitable, rejects any idea of a negotiated settlement, the leaders of the Soviet Union are apparently less intransigent. At the same time, they continue to pour significant amounts of military hardware into North Vietnam. Obviously, Mao does not desire a strong Soviet presence in Southeast Asia. But at present, aside from continuous castigation of the "modern revisionists" and denigration of their aid to Ho Chi-minh, there is little he can do to neutralize growing Soviet influence in Hanoi's councils. This frustrating situation tends to exacerbate his anti-Soviet prejudices.

Evidently, he opposes with equal vehemence any policies which would tend to dissipate the dynamic of his continuing revolution on the home front. For the Chairman, time is running out, as this poem suggests:

> On this tiny globe
> A few flies dash themselves against the wall,
> Humming without cease,
> Sometimes shrilling,
> Sometimes moaning.
> Ants on the locust tree assume a great-nation swagger
> And mayflies lightly plot to topple the giant tree.
> The west wind scatters leaves over Changan,
> And the arrows are flying, twanging.
> So many deeds cry out to be done,
> And always urgently;
> The world rolls on,
> Time presses.
> Ten thousand years are too long,
> Seize the day, seize the hour!
> The four seas are rising, clouds and waters raging,
> The five continents are rocking, wind and thunder roaring.
> Away with all pests!
> Our force is irresistible.[2]

It seems possible that the "humming," "shrilling" and "moaning" flies who "dash themselves against the wall" symbolize those colleagues who oppose the Chairman's will. The "ants" may represent the leadership of the CPSU; the "mayflies," the government of the United States. But all are "pests," and all will be eliminated by the irresistible force of Mao's revolution.

The poem also expresses the sense of urgency that animates the Chairman. This was manifested in the disastrous Great Leap Forward, in which twenty years were to be as one day. There are many indications now that another Great Leap is in the making, and that it was opposed by some of Mao's more pragmatic colleagues who do not share his conviction that spiritual force alone can transform China.

All these conflicting tendencies are closely connected with the problems of succession. Mao has been surrounded for many years by a cohesive group. But these men, too, are ambitious to lay their hands on the instruments of power. Apparently, some of the back-stage maneuvering has been less than discreet.

After the countless rectification campaigns endured by the armed forces during the past decade, it seems incredible that "a struggle between the two lines—the proletarian revolutionary line repre-sented by Chairman Mao and the bourgeois reactionary line," can exist within the PLA.[3] But *The Liberation Army Daily* asserted on January 14, 1967, that this struggle exists; that it is "acute and complicated," and exhorted the troops "truly loyal" to the Chair-man to grasp their rifles firmly and eliminate from their midst the opponents of Chairman Mao "who have wormed their way into the PLA."

This purge is to be inclusive. As announced, it will extend to "high-ranking leading organs" (presumably both political and mili-tary), military colleges and schools "and (existing) cultural organi-zations of our army." All those in the armed forces who fail to arm themselves with Mao's thought are to be "dragged out," "pulled down" and "discredited."

Several inferences—not mutually exclusive—may be drawn. One is that Mao and Lin are preparing to inject the PLA into the nation-wide struggle. A second is that Lin has mounted this campaign primarily to settle old scores that for one reason or other he had not found opportunity to settle earlier. A third is that the Peking leadership fears that regional tendencies may be exploited by PLA commanders distant from the capital.

Certainly, we have learned during the past ten years that any-thing may happen in China. Still, the possibility of a Latin-American type *pronunciamento* in which a military leader, or a military junta takes power, is remote. Mao, so it is reported, has recently co-opted Hsü Hsiang-ch'ien, Yeh Chien-ying and Nieh Jung-chen as mem-bers of the Politburo. If this is true, it reflects the old man's ap-prehensions. Of course, he would not hesitate for a moment to call in the PLA if he conceived his continuing revolution to be seriously threatened. But it is difficult to see how the fragmented opposition, under constant attack, can create a sufficiently strong power base to challenge him successfully. As long as Mao and the group aligned with him control the gun, they will wield the power. And there is not yet any indication that they do not hold the gun firmly in their hands.

Marshals of the People's Republic of China

The following brief biographies of the ten men who were named marshals of the People's Republic of China in September 1955 have been compiled from materials kindly made available by the Union Research Institute, Hong Kong, and by Mrs. Anne B. Clark and Donald W. Klein of the East Asian Research Center, Harvard University.

Ch'en Yi, Marshal, P.R.C.

Member, Central Committee
Member, Politburo
Vice-Chairman, National Defense Council
Vice-Premier, State Council
Former Mayor, Shanghai Municipality
Former Chairman, Commission for Scientific Planning
Foreign Minister
Member, Military Affairs Committee

Ch'en Yi, the most active of Communist China's fifteen vice-premiers, has had a long and successful career in the Party. He was born in Loshan *hsien*, Szechwan, in 1901, the son of a magistrate. After the family moved to the city of Chengtu, he attended a first-class commercial school and distinguished himself on the school's soccer team. As a youth, he was greatly interested in classical poetry and spent much time in teahouses enthusiastically discussing politics, philosophy, and government.

In 1919, Ch'en Yi went to France on a government scholarship, but illness interfered with his studies. Running out of money, he eventually took a job as an ironworker in an arsenal. In 1921, he led a number of other Chinese students living in Paris to the Chinese legation to protest terms of a Sino-French loan. Shortly after this episode, he returned to China, where he served as adjutant for a Szechwan war lord. But he did not get along well with either the troops or the other officers and left the army to become editor of the *Hsin Shu Pao* (New Szechwan *News*). He joined the Communist Party in 1923, took part in the northern expedition, and on Chu Teh's recommendation was appointed magistrate of Yungfen *hsien*, Kiangsi.

Later Ch'en Yi went to Nanch'ang, where he served under Yeh T'ing. He participated in the abortive Nanch'ang uprising of August 1, 1927. He then fled with Yeh T'ing to Swatow; after Yeh left for Germany, Ch'en Yi led some 700 troops to join Chu Teh in Hunan. At Chingkangshan, he received command of one of the three divisions (the 12th) of the 4th Army. He allegedly adhered to the Li Li-san "line" at this time but later gave his support to Mao.

When the Long March began, Ch'en Yi and Hsiang Ying remained in the Kiangsi–Kwangtung border area. When the 4th Army was formed from guerrilla forces south of the Yangtze River in 1938, with Yeh T'ing as commander, Ch'en Yi took command of the First Column and moved with it north of the Yangtze.

Shortly after the "South Anhwei Incident" of January 1941, in which Nationalist troops cut up the 4th Army, captured Yeh T'ing, and killed his deputy commander, Hsiang Ying, Mao ordered the organization of the New 4th Army. The Central Committee named Ch'en Yi acting commander. He was later formally named commander, with the concurrent position of political commissar.

The New 4th Army expanded rapidly and assured the Communists a solid postwar position in East China. After the defeat of Japan, Ch'en Yi's force became the East China Liberation Army; shortly thereafter, it was designated the 3rd Field Army, PLA. During the civil war, Ch'en Yi won several important victories, notably in Shantung in May 1947 and during the Hwai-Hai campaign (November 1948–January 1949). On April 20, 1949, his field army crossed the Yangtze; he subsequently occupied Nanking (April 20, 1949), Shanghai (May 27, 1949), Foochow (August 17, 1949), and Amoy (October 17, 1949).

When the Communist regime established itself in Peking, Ch'en Yi was named to the Central People's Government Council and the People's Revolutionary Military Council and concurrently became mayor of Shanghai. He received new posts after the reorganization of the government in September 1954. In September 1955, he was accorded the title of marshal of the People's Republic of China and awarded the three highest military decorations: the Orders of August 1, of Independence and Freedom, and of Liberation. In March 1956, he was named first chairman of the Scientific Planning Commission, a post he held until May 1957. In 1958, he became foreign minister.

Ch'en Yi has traveled extensively. In October 1954, he led a delegation to East Germany. During this trip, he also visited Warsaw and Moscow. In April 1956, he headed the delegation that went to Lhasa to attend the inauguration of the Preparatory Committee for the Autonomous Region of Tibet. He is well known in Southeast Asia and was a delegate to the Geneva Conferences on Laos (May–July 1961 and July 1962). In May 1963, he accompanied Lui Shao-ch'i on state visits to Indonesia, Burma, Cambodia, and North Vietnam. He visited Afghanistan, Pakistan, and Nepal in March 1965 and in the following month accompanied Chou En-lai to Djakarta.

Chu Teh, Marshal, P.R.C.

Member, Central Committee
Vice-Chairman, Central Committee
Member, Politburo
Vice-Chairman, Politburo
Member, Standing Committee, Politburo
Member, Military Affairs Committee

Chu Teh, senior marshal of the ten created in September 1955, was born of peasant parents in 1886 in Szechwan province. In 1909, he left home to enroll as a cadet in the newly established Yunnan Military Academy. There he joined Sun Yat-sen's *T'ung Meng Hui*, an association devoted to furthering the cause of the revolution. He was active in the movement from 1909 to 1915.

In 1921, Chu decided to abandon his military career and seek other employment. It is alleged that until this time he had for some years led a debauched life—had drunk to excess, gambled, smoked opium, and kept four concubines.

In Shanghai, he met Sun Yat-sen and became intimate with Ch'en Tu-hsiu, the leading Chinese Marxist. Ch'en is said to have influenced Chu Teh to give up his bad habits and to go abroad to study.

In the autumn of 1922, Chu sailed to Marseilles; in October, he moved to Germany, where he settled in Berlin. There he met Chou En-lai and in 1922, at the age of thirty-six, joined the CCP. In 1925, the German government deported him for subversive political activity, and he returned to China via the U.S.S.R. Shortly after his return, he was made director, Political Department, 20th Nationalist Army.

He participated in the Nanch'ang uprising and after the Communists left the city marched south with his troops to Swatow. Following the failure of the Swatow uprising, he fled with a few troops to Hunan, where in January 1928 he attempted to establish a Soviet regime. In April of that year, he led his column to Chingkangshan, where he joined forces with Mao. The product of this alliance was "The 4th Army, Chinese Workers' and Peasants' Red Army," with Chu as commander and Mao as commissar. In August 1930, Chu was named commander in chief of the Red armies. At this time, he and Mao were the most powerful individuals in the Party. He was a member of the Central Committee, chairman of the Revolutionary Military Committee, and the Party's most respected military commander.

In June 1935, Chu Teh's 1st Front Army from the Kiangsi Soviet joined Chang Kuo-t'ao's 4th Front Army at Maokung in West Szechwan. After the Maoerhkai conference of the Central Committee in August 1935, the two armies marched westward into Sikang. In June 1936, what remained of Ho Lung's 2nd Front Army joined Chu and Chang at Kantzu, Sikang. Later, Chu Teh, Ho Lung, and Jen Pi-shih prevailed upon Chang Kuo-t'ao to join forces with Mao Tse-tung in North Shensi.

After the outbreak of the Sino-Japanese War, Chu Teh was named commander in chief, 8th Route Army, and concurrently deputy commander in chief (to Yen Hsi-shan) of the First War Zone. He was also vice-chairman of the People's Revolutionary Military Council.

Chu Teh commanded the Party's Liberation armies during the civil war. He has occupied many posts of importance since 1946. He is vice-chairman of the Party's Politburo, a member of its Standing Committee, a vice-chairman of its Central Committee, and a member of the Military Affairs Committee. He has led Chinese delegations to Moscow, the German Democratic Republic, Hungary, Czechoslovakia, and Poland.

Ho Lung, Marshal, P.R.C.

Member, Central Committee
Member, Politburo
Member, State Council
Vice-Premier, State Council
Vice-Chairman, National Defense Council
Member, Military Affairs Committee

Ho Lung was born in Sangchi *hsien*, Hunan province, in 1896. He had little formal schooling. In 1912, at the age of sixteen, he assassinated a government official and fled into Szechwan. He organized the peasants there and in neighboring areas and by 1919 controlled a force of some 19,000. In 1920, this personal army was assimilated as a brigade into the National Revolutionary Army.

In 1927, Ho was admitted to the Communist Party and later that year given command of the Kuomintang's 20th Army, then part of Chang Fa-k'uei's 4th ("Iron") Army. After the failure of the Nanch'ang uprising, in which he played a leading part, he marched south with Yeh T'ing to

Swatow. After the defeat there, he escaped to Hong Kong. He proceeded thence to Shanghai, where he sought out and reported to the Central Committee. The CC instructed him to go to his native province to recruit a peasant army.

In November 1928, Ho organized the 2nd Red Army in western Hunan. He operated successfully in the Hunan–Hupeh Border Region for the next several years. In June 1930, his command was redesignated the 2nd Army Corps. In October 1934, he joined forces with the 6th Red Army (Hsiao K'o, Jen Pi-shih, Wang Chen) to form the 2nd Front Army, with himself as commander and Jen Pi-shih as political commissar.

In November 1935, a year after the Chu-Mao column set out, the 2nd Front Army began its Long March to Northwest China, and in the summer of 1936, it joined forces with the 4th Front Army (Chang Kuo-t'ao and Hsü Hsiang-ch'ien) near Kan Tzu in Sikang province. During its march to Shensi, the 2nd Front Army suffered severely.

When the 8th Route Army was formed, Ho took command of the 120th Division, with Hsiao K'o as vice-commander and Kuan Hsiang-ying as political commissar. In 1938, he assumed command of 8th Route Army units in central Hopeh; in the following year, he was ordered to establish the Northwest Shansi Military Region. Shortly thereafter, this was redesignated the Shansi–Suiyuan Military District. In 1940, the Shansi–Suiyuan Military District was merged with the Shen-Kan-Ning Border Region, and Ho took over the enlarged command.

In 1943, Ho returned to Yenan and in 1945 was elected to the Seventh Central Committee.

At the close of the civil war, Ho was in command of the 1st Field Army in southwest China. Ho and Liu Po-ch'eng (2nd Field Army) joined forces at Chengtu in Szechwan in November 1949. Shortly thereafter, he took command of the Southwest Region, which comprised Szechwan, Kweichow, Sikang, Yunnan, and Tibet. Here, he worked closely with Teng Hsiao-p'ing, then director of the Party's Southwest Bureau.

Although Ho's duties kept him in the Southwest for the next four years, he was elected to a number of Party offices. He was a PLA delegate to the First National People's Congress (1954) and a member of the Presidium. In the same year, he was elected to the State Council and named a vice-premier. He became concurrently a vice-chairman of the National Defense Council. In 1955, he was named a marshal of the People's Republic, and the nation's three highest military orders were conferred on him. In 1956, he was elected to the Eighth Central Committee and made a member of the Politburo.

Ho Lung has led a number of delegations to European and South Asian countries. In November 1963, he visited Djakarta and Rangoon and in the following year was a senior member of a delegation to Moscow.

He has devoted a great deal of attention in the past several years to the encouragement of athletics and in 1965 was named chairman of the Preparatory Committee for the Second National Games.

Hsü Hsiang-Ch'ien, Marshal, P.R.C.

Member, Central Committee
Vice-Chairman, National Defense Council
Member, Military Affairs Committee

Hsü Hsiang-ch'ien was born in 1902 in Wut'ai *hsien*, Shansi province. After an elementary education, he clerked in a bookstore, entered normal school, graduated, and then taught for several years. He was a member of the first class at Whampoa and participated in the 1926 Northern Expedition. He joined the CCP secretly in 1927 and took part in the Canton uprising in December of that year.

June 1929 found Hsü in the Hupeh-Honan-Anhwei Border Region, where with Chang Kuo-t'ao he established a Soviet area. In 1931, he organized the 4th Front Army. Breaking out of a Nationalist encirclement, he led his army into Szechwan (January 1933) and shortly thereafter set up the North Szechwan Soviet Area. He operated with great success in Szechwan and southern Shensi.

In June 1935, he met the column led by Chu Teh and Mao Tse-tung at Maoerhkai. After the Red Army split, Hsü's forces marched with Chu Teh's column into Sikang. In December 1936, Hsü's command—now styled "The West Route Army"—was practically annihilated by General Ma. In the spring of 1937, Mao ordered Hsü to proceed to Shensi.

In Yenan, after recuperating from a serious illness, Hsü was appointed vice-commander of Liu Po-ch'eng's 129th Division of the 8th Route Army. In 1939, Hsü led three regimental columns across southern Hopei into Shantung, where he established a base area. In 1945, he was elected a member of the Seventh Central Committee.

During the civil war, Hsü was vice-commander of the Shensi-Hopei-Shantung-Honan Military Region; commander and concurrently political commissar, 1st Army Corps, North China Field Army; commander, 18th Army Group, and, after capturing T'aiyuan in November 1948, chairman of the T'aiyuan Military Control Commissioin.

In October 1949, Hsü was appointed to the People's Revolutionary Military Council, a body later superseded by the Military Affairs Committee. He has been a PLA delegate to the First, Second, and Third National People's congresses and is a member of the Central Committee, of the National Defense Council, and of the Military Affairs Committee.

Lin Piao, Marshal, P.R.C.

Member, Central Committee
Member, Politburo
Vice-Chairman, National Defense Council
Vice-Premier, State Council
Minister of National Defense
Acting Chairman, Military Affairs Committee

Lin Piao, esteemed in the People's Republic as the nation's finest military strategist, was born into a peasant family in Huilungshan, Hupeh, in 1908. He attended middle school at Wuch'ang, where he began reading such magazines as *New Youth* and *Guide* and helped organize the school study society. He took part in the "May 30" movement and later joined the Kuomintang.

Lin enrolled as a cadet in the fourth class at the Whampoa Military Academy. During the Northern Expedition, he was a deputy platoon leader. For a time, he was adjutant to Gen. Chang Fa-k'uei but was dismissed following disciplinary charges. At this time, he appealed to Chiang Kai-shek for reassignment; when this request was refused, he joined the Communist Party. Shortly thereafter, he was reinstated in the army.

During the Nanch'ang uprising, Lin Piao was a company commander under Yeh T'ing. After its failure and the subsequent collapse of the Canton Commune, he left Canton for Hunan to organize peasant revolts under the direction of Chu Teh. He won his first military brush with the Nationalists and thus gained favor with Chu Teh. He was commanding a regiment by the time he reached Chingkangshan in 1928. During the Kiangsi period, he further enhanced his military reputation.

As the Long March began, Lin commanded units of the advance force. Shortly after the Communists arrived in Yenan, he was named president of the Anti-Japanese Military and Political University. At the beginning of the war against Japan, he commanded the 115th Division of the 8th Route Army. In late 1937, he was wounded while fighting the Japanese in northeast Shansi and was sent to Moscow for medical treatment. He availed himself of this opportunity to study military science. While in the U.S.S.R., he took part in the defense of Leningrad.

At the end of the war, Lin led a column from Shensi into Manchuria and there established the Northeast Democratic Alliance Army, which he commanded. With Soviet help, he re-equipped his army from surrendered Japanese stocks, and by the time the Nationalists arrived, his troops were in control of vast areas of the countryside.

Lin turned the tide of the civil war by his victories in the northeast.

He successively occupied Kirin, Changchun, and Mukden, and by November 1948, his Northeast Field Army controlled practically all Manchuria. After the defeat of the Nationalists, Lin's command was reorganized as the 4th Field Army.

With the establishment of the Communist regime, Lin held the positions of member, Central People's Government Council; commander, Central-South China Military Region; member, People's Revolutionary Military Council; commander and political commissar, 4th Field Army; chairman, Central-South Military and Administrative Committee; and secretary of the Central-South Bureau of the Party.

In 1950, Lin's troops were the first to enter Korea, but it is probable that he did not exercise field command. He has since served in a variety of important posts, including vice-chairman and later acting chairman, Military Affairs Committee; vice-premier; vice-chairman, National Defense Council; vice-chairman, Eighth Central Committee; and Minister of Defense.

In April 1955, Lin was made a member of the Politburo, and on September 23, 1955, Mao Tse-tung named him a marshal of the People's Republic and conferred on him the nation's three highest military orders. In September 1959, he succeeded P'eng Teh-huai as minister of National Defense. He is now also a member of the Standing Committee of the Politburo.

From the "Great Proletarian Cultural Revolution" which raged in China June–September 1966, Lin Piao seems to have emerged as Mao Tse-tung's "right-hand man" and probable successor. That Lin is a military professional would, however, very probably seriously militate against his selection as chairman of the CCP.

Liu Po-ch'eng, Marshal, P.R.C.

Member, Central Committee
Member, Politburo
Member, Standing Committee, National People's Congress
Vice-Chairman, Standing Committee, Third National People's Congress
Vice-Chairman, National Defense Council
Formerly Director, Training Department, PLA
Member, Military Affairs Committee

Marshal Liu Po-ch'eng, the "One-eyed Dragon," was born in 1892 in Kaihsien, Szechwan province. His father was a wandering musician, a calling much looked down upon in the old society. In order to give his son opportunities that he himself had been denied, Liu's father saved enough money to allow the youth to study for the *hsiu-tsai* examination.

Liu did not take the examination, however, but entered a military school in Chengtu, the provincial capital.

On the eve of the 1911 revolution, Liu joined the army as a junior officer and served in Szechwan under Hsiung K'o-wu. Under this revolutionary leader, Liu fought in many battles against other Szechwan militarists; in the course of one of these, he lost an eye.

Liu joined the Communist Party in May 1926 and took part in the Nanch'ang uprising of August 1, 1927. Later that year, he went to the U.S.S.R., where he studied first at the Military Institute in Moscow and then at the Frunze Academy. He returned to China in 1930, and in 1931 was made director of troop training in the Kiangsi Soviet. The following year, he was named chief of staff of the Central Revolutionary Military Committee.

Liu played a prominent part in the Long March. He personally directed the decisive river crossings that brought the army safely out of Chiang's reach but into the territory of hostile tribal peoples on the Szechwan-Sikang border. Here in May 1935, Liu, a Szechwanese himself, swore an oath of blood brotherhood with tribal leaders, who allowed the Communists to traverse the region unmolested.

When the war against Japan broke out, Liu had command of the 129th Division of the 8th Route Army, which was operating in southeast Shansi. Teng Hsiao-p'ing was with him as political commissar of the division, and Hsü Hsiang-ch'ien as deputy commander.

In the spring of 1944, the Shansi-Hopeh-Shantung-Honan-Anhwei Border Region was established, and Liu assumed command of its military forces. By the spring of 1945, he controlled 11 *hsien*. At this time, Liu built an extensive tunnel system along the north bank of the Yellow River to provide both air shelters and underground communications. (Chinese forces in Korea later developed this technique and constructed complex tunnel systems.)

In August 1945, Liu was elected a member of the Seventh Central Committee. On V-J Day, Liu's troops were in southern Hopeh. He cut off two Nationalist armies proceeding north along the Peip'ing–Hankow Railway and extended his control to the provinces of Shantung and Hunan. In June 1946, his troops crossed the Yellow River, cut the Lunghai Railway, and overran some 50 *hsien* from Kaifeng to Tungshan. When the Nationalists gathered their forces to give battle, Liu quickly withdrew north of the Yellow River.

In June 1947, his command, now designated the Central Plains Liberation Army, again crossed the Yellow River and occupied a large area extending from the Tientsin–Pukow Railway to the Peip'ing–Hankow Railway. In November 1948, the Central Plains Army, coordinating with Ch'en Yi's New 4th Army, launched the decisive Hwai-Hai campaign.

In September 1949, Liu was elected 2nd Field Army delegate to the First Chinese People's Political Consultative Conference. With the establishment of the new regime, he was named chairman of the Southwest Military and Administrative Committee and was appointed to the Central People's Government Council, to the board of directors of the Sino-Soviet Friendship Association, and to the People's Revolutionary Military Council. In 1951, he became president of the Military Academy of the Chinese People's Liberation Army, situated at Nanking.

In September 1954, Liu was elected to the Standing Committee of the First National People's Congress. He was subsequently named vice-chairman of the National Defense Council and superintendent of the Training Department of the PLA, while he still retained his post as president of the Nanking Military Academy. He was named a marshal of the Chinese People's Republic in September 1955 and awarded the nation's three highest military honors: the Orders of August 1, Independence and Freedom, and Liberation. In September 1956, he became a member of the Politburo.

Liu proved himself an extremely able tactician and is said to have executed Mao Tse-tung's theories of guerrilla warfare more effectively than any other Communist commander. He has written extensively on military affairs. His publications include works on strategy and tactics and translations of a number of Soviet military manuals.

Lo Jung-huan, Marshal, P.R.C. (d. 1963)

Formerly Member, National Defense Council
Formerly Vice-Chairman, National Defense Council
Formerly Member, Central Committee
Formerly Member, Politburo
Formerly Member, Military Affairs Committee
Formerly Director, General Political Department, PLA

Lo Jung-huan, who died in December 1963, was born in Hungshan, Hunan, in 1902. In 1921, he joined the Communist Youth League, and in the same year he became a member of the Party. As a junior political officer, he took part in the Nanch'ang uprising. His service with the army was spend almost entirely as a member of the Party's political organization.

In 1945, Lo was elected to the Seventh Central Committee, and in the late 1940s he succeeded P'eng Chen as political commissar of the Northeast Military Region (Manchuria). In 1948, he was appointed commissar of Lin Piao's Northeast Field Army. In 1949, he was made director of the Political Department, People's Revolutionary Military Council. There are unsubstantiated reports that he served as commissar of the Chinese People's Volunteers during the Korean War. Other reports have it that Lo was in charge of all PLA political activities from 1950 to 1954.

In the reorganization of 1954, Lo took over the General Political Department of the PLA, and in September 1955, he was named one of the ten marshals of the People's Republic. From September 1956 until his death, he was a member of the Politburo.

Lo held the nation's three highest military awards: the Orders of August 1, Independence and Freedom, and Liberation. At his funeral ceremony on December 22, 1963, the eulogy was delivered by Teng Hsiaop'ing, general secretary of the Party, who described Lo as "a close comrade in arms of Mao Tse-tung."

Nieh Jung-chen, Marshal, P.R.C.

Member, Eighth Central Committee
Vice-Premier, State Council
Vice-Chairman, National Defense Council
Chairman, Scientific and Technological Commission
Member, Military Affairs Committee

A skillful party organizer with a sound military background, Nieh Jung-chen was born in Chiang-ching *hsien*, Szechwan, in 1899, the son of well-to-do peasants. After elementary schooling in his village, he went on to the Chungking Middle School. He took part in the "May 4 Movement" in 1919 and the following year was one of the young Chinese who went to France on a work-study program. He spent some time studying natural science in Belgium but then returned to Paris, where he worked first in an arsenal and later in the Renault automobile plant. He joined the Communist Youth League in 1922 and the Party the following year.

In 1924, the Third International sent Nieh to the U.S.S.R. to attend the University of the Toilers of the East, but he soon transferred to the Red Army Military Academy to study military science. He returned to China in 1925 during the period of KMT-CCP cooperation. The Whampoa Military Academy had recently been established, and Nieh served on the staff as a political instructor and secretary of the Political Department.

Nieh participated in the Northern Expedition in 1926. At the time of the break between the left KMT and the Communists in Hankow, he was sent to work among the peasants in Hunan. In July 1927, he took part in the Nanch'ang uprising as a political commissar in Yeh T'ing's division. In December 1927, he participated in the Canton uprising. After its failure, he escaped to Hong Kong. By 1931, he was in the Kiangsi Soviet area as deputy director of the General Political Department of the Red Army. Later, he became political commissar of the 1st Army Corps, commanded by Lin Piao.

Nieh took part in the Long March, but little more was heard of him until the war against Japan started. He was then deputy commander and political commissar of Lin Piao's 115th Division of the newly formed 8th Route Army. When Lin took his division to South Shensi, he ordered Nieh to remain in the Wut'ai Mountains to organize base areas and conduct guerrilla warfare. In November 1937, Nieh drew up plans for the Shansi-Chahar-Hopeh Border Region, and when it was organized in early 1938, he was named commander and political commissar of its military forces. By the end of the war, these forces had grown to some 150,000 men.

Nieh was first elected to the Central Committee in 1945. In November 1946, after the breakdown of KMT-CCP negotiations, his troops occupied most of Chahar province. In 1948, he became commander of the North China Military Region, North China PLA, and second secretary of the Party's North China Bureau. When Fu Tso-yi surrendered Peking to the Communists in January 1949, Nieh became commander of the Peking-Tientsin Garrison Force. That year, he was a delegate to the Chinese People's Political Consultative Conference and on September 8, succeeded Yeh Chien-ying as mayor of Peking and commander, North China Military Region.

In October 1949, Nieh was named a member of the Central People's Government Council, a member of the board of directors of the Sino-Soviet Friendship Association, a member of the People's Revolutionary Military Council, deputy chief of staff of the PLA, and a member of the National Defense Study Group. He attended the First National People's Congress in September 1954 as an army delegate and shortly afterward was appointed a vice-chairman of the National Defense Council. He is said to have drafted the Military Service Law promulgated by the State Council in July 1955. In September 1955, he was named a marshal of the People's Republic of China and honored with the nation's three highest military orders. He accompanied Chu Teh to East Germany in December 1955 and later visited Hungary, Czechoslovakia, Rumania, and Poland.

Nieh was elected a member of the Eighth Central Committee in September 1956 and on November 16 was named a vice-premier. In May of the following year, he was appointed chairman of the Scientific Planning Commission. He was a member of the Presidium of the Third National People's Congress (1966). He is now chairman of the State Scientific-Technological Commission and a member of the Politburo.

P'eng Teh-huai, formerly Marshal, P.R.C.

Member, Central Committee *
Member, Politburo *

* As of January 1966, P'eng Teh-huai was still officially carried as a member of both the Central Committee and the Politburo.

Formerly Minister of National Defense
Formerly Member, Military Affairs Committee

P'eng Teh-huai, who until he was dismissed from his post as minister of national defense in September 1959 was one of the PLA's most successful and respected commanders, was born in 1902 in Hsiangtan *hsien*, Hunan province. He ran away from his stepmother's home while he was still a child; joined the army as a youth; and became a platoon commander at the age of eighteen.

P'eng joined the Kuomintang during the Northern Expedition; in 1928, at the age of twenty-five, he was appointed a brigade commander. In the summer of 1928, he led a peasant uprising in Hunan province, and in December of that year, he joined Mao and Chu Teh on Chingkangshan. By 1933, he was commanding the 3rd Army Corps, First Front Army. In October 1934, this corps marched out of Kiangsi as advance guard on the Long March.

After the Communists reached North Shensi, P'eng's corps merged with the 15th Army Corps (Hsü Hai-tung) to form a new 1st Front Army with P'eng as commander and Mao as political commissar. He was active in numerous responsible positions during the Anti-Japanese War and in 1945 became a member of the Seventh Central Committee.

P'eng Teh-huai commanded the Chinese People's Volunteers (CPV) in Korea, October 1950 to September 1954. In September 1954, he was appointed minister of National Defense, and a year later he was made a marshal of the People's Republic. He was a member of the Eighth Central Committee and the Politburo.

P'eng led a Chinese delegation to East Germany in 1955 and attended the Warsaw Conference (where the Warsaw Pact was signed) as an observer. Afterward, he visited the Soviet Union. In November 1957, he again went to Moscow, and in April 1959, he headed a delegation to the East European Communist countries, the U.S.S.R., and Mongolia.

In September 1959, P'eng was dismissed from his post as minister of Defense and officially has not been heard of since. The precise reasons for his fall from grace are not clear, but it is known that his strategic views as of 1959 were in conflict with those of Mao Tse-tung, who was apparently supported by Chu Teh, Lin Piao, and other leading military figures. (See David A. Charles, "The Dismissal of Marshal P'eng Teh-huai," *The China Quarterly*, no. 8, October–December, 1961. pp. 63–76.)

Yeh Chien-ying, Marshal, P.R.C.

Member, Central Committee
Vice-Chairman, National Defense Council
Member, Presidium, Third National People's Congress

Member, Standing Committee, Third National People's Congress

Director and Political Commissar, Academy of Military Science, PLA

Member, Military Affairs Committee

Yeh Chien-ying, reported to be a key figure in Communist China's program for modernizing her armed forces, was born of Hakka parents in P'ing-tsun, Kwangtung, in 1897 or 1898 but spent some of his early years with relatives in Singapore and Hanoi.

Yeh graduated with the twelfth class of the Yunnan Military Academy and then served for a time as a junior officer in Canton under Ch'en Ch'iung-ming. He was an instructor at the Whampoa Military Academy in 1924 and joined the CCP in that year. He commanded the 21st Division of the National Revolutionary Army during the Northern Expedition and later was chief of staff of the "Iron Army," commanded by Chang Fa-k'uei. He participated in the preparatory conference for the Nanch'ang uprising. After the failure at Nanch'ang, he fled to Hong Kong but subsequently returned to Canton to help organize the uprising there (December 1927). When this, too, failed, he escaped to Shanghai.

In 1928, Yeh was sent to the Soviet Union to study military science and was put in a special class at Sun Yat-sen University with Tung Pi-wu, Lin Po-c'hü and others. (One source states that while in Russia. Yeh was criticized for living luxuriously—a bourgeois tendency that manifested itself many years later when foreigners who met him during the negotiations at the time of the Marshall mission found him the most affable and convivial of the Chinese Communists, fond of good food and drink.)

Yeh returned to China in 1931 after a visit to France en route. He immediately made his way to the Soviet base area in Kiangsi, where he served first as director of the Red Army College and chief of staff of the Revolutionary Military Committee. In 1933, he was appointed chief of staff, 1st Front Army. He drafted the original plans for the first phase of the Long March and at Maoerhkai in 1935 supported Mao in Mao's power struggle against Chang Kuo-t'ao.

During the negotiations between the KMT and the CCP after the Sian incident, Yeh acted as the CCP's liaison officer, first in Sian and then in Nanking and Hankow. From 1938 to 1945, he was chief of staff, 8th Route Army. After the Japanese surrender, he was the chief Communist representative at executive headquarters in Peip'ing, in which Nationalists, Communists, and Americans participated. He then held the rank of lieutenant general. Following the breakdown of peace negotiations, he was named deputy chief of staff of the People's Revolutionary Military Council, and chief of staff of the Liberation armies.

In January 1949, when Fu Tso-yi surrendered Peip'ing to the Communists, Yeh was named mayor of the city and chairman of the Peip'ing

Military Control Commission. In April 1949, he again represented the Communists in further abortive peace talks with the KMT. He moved south to Kwangtung in the wake of the 4th Field Army and was subsequently named acting secretary of the Central Committee's South China Bureau, chairman of the Kwangtung Provincial People's Government, mayor of Canton, commander and concurrently commissar of the Kwangtung Military Region, and chairman of the Canton Military Control Commission. He was appointed to the board of the Sino-Soviet Friendship Association and to the People's Revolutionary Military Council and was named vice-chairman of the Central-South China Military and Political Council.

With the reorganization of the governmental structure of 1954, Yeh was recalled to Peking and appointed vice-chairman of the National Defense Council and director of the Armed Forces Supervision Department of the PLA. He received the rank of marshal and was awarded the highest military honors in September 1955. A year later, he was re-elected to the Central Committee.

In December 1956, Yeh led a military delegation to Burma. In 1957, he was deputy chief of a military delegation to the U.S.S.R., and in the following year, he led a similar delegation to India.

Yeh was a member of the Presidium of the Third National People's Congress (1964–65) and is a member of the Congress's Standing Committee. He is now a member of the Politburo.

APPENDIX B

*(The following material will be found in the pocket
attached to the inside back cover of this volume)*

Figure 1: Chinese Communist Government Organization

Figure 2: Chinese Communist Party Organization

Figure 3: Chinese Communist Military Forces Organization
and List of Key Personnel

Notes

BOOK I

Chapter 1

1. Although Marxist "study groups" had existed for several years at Peking University and elsewhere, the CCP was not founded until May 1921 in Shanghai. The Party held its first "Conference" (Congress) there in July. During the first few years of its existence, the Party remained "an academic group without definite policies and even less action." Sing-ming Chiu, *A History of the Chinese Communist Army* (unpublished doctoral dissertation, University of Southern California, 1958).

   Chiang Kai-shek describes the Party at the time as "little more than an association of intellectuals who had accepted Karl Marx's dogmas, who felt friendly toward Soviet Russia, and who sought to develop their party organization by means of labor movement [sic]." *Soviet Russia in Asia: A Summing-up at Seventy* (New York: Farrar, Straus and Cudahy, 1957), p. 15.

   Conrad Brandt calls the early leaders "groping intellectuals" who had no experience in political work. "Clearly such men required firm guidance by experienced Comintern hands in order to convert a Marxist sect into a Communist Party." *Stalin's Failure in China* (Cambridge: Harvard University Press, 1958), p. 20. The Comintern was eager to furnish the "firm guidance," but only in return for unquestioning obedience to its directives.

2. See, for example, *The First Manifesto of the CCP on the Current Situation* (June 10, 1922).

> "Workers, peasants, students, soldiers, policemen and merchants! So long as the authority of the military is not overthrown, there will be no hope of disarming the provincial armies and abolishing the *tu-chün* [war lord] system. So long as the authority of the military is not overthrown, there will be no hope of reducing the demands for national funds, which are used to cover war expenses and further to disrupt the entire national and local financial system. So long as the authority of the military is not overthrown, all conditions will be present to allow the military to secure new loans from foreigners and thus bring about an intensification of foreign influence in China. So long as the authority of the military is not

overthrown, there will be no hope that the military will cease imposing heavy imposts on the citizens of China; there will be no hope that looting may cease, no hope that order may be restored in all regions of China. So long as the authority of the military is not overthrown, there will be no hope of a broad development of education in China and of industrial progress in our country. So long as the authority of the military is not overthrown, there will be no hope that the struggle among militarists for the expansion of their own spheres of influence may cease. Peasants and merchants are always war victims. These wars will be inevitable and endless if they are not stopped by the people themselves."

This manifesto also called for a "united front" of the Communist Party with the Kuomintang "to struggle against war lords of the feudal type . . . to liberate the Chinese people . . . from the yoke of foreigners and the yoke of the powerful militarists." Conrad Brandt, Benjamin Schwartz, and John K. Fairbank, *A Documentary History of Chinese Communism* (Cambridge: Harvard University Press, 1962), pp. 54–63.

Although the First, Second (held in Canton in June or July 1922), and Third (held in 1923) Party conferences each passed "resolutions" or "decisions" and the Third issued a "manifesto" as well, none of these documents contained any mention of need for an army under Party control. For these documents, which are presumed to be authentic, see Ch'en Kung-po, *The Communist Movement in China*, ed., with an introduction, by C. Martin Wilbur (Columbia University East Asian Institute Series, no. 7; New York: Columbia University, September 1960).

3. The Russians repeatedly denied that they were "interfering" in China's "internal affairs." All such allegations they branded as slanders; "absurd . . . lies from beginning to end." See Foreign Minister Chicherin's statement in *Izvestia*, July 2, 1925, reprinted in Jane Degras, ed., *Soviet Documents on Foreign Policy*, v. 2 (London: Oxford University Press, 1952), pp. 51–52.

4. F. F. Liu, *A Military History of Modern China* (Princeton University Press, 1956), p. 8.

5. C. Martin Wilbur and Julie Lien-Ying How, eds., *Documents on Communism, Nationalism, and Soviet Advisers in China 1918–1927* (New York: Columbia University Press, 1956), pp. 176–180, 191, 200–202.

6. M. N. Roy, *Revolution and Counter-Revolution in China* (Calcutta: Renaissance Publishers, 1946), pp. 411–412.

"Never did Chiang prove more astute as a political leader than during the Northern Expedition when he used—and outwitted—the Communists. Arms alone, he knew well at that time, could not win so swiftly and surely as arms preceded by propagandists bearing a popular message. By leaving the Communists a free hand in the lower Kuomintang echelons, he secured for his armies the mass support which the 'youngsters' knew best how to rally." Brandt, cited, pp. 81–82.

7. In early 1927, the Party was said to have 90,000 members, and the Youth Branch more than 60,000. "Bolshevistically inclined trade-unionists" were estimated as 3 million and peasant association members, at 10 million. V. K. Wellington Koo, *Memoranda Presented to the Lytton Commission* (New York: Chinese Cultural Society, 1932–33), v. 2, p. 737.

8. *International Press Correspondence (INPRECORR)*, v. 6, nos. 90 and 91, December 23 and 30, 1926.

The principal mechanisms the Party used to "increase its work in the armies" and to "entrench its influence" were the activist and the political representative. The "activist" (*hsia-chi kan-pu*), or "cadre," was a Party member but *not* a functionary in the political structure, which paralleled the command structure in the army. The "political representative" (*cheng-wei*), also a Party member, *was* a functionary with specific responsibilities and commensurate authority.

The *kan-pu* were agitators and propagandists working at company, platoon, and squad levels. The *cheng-wei* prescribed the propaganda lines and the general nature of the cadres' activities, which were not exclusively confined to work in the ranks of the army. An important complementary task assigned the *kan-pu* was that of influencing the population in the zone of operations to receive the army favorably and to support it actively. To paraphrase the picturesque language later used to describe an important concept, the *kan-pu* were responsible for creating proper "temperature" in the "water" (the masses) in which "the fish" (the army) could "swim."

9. Same. Comrades Petroff and Duncan are not otherwise identified.

10. The split between the "left" Kuomintang and the Communists in Hankow was a direct reflection of the split between the factions led by Stalin and Trotsky in Moscow. Trotsky had all along recommended a much more radical and aggressive line in China than had Stalin, whose policies prevailed. Both men misread the situation, and neither would listen to advice from those who knew more about it than they did. An authoritative treatment of this period in China, with analysis of the intra-party fight in Moscow, is that of Harold Isaacs in his *Tragedy of the Chinese Revolution* (2nd rev. ed.; Stanford University Press, 1961).

11. Xenia J. Eudin and Robert C. North, *Soviet Russia and the East, 1920–29: A Documentary Survey* (Stanford University Press, 1952), p. 306.

12. Order of Battle, 2nd "Front" (Group) Army, August 1927, according to information supplied by General Chang Fa-k'uei:

2nd Front Army	Chang Fa-k'uei
4th Army	Huang Chi-hsing
Chief of Staff	Yeh Chien-ying
12th Division	Mao P'ei-lan
25th Division	Li Han-yun
21st Division	Fu Hsiang-ying
11th Army	Chu Hui-jih
24th Division	Yeh T'ing
10th Division	Tsai T'ing-k'ai
26th Division	Hsu Chih-jui
20th Army	Ho Lung

(consisting of one division, formerly 20th Division)

13. Conversations with General Chang Fa-k'uei in February 1964 and subsequent correspondence in 1964–65.

14. For reconstructions of the circumstances of the August 1 *pao-tung* and the aftermath, see Colonel J. Guillermaz, "The Nanchang Uprising," *China*

Quarterly, no. 11, July/September 1962, pp. 161–168; and C. Martin Wilbur, "The Ashes of Defeat," same, no. 18, April/June 1964, pp. 3–54.

15. J. V. Stalin, "The Perspectives of the Chinese Revolution," in Degras, cited, pp. 193–198.

16. Quoted in C. Martin Wilbur, "The Ashes of Defeat," cited, pp. 12–13. Chou I-chun, another Communist who made this march, described it in equally dramatic language:

> A great many soldiers and porters fell and died . . . there was no medicine for the sick . . . no one to give a peaceful burial to the dead— a condition too pitiful for pen to describe . . . the morale of the officers and troops became utterly ashen hearted . . . men and horses were so exhausted they could not revive interest in life. [Quoted in same, p. 27.]

17. Same, p. 31.
18. Same, pp. 18–19.
19. Same, p. 21.
20. Same, p. 24.
21. Mao Tse-tung, *Selected Works*, v. 1 (New York: International Publishers, 1954), p. 22.
22. Same, p. 32.
23. Yeh T'ing's "Report on the Canton Insurrection." Quoted by M. N. Roy, cited, p. 558.
24. Same, pp. 562–563.

The abortive Canton uprising was ordered by Stalin, who professed to believe that the Chinese revolution was at the point of a new "upsurge." Later, Trotsky wrote:

> At the end of 1927, Stalin's faction, frightened by the consequences of its own mistakes, tried to make up at one stroke what it had failed to do over a number of years. . . . In reality, the revolutionary tide had already been replaced by a downward movement.

As cited by Jerome Ch'en, *Mao and the Chinese Revolution*. (London: Oxford University Press, 1965), p. 137.

25. Many years before, in his essay "The Revolutionary Act," Frederick Engels had written:

> The time is past for revolutions carried through by small minorities at the head of unconscious masses. When it gets to be a matter of the complete transformation of the social organization, the masses themselves must participate, must understand what is at stake, and why they act.

Frederick Engels. *The Revolutionary Act* (New York: New York Labor News Company, 1935), p. 24.

Chapter 2

1. Jerome Ch'en, *Mao and the Chinese Revolution* (New York: Oxford University Press, 1965), p. 131.

2. Quoted by Edgar Snow, *Red Star Over China* (New York: Random House, 1938), pp. 153–154.
3. Mao Tse-tung wrote in 1928:

> "Amid the encirclement of White forces, serious problems have arisen because of shortage of daily necessities for the army and the people and shortage of cash. Since last year, because of the enemy's tight blockage, daily necessities like salt, cloth and medicine have at all times been quite scarce and dear in the area under the independent regime, and this has caused discomfort, sometimes to extreme degree, to the masses of workers, peasants and the petty bourgeoisie, as well as the soldiers of the Red Army. . . . Many soldiers have fallen ill of malnutrition, and the wounded in the hospitals are suffering even more."

Selected Works, v. 1 (New York: International Publishers, 1954), pp. 69–70.
4. Same, p. 74.
5. Nym Wales, *Inside Red China* (New York: Doubleday, Doran, and Company, 1939), p. 247.
6. Mao Tse-tung, cited, p. 83.
7. These were known as "The Three Rules." The "Eight Observances" (of behavior) which supplemented them were:
   (1) Replace all doors when you leave a house. [At night, doors were unhinged, laid across sawhorses, and used as beds.]
   (2) Return and roll up the straw matting on which you sleep.
   (3) Be courteous and polite to the people, and help them when you can.
   (4) Return all borrowed articles.
   (5) Replace all damaged articles.
   (6) Be honest in all transactions with the peasants.
   (7) Pay for all articles purchased.
   (8) Be sanitary, and especially establish latrines a safe distance from people's houses.

Snow, cited, p. 158.
These "Rules" and "Observances" had the force of holy writ in the Communist army. After he returned from Yenan, Colonel Evans Carlson, USMC (who had been an observer there), wrote them down in Chinese for me. This memento of a friendship is unfortunately lost. Both "Rules" and "Observances" have been modified several times. A more recent official version, issued by headquarters, PLA, in October 1947, gives them as follows:

The Three Cardinal Rules of Discipline:
   (1) Obey orders in all actions.
   (2) Do not take a single needle or piece of thread from the people.
   (3) Turn all booty over to H.Q.
The Eight Reminders:
   (1) Talk to people politely.
   (2) Be fair in all business dealings.
   (3) Return everything you have borrowed.
   (4) Pay for anything you have damaged.
   (5) Don't beat or bully people.

    (6) Don't damage crops.

    (7) Don't flirt with women.

    (8) Don't ill treat prisoners of war.

Mao Tse-tung, *Selected Works*, v. 4 (New York: International Publishers, 1954), p. 343.

8. "Resolution of the Sixth National Congress [of the CCP] on the Peasant Movement" (September 1928) in Conrad Brandt, Benjamin Schwartz, and John K. Fairbank, *A Documentary History of Chinese Communism* (Cambridge: Harvard University Press, 1952), p. 162.

    Mao's choice of words is interesting. What worried him was indiscriminate "killing and burning." Purposeful "killing and burning," that is, the deliberate, discriminating use of terror, was then a Communist tactic in China as it has since been elsewhere.

9. Mao Tse-tung, *Selected Works*, v. 1, cited, p. 81.

10. Stuart R. Schram, "The Military Deviation of Mao Tse-tung," *Problems of Communism*, v. 23, no. 1, January/February 1964, pp. 49–56.

11. Mao Tse-tung, *Nineteen Poems* (Peking: Foreign Languages Press, 1958), p. 12.

12. Mao Tse-tung, *Selected Works*, v. 1, cited, pp. 105–115.

13. Brandt, Schwartz, and Fairbank, cited, pp. 166–179. In *Chinese Communism and the Rise of Mao* (Cambridge: Harvard University Press, 1952), chapters IX and X, "The Li Li-san Leadership" and "Changsha and the Li Li-san Line," Benjamin Schwartz describes the several policy conflicts which rent the CCP from 1928 until Li Li-san was forced to resign from the Politburo in November 1930.

    Schwartz quotes Li Li-san as writing in *Hung Ch'i* [*Red Flag*] of March 29, 1930: "Simply to rely on the Red Army to take one or several provinces in order to set up a national revolutionary regime would be a most serious error. Not only is such an idea preposterous, but it might even lead us to neglect our most vital activity—the organization of the worker's struggle and the organization of political strikes by armed workers' units." The cities, he maintained, are the "brains and heart" of the ruling class (p. 138). Again in April, he insisted: "Unless we have the industrial cities and industrial zones we shall never gain a victory in one or several provinces. All talk of 'encircling the city with the country' or of relying on the Red Army to take the cities is sheer nonsense" (p. 139).

    But by June 11, Li Li-san had changed his mind; his letter of that date to the Comintern admits for the first time that the Red Army could be a powerful, if not decisive, factor in the triumph of the revolution (pp. 141–142).

14. Hu Chiao-mu, *Thirty Years of the Communist Party of China* (4th ed.; Peking: Foreign Languages Press, 1959), p. 40.

15. Snow, cited, pp. 159–160.

16. Same, p. 161.

17. V. K. Wellington Koo, *Memoranda Presented to the Lytton Commission* (New York: The Chinese Cultural Society, 1932–33), v. 2, p. 479.

18. I have examined Nationalist materials dealing with this and subsequent "Extermination Campaigns." They are not entirely reliable. Communist strength is invariably exaggerated, as that of the Nationalists is minimized. All sorts

of reasons (bad weather, difficult terrain, trouble with recalcitrant war lords, the Japanese intervention in Manchuria) are given for Nationalist failures, but they do not include the basic ones: inept command, poor intelligence, half-baked plans, and the low morale of the provincial troops.

19. T. A. Bisson writes:

> "During the heavy fighting in the last two weeks of May, the Red armies were reported to have captured more than 20,000 rifles, about 80 machine guns, some trench mortars and artillery, and large quantities of supplies. In addition, numerous units of the government troops, estimated at 20,000 men, had deserted and been incorporated into the Communist armies."

See *The Communist Movement in China* (Foreign Policy Reports, v. 9, no. 4; New York: Foreign Policy Association, Inc., April 26, 1933).

Bisson's figures are probably somewhat exaggerated but do reflect the incontrovertible fact that Communist strength was increasing during 1930–32 and not diminishing, as the Nationalists persistently claimed.

20. This poem, "The Second Encirclement," is one of those translated in Ch'en, cited, p. 332.

21. Koo, cited, p. 790.

22. Two books which the KMT historian T'ang Leang-Li describes as consisting largely of travesties of "the facts relating to Communism in China" are obviously biased, but scarcely more so than the apologia for the Nationalists which he edited: *Suppressing Communist Banditry in China* (rev. ed.; Shanghai: China United Press, December 1934). As I have observed above, no dispassionate history of the Extermination campaigns exists, and it is exceedingly unlikely that one will ever be produced. The two books to which T'ang refers are Victor A. Yakhontoff, *The Chinese Soviets* (New York: Coward-McCann, Inc., 1934) and Agnes Smedley, *China's Red Army Marches* (New York: Vanguard, 1934). The latter is almost pure propaganda. Yakhontoff's report, based on hearsay evidence, was compiled in Shanghai. He never reached the Soviet areas.

23. Koo (cited, p. 750) states that the government "was obliged to recall its troops" because of the Japanese threat to Manchuria. This did, indeed, provide a convenient pretext for ringing down the curtain in Kiangsi, where the Reds, "thus made bold, launched a counteroffensive. The conquered regions had to be evacuated and the gains realized in the course of the campaign were almost completely lost. . . . A lesson was, however, learned: that with well-organized forces carefully conducted, it was possible to reach Communist dens even in the most inaccessible parts of the interior."

24. The "Final Decision Concerning Red Army Problems" is perhaps the most important single document dealing with the function and character of the Red Army. Because it is not readily available in English elsewhere, it is reproduced in full below. The text is taken from *Su-wei-ai Chung-kuo* [*Soviet China*] (Moscow: Soviet Foreign Workers' Publishing House, 1933), pp. 175–181.

FINAL DECISION CONCERNING RED ARMY PROBLEMS

(Adopted by the First National Congress of the Representatives of Chinese Workers', Peasants', and Soldiers' Soviets, December 1931)

"In the line of fire of the national revolutionary struggle, in the obdurate struggle of the broad masses of the distressed workers and peasants against feudal landlords, bullying gentry, capitalists, and foreign imperialists, the fragments of workers' and peasants' guerrillas in various parts of China, under the leadership of the Chinese Communist Party, already have built the Workers' and Peasants' Red Army.

"In the process of the heroic struggle of the past three years, the Red Army has displayed that it is the most determined executor of the agrarian reform and the struggle against imperialism. Although there were some temporary partial defeats and failures, nevertheless, its heroic prominence served to establish Soviet China and uninterruptedly and strongly advance the determined struggle with all counterrevolution.

"The Chinese Red Army already has attracted the highest degree of enmity and jealous hate of all enemies of the revolution (imperialists, Kuomintang, capitalists, landlords, slave masters, bureaucrats, police, executioners, detectives, preachers, and White Russians), and they have mobilized all counterrevolutionary strength and war-lord units to assault the Red Army. Moreover, although the present enemy has exceedingly large military forces and clever expertise, and, in addition, operates with the fullest assistance of the imperialists, nevertheless, it is still incapable of destroying the inexperienced and still clumsy and inferior Red Army.

"At present, the workers, peasants, and toiling masses of the nation and of the whole world all express unlimited pleasure and affection in and for the Chinese Workers' and Peasants' Red Army.

"These circumstances completely prove that the Chinese Workers' and Peasants' Red Army is the armed strength of the agrarian revolution and the anti-imperialist revolutionary struggle; they also prove that the struggle of the masses of Chinese workers and peasants for liberation from long-term slave life and all oppression (imperialist, landlord, gentry, cruel and vindictive militarist oppression, and flaying connected with blood-smelling feudalistic capitalism) has already begun and will successfully develop in the future. The Chinese revolution already has succeeded in attaining Soviet political power and the stage of struggle.

"Determined class struggle already has begun; moreover, it will develop in the future. However, the final victory in the total national revolution—to set forth the difficult path of struggle in the future of the Chinese working class and revolutionary peasantry because of the strength of China's counterrevolutionaries and the imperialists, who are just on the point of utilizing all available power to assault the revolutionary Workers' and Peasants' Red Army—the success or failure of this historical class struggle which already has begun will be decided by armed strength.

"In order to protect the Soviet political power and the broad Soviet regions, in order to guarantee the victory of the revolution, and in order to strengthen the bitter struggle with the Chinese counterrevolutionary forces and imperialism, the worker and peasant masses of China must put forth great effort, in numbers and in mass, to strengthen the Red Army.

"The Red Army is the most important defender of the Soviet political power; it is a class army, and in mission or in spirit, it is fundamentally dissimilar from the Kuomintang army and the imperialist armies.

"The imperialist armies and war-lord armies are isolated from the masses; they are instruments to oppress the workers and peasants and to ravage colonies, and they are advancing aggressive wars and war-lord coalition wars. But the Red Army is the army of the masses of workers and peasants themselves; it is the armed power of liberation of the masses of workers and peasants, and, moreover, it is the army which has a great international mission. The armed might of the Red Army is the armed might which is capable of accelerating the collapse of the reactionary ruling class and of destroying the capitalist and imperialist armies.

"The Red Army is the army which is trained and acts in obedience to the international mission and spirit of the toiling masses, and in the history of China it is the one organized with consciously revolutionary warriors. Every combatant in the Red Army knows that it exists to struggle for the interests of his own class, to serve all of the toiling masses, and that it absolutely does not exist to represent the flayers and capitalists in oppressing the workers and peasants.

"The Red Army Political Commissariat is the direct representative of the Communist Party and the Soviet Government in the Red Army, and the Communist Party and the Communist Youth League are inseparable organizational constituents of the Red Army.

"All toilers, workers, hired farmers, poor peasants, middle peasants, and urban poor have the right and privilege to take up arms to defend the Soviet political power; all who belong to the ruling classes and flayers—war lords, landlords, bullying gentry, bureaucrats, capitalists, rich peasants, and those who belong to their families—are not permitted to join the Red Army.

"To serve the interests of the revolution, a strict, self-conscious discipline must be established in the Red Army. All command, managerial, and supply organizations must be completely integrated; they must use all their power regularly to strengthen and raise the fighting capacity of the Red Army, and at the same time, with all their power, they must increase the ability of the Soviet political power to maintain its authority within the Red Army.

"The First National Congress of the Representatives of the Chinese Soviets commissions the Presidium of the Central Executive Committee to apply all necessary political methods to organize and strengthen the fighting power of the Red Army, and the Congress, more concretely, commissions the following:

"1. Designates the supreme military affairs organization—the Revolutionary Military Affairs Council, Commander in Chief of the Chinese Red Army—to administer the supply and organization of the Red Army and military training and to command the combat activities of the Red Army. Only under conditions of the strictest concentrated leadership (embracing the entire Red Army), of planning and unification of activities carried into effect at the highest level of leadership can the Red Army fight to victory over the war lords' and imperialists' power, can the military base of operations of the Soviet regions be expanded. Hence, the Red Army must immediately and determinedly carry into effect all of the instructions of the Revolutionary Military Affairs Council and its subordinate organs.

"2. To devise means of augmenting the increment of workers and hired farmers in the Red Army and to strengthen the assimilation and participation of workers and hired farmers in the Red Army, the Congress simultaneously summons workers' organizations in non-Soviet regions regularly to send revolutionary workers to the Red Army; only if there is an increase in the increment of workers and hired farmers, a strengthening of the work of the Political Commissars and the Political Department, and a strengthening of the organs of the Communist Party and the Youth League in the Red Army, can the proletarian leadership of the Red Army be guaranteed.

"3. The Congress especially points out: The Political Commissariat, the Communist Party, and the Youth League in the Red Army are to carry into effect the class mission which is the function of political education and the strengthening of the Red Army's fighting power by the Red Army political personnel. The government and the Revolutionary Military Affairs Council must compose the various rules for the responsibilities and necessary limits of authority of Political Commissars, the Political Departments, and the various political organizations in the Red Army; and they must insure that every soldier is capable of expounding the contents of these rules.

"4. Regular attention to the improvement of the mass of Red Army Army leaders requires, first of all, bringing forward workers, hired farmers, poor peasants, and revolutionary warriors who have displayed loyalty and sincerity in past revolutionary struggles and who have rich experience to undertake military leadership and political work.

"5. To adopt all strong methods to expand the numbers of the Red Army (to organize new groups, instructors, and armies) and to reconstruct the mass of the Red Army (in accordance with strategic conditions, to organize fighting units, construct military schools, publish military regulations, and various types of books) so as to assist the fighting strength of the Red Army to fight to victory over the enemies of the revolution.

"6. In order to guarantee the supply of weapons and all necessary goods to the Red Army, works to manufacture ammunition, arsenals, and unified supply organs must be organized.

"7. Without the positive assistance of the Soviet political power in various ways, the fight to victory of the Red Army is impossible. The Soviet Government must construct revolutionary laws and fix the rights and privileges and the obligations of the various levels of Soviets and various levels of organizations vis-à-vis the Red Army so as to strengthen the Red Army and assist the fighting activities of the Red Army.

"8. It is necessary to draw up and publish the oath of Red Army personnel.

"The Congress of Soviets summons the Soviets of various levels, the Communist Party, the Youth League, Workmen's Associations, and all other revolutionary bodies and the broad masses of workers, peasants, and toilers to give the Red Army greater assistance. If there is anyone who does not assist the Red Army, does not assist the Red Army's strength, does not assist the Red Army's discipline, objectively he is a counterrevolutionary and opposes the Red Army."

At this time, the Japanese government estimated the class composition of the Red Army to be roughly as follows:

Poor peasants	57 per cent
Surrendered Nationalists	28 per cent
Vagabonds and bandits	9 per cent
Workers	6 per cent

See Japan, *Documents Relating to the Sino-Japanese Dispute* (rev. ed.; n. pl; n. pub., July 1932), Document A, Appendix A-3.

25. T'ang, cited, p. 115. The Chinese, it should be noted, are inclined to use the character *tui* to indicate a formation or detachment which cannot be described in more specific terms. In this particular case, the character was incorrectly translated as "corps." The names of the commanders are as given by T'ang.

If we reduce the figures to more meaningful terms, i.e., to 2,000-man regiments of three 600-man battalions (a figure then *generally* applicable), the table would show Chu Teh commanding 10 such regiments; Ho Lung, four to five; P'eng Teh-huai, about six; Li Nien-hui, three; and so forth. The Reds thus mustered about 50 regiments at this time.

26. *China Year Book, 1933* (Shanghai: North China Daily News, 1933), p. 253.

27. The role which the German advisers to the Nationalists played in the formulation of strategy for the Fifth Campaign remains obscure. Certainly, some German advisers were in the field at division and army headquarters. I have discussed their role with one German who served as adviser to a division commander during the campaign, and although he was not present in Nanch'ang and could not say how importantly his colleagues there figured in the planning, he did say that in the field he made operational decisions.

The Comintern publication, *Inprecorr*, obviously a highly suspect source, claimed in October 1933 that "70 German officers" were at the Generalissimo's advanced headquarters in Nanch'ang planning the final Kiangsi campaign. (See *International Press Correspondence*, v. 13, no. 44, October 6, 1933.) As early as May 1933, however, Chiang presided over a "bandit-extermination" conference in Nanch'ang where it was decided that the policy to pursue in the future for "internal pacification" and "expulsion of the aggressor" was to be "three parts military and seven parts political guidance, using a combination of government, party, and military resources in a strategy of dividing, blockading, surrounding, and exterminating." *Chung-hua Min-kuo Chan-shih T'u-chi* [Military (War) History of the Chinese Republic Compiled with maps] (Taipei: Republic of China, Ministry of Defense, Historical Division, 1961), pp. 78–80.

28. General L. M. Chassin, *L'Ascension de Mao Tse-tung (1921–1945)* (Paris: Payot, 1953), pp. 112–113. (My translation.)

29. Sun Tzu, *The Art of War*, trans., with an introduction, by Samuel B. Griffith (Oxford University: Clarendon Press, 1963), p. 66.

30. In "Strategic Problems of China's Revolutionary War" (1936), Mao castigated those who in Kiangsi had advanced such slogans as "Halt the enemy beyond the gate"; "Don't abandon an inch of territory," etc., for manifesting "revolutionary hysteria." These "theories and practices of hotheads and ignoramuses" were "anti-Marxist." The Chairman continued: "The object of strategic retreat is to conserve forces and prepare for the counteroffensive. . . . " See *Selected Works*, v. 2 (New York: International Publishers, 1954), pp. 214, 215.
      We can do no more than sense the general nature of the bitter struggle that obviously divided the Party's hierarchy before the decision to abandon the Kiangsi Soviet was made. But in assessing Mao as a strategist, one must remember that he (probably with the support of Chu Teh, P'eng Teh-huai, and other generals) advocated immediate withdrawal from Kiangsi and that this opinion prevailed.

Chapter 3

1. Mao Tse-tung, *Selected Works*, v. 1 (New York: International Publishers, 1954), p. 61.
      Although in both history and legend the term "Long March" has come to refer specifically to the great trek led by Mao Tse-tung and Chu Teh, there were in fact four dramatic marches made by Communist armies between 1933 and 1936 in displacing from Soviet areas in South, Central, and West China to the far Northwest. The three others were led by Li Chih-tan from Central China to the original base area in Shensi; Ho Lung, Hsiao K'o, and Jen Pi-shih from the Hunan-Hupeh-Kweichow Soviet; and Chang Kuo-t'ao and Hsü Hsiang-ch'ien from the Szechwan Soviet. Each, a superb achievement of enduring significance to the participants, has been overshadowed by *the* Long March. Today, they receive but little attention in the growing body of "Long March literature" and have perhaps undeservedly been relegated to footnotes, as they are in these pages.

2. Chen Chang-feng, *On the Long March with Chairman Mao* (Peking: Foreign Languages Press, 1959), p. 22.

3. Same.

4. Mao Tse-tung, "Problems of Strategy in China's Revolutionary War," *Selected Military Writings* (Peking: Foreign Languages Press, 1963), p. 127. Hu Chiao-mu ascribes the defeat in Kiangsi "to the completely wrong military strategy of remaining solely on the defensive and certain other wrong policies produced by the Party's Central Committee." See *Thirty Years of the Communist Party of China* (4th ed.; Peking: Foreign Language Press, 1959), p. 42.

5. "Problems of Strategy in Guerrilla War against Japan," *Selected Military Writings*, cited, p. 162.

6. Nym Wales, *Red Dust: Autobiographies of Chinese Communists* (Stanford University Press, 1952), p. 65.

7. A reasonably reliable source, a man who has asked that he not be identified but who was at the time situated where he had access to highly classified information gathered by the Nationalists, has asserted unequivocally that the

Red Army Command paid Mex (silver) $250,000 to the provincial command in Kwangtung to permit the Communists to pass the lines of the provincial forces without fighting. This is possible. Even Hsü Meng-ch'iu, in describing the episode to Nym Wales, stated that when the Communists met the Kwangtung army, they "scattered it easily." Wales, cited, p. 65.

8. Liu Po-ch'eng, "Looking Back on the Long March" in *The Long March: Eye-witness Accounts* (Peking: Foreign Languages Press, 1963), p. 208.

9. Same, pp. 207–208.

10. Same, p. 209.

11. Same, p. 210. All accounts the Communists have made public conform generally to that of Liu Po-ch'eng. Obviously, the crux of the matter was the question of correct strategy and tactics in the circumstances. The so-called "returned students group" on the Central Committee still adhered rigorously to the Moscow line, which demanded seizure of cities. The German military specialist with the Communists, a former officer known as Li Teh, also apparently recommended this. To Mao, as no doubt to Chu Teh, the essential point at issue was preservation of the army. After the Tsunyi conference, both Li Teh and members of the "returned students group" were completely discredited.

12. Norman Hanwell, "The Chinese Red Army," *Asia*, v. 36, no. 5, May 1936, pp. 317–322. Hanwell spent three months in Communist areas in Szechwan in the spring of 1934. Apparently, he was permitted to travel freely and collected a considerable amount of information, which he augmented with material contained in a series of articles by one Hsun Shih, published in the *Kuo-wen Chou-pao* in 1935.

A table in Hanwell's article (p. 319) shows principal command and staff personnel, 4th Front Army, as of May 1934. These included:

4TH FRONT ARMY

Army Commander	Hsü Hsiang-ch'ien
Political Commissar	Ch'en Ch'ang-hao
Vice Commissar	Wang Shu-shan
Chief of Staff	Ni Chih-liang

4TH ARMY

Commander	Wang Hung-k'un
Political Commissar	Hsu ?

9TH ARMY

Commander	Ho Wei
Political Commissar	Chang Ts'ai-fang

30TH ARMY

Commander	Yu T'ien-yan
Political Commissar	Li Hsien-nien

31ST ARMY

Commander	Sun Yu-ch'ing
Political Commissar	Tseng Ch'uan-liu

33RD ARMY

Commander	Wang Wei-chou
Political Commissar	T'ao Hsien-li

However, Hsü Hsiang-ch'ien told Nym Wales (cited, p. 159) that the chief of the Political Department of the army was Fu Chung.

In addition, Hanwell gives total Communist strength as 25,000 whereas Hsü

Hsiang-ch'ien alleges it was 60,000 to 80,000. The Communist commander claimed his armies inflicted more than 100,000 casualties, principally on troops commanded by Liu Hsiang. He admitted that the Communist wounded amounted to more than 10,000 but gave no figures for those killed.

The question of Communist casualties on the various marches will probably never be answered. At this period of their history, the Communists were occupied with matters more important than personnel accounting. Basing figures on information he gathered from leading Communists in Pao-an in September 1935, Edgar Snow calculated *total* "Long March" losses at 140,000. Chou En-lai thought that some 40,000 had been left behind to form partisan nuclei. Edgar Snow, *Random Notes on Red China (1936–1945)* (Cambridge: Harvard University Press, 1957), pp. 100–102.

13. Anthony Garavante, in his detailed study, "The Long March" (*The China Quarterly*, no. 22, April/June 1965, pp. 89–124), argues convincingly that the Kiangsi leaders planned originally to go to Szechwan, unite with the 4th Front Army there, and establish a new base. However, as we have seen, the meetings at Maoerhkai produced not the hoped-for unity but discord.

In discussing the causes of the split, Garavante concludes (pp. 121–122) that Mao Tse-tung wanted to march to Shensi "because Chang [Kuo-t'ao] had too much influence in the Hsikang-Szechwan region" and that Chang Kuo-t'ao wanted to stay in this area "because he feared the loss of power once his 'Szechwanese' 4th Army left the region of its home province. Mao's strength lay mainly in his formal leadership of the Party; Chang's by the fact that the Communists were in his territory and that he led a larger, healthier army. In the end, Chang was overruled. . . ."

Chu Teh's position at this time is a mystery. Did Mao order him to stay, did he wish to stay, or was he "detained" by Chang Kuo-t'ao, as some Chinese accounts allege? The first possibility seems most likely, for when Chu arrived in Shensi, he immediately assumed the role of commander in chief, a position Mao would certainly never have accorded him had he voluntarily thrown in his lot with Chang Kuo-t'ao.

14. Nym Wales, *Inside Red China* (New York: Doubleday, Doran, and Company, 1939), p. 28.

15. Same.

16. Mao Tse-tung, *Selected Works*, v. 1, cited, p. 161.

17. Mao Tse-tung, *Nineteen Poems* (Peking: Foreign Languages Press, 1958), p. 18.

Chapter 4

1. A carefully documented study of this period by Donald G. Gillin of Duke University appeared as a review article in the *Journal of Asian Studies*, v. 23, no. 2, February 1964, pp. 269–289, under the title "Peasant Nationalism in the History of Chinese Communism." Professor Gillin, using hitherto untranslated materials, analyzes the impact of the Red Army's invasion of Shansi in February–April 1936. He concludes that the primary content of the appeal the army's political workers made to the poor peasants was revolutionary rather than nationalistic. At the same time, the Communists cleverly employed slogans designed to arouse the spirit of nationalism in all social groups.

In existing circumstances, the Communist formula was practically infallible. The great majority of peasants urgently desired land reform; thousands of those who dwelt in cities and towns were eager to see the civil war stopped and the Nanking government take the lead in active resistance to Japanese aggression. One must realize, however, that the propaganda had two separate, although related, thrusts.

2. Same, p. 271.
3. See, for example, Madame Chiang Kai-shek, *Sian, a Coup d'Etat: A Fortnight in Sian, Extracts from a Diary by Chiang Kai-shek* (Shanghai: The China Publishing Company, 1937); James M. Bertram, *First Act in China: The Story of the Sian Mutiny* (New York: The Viking Press, 1938); Hu Shih, "China in Stalin's Grand Strategy," *Foreign Affairs*, v. 29, October 1950, pp. 11–40; and Edgar Snow, *Random Notes on Red China (1936–1945)* (Cambridge: Harvard University Press, 1957).

   Hu Shih, cited, speculated that the Kremlin ordered the CCP to release the Generalissimo. His conclusion was strongly supported in the later account by Edgar Snow, cited. In his Preface, Snow writes:

   "It now seems probable that the Communists had encouraged Chang Hsüeh-liang to detain the Generalissimo. Their chief delegate at the Young Marshal's headquarters in Sian (Liu Ting) was in close touch with the young officers who led the coup. The Politburo at first meant to exploit it as a means of setting up a national anti-Japanese government in Sian, isolating if not totally discrediting Chiang Kai-shek, their chief internal enemy. Moscow's sudden intervention undercut previous plans . . . *Pravda's* shattering denunciation of Chang [Hsüeh-liang] as a traitor and a Japanese agent enormously weakened the Chinese Communists in their relations with him and threw them into confusion. . . ."

   Later (pp. 1–2), Snow quotes an anonymous source, identified only as "X," as saying that a cable from Moscow to Pao-an threatened that the Russians would cut all relations with the CCP, repudiate it, and denounce the Chinese Communists as "bandits" if Mao did not use his influence to secure Chiang's release. Accordng to X,

   "Mao Tse-tung flew into a rage when the order came from Moscow to release Chiang. Mao swore and stamped his feet. Until then they had planned to give Chiang a public trial and to organize a Northwest Anti-Japanese defense government."

   David J. Dallin has provided evidence from Soviet sources which substantiates that provided by Snow and seems clearly to establish that the CCP obeyed orders from Moscow, albeit much against Mao's will. "Moscow . . . valued a pact with Chiang more highly than one with the irregular forces of the insurrectionists; it adopted an unequivocally hostile attitude toward the Sian rebellion. . . . The very day that the first news reached Moscow, *Izvestia* sharply attacked Chang Hsüeh-liang." On the day following, *Pravda* came out with an even more blistering attack on the Young Marshal. See *Soviet Russia and the Far East* (New Haven: Yale University Press, 1948), p. 69.
4. Mao Tse-tung, *Selected Works*, v. 1 (New York: International Publishers, 1954), pp. 254–257.

5. Same, p. 165.

6. As the author did on several occasions.

7. Chu Teh's account of the battle, the best description of it available, is in Evans Fordyce Carlson, *Twin Stars of China* (New York: Dodd, Mead, and Company, 1940), pp. 70–71. There was a play-by-play reprise of this tactic in Korea on November 30, 1950, when the Chinese trapped and severely punished a combat team of the U.S. 2nd Division.

8. Same, p. 110. Carlson also observed that the extent to which the men of the 8th Route Army had broken with Chinese tradition was "unprecedented." The Communists expected the soldier to cut all family ties. They frowned upon "face-saving" and did not permit any soldier to "salvage his pride at the expense of truth or efficiency." They regarded lethargy and procrastination as cardinal sins. Nor did they observe time-honored courtesies—the traditional Chinese *k'o ch'i* had been "cast aside." Evans Fordyce Carlson, *The Chinese Army* (New York: Institute of Pacific Relations, 1940), p. 42.

9. *Twin Stars of China,* cited, p. 80.

10. Same, p. 79.

11. "Interview with the British Correspondent James Bertram," October 24, 1937, in *Selected Works,* v. 2 (New York: International Publishers, 1954), pp. 96–97.

12. *Twin Stars of China,* cited, p. 109.

13. The author had an opportunity (albeit a most superficial one) to confirm some of Carlson's impressions in early December 1937 when he was permitted to interview six 8th Route Army prisoners at a Japanese regimental headquarters near Niang Tzu Kuan, the mountain gates to eastern Shansi. These men, of medium height, were lean, wiry, and obviously in top physical condition. They were not averse to recounting the circumstances of their capture on the previous night. They formed the rear guard of a small 8th Route Army detachment attacking a Japanese-manned station on the Cheng-T'ai (Shihchiachuang-T'aiyuan) Railway, which winds tortuously upward through the pass leading from the rich plains of central Hopeh to Shansi. To the attackers' surprise, the Japanese garrison, unexpectedly reinforced during the preceding day, sallied out of the station and adjacent blockhouses and managed to cut off the rear guard of the combat group.

The captives were warmly dressed in well-padded, clean, slate-colored jackets and trousers, wore foot wrappings, cloth shoes with thick woven soles, and cloth puttees which enclosed the ankles and kept the cold air from seeping up the legs of their trousers. Each had carried a Krag-type bolt-action rifle, three "potato-masher" grenades, and about 30 rounds of ammunition in a canvas pouch. Each had a sausage-shaped cloth tube draped over the left shoulder. The ends of this sausage, which held four pounds of millet flour, were tied together at the waistband on the right side. Each also carried a water bottle and two small packets, one containing tea and the other a few grains of salt. Sewn above the visor of their slate-colored cloth caps was the Kuomintang star. In terms of uniform, at least, they had been integrated.

There could have been little doubt in the minds of these soldiers what was going to happen to them. They were going to be intensively interrogated, probably tortured, and ultimately shot. But if they contemplated this fate, they succeeded in preserving a remarkable equanimity.

Under the circumstances, the questions I posed had to be superficial and couched in general terms, for questioning them more closely in the presence of their captors might have prejudiced their slim chance to live long enough to see the sun sink one more time behind the barren mountains of East Shansi. But I did form an impression from the answers: these young men were physically tough and mentally alert. Possibly they were illiterate or semi-literate, although I had no opportunity to determine so positively.

14. *Selected Works*, v. 1, cited, p. 163.
15. For the sake of historical accuracy, it should be made clear that the 8th Route Army received assistance in the formation of these "border region" governments from various anti-Japanese groups, by no means all of which were Communist-oriented. In *Peasant Nationalism and Communist Power* (Stanford University Press, 1962), chapter 4, Chalmers W. Johnson deals with this matter in considerable detail.
16. *Selected Works*, v. 2, cited, p. 139.
17. Same.
18. Same, pp. 116–118.
19. F. F. Liu, cited, pp. 205–206.
20. Chalmers A. Johnson, cited, offers a radically different view of the political situation which impelled the Communists to embark on the "Hundred Regiments Offensive." Johnson believes "the most important consideration" from Yenan's point of view "was that the deteriorating international situation . . . had given rise to a great wave of pessimism" in Nationalist circles and had "strengthened the pro-Japanese elements" in the Kuomintang. The Communists, he avers, "feared a peace settlement between Chungking and Japan which would be at their expense. One way to keep Chunking in the war was to keep the war alive, and the Hundred Regiments accomplished just that." See pp. 208–209, note 57. The Japanese document he paraphrases there is the only evidence he adduces to support this thesis. Testimony from such a source is scarcely unimpeachable. But this feeling may have contributed to the decision to take the offensive.
21. U.S. Senate, Committee on the Judiciary, *Institute of Pacific Relations*, Hearings before the Subcommittee to Investigate the Administration of the Internal Security Act and Other Internal Security Laws, 82nd Cong., 1st sess. (Washington, D.C.: GPO, 1951–52), Part 7A, Appendix 2, "The Chinese Communist Movement," p. 2366.
22. Same.
23. Lest the author be accused of ascribing to the Communist command an undue prescience, he must point out that the pattern of guerrilla raid-Japanese reprisal-increased Communist influence was standardized by the spring of 1941 in North China. The fiercer the raids, the more brutal the reprisals, and the more conditioned the peasants to accepting what the Communists offered.
The official Japanese account of "The Hundred Regiments Offensive" is contained in U.S. Army, Forces in the Far East, *North China Area Operations Record, July 1937–May 1941* (Tokyo: Military History Section; Headquarters, Army Forces Far East, 1955), "Japanese Monograph 178," pp. 316–320. (This monograph was written by Lieut. Gen. Shimoyama Takuma, former staff officer, North China Area Army, and Lieut. Gen. Hashimoto Gun, former chief of staff, 1st Army.) The Japanese admitted that "those totally

unexpected attacks caused serious damage, and it was necessary to spend much time and money in restoration work." Guerrilla suppression was thorough. According to the Japanese account, the Imperial Army administered such a "heavy blow" to the Communists and their bases that "thereafter they offered very little resistance in this area."

24. Statement by Generalissimo Chiang Kai-shek to the Fifth Central Executive Committee of the Kuomintang, September 13, 1943, in U.S. Department of State, *United States Relations with China* (Washington, D.C.: Author, August 1949), pp. 530–531.

25. In North China, the Red Army was always *Ti-pa-lu-chün* or "8th Route Army." The appellation preferred by the central government did not stick, and I have not used it.

26. Excluding partisan formations. *United States Relations with China*, cited, p. 533. The central government agreed to four armies of 10 divisions. Same, p. 538.

27. Same, p. 545. At one point in the discussions at this time, Yenan asked for six armies, totaling 18 divisions. Same, p. 547. In May 1944, Lin Tsu-han, the Communist delegate to conversations held in Sian and Chungking, gave Red Army strength as 475,000 troops. Same, p. 545.

28. Later, Col. Evans Carlson, USMC, organized the squads of his 2nd Raider Battalion, U.S. Marine Corps, along these lines. The author, when in command of the 1st Marine Raider Battalion, copied Carlson. Later still, the U.S. Marine Corps officially adopted a similar squad structure, which remains in effect.

29. Mao Tse-tung, *Selected Works*, v. 2, cited, p. 224.

30. Same, p. 222.

31. Theodore H. White and Annalee Jacoby, *Thunder out of China* (New York: William Sloane Associates, 1946), p. 152.

32. Chu Teh, *The Battle Front of the Liberated Areas* (2nd ed.; Peking: Foreign Languages Press, 1962).

33. This figure for over-all strength tallies with that given by Tung Pi-wu, a Yenan representative in the Chinese delegation to the San Francisco Conference of 1945, in a "Memorandum of China's Liberated Areas." The common source is the "Report on the General Military Situation of the Chinese Communist Party," prepared by General Yeh Chien-ying of 8th Route Army Headquarters in Yenan in late 1944 and updated in the spring of 1945. Both Tung's memorandum and Yeh's report are cited in Hsu Yung-ying, *A Survey of Shensi-Kansu-Ninghsia Border Region* (New York: Institute of Pacific Relations, 1945), v. 2, p. 150.

General Yeh's report gives the strength of Chinese Communist "liberation" armies from 1937 to 1945 as follows:

	8th Route	New 4th	East River	Hainan	Total
1937	80,000	12,000			92,000
1938	156,700	25,000			181,700
1939	270,000	50,000			320,000
1940	400,000	100,000			500,000
1941	305,000	135,000			440,000
1942	340,000	110,960			450,960
1943	339,000	125,892			464,892

	8th Route	New 4th	East River	Hainan	Total
1944 (summer)	320,800	153,676			474,476
1944 (December)	550,835	293,982		20,730	865,547
1945 (spring)					910,000

It is interesting to note the marked reduction in 8th Route Army strength from 400,000 in 1940 to an average of 326,000 for 1941 to mid-1944. These figures support Japanese General Okamura's statement to me (1963) that between 1940 and 1943 Japanese punitive expeditions inflicted more than 100,000 casualties on the 8th Route Army.

The December 1944 figure of 865,547 is almost twice that estimated by U.S. sources. According to the U.S. Army's Military Intelligence Division (MID), Red Army strength in October 1944 totaled 475,000, of whom 346,000 were in "field armies," i.e., the 8th Route and reconstituted New 4th. The remaining 129,000 were in "local" guerrilla forces. At this time, MID estimated militia strength at 2 million. *Institute of Pacific Relations,* cited, Part 7A, Appendix 2, p. 2448.

The regular forces were organized into "A"-, "B"-, and "C"-type regiments. The 59 "A"-type were reasonably well equipped—with rifles, carbines, pistols, automatic rifles, light and heavy machine guns, and medium and light mortars. "B"- and "C"-type regiments were smaller and not equipped to Type-"A" standards.

Hsu Yung-ying, cited, gives a summary of the strength of the People's Militia as of March and December 1944. These figures were extracted from Yeh Chien-ying's report. I would consider them reasonably reliable, although probably slightly inflated.

Military Areas	March 1944	December 1944
Shansi-Hopeh-Honan	630,000	
Shansi-Hopeh-Honan	320,000	
Hopeh-Shantung-Honan	80,000	
Shantung	500,000	
Shansi-Suiyuan	50,000	
Total Northern China	1,580,000	1,615,000
Central Kiangsu	130,000	
South Hwai Valley	55,000	
Northern Kiangsu	85,000	
North Hwai Valley	70,000	
Hupeh-Honan-Anhwei	150,000	
Southern Kiangsu	25,000	
Central Anhwei	25,000	
Eastern Chekiang	10,000	
Total Central China	550,000	580,000
Total Central and Northern China	2,130,000	
Total Southern China		5,000
Total Northern, Central, and Southern China		2,200,000

It is not clear what the situation in Manchuria was at this time. Apparently, a total of seven guerrilla "columns" operated there under various appellations. There was, for instance, "The Anti-Japanese League 5th Corps," which operated in east Kirin. "The People's Revolutionary 3rd Corps" also operated in Kirin. The Japanese Kwantung Army, which garrisoned Manchuria, succeeded in holding down the Communists; for their part, the Reds concentrated primarily on organizing peasant villages in remote areas. A large number of Koreans served in these Manchurian anti-Japanese columns and gained valuable experience.

34. Conversations with Gen. Okamura Yasuji, Office of War History, Tokyo, November 1963. As I have already remarked (see note 33), his estimate of casualties inflicted on the Communists corresponds reasonably well with Communist figures on 8th Route Army strength during the period.

35. These claims are in Chu Teh, cited. I have concentrated primarily on the North China area in which the 8th Route Army operated. The Red High Command assigned similar guerrilla and organizational missions to Yeh T'ing's 4th Army in the Yangtze Valley. I have purposely omitted reference to the "4th Army Incident," a skein which need not be untangled in these pages.

The New 4th Army was organized in the spring of 1938 in eastern Kiangsi and southern Anhwei with Yeh T'ing as commander and Hsiang Ying as vice-commander. Ch'en Yi commanded a column, as did Su Yü. The area of operations which the central government assigned the New 4th was roughly the triangle Nanking-Hangch'ow-Kiukiang, but detachments also operated north of the Yangtze. A portion of this army was surrounded, attacked, and wiped out by the Nationalists in early January 1941. Yeh T'ing was captured. Ch'en Yi, who had previously led his column to the area north of the Yangtze, escaped. Shortly thereafter, Mao directed him to organize the New 4th Army, with Chang Yun-i as vice-commander, Liu Shao-ch'i as political commissar, Lai Chuan-chu as chief of staff, and Teng Tzu-hui as chief of the Political Department.

The growth of the New 4th Army was phenomenal. From Ch'en Yi's group, which did not exceed 2,000, the New 4th Army had expanded by 1944 to a strength of some 200,000 and effectively controlled large areas of central and southeast China from which Japanese arms effectively excluded the Nationalists. As of the end of 1943, the New 4th Army administered the East China Military Region (Jao Su-shih); the Hunan-Hupeh Border Area (L Hsien-nien); the Honan-Anhwei Border Area (Chen Shao-min); the Yellow River Flooding Area (Wei Feng-lou and Wang Cheng-hua); the Kwantung Kwangsi Border Area (Wen Cho-hua); the Kiangsi-Anhwei Border Are (Yeh Fei); the Central Kiangsu Area (Su Yü), and the Hwai-Hai Area.

In these, as in other areas they controlled, the Communists devoted thei energies primarily to organizing the countryside and building armed force militia, and People's Self-Defense Corps and not to engaging the Japanese.

36. The official American history of World War II records remarks by Gener Hata Shunroku which suggest the possibility that in 1944 Yenan surrept tiously worked out at least a verbal *modus vivendi* with the Japanese Nort China Command. In 1952, General Hata, who had commanded the China E peditionary Army in 1944, stated that in the summer of that year the Japa ese were "planning" to use Chinese Communist forces against the Nationalis Hata, incidentally, did not think much of Communist military capabiliti and observed that the Communists "merely resorted to guerrilla warfare a planned the expansion of the area under their influence and the weakeni

and disintegration of the Nationalist forces through the war against Japan." Charles F. Romanus and Riley Sunderland, *The China-Burma-India Theater: Stilwell's Command Problems*, v. 23: *The United States Army in World War II* (Washington, D.C.: Office of the Chief of Military History, Department of the Army, 1956), p. 433, 433*n*.

37. *United States Relations with China*, cited, p. 565.

38. Same, p. 566.

Chapter 5

1. U.S. Department of State, *United States Relations with China* (Washington, D.C.: Author, August 1949), p. 760.

2. *Selected Works*, v. 4 (New York: International Publishers, 1954), pp. 331–332. (Italics added.)

3. Same, p. 332.

4. "Volunteer" partisan groups led by Chinese and Korean Communists had existed in East and Northeast Manchuria since the Japanese takeover of September 1931. They were not, however, "a very effective force for resistance because they lacked money, supplies, equipment, and strong, inspiring leadership. Until the Japanese carried the conflict into China in 1937 the Volunteers had little support from China." Evans Fordyce Carlson, *The Chinese Army* (New York: Institute of Pacific Relations, 1940), p. 44.

In 1937, Mao wrote that the guerrilla movement in the northwestern provinces had become "an important and powerful influence. Already seven or eight guerrilla regiments and a number of independent platoons have been formed, and their activities make it necessary for the Japanese to send troops after them month after month." These guerrillas hampered Japanese efforts at pacification and, according to Mao, "inspired" revolutionary ferment in Korea. But there were many weaknesses in the movement, the most important of which were that organization was still in its "primary stages" and participation of the people was not general. Mao was optimistic: "If present policy is continued tenaciously, all these weaknesses will be overcome. Experience proves that guerrilla warfare will develop to even greater proportions and that in spite of the cruelty of the Japanese and the many methods they have devised to cheat the people, they cannot extinguish guerrilla activities in the three northeastern provinces." Mao Tse-tung, *On Guerrilla Warfare*, trans., with an introduction, by Samuel B. Griffith (New York: Praeger, 1961), p. 64.

Carlson met several Manchurian leaders in Yenan in 1938, and they told him that the Manchurian partisans at that time numbered some 100,000 and were organized as 10 columns. Seven operated in Kirin, two in Heilangkiang, and one in Liaoning—all under the command of a Gen. Li Tu. Apparently in 1938, the Yenan Communists did not have much confidence in the Manchurian "volunteers." Carlson says: "The Manchurians" lacked "a strong militant leadership," which could possibly be provided "by the 8th Route Army." (Carlson, cited, pp. 44–45.) This leadership was not available until the autumn of 1945 when Lin Piao arrived in northern Manchuria with his division of the 8th Route Army, established contact, assumed command, and assimilated all such "volunteer" groups.

The assimilation of these forces, which included many thousand Koreans, explains the amazing growth of Communist forces in Manchuria during 1946. It also helps explain the combat efficiency of Kim Il Sung's North Korean People's Army during the early phases of the Korean War, for the Koreans who served with the Chinese Communist armies during the decisive period of the Chinese civil war were ultimately transfered to the NKPA.

5. Mao Tse-tung, *Selected Works*, v. 5 (New York: International Publishers, n.d.), pp. 11–26.

6. Mao's charge that the Generalissimo had been waiting for the victory over Japan to be won by someone else is not without foundation. In a study dated July 5, 1945, the Military Intelligence Division, U.S. War Department, observed:

> "After the United States entered the war and American military aid was extended to China, Chungking's unwillingness to commit its best armies to fight the Japanese became even more apparent. American observers came to believe that many leading Chinese Government officials felt that China had done her part in fighting Japan and that it was henceforth up to the United States and Britain to defeat Japan. American officials in China repeatedly complained in their reports about the Chinese Government's lack of interest even in supporting the American war effort in China, and emphasized that Chinese troops 'that could be used for the protection of our air bases are stationed elsewhere to blockade Chinese Communist areas.' In September 1943 General Wu T'ieh-ch'eng, Secretary-General of the Central Executive Committee of the Kuomintang, agreed with an American observer in Chungking that it was 'unfortunate' that so many Government troops were immobilized because of the Chinese Communists. He said that 'about 20 divisions of good soldiers' were 'prevented from fighting Japan.' "

See U.S. Senate, Committee on the Judiciary, *Institute of Pacific Relations*, Hearings before the Subcommittee to Investigate the Administration of the Internal Security Act and Other Internal Security Laws, 82nd Cong., 1st sess. (Washington, D.C.: GPO, 1951–52), Party 7A, Appendix 2, p. 2355.

The same study, however, also makes the point that *both* Yenan and Chungking were conserving their forces for the civil struggle they saw as the inevitable aftermath of Japanese defeat.

> "The record indicates that neither the Communists nor the Kuomintang have expended their main efforts against the Japanese, except as both have been compelled to defend themselves. Both have done everything they could to prepare to maintain their own positions after the war. The evidence substantiates the statement made by Congressman Mansfield in his report to the Congress in January this year, after his return from hi mission to China: 'On the basis of information which I have been able to gather, it appears to me that both the Communists and the Kuomintang are more interested in preserving their respective parties at the present time, and have been for the past two years, than they are in carrying on

the war against Japan. Each party is more interested in its own status because both feel that America will guarantee victory.' "

Same, p. 2363.

7. Sun Tzu, *The Art of War*, cited, p. 84, (Literally: "Know the enemy, know yourself; one hundred battles, one hundred victories.").

8. Theodore H. White and Annalee Jacoby, *Thunder out of China* (New York: William Sloane Associates, 1946), pp. 106–107.

9. *United States Relations with China*, cited, pp. 758–763. This address delivered on August 22, 1947, to a joint meeting of the State Council and all ministers of the National Government, was not specifically descriptive of conditions at that date. The conditions had existed for years.

10. This inner-Party directive was drafted by Mao. See *Selected Works*, v. 5, cited, pp 89–95.

11. As of June 1946, the Chinese Communist Army consisted of three major groupings:

(1) THE NORTHEAST DEMOCRATIC UNION ARMY
Commander in Chief	Lin Piao
Deputy Commander in Chief	Hsiao Chin-kuang
Chief of Staff	Liu Ya-lou
Commissar	P'eng Chen

(2) THE 18TH ARMY GROUP (THE 8TH ROUTE ARMY)
Commander in Chief	Chu Teh
Deputy Commander in Chief	P'eng Te-huai
Chief of Staff	Teng Tai-yuan
Commissar	?

(3) THE NEW 4TH ARMY
Commander in Chief	Ch'en Yi
Deputy Commander in Chief	Chang I-yün
Chief of Staff	Chen Shih-chu
Commissar	Liu Shao-ch'i

My sources (all in Chinese) are: Government of the Republic of China, *Outline of Battle during the Civil War* (Taipei: Military History Bureau, Ministry of National Defense, n.d.), v. 1 and 2; Chang Ta-chun, *Who's Who in Communist China* (Hong Kong: Freedom Press, June 1956); Ch'en Hsiao-wei, *Why We Lost the Mainland* (Taipei: China Art Press, 1964).

12. Mao Tse-tung, *Selected Works*, v. 5, cited, pp. 113–118.

13. Same, pp. 103–107.

14. Sun Tzu, cited, p. 66.

15. *United States Relations with China*, cited. Chiang's address of November 15 appears as Annex 110; Chou's statement of the following day, as Annex 111.

16. Same, p. 209.

17. *Selected Works*, v. 5, cited, p. 129.

18. Sun Tzu, cited pp. 65–66.

19. *United States Relations with China*, cited, p. 209.

20. Same, p. 211.

21. Same, p. 759.

22. Same, pp. 315–316.

At this time, the Chinese Communist armed forces were organized into the five People's Liberation Armies, shown below:

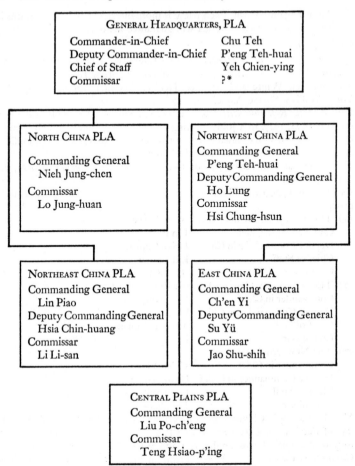

GENERAL HEADQUARTERS, PLA

Commander-in-Chief	Chu Teh
Deputy Commander-in-Chief	P'eng Teh-huai
Chief of Staff	Yeh Chien-ying
Commissar	?*

NORTH CHINA PLA

Commanding General
  Nieh Jung-chen
Commissar
  Lo Jung-huan

NORTHWEST CHINA PLA

Commanding General
  P'eng Teh-huai
Deputy Commanding General
  Ho Lung
Commissar
  Hsi Chung-hsun

NORTHEAST CHINA PLA

Commanding General
  Lin Piao
Deputy Commanding General
  Hsia Chin-huang
Commissar
  Li Li-san

EAST CHINA PLA

Commanding General
  Ch'en Yi
Deputy Commanding General
  Su Yü
Commissar
  Jao Shu-shih

CENTRAL PLAINS PLA

Commanding General
  Liu Po-ch'eng
Commissar
  Teng Hsiao-p'ing

*It is probable that Yeh Chien-ying was both chief of staff and commissar, GHQ, PLA.

(For my sources, see note 11.)

23. *United States Relations with China*, cited, p. 316.
24. *Selected Works*, v. 5, cited, pp. 141–46.
25. *United States Relations with China*, cited, p. 774.
26. His full report on the Chinese situation may be found in same, pp. 764–81⸺
27. Chiang Kai-shek, *Soviet Russia in China: A Summing Up at Seventy* (Nev York: Farrar, Straus and Cudahy 1957), pp. 232–233.
28. *United States Relations with China*, cited, pp. 317–318.
29. *Selected Works*, v. 5, cited, pp. 157–176.
30. On January 9, 1948, the U.S. Ambassador in China, John Leighton Stuar

cabled his analysis of Mao's statement to Washington (*United States Relations with China,* cited, pp. 840–841). Stuart said that the Embassy, after examining the statement, had gained two dominant impressions:

> "(1) the note of triumphant conviction that the essentials of the Communist struggle for victory in China have been achieved, though Mao is careful to point out that additional great sacrifices will be required, and (2) the continuous and vitriolic attacks on the United States as the great enemy of the world and the agent responsible for the continuing civil war in China. Endlessly Mao reiterates the point that reactionary American imperialism is a major enemy of the people of China. Even though the recent months have witnessed heightening attacks on the United States, this is the first time that one of the top leaders of the Party has publicly joined the hue and cry.
>
> Mao's elaboration of Communist military tactics and strategy is a remarkably candid explanation of how precisely Communist armies operate as far as the Embassy has been able to determine. It is perhaps a mark of Communist contempt for Nationalist military thinking and intelligence that the Communists have so little hesitation in explaining their strategy, which, it must be admitted, has to date not been without success."

31. *United States Relations with China,* cited, p. 325.
32. Same, pp. 334–335. In Communist parlance, the final operation in Manchuria is known as "The Liaosi-Shenyang Campaign." Hu Chiao-mu claims that 472,000 Kuomintang troops were "put out of action" between September 12 and November 2, 1948. See *Thirty Years of the Communist Party of China* (4th ed.; Peking: Foreign Languages Press), p. 88. General Barr's figure may be accepted as the more accurate.
33. *Selected Works,* v. 5, cited, pp. 279–282.
34. O. Edmund Clubb, "Chiang Kai-shek's Waterloo: the Battle of the Hwai-Hai," *Pacific Historical Review,* v. 25, November 1956, pp. 389–399.
35. *United States Relations with China,* cited, p. 919.
36. Same, p. 336.
37. Same, pp. 336–338.
38. *Selected Works,* v. 5, cited, pp. 387–396.
39. As of this time, the major elements of the People's Liberation Army were as shown at the top of the following page.
40. *United States Relations with China,* cited, p. 305.
41. I do not propose here to enter the futile discussion about the so-called "loss" of China to the Communists which certain groups claim was the result of wrong-headed U.S. policy, a failure to render adequate support to the Nationalist government, and so on. Nevertheless, it is germane in this connection to recall General Barr's report of November 16, 1948: "No battle has been lost since my arrival due to lack of ammunition or equipment. Their [Nationalist] military debacles in my opinion can all be attributed to the world's worst leadership and many other morale-destroying factors that lead to a complete loss of the will to fight." General Barr thought that "the complete ineptness of high military leaders, and the widespread corruption and dishonesty throughout the Armed Forces" might have been "in some

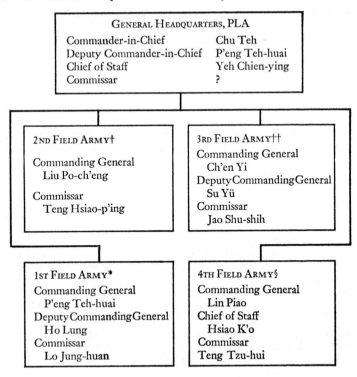

GENERAL HEADQUARTERS, PLA

Commander-in-Chief	Chu Teh
Deputy Commander-in-Chief	P'eng Teh-huai
Chief of Staff	Yeh Chien-ying
Commissar	?

2ND FIELD ARMY†

Commanding General
  Liu Po-ch'eng

Commissar
  Teng Hsiao-p'ing

3RD FIELD ARMY††

Commanding General
  Ch'en Yi
Deputy Commanding General
  Su Yü
Commissar
  Jao Shu-shih

1ST FIELD ARMY*

Commanding General
  P'eng Teh-huai
Deputy Commanding General
  Ho Lung
Commissar
  Lo Jung-huan

4TH FIELD ARMY§

Commanding General
  Lin Piao
Chief of Staff
  Hsiao K'o
Commissar
  Teng Tzu-hui

  * Reorganized from Northwest China PLA and North China PLA
  † Reorganized from Central Plains PLA
 †† Reorganized from East China PLA
  § Reorganized from Northeast China PLA

(For my sources, see note 11.)

measure controlled" had major U.S. command and logistics organizations
with complete power and authority, been present, but he felt that U.S. forces
would also have been required to take the field, a measure he "certainly"
did not recommend. Same, pp. 358–359.

42. Hu Chiao-mu, cited, p. 90, and Sing-ming Chiu, *A History of the Chinese
Communist Army* (unpublished doctoral dissertation, University of Southern
California, 1958), p. 131.

  Some idea of the tremendous amount and variety of military supplies provided Nationalist China (practically all of which were lost to the Communists) may be had from perusal of *United States Relations with China,* cited
Annexes 170–174.

43. For example, the embassy reported to the Department of State in early November 1948 that in the battles of Tsinan, the Liaoning Corridor, Chiang ch'u
and Mukden (Shenyang), the Nationalists lost 33 divisions—more than 32c

ooo men—including eight divisions which had been 85 per cent U.S. equipped. The equipment losses incurred included 100,000 U.S. rifles. A month later, a total of "17 originally U.S. equipped divisions" had been lost. After the fall of Manchuria, the Nationalists estimated that 80 per cent of the U.S. arms and equipment supplied their ground forces had been lost and that practically all these had fallen intact into the hands of the Communists. See *United States Relations with China,* cited, p. 357.

Chapter 6

1. The President used this phrase in his July 19, 1950, message to the Congress describing the North Korean attack on the Republic of Korea. U.S. Senate, *Military Situation in the Far East,* Hearings before the Committee on Armed Services and the Committee on Foreign Relations, 82nd Cong., 1st sess. (Washington, D.C.: GPO, 1951), p. 3464.
2. The attack had been launched seven hours earlier—that is, at 4 A.M., June 25, Korean time. Since there is a fourteen-hour time difference between Washington, D.C., and Seoul, this time/date corresponded to 2 P.M., Saturday, June 24, in Washington. To avoid confusion, all times/dates in this narrative will be local.
3. Roy E. Appleman, *South to the Naktong, North to the Yalu: June–November 1950,* v. 1: *The United States Army in the Korean War* (Washington, D.C.: Office of the Chief of Military History, Department of the Army, 1961), p. 21.
4. U.S. Department of State, *United States Policy in the Korean Crisis* (Washington, D.C.: GPO, 1950), Document 1, p. 11.
5. Testimony of William C. Foster, deputy administrator of the Economic Cooperation Administration, before the Senate Appropriations Committee on June 13, 1950. Quoted in *Military Situation in the Far East,* cited, p. 2009.
6. Charles A. Willoughby and John Chamberlain, *MacArthur 1941–1951* (New York: McGraw-Hill, 1954), p. 352.
7. Robert K. Sawyer, *Military Advisors in Korea: KMAG in Peace and War* (Washington, D.C.: Office of the Chief of Military History, Department of the Army, 1962), p. 105.
8. U.S. Department of State, *North Korea: A Case Study in the Techniques of Takeover* (Washington, D.C.: Author, January 1961), pp. 114–115. This statement is not entirely accurate. Three agreements (covering postal services, telecommunications, and telephone services) were concluded in December 1949.
9. Edgar Snow, *The Other Side of the River: Red China Today* (New York: Random House, 1961), p. 714.
10. U.S. Senate, *Military Situation in the Far East,* Hearings before the Committee on Armed Services and the Committee on Foreign Relations, 82nd Cong., 1st sess. (Washington, D.C.: GPO, 1951), p. 3439.
11. Allen S. Whiting, *China Crosses the Yalu: The Decision to Enter the Korean War* (New York: The Macmillan Company, 1960), p. 45.
12. Radio news broadcasts, New China News Agency (NCNA), Peking, June

27, 1950. The reference in the quotation is to Ambassador John Foster Dulles, later secretary of state.

13. Radio news broadcast, Taipei, Taiwan, June 27, 1950.
14. Quoted in a radio news broadcast, Kyoto, Tokyo, June 29, 1950.
15. Radio news broadcast, Chinese International Service (CIS), June 29, 1950.
16. London *Daily Mail*, March 2, 1949.
17. Testimony of General Hoyt S. Vandenberg, USAF, chief of staff, U.S. Air Force, in U.S. House of Representatives, *The National Defense Program— Unification and Strategy*, Hearings before the Committee on Armed Services, 81st Cong., 1st sess. (Washington, D.C.: GPO, 1949), p. 472. Italics added.
18. Same.
19. Testimony of Adm. Arthur W. Radford, USN, in same, p. 41.
20. Testimony of Fleet Admiral William F. Halsey, USN, in same, p. 237.
21. In this address, made before the National Press Club in Washington, Acheson said. "This defensive perimeter [i.e., in the Far East] runs along the Aleutians to Japan, and then goes to the Ryukyus . . . [it then] runs from the Ryukyus to the Philippine Islands." *Department of State Bulletin*, v. 22, January 23, 1950, p. 116.

Both MacArthur's statement and that of the Secretary must be placed in the context of a policy decision made as early as September 1947. At that time, the Joint Chiefs of Staff, in response to a query from the Secretary of State, concluded that the United States "had little strategic interest in maintaining the present troops and bases in Korea." The troops could be used to greater advantage elsewhere. Moreover, should hostilities with Russia suddenly break out, these hostages to fortune would inevitably be trapped. Phased withdrawal of occupation forces from South Korea began in 1948. On January 15, 1949, headquarters, U.S. XXIV Corps, was transferred to Japan for deactivation. As of June 30, 1949, all U.S. troop units had left Korea. Officers and men assigned to the Military Advisory Group (KMAG) were at that time the only U.S. military personnel remaining in South Korea.

22. Address by Secretary of State John Foster Dulles to the American Legion Convention, St. Louis, Missouri, September 2, 1953, in same, v. 29, September 14, 1953, p. 339.
23. During the Potsdam conference in July 1945, division of Korea along the 38th parallel was suggested to General George C. Marshall, chief of staff, U.S. Army, by his chief of operations, Lieut. Gen. John E. Hull, USA, as a device to facilitate orderly acceptance of the Japanese surrender. As the heads of state had expressed their common desire to create a unified Korea with a freely elected government, the line was conceived by both Marshall and Hull not as a boundary between a "Soviet zone" to the north and an "American zone" to the south but as a transient device of no political or military significance. In fact, they did not even discuss the matter with their Soviet opposites. (Appleman, cited, pp. 2–3.)

On August 15, 1945, President Truman approved General Order 1, which prescribed that American forces would accept surrender south of the parallel while Soviet forces accepted surrender north of it. Both Soviet and British governments agreed to this arrangement.

For two years, no steps were taken by the great powers, or the United Nations, to create an independent Korea. Finally in November 1947, the United

Nations established a Temporary Commission on Korea (UNCOK). UNCOK's mission was to supervise election of representatives to a national assembly which would draft a constitution and establish the government. The Soviet Union, however, refused permission to UNCOK to conduct such elections in North Korea. The impasse had not been resolved in May 1949, when South Koreans went to the polls to elect their representatives. On August 15, the Republic of Korea, with Syngman Rhee as its first president, was formally inaugurated. This government was recognized as legal by the United Nations in December and by the United States on January 1, 1949.

In the meantime, the Russians had set up a rival government with its capital at P'yongyang, and on September 10, 1948, Kim Il Sung, a Moscow-trained Korean, became premier of the Democratic People's Republic of Korea.

> "Thus, three years after U.S. military authorities accepted the surrender of the Japanese south of the 38th parallel there were two Korean governments in the land, each hostile to the other and each claiming jurisdiction over the whole country. Behind North Korea stood the Soviet Union; behind South Korea stood the United States and the U.N. Temporary Commission on Korea." [Same, p. 5.]

24. Same, p. 6. Senator Taft was later to state: "Certainly the fact of our policy toward the arming of South Korea was well known to the North Koreans, and certainly it was a policy which invited the attack which has occurred." *Military Situation in the Far East,* cited, p. 3213.

25. Appleman, cited, pp. 9–10. General MacArthur reported to the United Nations on September 17, 1950, that the Chinese "furnished substantial if not decisive military assistance to North Korea" by releasing 40,000 to 60,000 seasoned troops for integration in the NKPA. *Military Situation in the Far East,* cited, pp. 3402–3403. MacArthur's estimate is probably the more accurate as Appleman apparently did not take full account of North Koreans who served with the Soviet Far Eastern Army or other Soviet forces. Also, several thousand had received basic training in the Japanese Kwantung Army.

It has sometimes been asserted that the transfer of ethnic Koreans from the People's Liberation Army to the NKPA tends to prove that the Chinese were aware of Stalin's plans for Korea. But such an arrangement between two neighboring Communist states would seem normal enough under the circumstances. The Communists had won the "Third Revolutionary War," were rapidly consolidating, and had publicly announced plans for reducing and reorganizing the PLA. In this connection, Allen S. Whiting (cited, p. 44) writes:

> "While this move [the transfer of ethnic Koreans from the PLA to the NKPA] suggests Chinese Communist participation in preparations for the North Korean attacks, it is susceptible to alternative interpretations. . . . If friction between Peking and P'yongyang was resolved through Soviet good offices at this time, transfer of experienced Korean fighting units from the PLA to the KPLA may have been part of a general settlement of outstanding differences. In addition, Chinese Communist concern over military expenditures and preparations for a cutback in its own

armed forces during 1950 made such a transfer expedient from Peking's point of view."

26. Douglas MacArthur, *Reminiscences* (New York: McGraw-Hill, 1964), p. 333.
27. Walter Millis, Harvey C. Mansfield, and Harold Stein, *Arms and the State* (New York: The Twentieth Century Fund, 1958), p. 264.
28. *Military Situation in the Far East,* cited, p. 3381.
29. Richard H. Rovere and Arthur M. Schlesinger, Jr., *The General and the President* (New York: Farrar, Straus and Young, 1951), p. 126.
30. K. M. Panikkar, *In Two Chinas* (London: George Allen and Unwin, Ltd., 1955), p. 108. The "border" in the context was the Sino-Korean border and not the 38th parallel, as has sometimes been presumed.
31. *Military Situation in the Far East,* cited, p. 3411.
32. Radio news broadcast, NCNA, October 1, 1950.
33. Panikkar, cited, p. 110.
34. Jawaharlal Nehru, *India's Foreign Policy* (Delhi: Publications Division, Ministry of Information and Broadcasting, Government of India, August 15, 1961), p. 417.
35. Harry S Truman, *Years of Trial and Hope,* v. 2: *Memoirs* (New York: Doubleday, 1956), p. 362.
36. *Time,* v. 56, October 9, 1950, p. 35.
37. Testimony of General of the Army Douglas MacArthur, *Military Situation in the Far East,* cited, p. 20.
38. Lynn Montross and Nicholas A. Canzona, *U.S. Marine Operations in Korea, 1950–1953,* v. 3 (Washington, D.C.: headquarters, U.S. Marine Corps, 1957), p. 5.
39. U.N. General Assembly, *Documents, Fifth Session,* A/1435, October 7, 1950. Italics added.
40. Peking *People's Daily,* October 10, 1950.
41. All ROK divisions except the 1st (attached to U.S. I Corps) crossed the 38th parallel before any U.S. forces crossed.
42. The full texts of General MacArthur's messages of October 1 and October 9 are available in *Military Situation in the Far East,* cited, pp. 3425–3426.
43. Radio news brodacast, NCNA, October 10, 1950.
44. *Military Situation in the Far East,* cited, p. 3483.
45. Same, p. 1835.

Chapter 7

1. From the introduction to General MacArthur's Ninth Report to the United Nations (period November 1–15), dated December 27, 1950. U.S. Senate, *Military Situation in the Far East,* Hearings before the Committee on Armed Services and the Committee on Foreign Relations, 82nd Cong., 1st sess. (Washington, D.C.: GPO, 1951), p. 3432.
2. Testimony of Secretary of State Dean Acheson in same, p. 1933.
3. Appleman, cited, p. 761.
4. Same, p. 759.
5. This was the second of two "restraining lines" established by MacArthur.

The first, that of September 27, ran east to west, generally from Hungnam to Chonju, a few miles below the 38th parallel.

6. The JCS policy directive of September 27 read, in part: "No non-Korean ground forces will be used in the northeast provinces bordering the Soviet Union or in the area along the Manchurian border." *Military Situation in the Far East*, cited, p. 1230. MacArthur's action was a violation of this directive. "He sent American forces directly to the frontier without advising us ahead of time on it, and when we asked him, challenged his doing it, he said that he did it because of military necessity. . . ." Testimony of Gen. J. Lawton Collins, USA, in same, p. 1216.

7. Same, p. 974. Actually, X Corps was not a part of 8th Army but a separate operational command.

8. Montross and Canzona, cited, p. 44.

9. Sun Tzu, *The Art of War*, trans., with an introduction by Samuel B. Griffith (Oxford University: The Clarendon Press, 1963), p. 66.

10. Appleman, cited, p. 671.

11. Same, p. 761.

12. *Military Situation in the Far East*, cited, p. 3427.

13. The Order of Battle of Chinese Communist Forces (CCF) in Korea as of November 3, 1950, was:

ARMY	COMMANDER	DIVISIONS
38th	Liang Pi-yeh	112th, 113th, 114th
39th	Liu Chen	115th, 116th, 117th
40th	Han Hsien-chu	118th, 119th, 120th
42nd	Sung Chi-huan	124th, 125th, 126th
50th	Tseng Tse-sheng	148th, 149th, 150th
66th	Su Ching-huai	196th, 197th, 198th

Appleman, cited, p. 768; Charles A. Willoughby and John Chamberlin, *MacArthur 1941–1951* (New York: McGraw-Hill, 1954), p. 394. The names of the army commanders are omitted in Appleman.

The Chinese infantry divisions were at an average strength of 8,000 to 9,000. As is noted in the text, two complete and one partial artillery divisions plus the 42nd Truck Regiment and a regiment of cavalry were also present.

For purposes of comparison, U.N. strength as of September 30, 1950, is listed below:

	U.N. Forces	Attached Koreans
Ground Combat Forces	198,211	22,404
U.S. Ground Combat Forces	113,494	22,404
8th Army	1,120	
I Corps	4,141	267
1st Cavalry Division	13,859	2,961
24th Infantry Division	15,591	3,606
IX Corps	4,224	1,009
2nd Infantry Division	14,122	2,756
25th Infantry Division	14,617	3,230
X Corps	8,344	600
7th Infantry Division	15,865	7,975
1st Marine Division (reinforced)	21,611	

Other Ground Combat Forces

ROK Army	81,644	
British Ground Combat Forces	1,704	
Philippine Ground Combat Forces	1,369	
Air Forces		
FEAF	36,677	
Other U.N. Air Forces	330	
NAVFE	59,438	7,045
Ground Service Forces	20,608	444
8th Army	2,820	
I Corps	1,235	305
IX Corps	187	110
X Corps	2,039	29
Pusan Base	9,792	
Inch'on Base	4,452	
Seoul Area Command	83	

By the end of September, 8th Army had suffered 24,172 battle casualties —5,145 killed in action; 16,461 wounded in action, of whom 422 died of wounds; 402 reported captured; and 2,164 missing in action. Many of the latter were prisoners of war. Appleman, cited, p. 605.

14. Sun Tzu, cited, p. 104.
15. Radio News Broadcast, NCNA, November 24, 1950.
16. Appleman, cited, p. 677.
17. On November 6, 1950, the American Ambassador to Nationalist China, Karl Lott Rankin, cabled the Department of State that the Chinese Communists planned "to throw the book at the U.N. Forces" in Korea. The Ambassador also speculated as to the motives of the Chinese Communists in delaying large-scale intervention. This dispatch is quoted in full below:

"Chinese military intelligence forwarded to Washington by the Embassy's service attachés during the past few days lends strong support to the assumption that the Chinese communists plan to throw the book at the United Nations forces in Korea and in addition to step up their pressure in Indochina. Allowance evidently should be made for wishful thinking among the Chinese military, most of whom regard a general conflict as the only means of liberating China from the communists. In the present instance, however, such a caveat still leaves an imposing array of apparently established facts, as well as evidence of sincerity among the best informed Chinese, such as to render quite possible the correctness of their consensus of opinion that all-out action in Korea by the Chinese communists should be expected.

"The reasons why the Chinese communists have so far delayed their entry into Korea in force, quite aside from any speculation on influences exerted by Moscow, may include:

"1. The Chinese communists had assumed that the North Koreans would win; hence they had not prepared to intervene earlier.

"2. Postponing any major effort on their part until the fighting reached the region of the Korean–Manchurian frontier served to shorten their lines of communication—a particularly important point in view of the fact that United Nations forces control sea and air—and also gave them the maximum time for preparation. In addition to bringing up forces from other parts of China, it was necessary to replenish stocks of equipment and supplies in Manchuria which had been seriously depleted in extending aid to the North Koreans.

"3. In the above-mentioned frontier area full advantage can be taken of the degree to which world opinion has been conditioned to acts of aggression and now looks upon a few regiments being identified on the wrong side of a border as indicating rather less than overt action. Meantime the United Nations forces can be weakened and the exposure to bombing of Chinese communist lines of communications and bases can be postponed. Evidence of an all-out effort, including the expenditure of the Chinese communist Air Force, probably will be delayed as long as possible for the reasons mentioned in paragraph 2.

"4. The support of public opinion in communist China for major military operations can be whipped up much more easily if it can be represented that an immediate threat to the Manchurian border exists; this notwithstanding the general assumption that Chinese communist leaders are aware United Nations forces do not intend to cross the frontier and would not attempt an invasion of Manchuria with a force of only ten divisions in any case.

"5. United Nations successes to date can be most effectively countered by a crushing Chinese communist victory in North Korea, thereby enhancing Asian and communist prestige in relation to Western imperialism and eliminating as a fighting force an important part of the U.S. Army.

"The above points necessarily are matters of opinion to a considerable degree, but the Chinese military on Formosa have access to more China mainland sources of information and have had more experience in this field of estimating Chinese communist intentions than others outside the Curtain; their opinions therefore warrant the most careful attention at this time."

Karl Lott Rankin, *China Assignment* (Seattle: University of Washington Press, Washington, 1964), pp. 65–66.
18. Special Report of General MacArthur to the Security Council, United Nations, November 5, 1950, in *Military Situation in the Far East*, cited, pp. 3492–3493.

MacArthur's Eighth Report to the United Nations (period October 16–31) was dated November 6, 1950. In it, he failed to mention some of the unpleasant events that had occurred in the last days of October in the zone of action of the 8th Army, although he did observe that Chinese soldiers had been captured, identified as such, and interrogated:

"For the first time in the Korean war, Chinese soldiers of the Chinese Communist forces were captured in combat in Korea. They wore North Korean uniforms and may have been volunteers. There is no positive evidence that Chinese Communist units, as such, have entered Korea, although incomplete interrogation of these prisoners of war indicates that possibility (Same, p. 3427)."

But in the next report, which covered the period November 1–15, CINCUNC informed the United Nations that the "possibility" had become fact:

"Chinese Communist forces in significant strength have moved across the Yalu River and attacked United Nations forces. This constitutes an act of international lawlessness far exceeding that of mere brigandage. The course of operations of United Nations forces in Korea has in consequence changed from that of pursuit of defeated and routed North Korean Army remnants to that of a new campaign against a fresh enemy force. (Same, p. 3432.)"

In this report, MacArthur stated that the "complete air supremacy" hitherto enjoyed by U.N. aircraft over Korea had been "challenged—by a modern high-performance jet-type aircraft." (Same, p. 3434.) These were MIG 15s, which entered combat on November 1. MacArthur also for the first time mentioned the Manchurian "sanctuary" available to the Chinese and mildly complained of the "handicaps" under which he was forced to operate by "refraining from attack on Manchurian bases." This plaint was soon to become a theme.

19. Montross and Canzona, cited, p. 12.
20. Appleman, cited, p. 716.
21. Same, p. 764.
22. Montross and Canzona, cited, p. 131. In his later testimony at Senate hearings, MacArthur would describe the November movement north as "a reconnaissance in force." *Military Situation in the Far East*, cited, p. 21.
23. Appleman, cited, p. 765.
24. Robert F. Futrell, *The United States Air Force in Korea, 1950–1953* (New York: Duell, Sloan & Pearce, 1961), pp. 210–211.

Chapter 8

1. Mao Tse-tung, *Selected Military Writings*, cited, p. 226. The context reads:

"Our commanders should have not only the boldness to overwhelm the enemy but also the ability to remain masters of the situation throughout the changes and vicissitudes of the entire war. Swimming in the ocean of war, they must not flounder, but make sure of reaching the opposite shore with measured strokes. Strategy and tactics, as the laws for directing war, constitute the art of swimming in the ocean of war."

2. Same, p. 193.
3. Montross and Canzona, cited, p. 142.
4. Same, p. 144.
5. Same.
6. *Military Situation in the Far East*. cited, p. 1834.
7. *The Travels of Marco Polo*, trans. by William Marsten with an introduction by F. W. Mote (New York: Dell, 1961), p. 151.
8. Sung Shih-lun commanded 9th Army Group:

ARMY	COMMANDER	DIVISIONS
20th	Liu Fei	58th, 59th, 60th, 89th
26th	Sun Chi-kuang (or Sun Chi-hsien?)	76th, 77th, 78th, 88th
27th	Nieh Feng-chien (or Ch'un Yi-kung?)	79th, 80th, 81st, 90th

Montross and Canzona, cited, Appendix G, "Enemy Order of Battle," pp. 397–398. Names of army commanders supplied. Of the above units, the 78th, 88th, and 90th divisions were not in contact but apparently either were held in reserve or did not reach the area of operations in East Korea.

9. Same, p. 163.
10. *1st Marine Division Special Action Report: Wonsan-Hamhung-Chosin, 8 October 1950–15 December 1950* (Historical Library, Headquarters, U.S. Marine Corps), pp. 34–35.
11. Same, pp. 29–30.
12. Maj. Gen. Courtney Whitney, USA, General MacArthur's aide-de-camp and confidant, attended this meeting and describes it thus:

> ". . . both Walker and Almond were optimistic. Walker felt that he could hold at least the P'yongyang area. Almond, who had not as yet been subjected to the full force of the enemy's counter offensive in the northeast, felt that the 1st Marine Division could press forward to the corridor that the enemy had used in the west and attack him from the rear."

Courtney Whitney, *MacArthur: His Rendezvous with Destiny* (New York: Alfred A. Knopf, 1956), p. 394.
13. In a special communiqué issued on November 28, 1950, General MacArthur stated:

> "Enemy reactions developed in the course of our assault operations of the past four days disclose that a major segment of the Chinese continental armed forces in army, corps, and divisional organization of an aggregate strength of over 200,000 men is now arrayed against the U.N. forces in North Korea.
> "There exists the obvious intent and preparation for support of these forces by heavy reinforcements now concentrated within the privileged sanctuary north of the international boundary and consistently moving forward.
> "Consequently, we face an entirely new war. . . ."

See the *New York Times*, November 29, 1950.

14. Mao Tse-tung, cited, p. 233.
15. Maj. Gen. Oliver P. Smith, USMC.
16. Allied Translator and Interpreter Service, Far East Command, Interrogation Report KG0252. Other interrogation reports examined in this context are similar.
17. *Military Situation in the Far East*, cited, p. 3496.
18. S. L. A. Marshall, *The River and the Gauntlet* (New York: William Morrow, 1953), p. 1.
19. Radio News Broadcast, NCNA, December 2, 1950.
20. Douglas MacArthur, *Reminiscences* (New York: McGraw-Hill, 1964), p. 374. Italics added.
21. Same.

22. Whitney, cited, p. 42.
23. Same.
24. MacArthur, cited, p. 374.
25. Same, p. 376.

Chapter 9

1. The complete text of "Report to the General Assembly from Group on Cease-fire in Korea, January 2, 1951," together with annexes containing Chinese replies, is reproduced in U.S. Senate, *Military Situation in the Far East*, cited, pp. 3505–3513.
2. The complete text of General Wu Hsiu-chüan's statement, as published in the *New York Times* on December 17, 1950, follows:

> "We have come here to strive for peace. We have proposed to the United Nations Security Council that effective measures be adopted, in order to stop aggression and to restore peace, to bring about the withdrawal by the United States Government of its armed forces of aggression against China's territory, Taiwan [Formosa], the cessation of its intervention in Korea and the withdrawal of all its armed forces of intervention in Korea. But unfortunately, though not unexpectedly, the United Nations Security Council, under the manipulation of the Anglo-American bloc, rejected the rightful proposal for peace of the Central People's Government of the People's Republic of China. Against this, we must raise our resolute opposition and protest.
>
> "The Central People's Government of the People's Republic of China has also accepted the invitation of the United Nations and sent me to participate in the discussion of the charge of United States aggression against China levelled by the representative of the Soviet Union in the Political and Security Committee of the fifth session of the United Nations General Assembly. But, up to date, in spite of the vigorous advocation by the representative of the Soviet Union that the Political and Security Committee continue to discuss this charge without interruption, the Political and Security Committee, under the manipulation of the United States Government, has not taken up the discussion of this important charge. Thus, though we have been invited to come and have waited for a long time, yet up to now we have not had an opportunity to speak. But it is our belief that the voice of the People's Republic of China should be heard by the whole world. We cannot but express our indignation against such manipulation of the United Nations by the United States Government denying me of the right to speak.
>
> "The small group of the United States ruling circle has obstinately refused to recognize the existence of the People's Republic of China and has denied its rights of expression and representation on important Far Eastern problems concerning China. It has obstinately carried on a policy of wanton intervention in China's internal affairs, of supporting the Chiang Kai-shek reactionary remnant clique, who has been forsaken by all the people of China and the whole world, of open aggres-

sion against China, and of making enemies of the 475 million people of the People's Republic of China. But facts prove that the People's Republic of China cannot be forcibly denied of a major voice in Asian affairs and of its position in the United Nations. Only on the basis of a full recognition of this fact may the efforts to solve by peaceful means the present-day important problems of the world reach any result.

"We have always advocated that the Korean problem should be solved by peaceful means and that it should be localized. This is why we uphold resolutely the stand that all foreign troops be withdrawn from Korea and that the Korean problem be solved by the Korean people themselves. Yet the United States ruling circle has carried out, simultaneously with its armed intervention in Korea, armed aggression against Taiwan and bombing against China's mainland and is extending its aggression to Eastern Asia. The peace-loving people of the whole world are demanding that the Korean problem be solved peacefully. Yet the Anglo-American bloc insists to maintain its aggressive forces and its aggressive actions in Korea, to continue its invasion and occupation of China's Taiwan and to carry out even more persistently its aggressive and war policy against the whole world. We have only to look for proof in the statement of President Truman, which threatened to use the atomic bomb, in the joint communiqué of President Truman and Prime Minister Attlee and in the proclamation of a state of national emergency by the United States Government.

"From these, one can also come to understand the real intention of the proposal of 'cease fire first' in Korea, a proposal which has met the approval of Mr. Austin. The real intention is to demand that the Korean People's Army and the Chinese volunteers tie their own hands so that the United States armed forces of aggression may continue their aggression in Korea. The real intention is to demand that Taiwan be kept under the invasion and occupation of the United States armed forces. It is to demand that Japanese militarism be revived again by MacArthur. It is to demand that the American people be driven at will by the United States ruling circle into the abyss of war. Such a trap was set many times in China by Chiang Kai-shek with the help of General Marshall. Hence, it is not unfamiliar to the Chinese people. We wish to unmask such trap of the United States ruling circle to the peace-loving people of the whole world.

"The Chinese people love peace ardently. They fervently hope that they will be able to construct their own country in peace without being subject to aggression and aggressive threats. The Chinese Government has always advocated that all the present-day important problems of the world be solved by peaceful means, particularly the problem in the Far East arising from the policy of the United States ruling circle, of armed aggression against China and Korea. Although the United Nations Security Council, under the manipulation of the Anglo-American bloc, rejected this time the basic proposal of China to solve peacefully the problem of the Far East, we shall still do our utmost to strive for a peaceful solution to the problem of the Far East. We are also willing to try to advise the Chinese volunteers to bring to an early conclusion the military operations which they have been forced to undertake together with the Korean People's Army in their resistance against the United States armed forces of aggression.

"In coming here, we have received a friendly welcome expressed by the American people in various ways. To them, we are sincerely thankful. We earnestly believe that the friendship between the Chinese people and the American people, though threatened at the present time by the policy and the actions of the United States ruling circle in its aggression against China, will definitely continue under the joint efforts of the peace-loving peoples of the two countries."

3. Tokyo-monitored Peking broadcast, the *New York Times*, December 22, 1950.
4. Matthew B. Ridgway, *Soldier* (New York: Harper & Brothers, 1956), p. 210.
5. Same, p. 215.
6. Douglas MacArthur, *Reminiscences* (New York: McGraw-Hill, 1964), pp. 376–377.
7. Leon Trotsky, *My Life* (New York: Charles Scribner's Sons, 1930), p. 428.
8. James F. Schnabel, "Ridgway in Korea," *Military Review*, v. 44, no. 3, March 1964, p. 8.
9. MacArthur, cited, pp. 381–382.
10. John W. Spanier, *The Truman-MacArthur Controversy and the Korean War* (Cambridge: Harvard University Press, 1959), p. 144.
11. *Military Situation in the Far East*, cited, p. 1211.
12. Same. Italics added.
13. The information in this and subsequent paragraphs is drawn from General Headquarters, Far East Command, "G-2 Staff Section Report of 30 January, 1951," Master Annex 3, pp. 15–20.
14. Headquarters, 8th U.S. Army, Korea, "Command Report, 30 November, 1951," Section II, Enclosure 6 G.
15. Mark W. Clark, *From the Danube to the Yalu* (New York: Harper & Brothers, 1954), pp. 2–3. Italics added.
16. Malcolm W. Cagle and Frank A. Manson, *The Sea War in Korea* (Annapolis: U.S. Naval Institute, 1957), p. 232.
17. Same. Italics added.
18. Lynn Montross, Hubard D. Kuokka, and Norman W. Hicks, *U.S. Marine Operations in Korea, 1950–1953*, v. 4 (Washington, D.C.: Headquarters, U.S. Marine Corps, 1962), p. 144.
19. S. L. A. Marshall, *Operation PUNCH and the Capture of Hill 440, Suwon, Korea, February 1951* (Baltimore: Johns Hopkins University, 1952), p. 9.
20. This unique brigade consisted of one Australian, one Canadian, one English, and one Scottish battalion plus a New Zealand Field (Service of Supply) regiment, an Indian Field Ambulance unit, and the 2nd U.S. Heavy Mortar Battalion (36 4.2-inch mortars). There was at the same time a full British brigade (the 29th) in Korea.

During the fighting at Chipyong-ni, an incident occurred which reflects the spirit the commander of the revitalized 8th Army had conveyed to the front-line fighting men in six short weeks. Although the thermometer hovered around twelve degrees below zero, the regulation that there were to be no exposed fires at night was enforced. (Troops were sent in relays to blacked-out "warming tents.") This order "had never appealed to the French," who invariably had a few fires going. An American officer telephoned the French battalion to remonstrate:

" 'Get those fires out at once, or you'll have all the Chinese in Korea around you,' he said.

" 'But, Monsieur,' replied the French officer, 'that is magnificent. As you say, the Chinese will see our fires; they attack us, we kill them.' "

Cyril Nelson Barclay, *The New Warfare* (New York: Philosophical Library, 1954), p. 51.
21. *Military Situation in the Far East*, cited, p. 3456.
22. Ridgway, cited, p. 219.
23. Futrell, cited, p. 337.
24. *Operations in Korea* (West Point: U.S. Military Academy, 1956), p. 37.
25. Barclay, cited, p. 67.
26. Montross, Kuokka, and Hicks, cited, p. 126.
27. Same, p. 120.
28. Allied Translator and Interpreter Service, Far East Command, Interrogation Report KT 1671, October 3, 1951.
29. Same.
30. "Far East Command Intelligence Summary No. 3214, June 28, 1951." Quoted in Futrell, cited, pp. 342–343.
31. Montross, Kuokka, and Hicks, cited, p. 127.
32. James A. Van Fleet, "The Truth about Korea," *Life*, May 11, 1953, p. 127.
33. Asher Lee, *The Soviet Air Force* (New York: The John Day Company, 1962), p. 115.
34. Same, p. 119.
35. Futrell, cited, p. 279.
36. See Shen Ch'ih-ch'ing. "The Vast Skies Are Shaken," *Current Background*, no. 596, October 7, 1959, pp. 25–28.
37. By January 1953, Chinese Communist combat aircraft inventory had risen to a figure of 2,200, all crewed by Soviet-trained Chinese. The great majority of these were deployed in Manchuria. Contemporary evaluations showed:

1300 MIG 15 fighters (jet)
200 fighters (piston)
100 IL-28 light bombers (jet)
250 TU-2 light bombers (piston)
175 IL-10 ground attack (piston)

U.S. Pacific Fleet, "Interim Evaluation Report No. 5, July 1, 1952–January 31, 1953," U.S. Marine Corps Historical Archives, File 132 683.
38. Lee, cited, p. 207. Far East Air Force admitted the loss of 1,041 aircraft of all types to enemy action during the period June 26, 1950–July 27, 1953. Of these, only 139, or less than 14 per cent, were lost in air combat. Of this number, 78 were Sabres.

Sabre pilots claimed 792 MIGs. These figures indicate a ten-to-one superiority in air combat. The figure is reasonably reliable as claimed kills in air combat could almost always be confirmed by photographic evidence.

In all, FEAF claimed to have destroyed a total of 900 Communist aircraft, "probably destroyed" 168, and "damaged" 973. U.S. Marine Corps pilots claimed 35 MIGs, and Navy pilots, 16. Other U.N. pilots claimed 3. Thus, the grand total of Chinese aircraft claimed destroyed in air-to-air combat was 846. Futrell, cited, p. 645.

39. Futrell, cited, pp. 651–655.

40. Same.

41. U.N. and Chinese Communist/NKPA Orders of Battle, March 1952. (Listed west to east.)

    (1) *U.S. I Corps Zone:*
          1st Marine Division
          1st Commonwealth Division
          1st ROK Division
          45th U.S. Division (Reserve)
        Opposing:
          65th Chinese Army
          63rd Chinese Army
          40th Chinese Army
          39th Chinese Army
          38th Chinese Army (less one division)
          64th Chinese Army (Reserve)

    (2) *U.S. IX Corps Zone:*
          9th ROK Division
          7th U.S. Division
          2nd ROK Division
          40th U.S. Division (Reserve)
        Opposing:
          One division, Chinese 38th Army
          15th Chinese Army
          42nd Chinese Army (Reserve)

    (3) *ROK II Corps Zone:*
          6th ROK Division
          Capital Division
          3rd ROK Division (Reserve)
         Opposing:
          12th Chinese Army
          68th Chinese Army (less one division)
          60th Chinese Army (Reserve)
          67th Chinese Army (Reserve)
          20th Chinese Army (General Reserve)

    (4) *U.S. X Corps Zone:*
          7th ROK Division
          25th U.S. Division
          8th ROK Division (Reserve)
         Opposing:
          One division, 68th Chinese Army
          NKPA II Corps

NKPA III Corps (less one division)
(5) *ROK 1 Corps Zone:*
11th ROK Division
5th ROK Division
Opposing:
One Division, NKPA III Corps
NKPA I Corps

U.S. Pacific Fleet, "Interim Evaluation Report No. 4, January 1, 1952–June 30, 1952," U.S. Marine Corps Historical Archives, File 121. 217/9. 117890–4.
42. Same.
43. U.S. Pacific Fleet, "Interim Evaluation Report No. 5," cited.
44. Clark, cited, p. 296.
45. Ridgway, cited, pp. 219–220.
46. Testimony of General of the Army Omar N. Bradley in *Military Situation in the Far East*, cited, p. 732.
47. Same, p. 937.
48. Personal correspondence, General Matthew B. Ridgway, U.S.A. (Ret.).

Chapter 10

1. *Survey of China Mainland Press (SCMP)*, no. 597, June 25, 1953, p. 1.
2. *SCMP*, no. 629, August 12, 1953, pp. 2–3.
3. *SCMP*, no. 649, September 12/14, 1953, pp. 2–14.
4. According to P'eng, "from June 23, 1950, up to the Armistice on July 27, 1953, the Korean and Chinese People's forces killed, wounded, and captured more than one million and ninety thousand of the enemy. Of these, over three hundred and ninety thousand were U.S. troops." This figure exaggerates U.S. casualties by a factor of three. Final figures showed:

UNITED STATES

Killed in action (KIA) or died of wounds (DOW)	25,801
Missing, presumed dead	7,828
Wounded in action	103,284
Missing after exchange of prisoners	24
Total	136,937

OTHER ALLIED FORCES
(exclusive of South Koreans)

KIA or DOW	3,000
WIA	12,000
MIA	4,000
Total	19,000

SOUTH KOREA
(estimates)

KIA and WIA	200,000
MIA	?

Operations in Korea (West Point: U.S. Military Academy, 1956), p. 58.
5. See Shih Ch'eng-chih's study, *People's Resistance in Mainland China 1950–*

1955, Communist China Problem Research Series, No. EC 17 (Hong Kong: The Union Research Institute, December 1956).

6. Theodore Hsi-En Chen and Wen-hui C. Chen, "The 'Three-Anti' and 'Five-Anti' Movements in Communist China," *Pacific Affairs.* v. 26, no. 1, March 1953, p. 9.

7. Same, p. 13.

8. Same.

9. Same, p. 18.

10. Same.

11. Same, p. 19.

12. Futrell, cited, p. 648.

13. Same, pp. 471–473.

14. Same.

15. General Headquarters, Far East Command, "Order of Battle Information, Chinese Communist Forces in Korea," Code 19322, Office of the Chief of Military History, Department of the Army. The Political Section, Army, consisted of 72 officers and 147 enlisted men; the Staff Section, of 54 officers and 169 enlisted men.

16. Allied Translator and Interpreter Service, Far East Command, Interrogation Report KG 0227. Unless otherwise noted, other quotes in this section are from the same document.

17. All air force officers, or at least all pilots, were required to be Party members.

18. Allied Translator and Interpreter Service, Far East Command, Interrogation Report KG 0248.

BOOK II

Chapter 11

1. William Theodore de Bary, Wing-Tsit Chan, and Burton Watson, *Sources of Chinese Tradition* (New York: Columbia University Press, 1960), p. 178.

2. Henry L. Kissinger, *Nuclear Weapons and Foreign Policy* (New York: Harper & Brothers for the Council on Foreign Relations, 1957), p. 316.

3. Quoted by Chou En-lai in his "Report on the Work of the Government" to the Third National People's Congress, text as broadcast by the New China News Agency (NCNA) International Service, December 30, 1964. The quotation is from a statement Mao issued on November 28, 1964, "in support of the people of the Congo (Léopoldville) against U.S. aggression." The relevant portion of NCNA's original version of the statement read:

> People of the world, unite, defeat the U.S. aggressors and all their flunkeys! People of the whole world, have courage, dare to fight, defy difficulties, advance one after the other, so that the world shall belong to the people. Each and every evil-doer shall be liquidated.

4. "Report on the Work of the Government," cited.

5. Lo Jui-ching, "Commemorate the Victory over German Fascism! Carry the Struggle against U.S. Imperialism through to the End," *Red Flag*, May 11, 1965, text as broadcast by NCNA International Service, May 10, 1965.

6. Lin Piao, "Long Live the Victory of the People's War," NCNA International Service, September 1965.
7. "Report on the Work of the Government," cited.
8. See his press conference of September 29, 1965, *Peking Review*, no. 41, October 8, 1965, pp. 12–13.
9. The *Bulletin of Activities* (*Kung-tso T'ung-hsün*) is, according to the General Political Department of the PLA, an irregular secret publication for officers at regimental level or above who belong to the Party. Top-secret issues are distributed only to divisional officers. The *Bulletin* was first published on January 1, 1961.

    Copies of twenty-nine issues of the *Bulletin*, covering the period January 1–August 26, 1961, apparently found their way out of China and thence into the hands of the U.S. State Department after Khambas overran a Chinese regimental post in Tibet in the late summer of 1961. The State Department released them to the public on August 5, 1963.

Chapter 12

1. Huang Tsung-hsi, *A Plan for the Prince*, trans. and explained by William Theodore de Bary (unpublished doctoral dissertation, Columbia University, April 1963), p. 356.
2. Same, p. 359.
3. Same, p. 361.
4. Same, p. 368.
5. Same.
6. John Magruder, "The Chinese as a Fighting Man," *Foreign Affairs*, v. 9, no. 3, April 1931, p. 369. (Italics added.)
7. James Legge, *The Chinese Classics*, v. IV, *The She Ching* (London: Trubner & Company, 1871), Book I, Ode VII; Book VII, Ode VI.
8. Same, Book XI, Ode III.
9. Same, "Minor Odes of the Kingdom," Book I, Ode VIII; Book III, Ode III.
10. Same, Book III, Ode VIII.
11. *The Chronicle of the Three Kingdoms* (*220–265*), trans. and annotated by Achilles Fang (Cambridge: Harvard University Press, 1952), pp. 15–17.
12. Sun Tzu, cited, Foreword.
13. In its issue of March 11, 1947, the Soviet periodical *Kultura i Zhizn* [*Culture and Life*], in a *diktat* defining the function of literature in a Communist state, said: "It is the highly noble task of Soviet literature to educate the people, and especially our youth, to respect and love the valiant Soviet Army and to educate them in the spirit of the great military traditions of the Soviet people, in the spirit of the willingness of every Soviet individual to fulfill his military duty." It is "the highly noble task" of writers and artists to perform precisely the same duty in China today.
14. Nym Wales, *Red Dust: Autobiographies of Chinese Communists* (Stanford University Press, 1952), p. 183.
15. Same, p. 188.
16. Mao Tse-tung, "Talks at the Yenan Forum on Art & Literature," *Selected Works*, v. 4 (New York: International Publishers, 1954), pp. 63–93. These

"Talks" were reprinted in *Peking Review*, July 8, 1966. According to the editor, the reprinting of the Chairman's "Talks" marked "the beginning of a new stage in the great proletarian cultural revolution." Mao's "Talks," the editor went on to say, are "the compass, the 'magic mirror' to detect demons, and the clarion call that sounds the advance."

17. Same, p. 71.
18. *China Quarterly*, no. 13, January–March 1963, contains a comprehensive survey of Chinese Communist literature.
19. Part Two of Jerome, Ch'en, *Mao and the Chinese Revolution* (New York: Oxford University Press, 1965), consists of translations by Ch'en and Michael Bullock of thirty-seven poems written by Mao between 1926 and 1963. The English versions are elegantly done and convey the flavor of the poetry without loss of its frequent delicacy. The same cannot be said for the English version of *Nineteen Poems* published by the Foreign Languages Press, Peking, in 1958.
20. Joint Publications Research Service, *Reports*, no. 23669, February 8, 1965, pp. 78–80.
21. Prof. T. A. Hsia of the University of California has written a most perceptive study which describes how the Party invoked Chinese legends and the martial tradition during the first period of the People's Communes. This fascinating essay is *Metaphor, Myth, Ritual and the People's Communes*; no. 7, *Studies in Chinese Communist Terminology* (Berkeley: Center for Chinese Studies, University of California, June 1961).
22. Some recent PLA "heroes" who have been "brought up on Chairman Mao's thought" include Lei Feng, Ouyang Hai, Wang Chieh, Mai Hsien-teh, Lin Ying-chun, Chang Chung-yu, Wang Yu-chang, and Ho Hsiang-kuei. Whether these paragons really existed or were fabricated is not relevant. Their "deeds" are recounted at great length in the Chinese press, which has extolled them as "illustrious models for the whole nation."

Wang Chieh is a good case study. In November 1965 the PLA was exhorted to "unfold a campaign" to learn from the exemplary life and heroic deeds of this successor to Lei Feng. The fact that his personal name—Chieh—means "hero" suggests the possibility that he is fictional. The "entries" in his alleged diary support this supposition. As might be expected, the Chinese press and radio never reveal the unit in which these "heroes" served.

Chapter 13

1. *Selected Works*, v. 2 (New York: International Publishers, 1954), p. 272.
2. People's Republic of China, *Documents of the First Session of the First National People's Congress of the People's Republic of China* (Peking: Foreign Languages Press, 1955), p. 140.
3. Same, p. 147.
4. Same.
5. The Constitution does not prescribe the composition of the NPC. The number of members has varied from time to time. Although the Third Na-

tional People's Congress (December 1964) formally removed P'eng Teh-huai and Marshal Lo Jung-huan had died earlier in 1964, the NPC filled only one of the two vacancies for vice-chairman. The appointment went to Lo Jui-ch'ing, who at that time was chief of the General Staff Department, PLA, but has since fallen from official grace.

6. On May 24, 1965, according to a New China News Agency radio broadcast, it was announced that "the ninth meeting of the NPC Standing Committee had decided to abolish the current system of military rank in the PLA" as of June 1. In order that "the revolutionary spirit and glorious tradition of the PLA . . . should have full expression and so there should be identity between the three services and between officers and men":

> "(1) Every member of the army, navy, and air force and the public security forces shall wear a red star insignia on his hat and a red badge on his collar. The present cap insignia, the present epaulettes and collar badge showing military rank, and the present insignia indicating the various services, arms, and branches shall be abolished.
>
> "(2) The "Chieh Fang" [liberation] cap shall be worn by all officers and men. The present hard-peak hat, the present hat without a peak worn by women, and the present round naval hat shall be abolished.
>
> "(3) The uniform worn by the navy shall be the same as that worn by the army and the air force except that the color shall be gray.
>
> "(4) A belt shall be issued to every officer and man. The belt over the shoulder worn by officers shall be abolished.
>
> "(5) The western style of military dress worn by field grade officers and above, and the skirt and blouse style of dress worn by women, shall be abolished."

7. *Documents of the First Session of the First National People's Congress of the People's Republic of China,* cited, pp. 148–150.

8. According to an August 1, 1966, dispatch to *The New York Times* from Hong Kong, Yang Cheng-wu was officially listed as acting chief of staff (i.e. chief of the General Staff Department) on the preceding day. The same report speculated that Hsiao Hua had been dismissed from his post as chief of the General Political Department and that Hsiao Ching-Kuang had been relieved as commander in chief of the navy. The *New York Times,* August 2, 1966.

9. For an enlightening discussion of the careers of Kao Kang and his alleged fellow-conspirator, Jao Shu-shih, see Albert Ravenholt's "Feud Among the Red Mandarins," *American Universities Field Staff, East Asia Series,* v. 11, no. 2.

10. Hsiao Hua, in *Survey of the China Mainland Press,* no. 2270, June 2, 1960, p. 4.

11. Same, no. 2358, October 14, 1960, p. 2.

12. Same, no. 2433, February 7, 1961, pp. 1–3, 5–6.

13. *Peking Review,* no. 4, January 21, 1966, pp. 5–6.

Chapter 14

1. Arthur A. Cohen, *The Communism of Mao Tse-tung* (University of Chicago Press, 1964). See also Benjamin Schwartz, "On the 'Originality' of Mao Tse-tung," *Foreign Affairs*, v. 34, no. 1, October 1955, pp. 67–76.
2. Cohen, cited, p. 188.
3. Same.
4. Ho Chung-jen, "The Founding of the Fourth Red Army," *Current Background*, no. 208, September 10, 1952, pp. 43–49.
5. See Ch'en Yi, "Learn from the Marxist-Leninist Creative Style of Work of Chairman Mao," in same, pp. 9–16.
6. Ho Chung-jen, cited.
7. Mao Tse-tung, *On Guerrilla Warfare*, trans., with an introduction, by Samuel B. Griffith (New York: Praeger, 1961), p. 65.
8. Truong Chinh, *The August Revolution and the Resistance Will Win.* Published in the United States as *Primer for Revolt: The Communist Takeover in Viet-Nam*, with introduction and notes by Bernard B. Fall (New York: Praeger, 1965).
9. V. I. Lenin, *Selected Works*, v. 7 (New York: International Publishers, 1943), p. 177.
10. Same, p. 302.
11. Mao Tse-tung, *Selected Military Writings* (Peking: Foreign Publishing House, 1963), p. 79.
12. *Krasnaya Flot (Red Fleet)*, October 24, 1946.
13. "Theses of the VI World Congress of the Communist International, 1928," *International Press Correspondence*, no. 84, November 28, 1928, p. 1590. Ostensibly, the Soviet leadership has disavowed this thesis. The question of the dogma of the inevitability of war between the two competing systems and between capitalist states has been analyzed by Frederic S. Burin in "The Communist Doctrine of the Inevitability of War," *The American Political Science Review*, v. 57, no. 2, June 1963, pp. 334–354.
14. Mao Tse-tung, *Selected Works*, v. 2 (New York: International Publishing, 1954), p. 198.
15. See *Apologists of Neo-Colonialism* (Peking: Foreign Languages Press, 1963).
16. For the Chinese position, see, for instance, *Long Live Leninism* (Peking: Foreign Languages Press, 1960); *The Origin and Development of the Differences between the Leadership of the CPSU and Ourselves* (Peking: Foreign Languages Press, 1963); *Two Different Lines on the Question of War and Peace* (Peking: Foreign Languages Press, 1963); *Peaceful Coexistence—Two Diametrically Opposed Policies* (Peking: Foreign Languages Press, 1963); *Apologists of Neo-Colonialism*, cited; *The Leaders of the CPSU Are the Greatest Splitters of Our Times* (Peking: Foreign Languages Press, 1964). There are many similar subsequent statements.
17. *Long Live Leninism*, cited, p. 3.
18. Ellis Joffe, "The Conflict between Old and New in the Chinese Army," *The China Quarterly*, no. 18, April/June 1964, p. 125.
19. Sun Tzu, cited, p. 77.

20. B. H. Liddell Hart, *Strategy: The Indirect Approach* (London: Faber and Faber, Limited, 1954), p. 25.
21. *Bulletin of Activities*, no. 10, February 20, 1961.
22. Same, no. 7, February 1, 1961.
23. Same, no. 8, February 6, 1961.

Chapter 15

1. V. I. Lenin, *Selected Works*, v. 3 (New York: International Publishers, 1943), p. 338.
2. Mao Tse-tung, *Selected Military Writings* (Peking: Foreign Languages Press, 1963), p. 85.
3. Leon Trotsky, *My Life* (New York: Charles Scribner's Sons, 1930), p. 447. The Russian Communists were not the first to discover a need for a mechanism of control and indoctrination of the armed forces in the context of violent social revolution. The French Convention, more than one hundred years earlier, had built a similar political structure. In August 1792, the Convention sent propagandists to all field armies and six months later systematized political control by dispatching "representatives on special mission" to all superior headquarters. The Convention empowered its "representatives to promote, demote, relieve, or execute any officer who betrayed the revolution or conspired against it. This was necessary: there were thousands of former Royalists in the new army, and treason flourished—or did until the deterrent of the guillotine put a stop to Royalist conspiracies.
4. D. Fedotoff White, *The Growth of the Red Army* (Princeton University Press, 1944), p. 73.
5. Quoted in Isaac Deutscher, *The Prophet Armed, Trotsky: 1879–1921* (New York: University Press, 1954), p. 421.
6. Quoted by Maj. Pierre Krebs, French Army, in *The Political Institutions of the Soviet Army with Special Reference to the Role of the Political Commissar* (unpublished doctoral dissertation, St. Antony's College, Oxford University, May 1958). Major Krebs' dissertation is the most complete study of Party institutions in the Red Army I have seen.
7. Mao Tse-tung, *Selected Military Writings*, cited, p. 28.
8. Nym Wales, *Inside Red China* (New York: Doubleday, Doran, and Company), 1939, p. 37.
9. Montross and Canzona, cited, p. 355.
10. Jack G. Downing, *The Party Committee System in the Chinese Red Army and Its Impact on Small Unit Tactics and Combat Efficiency during the Chosin Reservoir Campaign in Korea, 1950* (unpublished thesis, Harvard University, December 1962).
11. Montross and Canzona, cited, pp. 185–186.
12. Same, p. 353.
13. Same, p. 354.
14. Liu Chao-jung, and others, *Stories of the Chinese People's Volunteers* (Peking: Foreign Languages Press, 1960), pp. 177 ff.
15. *Current Background*, no. 422, October 18, 1956, p. 8.

16. The Party's Political Section, its working organization at division level, was distinct from the Division Party Committee. This section consisted of 66 officers and 152 enlisted men as shown below left:

In Headquarters Company of each infantry regiment, the Political Section consisted of 22 officers and 12 enlisted men as shown below right:

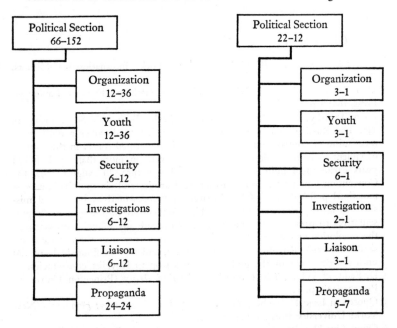

From General Headquarters, Far East Command, "Military Intelligence Summary, General Summary, 30 October, 1951," Office of the Chief of Military History, Code 19322.

17. Although most company commanders were Party members, some—a small proportion—were not. In such companies, the deputy company commander was invariably a Party man and sat on the Branch Committee. It is difficult to see how in this situation a company commander would enjoy any authority whatsoever.

18. Allied Translator and Interpreter Service (ATIS), Interrogation Reports KG 0273, 0237, 0189.

19. Same.

20. Same.

21. Same.

22. *Hung Ch'i (Red Flag)*, March 31, 1964, pp. 40-45.

Chapter 16

1. V. I. Lenin, *The Revolution of 1917* (New York: International Publishers, 1929), Book 1, pp. 45-46.

2. Mao Tse-tung, *Selected Works*, v. 1 (New York: International Publishers, 1954), pp. 67–68.

3. Same, p. 69.

4. Liu Yün-cheng, "The Militia in the People's Revolutionary Wars of China," *Survey of the China Mainland Press (SCMP)*, no. 2780, July 18, 1962, p. 5.
    Not unexpectedly, the Party today takes full credit for arousing and mobilizing the masses during the Anti-Japanese War. But the fact is that the invaders prepared the ground for the communists—particularly in North China, where their repressive and frequently brutal policies generated peasant hatred.
    In 1942, as has already been noted, the Japanese High Command, frustrated in its attempts to extirpate Eighth Route Army guerrillas, instituted the infamous "three-all" campaign: "kill all, burn all, destroy all." This stupid and inhuman policy, basically similar to that carried out by the Nazis in Russia, produced an identical effect: it estranged the peasant masses of North China from the Japanese and their Chinese puppets beyond any possible hope of reconciliation. The Communists were ready to take full advantage of the situation and instantly did so. However, it was not the Party, but a monumental and criminal blunder in Japanese Army policy, which played the critical generative role in the rural resistance movement.

5. Liu Yun-cheng, cited, p. 6.

6. *Nan-fang Jih-pao*, October 25, 1950.

7. *Liberation Army Daily*, May 14, 1957.

8. *SCMP*, no. 1833, August 15, 1958, pp. 1–5.

9. "Resolution on the Establishment of People's Communes in the Rural Areas, Central Committee of the Chinese Communist Party," August 29, 1958, *Peking Review*, no. 29, September 16, 1958, pp. 21–23. As is indicated in the text, the decision embodied in this resolution *had been made by the highest authorities some time previous to August 25*—that is, before the Taiwan Straits crisis reached a climax.

10. *Red Flag*, August 31, 1958.

11. John Gittings has described the movement as "perhaps the most ambitious military enterprise in the history of mankind." See "China's Militia," *China Quarterly*, no. 18, April/June 1964, p. 100.

12. *SCMP*, no. 1852, September 12, 1958, p. 5.

13. *Peking Review*, no. 29, September 16, 1958, p. 8, and no. 30, September 23, 1958, pp. 9–10.

14. Same, no. 33, October 14, 1958, p. 4.

15. Fu Ch'iu-t'ao, "The People's Militia—a Favorite System of Our People," *Extracts from China Mainland Magazines (ECMM)*, no. 159, March 2, 1959, p. 28. The most complete summary of the "Everyone a Soldier" movement as it developed in the autumn of 1958 may be found in *Current Background*, no. 530, October 31, 1958.

16. The methodical use of militant terminology in the context of the "people's communes" movement is analyzed by Dr. T. A. Hsia in a fascinating study entitled *Metaphor, Myth, Ritual, and the People's Communes*. Studies in Chinese Communist Terminology, no. 7. (Berkeley: Center for Chinese Studies, Institute of International Studies, University of California, June 1961.)

17. *Bulletin of Activities*, no. 4. The report cited is dated December 30, 1960, and the endorsement thereon, January 7, 1961. All quotations are from the "Report" or the "Endorsement."

18. Liu Yun-cheng, "The Role of People's Militia," *Peking Review*, no. 6, February 5, 1965, p. 18.

19. U.S. Joint Publications Research Service (JPRS), *Reports*, 26385, September 15, 1964, pp. 117–118.

20. Same, 26974, October 20, 1964, pp. 98–101.

21. Same, 27895, December 17, 1964, pp. 87–88.

22. Same, 26974, cited, pp. 91–92.

23. Quoted in same, 27895, cited, p. 85.

24. That the Party considered this Militia Political Work Conference an event of first importance is obvious from the list of those who with the Chairman received the delegates at an official reception: Liu Shao-chi, Chou En-lai, Chu Teh, Teng Hsiao-p'ing, Tung Pi-wu, P'eng Chen, Ch'en Yi, Li Fu-ch'-un, Ho Lung, Li Hsien-nien, Ulanfu, Lu Ting-yi, Ch'en Po-ta, Kang Sheng, Po I-po, and Teng Tzu-hui. (*SCMP*, no. 3340, November 19, 1964, p. 2.)

    The delegates listened to hortatory addresses by Marshals Lin Piao, Ho Lung, and Hsü Hsiang-ch'ien, who "issued important instructions"; P'eng Chen and Senior Gen. Lo Jui-ch'ing (chief GSD, PLA) "delivered important speeches"; Gen. P'eng Sho-hui (deputy director, General Staff, PLA) and Lieut. Gen. Hsü Li-ch'ing (deputy director, General Political Department, PLA) "spoke at the conference"; Lieut. Gen. Liang Pi-yeh (also a deputy director, General Political Department, PLA) merely "delivered a speech." (Same.)

25. Same, no. 3337, cited, p. 15.

26. The delegates were instructed that in view of the new situation prevailing both at home and abroad, the militia question had become one of significant strategic importance for "dealing with the anti-China plots of U.S. imperialism and all reactionaries, for preparations to shatter the war of aggression to be launched by the enemy, and for consolidating the people's democratic dictatorship." *SCMP*, no. 3340, cited, p. 2.

27. Quotation drawn from Liu Yün-cheng, "The Militia in the People's Revolutionary Wars of China," cited, p. 1.

28. Same.

29. Same.

30. Same.

31. The Security Forces assumed an active role in March 1963.

32. *Nan-fang Jih-pao*, February 14–20, 1962.

33. *Liu Yun-cheng*, cited, p. 18.

Chapter 17

1. Radio news broadcast, New China News Agency, October 6, 1965.

2. The British analyst P. J. Honey speculates that the war in Vietnam may drag on interminably if Le Duan assumes full control in North Vietnam. Implicit in this view, or so it seems to me, is the probability of eventual Chinese participation in combat operations. See P. J. Honey, "Vietnam: To the Bitter End?" *Survival*, v. 8, no. 2, February 1966, pp. 54–56.

3. NCNA radio broadcast, cited.
4. Maj. Gen. D. Som Dutt, *The Defence of India's Northern Borders,* Adelphi Papers, no. 25, January 1966.
5. A valuable summary of background materials relevant to China's first test detonation appears in Joint Publications Research Service (JPRS), *Reports,* no. 29529, April 12, 1965, pp. 1–7.
6. *Science,* v. 146, no. 3644, October 30, 1964, p. 601.
7. Same.
8. The *Washington Post,* December 30, 1965. The characteristics of the "G" Class ballistic missile submarine are:

Displacement:	2,350 tons surfaced
	2,800 tons submerged
Dimensions:	320 x 28 x 22 feet
Guided weapons:	Three vertical tubes for missiles
Torpedo tubes:	Six 21 inch (bow)
Machinery:	Three diesels. Three shafts
	Total h.p., 6,000—17.6 kn. surface
	Electric motors—17 kn. submerged
Radius:	22,700 mi. surface
Crew:	12 officers; 74 enlisted

Jane's Fighting Ships, 1965–1966 (New York: McGraw-Hill, 1966), p. 434. The "W" Class guided-missile submarine is equipped with a deck tank for housing guided missiles emplaced on ramp launchers. These submarines are reported to carry two such launchers. This is a long-range submarine with a radius of action between 13,000 and 16,500 miles. *Jane's,* cited, pp. 434, 436. *Jane's* (p. 52) credits the Chinese Communist navy with 21 such boats.
9. *Peking Review,* no. 41, October 8, 1965.
10. "Long Live the Victory of the People's War," text as broadcast by NCNA, September 2, 1965.
11. Same.
12. A number of guerrilla schools and training centers exist in China, and some Africans have received instruction there. Such a school was operated by the Chinese in Ghana before the overthrow of Kwame Nkrumah. Thus, China's direct assistance and her doctrinal contribution must be assessed as critically important.
13. *The New York Times,* February 19, 1965.
14. See, for example, protest notes delivered by the Ministry of Foreign Affairs to the Indian embassy in China, December 28, 1964, JPRS, no. 28766, February 16, 1965, pp. 47–48. These notes alleged that Indian military aircraft conducted repeated reconnaissances over Lhasa, Rudok, Gartok, Gyantse, and other critical areas.
15. Dispatch from New Delhi, the *Baltimore Sun,* December 30, 1965. This report may have been fabricated for the purpose of spurring aid from the United States, the United Kingdom, and the Soviet Union. Since that time, China has given (or sold) a few MIG-21 aircraft and 80 medium tanks to Pakistan.
16. New company regulations were issued in mid-September 1966. In these,

it was stated that owing to changes in the domestic and external situations, the increase in the arms and services, the complexity of modern technical equipment, and the growth of cadres at lower levels, it was necessary to impose greater demands in an effort to strengthen politico-ideological work, and improve management and educational work at company levels.

17. In this context, see Victor Zorza's "The Hidden Battle for Power in Red China," *Look*, August 23, 1966, pp. 25–28.
18. Radio news broadcast, NCNA International Service, January 24, 1966.
19. Radio news broadcast, Peking Domestic Service, January 18, 1966.

EPILOGUE

1. *People's Daily–Red Flag* editorial, 1 January, 1967.
2. This poem was reproduced in facsimile script on the front page of all Peking newspapers on December 31, 1966.
3. *The Liberation Army Daily*, 15 January, 1967.

On February 4, 1967, "some 100,000 revolutionary rebels" (Red Guards) assembled in Nanch'ang (where the PLA was born on August 1, 1927) with the avowed intention of "rebelling" against "the 1 August Army Day."

This date, so the Red Guards announced, had been "fabricated" by "a handful of schemers and careerists in the Party who have taken the capitalist road." These despicable characters, "with the guts of dogs," had "gone all out to distort . . . the history of the revolution, working hard to embellish the Nanch'ang 1 August uprising in order to sing the praises of their own virtues." Accordingly, the Red Guards seized their "iron brooms," and informed Chairman Mao, their "dearest, dearest, dearest great leader," that they were "sweeping away the 1 August Army Day," destroying the "1 August Uprising Memorial Hall," and "crushing to the ground and trampling underfoot" the "handful of counterrevolutionary revisionists" who had "turned history upside down" and maliciously stolen from Mao the credit of "personally creating the Red Army." The vilifications referred to former Marshals of the PLA Chu Teh, Ho Lung, Ch'en Yi and Liu Po-ch'eng, and Party Secretary Teng Hsiao-p'ing!

The fact that PLA Army, Navy and Air Force units took part in this frenetic demonstration supports the supposition that Defense Minister Lin Piao (who was a company commander in Yeh T'ing's rebellious division in August 1927) is manipulating the Red Guards to serve his own purposes. It it difficult to conceive that such aging figures as Chu Teh (now 81), Liu Po-ch'eng (now 75) and Ho Lung (now 71) could possibly threaten Lin's position, and it is therefore probable that his real targets are Ch'en Yi and Teng Hsiao-p'ing.

Nanch'ang Domestic Service

A Selected Bibliography

I. CHINESE SOURCES.

A. Books and articles
  1. Nationalist and Miscellaneous

Chang Ta-chun. *Chung Kung Jen Ming Tien* (*Who's Who in Communist China*). Hong Kong: Freedom Press, 1956.

Ch'en Hsiao-wei. *Wei Shen-ma Shih-ch'ü Ta-tu.* (*Why We Lost the Mainland.*) Taipei: China Art Press, 1964.

Chiang Kai-shek and Madame Chiang Kai-shek. *Sian, a Coup d'Etat: A Fortnight in Sian, Extracts from a Diary by Chiang Kai-shek.* Shanghai: 1937.

Chiang Kai-shek. *Soviet Russia in Asia: A Summing-up at Seventy.* New York: Farrar, Straus and Cudahy, 1957.

China, Government of the Republic of. *Chung-kuo Min-kuo Chan-shih T'u-chi.* (*A Military History of the Chinese Republic with Maps.*) Taipei: Military History Bureau, Ministry of National Defense, 1961.

———. *Kan-luan Chien-shih* (Brief History of Suppression Campaigns). Taipei: Military History Bureau, Ministry of National Defense, n.d.

China Year Book, 1933. Shanghai: 1933.

Hu Shih. "China in Stalin's Grand Strategy," *Foreign Affairs*, v. 29, October 1950, pp. 11–40.

Huang Tsung-hsi. *A Plan for the Prince.* Trans. and explained by William Theodore de Bary. Unpublished doctoral dissertation, Columbia University, New York, April 1963.

Koo, V. K. Wellington. *Memoranda Presented to the Lytton Commission.* New York: China Cultural Society, 1932–1933.

Legge, James. *The Chinese Classics*, v. 4: *The She Ching.* London: Trubner and Company, 1871.

Sun Tzu. *The Art of War.* Trans. and with an introduction by Samuel B. Griffith. Oxford: Clarendon Press, 1963.

T'ang Liang-li. *Suppressing Communist Banditry in China.* Rev. ed. Shanghai: China United Press, December, 1934.

371

2. Communist

Chen Chang-feng. *On the Long March with Chairman Mao*. Peking: Foreign Languages Press, 1959.

Ch'en Yi. "Learn from the Marxist-Leninist Creative Style of Work of Chairman Mao," *Current Background*, no. 208, September 10, 1952, pp. 9–16.

China, People's Republic of. National People's Congress. *Documents of the First National People's Congress of the People's Republic of China*. Peking: Foreign Languages Press, 1955.

Chu Teh. *The Battle Front of the Liberated Areas*. Report to the Seventh Congress of the Chinese Communist Party, April 25, 1945. Peking: Foreign Languages Press, 1962.

Fu Ch'iu-tao. "The People's Militia: A Favorite System of Our People," *Extracts from China Mainland Magazines*, no. 159, March 2, 1959.

Ho Chung-jen. "The Founding of the Fourth Red Army," *Current Background*, no. 208, September 10, 1952, pp. 43–49.

Hu Chiao-mu. *Thirty Years of the Communist Party of China*. 4th ed. Peking: Foreign Languages Press, 1959.

Liu Chao-jung and others. *Stories of the Chinese People's Volunteers*. Peking: Foreign Languages Press, 1960.

Liu Yun-cheng. "The Militia in the People's Revolutionary Wars of China," *Survey of the China Mainland Press*, no. 2780, July 18, 1962, pp. 1–12.

———. "The Role of the People's Militia," *Peking Review*, no. 6, February 5, 1965, pp. 17–20.

The Long March: Eyewitness Accounts. Peking: Foreign Languages Press, 1963.

Mao Tse-tung. *Nineteen Poems*. Peking: Foreign Languages Press, 1958.

———. *On Guerrilla Warfare*. Trans. and with an introduction by Samuel B. Griffith. New York: Frederick A. Praeger, 1961.

———. *Selected Military Writings*. Peking: Foreign Languages Press, 1963.

———. *Selected Works*. New York: International Publishers, 1954.

Shen Ch'ih-ch'ing. "The Vast Skies Are Shaken," *Current Background*, no. 596, October 7, 1959, pp. 25–28.

B. Periodicals

Current Background, American Consulate General, Hong Kong.

Extracts (Selections) from Chinese Mainland Magazines, American Consulate General, Hong Kong.

Hung Ch'i (Red Flag), Peking.

Jen-min Jih-pao (People's Daily), Peking.

Peking Review, Peking.

People's China, Peking.

Survey of the Chinese Mainland Press, American Consulate General, Hong Kong.

II. OTHER SOURCES

A. Books and articles

Appleman, Roy E. *South to the Naktong, North to the Yalu June–November 1950*, v. 1: *The United States Army in the Korean War*. Washington, D.C.: Office of the Chief of Military History, Department of the Army, 1961.

Arnold, Theodore. "The Technique of the Revolutionary War," *Bulletin*, Institute for the Study of the U.S.S.R., Munich, Germany, November 1960, pp. 3–12.

Barclay, Cyril Nelson. *The New Warfare*. New York: Philosophical Library, 1954.

Bargava, G. S. *The Battle of NEFA*. New Delhi: Allied Publishers, 1964.

Bertram, James M. *First Act in China: The Story of the Sian Mutiny*. New York: The Viking Press, Inc., 1938.

Bisson, T. A. *The Communist Movement in China*. Foreign Policy Reports, v. 9, no. 4. New York: Foreign Policy Association, April 26, 1933.

Brandt, Conrad. *Stalin's Failure in China*. Cambridge: Harvard University Press, 1958.

———, Benjamin Schwartz, and John K. Fairbank. *A Documentary History of Chinese Communism*. Cambridge: Harvard University Press, 1952.

Burin, Frederic S. "The Communist Doctrine of the Inevitability of War," *The American Political Science Review*, v. 57, no. 2, June 1963, pp. 334–354.

Cagle, Malcolm W. and Frank A. Manson. *The Sea War in Korea*. Annapolis: U.S. Naval Institute, 1957.

Carlson, Evans Fordyce. *The Chinese Army*. Institute of Pacific Relations Inquiry Series. New York: Institute of Pacific Relations, 1940.

———. *Twin Stars of China*. New York: Dodd, Mead & Co., 1940.

Chassin, General L. M. *L'Ascension de Mao Tse-tung (1921–1945)*. Paris: Payot, 1953.

Ch'en, Jerome. *Mao and the Chinese Revolution*. New York: Oxford University Press, 1965.

Ch'en Kung-po. *The Communist Movement in China*. Ed., and with an introduction, by C. Martin Wilbur. Columbia University East Asian Institute Series, no. 7. New York: Columbia University, 1960.

Chen, Theodore Hsi-en and Wen-hui C. Chen, "The 'Three-Anti' and 'Five-Anti' Movements in Communist China," *Pacific Affairs*, v. 26, no. 1, March 1953, pp. 3–23.

Cheng Chu-yuan. *Scientific and Engineering Manpower in Communist China, 1949–1963*. Washington, D.C.: National Science Foundation, 1965.

Chiu Sing-ming. *A History of the Chinese Communist Army*. Unpublished doctoral dissertation, University of Southern California, 1958. Ann Arbor: University Microfilms, 1964.

Clark, Mark W. *From the Danube to the Yalu*. New York: Harper & Brothers, 1954.

Clubb, O. Edmund. "Chiang Kai-shek's Waterloo: The Battle of Hwai-Hai," *Pacific Historical Review*, v. 25, November 1956, pp. 389–399.

———. *Twentieth Century China*. New York: Columbia University Press, 1964.

Cohen, Arthur A. *The Communism of Mao Tse-tung*. Chicago: University of Chicago Press, 1964.

Communist China, 1949–1959. 3 vols. Communist China Problem Research Series, Hong Kong: Union Research Institute, 1961.

Communist China, 1960. 2 vols. Communist China Problem Research Series, Hong Kong: Union Research Institute, 1962.

Communist China, 1961. 2 vols. Communist China Problem Research Series, Hong Kong: Union Research Institute, 1963.

Dallin, David J. *Soviet Russia and the Far East*. New Haven: Yale University Press, 1948.

de Bary, Wm. Theodore, Wing-Tsit Chan and Burton Watson. *Sources of Chinese Tradition*. New York: Columbia University Press, 1960.

Degras, Jane, ed. *Soviet Documents on Foreign Policy*. London: Oxford University Press, 1952.

Deutscher, Isaac. *The Prophet Armed. Trotsky: 1879–1921*. New York: Oxford University Press, 1954.

Downing, Jack G. *The Party Committee System in the Chinese Red Army and Its Impact on Small Unit Tactics and Combat Efficiency during the Chosin Reservoir Campaign in Korea, 1950*. Unpublished Master's thesis, Harvard University, December 1962.

Dutt, Maj. Gen. D. Som. *The Defence of India's Northern Borders*. Adelphi Papers, no. 25. London: Institute for Strategic Studies, January 1966.

Eckstein, Alexander. *Communist China's Economic Growth and Foreign Trade*. The United States and China in World Affairs Series. New York: McGraw-Hill for the Council on Foreign Relations, 1966.

Esposito, Col. Vincent J., ed. *The West Point Atlas of American Wars*. v. 2. New York: Frederick A. Praeger, Inc., 1959.

Eudin, Xenia J. and Robert C. North. *Soviet Russia and the East, 1920–29: A Documentary Survey*. Stanford: Stanford University Press, 1952.

Fang, Achilles, trans. *The Chronicle of the Three Kingdoms*. Cambridge: Harvard University Press, 1952.

Fisher, Margaret, Leo E. Rose, and Robert A. Huttenback. *Himalayan Battleground: Sino-Indian Rivalry in Ladak*. New York: Frederick A. Praeger, Inc., 1963.

Fitzgerald, C. P. *The Chinese View of Their Place in the World*. London: Oxford University Press for the Royal Institute of International Affairs, 1964.

Floyd, David. *Mao against Khrushchev*. New York: Frederick A. Praeger, Inc., 1964.

Futrell, Robert F. *The United States Air Force in Korea, 1950–1953*. New York: Duell, Sloan & Pearce, 1961.

George, Alexander L. *The Chinese Soldier in the Korean War*. Unpublished study. The Rand Corporation, 1965.

Gittings, John. "China's Militia," *China Quarterly*, no. 18, April/June 1964, pp. 100–117.

Guillermaz, Colonel J. "The Nanchang Uprising," *China Quarterly*, no. 11, July/September 1962, pp. 161–168.

Halperin, Morton H. *China and the Bomb*. New York: Frederick A. Praeger, Inc., 1965.

Hanwell, Norman. "The Chinese Red Army," *Asia Magazine*, v. 36, no. 5, May 1936, pp. 317–322.

Honey, P. J. "Vietnam: To the Bitter End?" *Survival*, v. 8, no. 2, February 1966. London: Institute for Strategic Studies, pp. 54–56.

Hsia, T. A. *Metaphor, Myth, Ritual, and the People's Communes*. Studies in Chinese Communist Terminology, no. 7. Berkeley: Center for Chinese Studies, Institute of International Studies, University of California, June 1961.

Hsieh, Alice Langley. *Communist China's Strategy in the Nuclear Era*. New York: Prentice-Hall, 1962.

India. Ministry of External Affairs. *White Paper VIII (October 1962–January 1963)*, and *White Paper IX (January 1963–July 1963)*. New Delhi: Author.

———. *The Chinese Threat*. New Delhi: Author, 1963.

Institute of Pacific Relations. *A Survey of the Shensi-Kansu-Ninghsia Border Region*. New York: Author, 1945.

Isaacs, Harold Robert. *Tragedy of the Chinese Revolution*, 2nd rev. ed. Stanford: Stanford University Press, 1961.

Joffe, Ellis. "The Conflict between Old and New in the Chinese Army," *China Quarterly*, no. 18, April/June 1964, pp. 118–140.

Johnson, Chalmers W. *Peasant Nationalism and Communist Power*. Stanford: Stanford University Press, 1962.

Karnik, V. B., ed. *China Invades India*. New Delhi: Allied Publishers, 1963.

Kashin, A. "Chinese Military Doctrine," *Bulletin*, Institute for the Study of the U.S.S.R., Munich, Germany, November 1961, pp. 36–44.

Kissinger, Henry L. *Nuclear Weapons and Foreign Policy*. New York: Harper & Brothers for the Council on Foreign Relations, 1957.

Krebs, Maj. Pierre. *The Political Institutions of the Soviet Army with Special Reference to the Role of the Political Commissar*. Unpublished doctoral dissertation, St. Anthony's College, Oxford University, May 1958.

Krishna Menon, V. K. *India and the Chinese Invasion*. Bombay: Contemporary Publishers, 1963.

Lee, Asher. *The Soviet Air Force*. New York: John Day, 1962.

Lenin, V. I. *Selected Works*. New York: International Publishers.

Lewis, John Wilson. *Leadership in Communist China*. Ithaca, N.Y.: Cornell University Press, 1963.

Liddell Hart, B. H. *Strategy: The Indirect Approach*. London: Faber and Faber Limited, 1954.

Liu, F. F. *A Military History of Modern China*. Princeton: Princeton University Press, 1956.

MacArthur, Douglas. *Reminiscences*. New York: McGraw-Hill, 1964.

Magruder, John. "The Chinese as a Fighting Man," *Foreign Affairs*, v. 9, no. 3, April 1931, pp. 469–476.

Marshall, S. L. A. *Operation PUNCH and the Capture of Hill 440, Suwon, Korea, February 1951*. Baltimore: Johns Hopkins University, 1952.

———. *The River and the Gauntlet*. New York: William Morrow, 1953.

Millis, Walter, Harvey C. Mansfield, and Harold Stein. *Arms and the State*. New York: The Twentieth Century Fund, 1958.

Montross, Lynn, and Nicholas A. Canzona, *U.S. Marine Operations in Korea*,

1950–1953, v. 3. Washington, D.C.: Headquarters, U.S. Marine Corps, 1957.

———, Hubard D. Kuokka, and Norman W. Hicks. *U.S. Marine Operations in Korea, 1950–1953*, v. 4. Washington, D.C.: Headquarters, U.S. Marine Corps, 1962.

Nehru, Jawaharlal. *India's Foreign Policy*. New Delhi: Publications Division, Ministry of Information and Broadcasting, Government of India, August 15, 1961.

Orleans, Leo A. *Professional Manpower and Education in Communist China*. Washington, D.C.: National Science Foundation, 1960.

Panikkar, K. M. *In Two Chinas*. London: George Allen and Unwin, Ltd., 1955.

Powell, Ralph L. *The Rise of Chinese Military Power 1895–1912*. Princeton: Princeton University Press, 1955.

———. "Everyone a Soldier: The Communist Chinese Militia," *Foreign Affairs*, v. 39, no. 1, October 1960, pp. 100–111.

Pusey, Merlo John. *Eisenhower, the President*. New York: Macmillan, 1956.

Rankin, Karl Lott. *China Assignment*. Seattle: University of Washington Press, 1964.

Ravenholt, Albert. "Feud Among the Red Mandarins," *American Universities Field Staff, East Asia Series*, v. 11, no. 2.

Rigg, Robert B. *Red China's Fighting Hordes*. Harrisburg, Penn.: Military Service Publishing Company, 1951.

Romanus, Charles F., and Riley Sunderland. *The China-Burma-India Theater: Stilwell's Command Problems*, v. 23: *The United States Army in World War II*, Washington, D.C.: Office of the Chief of Military History, Department of the Army, 1956.

Rovere, Richard H., and Arthur M. Schlesinger, Jr. *The General and the President*. New York: Farrar, Straus and Young, 1951.

Roy, M. N. *Revolution and Counter-Revolution in China*. Calcutta: Renaissance Publishers, 1946.

Sawyer, Robert K. *Military Advisors in Korea: KMAG in Peace and War*. Washington, D.C.: Office of the Chief of Military History, Department of the Army, 1962.

Schnabel, Lieut. Col. James F. "Ridgway in Korea," *Military Review*, v. 44, no. 3, March 1964.

Schram, Stuart R. "The Military Deviation of Mao Tse-tung," *Problems of Communism*, v. 23, no. 1, January/February 1964, pp. 49–56.

———. *The Political Thought of Mao Tse-tung*. New York: Frederick A. Praeger, Inc., 1963.

Schwartz, Benjamin. *Chinese Communism and the Rise of Mao*. Cambridge: Harvard University Press, 1951.

———. "On the 'Originality' of Mao Tse-tung," *Foreign Affairs*, October 1955, pp. 67–76.

Shih Ch'eng-chih. *People's Resistance in Mainland China, 1950–1955*. Communist China Problem Research Series. Hong Kong: Union Research Institute, December 1956.

Smedley, Agnes. *China's Red Army Marches*. New York: Vanguard, 1934.

Snow, Edgar. *The Other Side of the River: Red China Today*. New York: Random House, 1961.

———. *Red Star Over China*. New York: Random House, 1938.

———. *Random Notes on Red China (1936–1945)*. Cambridge: Harvard University Press, 1957.

Spanier, John W. *The Truman-MacArthur Controversy and the Korean War.* Cambridge: Harvard University Press, 1959.

Stanford Research Institute. *The Economic Potential of Communist China to Support Military Programs, 1965–1985.* Menlo Park, Calif.: Author, 1965.

Su-wei-ai Chung-kuo (Soviet China). Moscow: Soviet Foreign Workers Publishing House, 1933.

The Travels of Marco Polo, trans. by William Marsten with an introduction by F. W. Mote. New York: Dell, 1961.

Trotsky, Leon. *My Life.* New York: Charles Scribner's Sons, 1930.

Truman, Harry S. *Years of Trial and Hope,* v. 2: *Memoirs.* New York: Doubleday and Company, 1956.

Truong Chinh. *Primer for Revolt: The Communist Takeover in Viet-nam.* With introduction and notes by Bernard B. Fall. New York: Frederick A. Praeger, Inc., 1965.

U.S. Department of the Army. Office of the Chief of Military History. *North China Area Operations Record July 1937–May 1941.* Japanese Monograph no. 178. Tokyo: Military History Section, Headquarters, Armed Forces in the Far East, 1955.

U.S. Department of State. *Communist Perspective: A Handbook of Communist Doctrinal Statements in the Original Russian and in English.* Washington, D.C.: GPO, 1946.

———. *North Korea: A Case Study in the Techniques of Takeover.* Publication 7118. Washington, D.C.: GPO, January 1961.

———. *United States Policy in the Korean Crisis.* Publication 3922. Washington, D.C.: GPO, 1950.

———. *United States Relations with China.* Publication 3573. Washington, D.C.: GPO, August 1949.

U.S. Far Eastern Command. General Headquarters. *Order of Battle Information: Chinese Communist Forces in Korea.*

U.S. House. Committee on Armed Services. *The National Defense Program: Unification and Strategy.* Eighty-first Congress. Washington, D.C.: GPO, 1949.

U.S. Pacific Fleet. *Interim Evaluation Report No. 5.* (July 1, 1952–January 31, 1953.)

U.S. Senate. Committee on Armed Services and Committee on Foreign Relations. *Military Situation in the Far East.* Eighty-second Congress. First session. Washington, D.C.: GPO, 1951.

———. Committee on the Judiciary. *Institute of Pacific Relations.* Hearings before the Senate Committee to investigate the administration of the Internal Security Act and other internal security laws. Eighty-second Congress. First session. Washington, D.C.: GPO, 1952.

Van Fleet, James A. "The Truth about Korea," *Life,* May 11, 1953, pp. 127–142.

Wales, Nym. *Inside Red China.* New York: Doubleday, Doran and Company, 1939.

———. *Red Dust: Autobiographies of Chinese Communists.* Stanford: Stanford University Press, 1952.

White, D. Fedotoff. *The Growth of the Red Army*. Princeton: Princeton University Press, 1944.

White, Theodore H., and Annalee Jacoby. *Thunder out of China*. New York: William Sloane Associates, 1946.

Whiting, Allen S. *China Crosses the Yalu: The Decision to Enter the Korean War*. New York: The Macmillan Company, 1960.

Whitney, Courtney. *MacArthur: His Rendezvous with Destiny*. New York: Alfred A. Knopf, 1956.

Wilbur, C. Martin. "The Ashes of Defeat," *China Quarterly*, no. 18, April/June 1964, pp. 3–54.

———, and Julie Lien-ying How, ed. *Documents on Communism, Nationalism, and Soviet Advisers in China 1918–1927*. New York: Columbia University Press, 1956.

Willoughby, Charles A., and John Chamberlin. *MacArthur 1941–1951*. New York: McGraw-Hill, 1954.

Yakhontoff, Victor A. *The Chinese Soviets*. New York: Coward-McCann, 1934.

B. Periodicals

Allied Translator and Interpreter Service, Far Eastern Command.

The American Political Science Review, Washington, D.C.

The Annals of the American Academy of Political and Social Sciences, Philadelphia, Penn.

Asian Survey, Berkeley, California.

Bulletin of the Atomic Scientists, Chicago, Ill.

China News Analysis, Hong Kong.

China Quarterly, London.

Current History, New York, N.Y.

The Department of State Bulletin, Washington, D.C.

The Far Eastern Economic Review, Hong Kong.

Foreign Affairs, New York, N.Y.

India Quarterly, New Delhi.

International Press Correspondence, London.

New York Times, New York, N.Y.

Orbis, Philadelphia, Penn.

Problems of Communism, Washington, D.C.

Survival, London.

United Asia, Bombay.

The World Today, London.

Index

PUBLICATIONS

FOREIGN AFFAIRS (quarterly), edited by Hamilton Fish Armstrong.

THE UNITED STATES IN WORLD AFFAIRS (annual). Volumes for 1931, 1932 and 1933, by Walter Lippmann and William O. Scroggs; for 1934–1935, 1936, 1937, 1938, 1939 and 1940, by Whitney H. Shepardson and William O. Scroggs; for 1945–1947, 1947–1948 and 1948–1949, by John C. Campbell; for 1949, 1950, 1951, 1952, 1953 and 1954, by Richard P. Stebbins; for 1955, by Hollis W. Barber; for 1956, 1957, 1958, 1959, 1960, 1961, 1962 and 1963, by Richard P. Stebbins; for 1964, by Jules Davids; for 1965 by Richard P. Stebbins.

DOCUMENTS ON AMERICAN FOREIGN RELATIONS (annual). Volume for 1952 edited by Clarence W. Baier and Richard P. Stebbins; for 1953 and 1954 edited by Peter V. Curl; for 1955, 1956, 1957, 1958 and 1959 edited by Paul E. Zinner; for 1960, 1961, 1962 and 1963 edited by Richard P. Stebbins; for 1964 by Jules Davids; for 1965 by Richard P. Stebbins.

POLITICAL HANDBOOK AND ATLAS OF THE WORLD (annual), edited by Walter H. Mallory.

THE CHINESE PEOPLE'S LIBERATION ARMY, by Brig. General Samuel B. Griffith II U.S.M.C. (ret.) (1967).

THE ARTILLERY OF THE PRESS: Its Influence on American Foreign Policy, by James Reston (1967).

ATLANTIC ECONOMIC COOPERATION: The Case of the O.E.C.D., by Henry G. Aubrey (1967).

TRADE, AID AND DEVELOPMENT: The Rich and Poor Nations, by John Pincus (1967).

BETWEEN TWO WORLDS: Policy, Press and Public Opinion on Asian–American Relations, by John Hohenberg (1967).

THE CONFLICTED RELATIONSHIP: The West and the Transformation of Asia, Africa and Latin America, by Theodore Geiger (1966).

THE ATLANTIC IDEA AND ITS EUROPEAN RIVALS, by H. van B. Cleveland (1966).

EUROPEAN UNIFICATION IN THE SIXTIES: From the Veto to the Crisis, by Miriam Camps (1966).

THE UNITED STATES AND CHINA IN WORLD AFFAIRS, by Robert Blum, edited by A. Doak Barnett (1966).

THE FUTURE OF THE OVERSEAS CHINESE IN SOUTHEAST ASIA, by Lea A. Williams (1966).

THE CONSCIENCE OF THE RICH NATIONS: The Development Assistance Committee and the Common Aid Effort, by Seymour J. Rubin (1966).

ATLANTIC AGRICULTURAL UNITY: Is it Possible?, by John O. Coppock (1966).

TEST BAN AND DISARMAMENT: The Path of Negotiation, by Arthur H. Dean (1966).

COMMUNIST CHINA'S ECONOMIC GROWTH AND FOREIGN TRADE, by Alexander Eckstein (1966).

POLICIES TOWARD CHINA: Views from Six Continents, edited by A. M. Halpern (1966).

THE AMERICAN PEOPLE AND CHINA, by A. T. Steele (1966).

INTERNATIONAL POLITICAL COMMUNICATION, by W. Phillips Davison (1965).

MONETARY REFORM FOR THE WORLD ECONOMY, by Robert V. Roosa (1965).

AFRICAN BATTLELINE: American Policy Choices in Southern Africa, by Waldemar A. Nielsen (1965).

NATO IN TRANSITION: The Future of the Atlantic Alliance, by Timothy W. Stanley (1965).

ALTERNATIVE TO PARTITION: For a Broader Conception of America's Role in Europe, by Zbigniew Brzezinski (1965).

THE TROUBLED PARTNERSHIP: A Re-Appraisal of the Atlantic Alliance, by Henry A. Kissinger (1965).

REMNANTS OF EMPIRE: The United Nations and the End of Colonialism, by David W. Wainhouse (1965).

THE EUROPEAN COMMUNITY AND AMERICAN TRADE: A Study in Atlantic Economics and Policy, by Randall Hinshaw (1964).

THE FOURTH DIMENSION OF FOREIGN POLICY: Educational and Cultural Affairs, by Phillip H. Coombs (1964).

AMERICAN AGENCIES INTERESTED IN INTERNATIONAL AFFAIRS (Fifth Edition), compiled by Donald Wasson (1964).

JAPAN AND THE UNITED STATES IN WORLD TRADE, by Warren S. Hunsberger (1964).

FOREIGN AFFAIRS BIBLIOGRAPHY, 1952–1962, by Henry L. Roberts (1964).

THE DOLLAR IN WORLD AFFAIRS: An Essay in International Financial Policy, by Henry G. Aubrey (1964).

ON DEALING WITH THE COMMUNIST WORLD, by George F. Kennan (1964).

FOREIGN AID AND FOREIGN POLICY, by Edward S. Mason (1964).

THE SCIENTIFIC REVOLUTION AND WORLD POLITICS, by Caryl P. Haskins (1964).

AFRICA: A Foreign Affairs Reader, edited by Philip W. Quigg (1964).

THE PHILIPPINES AND THE UNITED STATES: Problems of Partnership, by George E. Taylor (1964).

SOUTHEAST ASIA IN UNITED STATES POLICY, by Russell H. Fifield (1963).

UNESCO: ASSESSMENT AND PROMISE, by George N. Shuster (1963).

THE PEACEFUL ATOM IN FOREIGN POLICY, by Arnold Kramish (1963).

THE ARABS AND THE WORLD: Nasser's Arab Nationalist Policy, by Charles D. Cremeans (1963).

TOWARD AN ATLANTIC COMMUNITY, by Christian A. Herter (1963).

THE SOVIET UNION, 1922–1962: A Foreign Affairs Reader, edited by Philip E. Mosley (1963).

THE POLITICS OF FOREIGN AID: American Experience in Southeast Asia, by John D. Montgomery (1962).

SPEARHEADS OF DEMOCRACY: Labor in the Developing Countries, by George C. Lodge (1962).

LATIN AMERICA: Diplomacy and Reality, by Adolf A. Berle (1962).

THE ORGANIZATION OF AMERICAN STATES AND THE HEMISPHERE CRISIS, by John C. Dreier (1962).

THE UNITED NATIONS: Structure for Peace, by Ernest A. Gross (1962).

THE LONG POLAR WATCH: Canada and the Defense of North America, by Melvin Conant (1962).

ARMS AND POLITICS IN LATIN AMERICA (Revised Edition), by Edwin Lieuwen (1961).

THE FUTURE OF UNDERDEVELOPED COUNTRIES: Political Implications of Economic Development (Revised Edition), by Eugene Staley (1961).

SPAIN AND DEFENSE OF THE WEST: Ally and Liability, by Arthur P. Whitaker (1961).

SOCIAL CHANGE IN LATIN AMERICA TODAY: Its Implications for United States Policy, by Richard N. Adams, John P. Gillin, Allan R. Holmberg, Oscar Lewis, Richard W. Patch, and Charles W. Wagley (1961).

FOREIGN POLICY: THE NEXT PHASE: The 1960s (Revised Edition), by Thomas K. Finletter (1960).

DEFENSE OF THE MIDDLE EAST: Problems of American Policy (Revised Edition), by John C. Campbell (1960).

COMMUNIST CHINA AND ASIA: Challenge to American Policy, by A. Doak Barnett (1960).

FRANCE, TROUBLED ALLY: De Gaulle's Heritage and Prospects, by Edgar S. Furniss, Jr. (1960).

THE SCHUMAN PLAN: A Study in Economic Cooperation 1950–1959, by William Diebold, Jr. (1959).

SOVIET ECONOMIC AID: The New Aid and Trade Policy in Underdeveloped Countries, by Joseph S. Berliner (1958).

NATO AND THE FUTURE OF EUROPE, by Ben T. Moore (1958).

INDIA AND AMERICA: A Study of Their Relations, by Phillips Talbot and S. L. Poplai (1958).

NUCLEAR WEAPONS AND FOREIGN POLICY, by Henry A. Kissinger (1957).

MOSCOW-PEKING AXIS: Strength and Strains, by Howard L. Boorman, Alexander Eckstein, Philip E. Mosley, and Benjamin Schwartz (1957).

RUSSIA AND AMERICA: Dangers and Prospects, by Henry L. Roberts (1956).